The Holy Spirit and Social Justice
Interdisciplinary Global Perspectives

Scripture & Theology

Antipas L. Harris and Michael D. Palmer, Editors

The Holy Spirit and Social Justice
Interdisciplinary Global Perspectives

Scripture & Theology

ISBN-10: 1-938373-22-7
ISBN-13: 978-1-938373-22-0
Library of Congress Control Number: 2019936859

SP

Copyright © 2019   **Seymour Press**
                    Lanham MD

Printed in the United States of American by

Endorsements

"This engaging collection of essays brings the Pentecostal tradition into a stimulating dialogue with the biblical concern for the poor and for social justice in all of its complexity. Christians in the Pentecostal tradition will no doubt be challenged and stimulated by these essays to take seriously both the scriptural witness and their own tradition in addressing contemporary social and economic problems. Students of the Bible outside of the Pentecostal tradition will also find illuminating the ways these essays call upon their theology of the Spirit to interpret biblical texts dealing with critical social issues."
Harold W. Attridge
Sterling Professor of Divinity
Yale Divinity School

"Antipas Harris is one of the most creative religious thinkers of this era. With judicious insight and wisdom, he analyzes and frames this important conversation around social justice, adeptly using the sources at his disposal. I would recommend this volume to anyone, whether academic or social activist, who wants to think deeply about how we build the Kingdom of God."
Michael Joseph Brown
New Testament Scholar and President
Payne Theological Seminary

"At last a raft of Pentecostal and charismatic academics brings pneumatology and social justice into play. No longer is the Spirit's work confined to the otherworldly or individual salvation and sanctification. The Spirit is shown also to be deeply concerned for the corporate, socio-political and creaturely world, including the poor and the marginalized. Through the individual essays and as a whole this volume makes a profound contribution not only to the fields of Spirit and social justice but also to the Church. Read it to be changed to bring change."

Graham H. Twelftree
Academic Dean and Professor of New Testament
and Early Christianity
London School of Theology

"This book has placed the discourse of social justice squarely in the center of both Pentecostal theology and holy living. It demonstrates that the true praxis of Pentecostal identity demands the capacity to constantly heed, nourish, and fulfill God's call to social justice. This is an insightful volume that will renew debates on Pentecostal ethics in the academy, in the churches, and on the street."

Nimi Wariboko
Walter G. Muelder Professor of Social Ethics
Boston University

"This work is much needed and awaited. Some of the leading Charismatic scholars give a thorough theological foundation for the move of the Spirit and the responsibility of the Church in the world.

Globally, Charismatic Christianity is the fastest growing religious group and strongest social movement. Led by the Spirit, a Pentecostal theological understanding of justice can change the world."

Ulrik Josefsson
Director, Academy for Leadership and Theology
Jonkping, Sweden

Table of Content

Following the Spirit

Co-editors and Contributors

Co-editors

Antipas L. Harris (D.Min., Boston University) is a practical theologian. He is the founding dean of the Urban Renewal Center in Norfolk, VA. He currently serves as president and dean of Jakes Divinity School in Dallas, TX. Harris holds degrees from Yale Divinity School, Emory University and LaGrange College. He has held teaching appointments at several universities, including the School of Divinity at Regent University, Sacred Heart University, New York Theological Seminary, Fuller Theological Seminary, and Portland Theological Seminary. An ordained minister, he has served on the pastoral staffs of churches for nearly 30 years. His research, teaching, and leadership aim to build bridges between education, ministry, and community leadership. He has led or participated in numerous educational symposia and professional conferences and is a frequent guest preacher in many churches.

Michael D. Palmer (Ph.D., Marquette University) serves as professor of philosophy in the School of Divinity at Regent University. His scholarly interests include moral theory and the history of philosophy, with special emphasis on the way classical philosophy has influenced Christian thought. He is the author of three scholarly books and numerous journal articles, book chapters, book reviews, and other professional writings. He was a co-editor of the *Willey-Blackwell Companion to Religion and Social Justice* (2012). He teaches courses on Christian ethics, Christian social teaching, and history of philosophy (ancient and medieval).

Contributors

Lisa Marie Bowens (Ph.D., Princeton Theological Seminary) serves as assistant professor of New Testament at Princeton Theological Seminary. She earned her BS (*cum laude*), MSBE and MLIS from the University of North Carolina at Greensboro, and her MTS and Th.M. from Duke Divinity School. Mohr Siebek published her recent book, *An Apostle in Battle: Paul and Spiritual Warfare in 2 Corinthians 12:1-10*, which is a revision of her dissertation. Bowens' work has been favorably reviewed and "highly recommended" for those interested in 2 Corinthians and Pauline cosmology and eschatology. Two of Bowens' significant articles include "Liberating Paul: African Americans' Use of Paul in Resistance and Protest" and "Divine Desire: Paul's Apocalyptic God of Rescue." Bowens' research interests include Paul and apocalyptic thought, Pauline anthropology, Pauline epistemology, discipleship in the gospels, African American Pauline Hermeneutics, and New Testament exegesis and interpretation. Bowens is a member of the Society of Biblical Literature, Society for Pentecostal Studies, and a past fellow at the Fund for Theological Education.

Alaine Thomson Buchanan (Ph.D., Regent University) serves as adjunct professor of Biblical Theology and Biblical Studies at the School of Urban Missions Bible College and Theological Seminary, and Evangel University. She is an ordained minister with the Assemblies of God, an active duty Army chaplain's spouse and a mom. Buchanan is an advocate for those who are treated as "less than" others, and her special research interest is in connecting social issues found in Scripture and in Second Temple Jewish Literature with social concerns throughout the world today.

Tommy Cásarez (Ph.D., Princeton Theological Seminary) currently serves as assistant professor of systematic and historical theology and chair of the Department of Religion at Vanguard University. He earned an M.Div. from Fuller Theological Seminary and an S.T.M. from Yale Divinity School. He teaches courses in church history, theology, and ethics. Cásarez also serves as Associate Pastor at Templo Calvario Church of Santa Ana, CA.

Enoch Sathiasatchi Charles, (Ph.D., Regent University) teaches as an adjunct lecturer at Bethel College, Pentecost Bible College, SUM Bible College and Theological Seminary, and Ashland University. His doctoral dissertation is entitled: *"Toward a Pneumatological-Participatory Theology of Divine Moral Assistance: An Apologetic Dialogue with Naturalistic and Kantian Ethics."* Charles' teaching and research interests include Christian theology, apologetics, ethics, and world religions. His professional writings have appeared in several peer-reviewed journals, including *Journal of Pentecostal Theology, Religious Studies Review,* and *International Journal of Pentecostal Missiology.*

Jacqueline N. Grey (Ph.D., Charles Sturt University) serves as associate professor of biblical studies in the Department of Theology at Alphacrucis College in Australia. She teaches courses in Old Testament studies. Grey has published numerous articles, book chapters, and books on Isaiah, prophetic literature of the Old Testament, Pentecostal hermeneutics, and women in leadership. She is a past president of the Society for Pentecostal Studies (2017) and also a member of the SBL Steering Committee for Biblical Ethics. Currently, Grey serves as a research fellow in the Department of Biblical and Ancient Studies at the University of South Africa.

Jin H. Han (Ph.D., Princeton Theological Seminary) serves as professor of biblical studies at New York Theological Seminary with responsibilities for First Testament, Exegesis, and Hebrew language. He is a contributor to the *Anchor Bible Dictionary*, the *Encyclopedia of Biblical Reception*, and other major reference works in the field. An ordained clergyperson of the Presbyterian Church (USA), he has deep love for the life of the parish and has led numerous workshops and retreats for churches. He has also been involved in the development of Bible study resources for churches with the United Methodist Publishing House and Westminster/John Knox Press.

Craig S. Keener (Ph.D., Duke University) serves as F. M. and Ada Thompson Professor of Biblical Studies at Asbury Theological Seminary. He has authored twenty-five books, seven of which have won national or international awards. The books include *The IVP Bible Background Commentary: New Testament*; the *New Cambridge Bible Commentary on 1-2 Corinthians and Galatians;* and a four-volume commentary on Acts published by Baker Academic Publishing. Keener has also authored approximately 100 academic articles and more than 150 popular articles. He is the editor of the *Bulletin for Biblical Research* and is vice president of the Evangelical Theological Society. Craig is married to Dr. Médine Moussounga Keener, a refugee from Congo. Médine's experience and

Craig and Médine's romance appear in *Impossible Love,* published by Chosen in 2016.

William L. Lyons (Ph.D., Florida State University) serves as associate professor of Old Testament and Semitic Languages in the Department of Theology at Oral Roberts University in Tulsa, Oklahoma. He has also taught at Regent University, Florida A&M University, Florida State University, and in multiple nations outside of the United States of America. He serves as a faculty mentor for the Scholars Initiative, the scholarly arm of the Museum of the Bible. Lyons' doctoral work was in religions of western antiquity. He has written on a number of topics, including war in the Hebrew Bible, ancient Near Eastern thought, women in the Bible, Old Testament character ethics, biblical hermeneutics (including feminist, rabbinic, and modern evangelical perspectives), and wisdom literature.

Herbert R. Marbury (Ph.D., Vanderbilt University) serves as associate professor of Hebrew Bible and Ancient Near East in the Divinity School at Vanderbilt University. His research focuses on history and hermeneutics; in particular, ancient Israel's scriptures in the Second Temple period and the way those texts have been interpreted in our time. In *Imperial Dominion and Priestly Genius: Coercion, Accommodation, and Resistance in the Divorce Rhetoric of Ezra-Nehemiah* (Sopher Press, 2012) he investigated meanings of the text for ancient Israel facing Persian imperial oppression. In his most work, *Pillars of Cloud and Fire: The Politics of Exodus in African American Biblical Interpretation* (New York University Press, 2015) he focused on the ways contemporary communities use the same scriptures to negotiate ongoing oppression.

Lee Roy Martin (D.Th., University of South Africa) serves as professor of Old Testament and Biblical Languages at Pentecostal Theological Seminary in Cleveland, Tennessee, and is an ordained pastor in the Church of God. He serves as editor of the *Journal of Pentecostal Theology* and is a past president of the Society for Pentecostal Studies. Martin's publications include articles on the book of Judges and on the Psalms and monographs on biblical Hermeneutics, fasting, worship, Jonah, Daniel, and soteriology. He has also edited volumes on holiness, preaching, worship, and hermeneutics. He is currently writing a commentary on the Psalms for the *Wesley One-Volume Bible Commentary*.

Néstor Medina (Ph.D., Emmanuel College) is a visiting scholar at the Emmanuel College Centre for Religion and Its Context, in the University of Toronto. He is an ordained Pentecostal minister. Medina studies the intersection of people's cultures, histories, ethno-racial relations, faith traditions, and theological knowledge. He was a recipient of the Louisville Book Grant for Minority Scholars (2014-15) and a Louisville Research Grant (2018). Medina has presented and published numerous articles on Latina/o Pentecostalism, contextual/liberation and Latina/o theologies, pneumatology, and post/decolonial theologies. He is also the author of *Mestizaje: (Re)Mapping "Race," Culture, and Faith in Latina/o Catholicism*, which was the winner of the 2012 Hispanic Theological Initiative's Book Award. His latest book is entitled *Christianity, Empire, and the Spirit: (Re)Configuring Faith and the Cultural* (Brill).

John T. Moxen (Ph.D., Regent University) is the national programs manager for FOCUS North America, a pan-Orthodox Christian basic needs organization that seeks to ameliorate the plight of the poor through social ministry. Moxen acquired his doctorate in organizational leadership research at Regent University's School of Business and Leadership with a focus on Ecclesial Leadership. He has published on the subject of Leadership Ethics in the *Journal of Biblical Perspectives on Leadership*. Moxen is also currently building a network of Orthodox Christian thought-leaders for a series of annual conferences on Social Justice and the poor.

Anthony Roberts (Ph.D. Candidate, University of Denver and the Iliff School of Theology) serves as the chair of the Department of Ministry and Theology in Southeastern University's School of Unrestricted Education, where he also serves as an assistant professor of Christian theology. His research interests are at the intersection of African American theology, pneumatology, and theories of human difference. Currently, Roberts is the Society for Pentecostal Studies Diversity Committee Chairperson and the book review editor for *Pneuma: The Journal of the Society for Pentecostal Studies*. In addition to his work in the academy, Roberts is an ordained bishop in the Church of God (Cleveland) and serves in the historically Black Florida-Cocoa region of the denomination.

J. Lyle Story (Ph.D., Fuller Theological Seminary) serves as professor of New Testament and Biblical Languages at Regent University School of Divinity. He teaches courses on the New Testament, including the areas of biblical interpretation, and biblical languages with a focus on *koiné* Greek. Story co-authored a widely acclaimed tool for learning Greek entitled *Greek To Me*, which is now in its 2nd Edition. He also created a fully online Greek course (GreekToMe.biz) for the general public. Most recently, Story published *Joyous Encounters: Discovering the Happy Affections in Luke-Acts* (Crossroads, 2018). Story has authored numerous journal articles, book chapters, and dictionary articles.

Richard E. Waldrop (D.Miss., Fuller Theological Seminary) is co-founder of Casa Shalom Home for Children in Guatemala, under the auspices of Church of God World Missions. He completed his B.A. degrees at Northwest Bible College and Lee University and received his M.A. degree from Bethel Theological Seminary, specializing in pastoral care and missiology. Waldrop served as a missionary with the Church of God World for over 40 years in five countries, including Guatemala, Costa Rica, Honduras, Ecuador and the United States. He has consistently championed holistic mission integrating evangelism and social action and has partnered in planting churches and establishing social ministry ventures among the most vulnerable sectors (impoverished children, battered women, drug addicts, under-served indigenous communities) within Latin American society. Most recently, he served as the Social Ministries Coordinator for the Church of God in that region and continues traveling extensively as a visiting professor of intercultural studies at colleges and seminaries throughout North and South America, Europe, Africa, and Asia.

Jordan Way (B.A., Oral Roberts University) studied Old Testament Literature and Northwestern Semitics at Oral Roberts

University. As a member of the Scholar's Initiative (the scholarly arm of the Museum of the Bible), he transcribed Bodmer Papyri texts for the Museum of the Bible's Greek Psalter Project. He plans to pursue doctoral work in Near Eastern Studies.

Adam White (Ph.D., Macquarie University) serves as senior lecturer in New Testament at Alphacrucis College in Parramatta, Australia. He teaches in the area of Pauline studies, with particular focus on the Corinthian correspondence and the historical context of the Graeco-Roman world. White's publications have appeared in *Library of New Testament Studies, Journal for the Study of the New Testament,* and *Journal of Pentecostal Theology.* White's current research is focused on the practice of excommunication and church discipline in Pauline communities.

Abbreviations

BBQ	*Catholic Biblical Quarterly*
CUB	*Common English Bible*
ECB	*Feminist Companion to the Bible*
INT	*Interpreter's Bible Commentary*
IVP	InterVarsity Press
JELL	*Journal of Biblical Literature*
JAB	*Jewish Bible Quarterly*
JIB	*Jewish Study Bible*
JOTS	*Journal for the Study of the Old Testament*
KJV	*King James Version*
NAB	New American Standard Bible
NISB	*New Interpreter's Study Bible*
NIV	New International Version
KJV	*King James Version*
NKJV	*New King James Version*
NRSV	*New Revised Standard Version*
SAP	Sheffield Academic Press
SBL	Society of Biblical Literature
WJKP	Westminster John Knox Press

Acknowledgments

We owe a debt of gratitude to many people for their assistance, advice, and encouragement in bringing to press this two-volume project called *The Holy Spirit and Social Justice*.

The core idea for the project originated at the 47th Annual Meeting of the Society for Pentecostal Studies, which convened in the spring of 2018 at Pentecostal Theological Seminary in Cleveland, Tennessee, in conjunction with the Wesleyan Theological Society. The theme of the conference was "The Good News of the Kingdom and the Poor of the Land." After listening to outstanding presentations, several colleagues discussed ways to share some of the conference insights with a broader audience. Key figures in these conversations were Estrelda Alexander, Lee Roy Martin, and Johnathan Alvarado. For their ideas and encouragement, which inspired this project, we thank them. We also wish to thank the Society for Pentecostal Studies for the opportunity to think deeply and critically with other scholars about the role of the Holy Spirit in public life.

We owe special thanks to Estrelda Alexander in her dual roles as publisher and chief editor at Seymour Press. She believed in the importance of the project enough to accept it for publication, and she supported the project with the press's highly competent editorial staff.

The Urban Renewal Center is concerned with the witness of faith in the public square. In partnership with First Presbyterian Church of Norfolk, Virginia, the center's mission is "to awaken transformation of personal health and spiritual wholeness, relentless pursuit of social justice, and racial and ethnic reconciliation." The center values the central role that local churches play in strengthening theological education and the practice of ministry within the church and society. Some of the editorial expenses associated with the project were underwritten by the Urban Renewal Center. We thank the Center for its support. We also wish to acknowledge Rev. Jim Wood and First Presbyterian Church of Norfolk, Virginia, for their encouragement to explore what it means to be people of the Spirit.

Finally, we wish to express our deep gratitude to the authors whose essays, gathered here under the title *The Holy Spirit and Social Justice*, have enriched our lives and made a distinctive contribution to an important and ongoing conversation.

Foreword

Amos Yong

The Holy Spirit and social justice!? I had to do a double-take when I saw the announced title to this two-volume set simply because, for over a hundred years now, those of us who count ourselves as children of the modern Pentecostal movement have been inoculated into thinking about the Holy Spirit in terms antithetical to the notion of "social justice." In effect there were—and in many circles, there still is and are—three strikes against making that connection. First, the Holy Spirit came down and touched down, Scripture itself tells us, on human flesh (see Acts 2:17), not on human society or societies as a whole; hence to link the work of the Spirit to the social sphere was inconceivable at best, and a case of mistaken extension at worst.

Second, the Spirit was concerned about human persons, in fact, about enabling human salvation and their being born again, which included regeneration, justification, and sanctification; hence, yes, the Spirit was at work to ensure that, as Scripture said, "The just shall live by faith" (Hab 2:4, Rom 1:17, Gal 3:11, Heb 10:38), which is about the justification of individual hearts and lives, not about social justice.

Last but not least, the work of the Holy Spirit is to apply the redemptive work of Christ for the salvation of all souls; hence, the goal of the Spirit's redeeming works had to do with the spiritual realm—with life-after-death, with eternal life in the heavenly presence of the transcendent God—not the socio-political domains of the terrestrial and creaturely world. In short, those of us who were caught up in the Spirit-filled, inspired, and empowered life were participants in God's mission to save souls from this world to prepare them for the one to come, and in this conception, the quest for social justice was at best a tangential aberration and at worst a deception of the devil to keep us from being more fully engaged with what really and eternally counted.

One might say that such a modernist, individualistic, and spiritualized understanding of the gospel is a caricature that mischaracterizes contemporary Pentecostal communities and their beliefs. Perhaps; but let's be even more precise than this: the preceding depiction is surely more prevalent among socially and economically privileged—read: Anglo—Pentecostal communities that have not had to deal, historically, with socio-political and economic marginalization. On the contrary, African American and Latino/a Pentecostal churches especially, while in some respects manifesting variously elements of the foregoing description prevalent across the spectrum of communities that have historically embraced the *Pentecostal* label, have done so under the conditions and constraints of measuring up to social (and ecclesial) structures established by European ideals, assumptions, and perspectives. For these groups of Pentecostals in North America, then, the good news of Jesus Christ empowers faithful discipleship amid and against oppressive social and—to be blunt—racialized conditions. For these brothers and sisters, the justification of individual souls and personal hearts has always been interrelated with social justice since the love of God and love of neighbor was not just a matter of incidental personal interactions but are part and parcel of the day-to-day and moment-to-moment structural realities making (im)possible relationship between those who were, as the Sunday School song intoned, "red and yellow, black and white."

The modern Pentecostal movement, as we know, saw glimpses at its inception at Azusa Street of, as the saying went, "the color line being washed away in the blood." If we had been able to maintain that fraternity and solidarity, the history of Pentecostalism in North America at least would have been very different over the last century. Unfortunately, as was the case with the economic mutuality and reciprocity of the earliest Messianists in Jerusalem that lasted only for an apparently short period, so also did the multi-raciality of Azusa Street persist for a few years before the segregationism of the North American polis divided whites from others too. My point is less to be inflammatory about this racialized history of the Pentecostal movement—I am only naming a past and persisting reality—than to observe that those who are either oblivious to the call for social justice or who would want to subordinate that task to the presumed "real work" of evangelism and mission are those who are fortunate enough, because of the color of their skin, to remain unconcerned about a holistic understanding of the demands of the gospel.

As an Asian American—Malaysian-born and North American raised (since I was ten)—Pentecostal minister, I have been a beneficiary of the faithfulness of white (Caucasian) Pentecostal missionaries under whose ministry my parents came to know Christ and who then sponsored our migration to the USA to work among Chinese speaking immigrants to Northern California. Our own imbibed Confucian ethic, internalized in ways consistent with the Puritan way of life behind the North American evangelical church, enabled embrace of this specific expression of the evangelical-Pentecostal ethos and embodiment of its European/white normativity as equivalent with a "biblical worldview." From that perspective, the Scriptures were understood and read according to a modernist mentality, one that did not allow recognition of social justice concerns that are manifest throughout the Bible. In fact, my reputation as a theologian was perhaps enhanced precisely because I was deemed to be so good in interpreting the Bible in ways privileged by my Asian American location aligned with the dominant North American evangelical

cultural milieu. Who knows? If I had been more insistent about calling attention to the historical, social, and economic forces at work in the world that are opposed to the priorities of biblical justice, maybe my work would have been dismissed and my voice marginalized.

Perhaps recent developments in our national (North American) political scene have confronted us with the fact that we don't actually have a "colorblind" society like our evangelical (historically predominantly white) pietism has presumed and prefers to self-describe and declare. The nationalism and anti-immigration platform of the current administration that has been supported by and remains popular among a large percentage of white evangelicals in this country has awakened us to the call of the biblical gospel that is for people of every tongue and tribe to and from the ends of the earth, and that message stands against the Caesars of this world. In fact, the essays to come all reflect, in one way or another, such a hermeneutical perspective. This perspective is one that has been formed to observe social justice as a major scriptural theme. Its authors are either persons of color who have experienced the underside of imperial society or have lived in some way in solidarity with such persons. Therefore they are more alert to how such locations and structures ("principalities and powers"— to use the

Pauline terminology) prompt attentiveness to the voices of the poor and marginalized that resonate throughout the Bible.

In short, the Pentecostal and Evangelical imagination that has always been committed to the authority of Scripture periodically needs to attend to voices coming from different socio-historical locations so that we can be renewed in our biblical commitments. The chapters in this and its companion volume gather together those who are devoted to the Spirit-filled/empowered renewal of the life of the mind in order to reconsider the scope of the gospel and of the mission of God. The book you hold in your hands is particularly relevant for those who want to ensure that the call to God's just order that has socio-political, not to mention economic, environmental, and other, implications needs to be rooted in the biblical witness. Fidelity to Scripture will, in turn, deepen our comprehension of the gospel and dedication to work displaying the divine compassion and love for the world. Those who are open to imagining otherwise from individualistic, spiritualized, and other-worldly theological and doctrinal horizons that have hampered the church's mission will not only be informed but be empowered by the many voices that speak through the following pages to herald the righteousness of the coming day and reign of the Lord.

Introduction

Antipas L. Harris and Michael D. Palmer

This book explores issues situated at the intersection of two broad themes: one theological (the Holy Spirit), the other ethical (social justice). That the conversation, centering on these two themes, should arise is not unexpected. From the beginning of the modern spiritual awakening (known as the Pentecostal movement), more than a century ago, those who emphasized a theology and *praxis* of the Holy Spirit also demonstrated social concern. What has changed—and therefore what is exceptional—is the scope and maturity of the conversations. In the past three decades, socially conscious Bible scholars, theologians, social scientists, pastors, historians, and others, have all added their voices, intensifying and focusing the conversations. Together they form a polyglot and global cohort. This book contributes to the growing body of work of those who seek to understand and assess questions of social justice from a pneumatological perspective. The contributing authors represent several ecclesial traditions, scholarly disciplines, and countries of origin.

Social Justice

The Italian Roman Catholic Jesuit scholar, Luigi Taparelli D'Azeglio (1793–1862), is generally credited with being the first to use the expression *social justice*. Drawing heavily on the moral teachings of the thirteenth century theologian Thomas Aquinas, D'Azeglio focused mainly on problems associated with the industrial revolution of the nineteenth century.

Today the expression *social justice* is used much more widely. The breadth of its semantic domain becomes apparent if we examine the constitutive terms: *social* and *justice*. Ethicists, philosophers, and theologians, use *justice* to refer to beliefs and practices by which peoples and individual persons do any one or more of the following: express concern for weak and vulnerable members of the community; sustain the com-munity; treat each other fairly; resolve disputes and grievances; distribute community resources; uphold the dignity of the human person; promote peaceful interaction; enhance political or economic participation in the community; or encourage a sense of stewardship for the natural world.

The word *social* suggests that social justice has to do with matters of justice at the societal level rather than the strictly personal level. Thus, for example, social justice is not principally about individual persons acquiring the virtue of justice. Depending on the context, it can be a near-synonym for any one of several forms of justice, including distributive justice, compensatory justice, restorative justice, or procedural justice. Moreover, it is not uncommon for actions having profound and positive social implications to be called something other than social justice. *Compassion*, *mercy*, and *hospitality* are examples. Let us briefly define and illustrate these expressions of justice.

Social Justice as Distributive Justice
Distributive justice (an ancient concept, explicated at least as early as Aristotle) is essentially a comparative concept having to do with

3

the just or fair allocation of benefits and burdens among the members of a social group. In "The Concept of Social Justice," William Frankena describes distributive justice as a purely formal principle: equals should be treated equally, and unequals should be treated unequally in proportion to their inequality.[1] More recently David Miller has described distributive justice more concretely:

> Very crudely, I think, we are discussing how the good and bad things in life should be distributed among the members of human society. When... we attack some policy or some state of affairs as socially unjust, we are claiming that a person, or more usually a category of persons, enjoys fewer advantages than that person or group ought to enjoy (or bears more of the burdens than they ought to bear), given how other members of the society in question are faring.[2]

Questions about distributive justice arise when avail-able resources (e.g., food, money, education, and healthcare) are insufficient to meet everybody's needs or when the available resources, even if sufficient, are allocated in a way that does not meet the needs of all members of the group. Questions about distributive justice also arise when burdens (e.g., onerous work, inadequate shelter, care of the very young, the very old, and those with disabilities) are excessive or unfairly imposed.

Distributive justice shows up as a theme in the Scriptures, nowhere more clearly than in the book of *Acts*.

4

Now during those days, when the disciples were increasing in number, the Hellenists complained against the Hebrews because their widows were being neglected in the daily distribution of food. And the twelve called together the whole community of the disciples and said, "It is not right that we should neglect the word of God in order to wait on tables. Therefore, friends, select from among yourselves seven men of good standing, full of the Spirit and of wisdom, whom we may appoint to this task, while we, for our part, will devote ourselves to prayer and to serving the word." What they said pleased the whole community, and they chose Stephen, a man full of faith and the Holy Spirit, together with Philip, Prochorus, Nicanor, Timon, Parmenas, and Nicolaus, a proselyte of Antioch. They had these men stand before the apostles, who prayed and laid their hands on them (Acts 6:1-6).

The problem that arose in the early days of the Church in Jerusalem was one of distributive justice: the widows among the Hellenists "were being neglected in the daily distribution of food." They were hungry. In response, the Apostles appointed seven men, "men of good standing, full of the Spirit and of wisdom." Foremost among them was Stephen, described as "a man full of faith and the Holy Spirit." These seven men, led by Stephen, were tasked with ensuring

5

that the widows among the Hellenists received adequate portions of food.

Social Justice as Compensatory Justice

As the name suggests, compensatory justice has to do with compensating someone or some social group. To compensate is to make whole, to make fair restitution to someone or some social group that has incurred loss or suffered injury because of someone else's wrongful act. The restitution may take many forms. It could be the replacement of a lost, damaged, or destroyed item; monetary compensation; or restitution by work.

Compensatory justice is governed by social rules, some of which are explicit and codified and others of which are implicit and context dependent. For instance, typically, the perpetrator of the loss or injury (not someone else) is expected to provide restitution to the victim. But what if the injury or loss occurred long ago, has persisted without remedy, and the actual perpetrators no longer survive? Then is anyone responsible to make restitution?

This question and other related questions are not simply hypothetical and rhetorical musings? They emerge with some measure of exigency in the way members of racial and ethnic minorities have been treated historically. For instance, African Americans have made claims of compensatory justice against the larger, dominant cultures in which their ancestors were enslaved. Their grievances are related to the social disadvantages from which they still suffer today due to their ancestors' loss of freedom and sometimes loss of life.

Social Justice as Restorative Justice

Restorative justice normally differs from compensatory justice in what it tries to achieve. The language of restoration is in fact sometimes used when talking about compensatory justice. But though there is no sharp or absolute line between compensatory justice and restorative justice, there is a practical distinction between the two. In practice, compensatory justice limits its attempts to restore or "make whole" to acts of exchanging products, money, or labor. If I damage your home, I must compensate you; i.e., I must pay to have your home repaired. Restorative justice, on the other hand, typically has more to do with human relationships than with property damage or loss.

An example of restorative justice among peoples associated with Pentecostal and Charismatic movements is the so-called "Miracle in Memphis." The history of race relations in classical Pentecostal circles is mixed but generally does not reflect well on Pentecostals. At the Azusa Street revivals in the early part of the twentieth century (1906 - 1913) people of many races worshiped together without apparent racial discord. At the time of the revival, Azusa was described by the press as a "colored" congregation that met in a "tumble-down shack." Yet according to historian Mel Robeck, "It was a church where whites, blacks, Hispanics, Asians, and others met together regularly and where from their own perspective the "color-line" was virtually nonexistent."[3] In the decades that followed, Pentecostals generally succumbed to the prevailing views of the popular culture. Few churches were integrated; the vast majority were single-race congregations.

The most notable single event involving racial recon-ciliation in Pentecostal circles occurred in 1994 at an inter-racial convocation of Pentecostal leaders, ministers, and scholars in Memphis, Tennessee. At that time the all-white Pentecostal Fellowship of North America (PFNA) was disbanded in favor of a racially inclusive association named the "Pentecostal and Charismatic Churches of North America"—the PCCNA. During the session–called by some "the Miracle in Memphis"–leaders of predominantly white Pentecostal de-nominations repented of the long-standing racial insensitivity and implicit racism in the denominations they represented. Unlike the all-white leadership structure of the disbanded PFNA, the leadership of the newly established PCCNA was racially balanced: six whites and six blacks and headed by Bishop Ithiel Clemmons of the Church of God in Christ. Commenting on the convocation, historian and eye-witness Vinson Synan observed:

> The high point of the historic gathering was the session where a white Assemblies of God pastor washed the feet of Bishop Clemmons while begging forgiveness for the sins of the past. After this Bishop Charles Blake of Los Angeles washed the feet of Thomas Trask, General Superintendent of the Assemblies of God.[4]

Social Justice as Procedural Justice
Procedural justice has its most direct application in legal and quasi-legal settings in which laws, rules, guidelines, protocols, or policies are enacted, administered, or adjudicated. The settings in which these actions are taken may be legislative settings, civil courts of law,

settings in which laws are administered or enforced (e.g., encounters between civilians and members of law enforcement agencies), or even ecclesiastical bodies.

Prophets in the Old Testament were often concerned in one way or another with matters of procedural justice. The prophet Amos decried the plight of people who were treated unfairly in ancient Israel. Amos was active during the first half of the eighth century BCE, during the long reign of Jeroboam II (788 - 747 BCE). During this time, Israel was at the height of its territorial expansion and in many ways was a prosperous country. But this prosperity did not extend to all of Israel's people. There were gross inequities between urban elites and the poor. The laws of the land were routinely used by wealthy land owners to manipulate the poor. Even small debts were used to divest people of their land and personal liberty. In this context, Amos says,

> Hear this, you that trample on the needy, and bring to ruin the poor of the land, saying, "When will the new moon be over so that we may sell grain; and the sabbath, so that we may offer wheat for sale? We will make the ephah small and the shekel great, and practice deceit with false balances, buying the poor for silver and the needy for a pair of sandals, and selling the sweepings of the wheat." The Lord has sworn by the pride of Jacob: Surely I will never forget any of their deeds. (Amos 8:4-7)

The prophet Isaiah leveled a similar charge against those who used the laws of the land to exploit the poor.

> Ah, you who make iniquitous decrees, who write oppressive statutes, to turn aside the needy from justice and to rob the poor of my people of their right, that widows may be your spoil, and that you may make the orphans your prey! (Isa 10:1-2)

The words of Amos and Isaiah were directed against those who exploited the weak and vulnerable. By manipulating existing laws and by enacting new onerous laws, the powerful violated the very procedures which were intended to guarantee fairness in public and private transactions.

The Holy Spirit

Links (both explicit and implicit) between the Holy Spirit and justice are evident throughout the Scriptures. We call attention to a few of them here in order to set the stage for what the contributing authors will say later.

In the book of Genesis, the Spirit, described as a wind (*ruach*, 1:2), is present at creation, bringing order out of chaos. *Order out of chaos* may seem to be something other than *justice* but linking the two concepts is not unprecedented. In the *Republic*, Plato defines justice both at the level of the individual and at the societal level as a harmony of the parts: in the individual, a harmony of the parts of the soul; in society, a harmony among the various social units. The

Spirit achieves something like this harmony when is brings order out of chaos at creation.

The book of Exodus uses the imagery of wind/spirit (*ruach*) to evoke the overwhelming power and awesome presence of God. It is God's *ruach* that divides the Red Sea (Ex. 14:21), thus allowing Israel to escape Egyptian bondage. By facilitating movement away from bondage and toward liberation, *ruach* evokes not only God's power and presence, but also God's redemptive purpose, an important precursor to an explicit conceptualization of justice.

The prophetic tradition is rich with links between the work of the Spirit of God and acts of justice. Nowhere is this more evident than in Isaiah 61, where the prophet announces his mission. Endowed with the spirit of God, he says that his mission is to proclaim good news to the poor and downtrodden and to proclaim the jubilee year of release from slavery.

In the New Testament (Lk 4:14-21), Jesus explicitly ties his own mission and ministry to the prophet's proclamation. Standing in the synagogue in Nazareth, he reads the words of the prophet:

> The Spirit of the Lord is upon me, because he has anointed me to bring good news to the poor. He has sent me to proclaim release to the captives and recovery of sight to the blind, to let the oppressed go free, to proclaim the year of the lord's favor.

After reading these words from the scroll (Is. 61:1), he declares, "Today this scripture has been fulfilled in your hearing" (Lk 4:21).

11

These passages by no means exhaust the scriptural links between the work of the Spirit and acts of justice. But they are enough to prepare the way for our contributing authors to share their insights.

Overview and Arrangement of Chapters

When we identify the Holy Spirit as one of two major themes in this volume, we are not thereby committing ourselves to the pneumatological teachings of any specific confessional group. Rather, we have left it to the contributing authors to explore, describe, explain, or envision for us what it means to say that the Holy Spirit empowers the church to undertake acts of justice. Some of the authors belong to Classical Pentecostal groups or denominations. Others, who call themselves Charismatic Christians, belong to traditional streams of the Christian tradition; e.g., Baptist, Eastern Orthodox, or Anglican. Diverse in theology and practice, they share a common interest in the historical and ongoing work of the Holy Spirit, particularly as that work relates to justice. We now summarize the contributions of these authors.

The lead chapter in this volume is Néstor Medina's theological reflection entitled "Thinking Pneumatology and Social Justice." Given that so many people seem oblivious to the role of the Holy Spirit in matters of social justice, Medina asks the reader to imagine two fundamental possibilities: (a) Can we imagine the Spirit being involved in social justice struggles, and (b) What would a Spirit-involvement in social justice look like? With these two questions clearly in focus, Medina says, "My goal is to reflect on how we can begin to imagine the activity of the Spirit in social justice movements and how we can theologize about it."

The remainder of the chapters in this volume are arranged into four sections: (I) The Holy Spirit in the Old Testament; (II) The Holy Spirit in the New Testament; (III) Living in the Spirit; and (IV) Following the Spirit.

Section I: The Holy Spirit in the Old Testament

Section I focuses mainly on the Holy Spirit's role in the prophetic tradition of the Old Testament. In "Elijah the Architect of a Spirit-Driven Prophetic Ministry," Jin H. Han explores themes of justice and mercy in the ministry of the prophet Elijah. He concludes that Elijah serves as a model for other prophets in the Old Testament. As Elijah did before them, the other prophets "deliver God's message and engage themselves in the ministry of justice and mercy as God directs them—only as the Holy Spirit leads them." Han surmises, "the present time is in critical need of such a prophet as Elijah, whose prophetic ministry can only be defined by his singlehearted service to God."

In "Social Justice in First Isaiah," Jacqueline N. Grey illuminates the often-overlooked message of justice in the prophetic ministry of Isaiah. She begins by situating her inquiry within her own Pentecostal tradition, which accentuates three themes: experience, empowerment, and eschatology. Drawing on these three themes, she explores social justice in the first 39 chapters of Isaiah. The eighth century BCE prophet of Judah experiences God from the moment of his call to ministry in Isaiah 6, and the totality of his theophany influences his message of social justice. Secondly, Grey examines the ways in which the Spirit empowers the prophet to address the injustices of his day. Thirdly, she attends to Isaiah's vision for a just society. Finally, Grey asks how Isaiah's message of social justice speaks to a contemporary Spirit-filled community. She concludes that his message calls for the people of God to be inwardly renewed and to affirm the Spirit's call for solidarity with the disenfranchised.

The last two chapters in this section are treatments of books from the Writings of the Old Testament – the Psalms and Ruth. In "He Raises the Poor from the Dust," Lee Roy Martin shows that issues of justice are addressed not only in Old Testament prophetic literature but also in the Psalms, where it is clear that God intended Israel to be an advocate for justice. Martin shows that the Psalms are a rich source of theology regarding economic concerns and calls attention to the relationships in the Psalms between the poor and the worshipping community. According to Martin, the Psalms show that God acts on behalf of the destitute and holds the worshiping community accountable for caring for and advocating on behalf of them.

In "Waiting for a Hero: Will Someone Do the Right Thing?" William L. Lyons and Jordan M. Way offer their interpretation of the book of Ruth, the narrative about a Moabite woman, who, despite personal tragedies, emerges as a notable figure in ancient Israelite society. Ruth is identified in the Scriptures as standing in the ancestral line of King David into whose family the New Testament messiah was born. For Lyons and Way, Ruth's story calls attention to the needs of disenfranchised and marginalized people in antiquity and holds lessons for people of faith today.

Section II: The Holy Spirit in the New Testament

The second arrangement of essays focuses on themes in the New Testament. In "The Gospel and Racial Reconciliation" Craig Keener offers a scriptural response to the contemporary problem of racism. He points out that the racial history of America provides abundant illustrations of the biblical principle of human depravity. At the same time, the Gospel of Christ offers hope for restoring the relationship between God and human beings and for healing the damaged relationships among human beings, particularly where racism is an issue. But there is more work to do. "Those who are really serious about reconciliation," says Keener, "must be willing to cross ecclesiastical as well as color boundaries. Such barriers can be crossed only if we unite on the basis of our common need before our Lord Jesus Christ, who has reconciled us all to the Father in one body by His cross."

In "The Spirit of Christ, Identity and the Undocumented in Our Midst," Tommy Cásarez undertakes a theological analysis of "space-making," his metaphor for welcoming the "other" into one's personal, familial, and communal life. The "other" is anyone we regard as different from ourselves—such as those who live among us but who lack official legal status (the "undocumented"). Cásarez explores how followers of Christ must understand Christian identity in relation to the "other." Specifically, he investigates how Christ's identity "shapes, defines, and determines not only our identity but also the shape and character of flourishing Christian life. It is from a theological understanding of identity," he says, "that we will find resources for better understanding ourselves and the undocumented other in our midst." His larger aim is to sketch out what he calls "a space-making theological ethic."

Alaine Thomson Buchanan's "God's Image and Likeness through Christ" takes a biblical-theological-historical turn away from the New Testament to re-examine Genesis 1-3. She proposes that understanding of Genesis 1-3 and key elements in the history of interpreting these passages can help us understand why the Genesis passages have been wrongly taken to authorize unequal treatment of certain people because of their gender, race, or ethnic heritage. At the same time, says Buchanan, looking more closely at Jesus' life and teachings can "jolt His followers' consciousness to the life and work of the Spirit that empowers them to live into the fullness of what God intends to be an equal human reflection of divine image and likeness."

Section II concludes with Adam White's chapter, "God Chose the Poor: Recapturing the Radical Vision of Early Pentecostalism and the Original Pauline Communities." White argues that modern Pentecostalism, at its heart, reflects the same egalitarian values that Paul attempted to establish in the churches he established in the first century. However, just as first-century Pauline churches (e.g., Corinth) departed from Paul's instructions against giving certain people preferential treatment, so too modern Pentecostals quickly lost sight of their egalitarian beginnings. Like the first-century Pauline churches, modern Pentecostals acquiesced to pressures to conform to the broader culture's values. "Equality and commonality quickly gave way to divisions along traditional social lines. The Pentecostal community, in other words, lost sight of its original ideals and continues in many ways to do so today." For White, the challenge remains to recapture the original vision.

Section III: Living in the Spirit

Chapters in Section III attend to the ethics of the Spirit. The first of these chapters is Lisa Bowens' "Spirit-Shift," in which she raises several questions in light of St. Paul's message to the Spirit-filled urban church of Corinth. For example, what does it mean that such a Spirit-filled congregation could be so beset by divisions and rifts, and how does Paul's reprimands about their observance of the Lord's Supper speak to us today about the Spirit and issues of social justice, especially economic justice? Responding to these questions, Bowens provides a brief history of the city of Corinth, reviews Paul's "Spirit-speech," provides a short exegetical analysis 1 Corinthians 11:17-26 and reflecting on this analysis. In essence, Bowens illuminates Paul's inclusive ethic of the Spirit and Eucharistic theology in light of his pastoral interests in marginalized persons. She concludes the chapter with some thoughts on the implications of Paul's words for today.

J. Lyle Story's "Indictment of Partiality and Redirection" is an examination of an important ethical theme in the book of James. Based on a careful examination of James 2:1-13, Story builds a case against an unethical attitude/behavior which he calls *partiality:* favoritism, prejudice, sexism, classism, racism, and other forms of preferential or discriminatory treatment. He argues that James seeks to influence the communities to whom he is writing—communities of the diaspora—to abandon attitudes and behaviors of partiality and to adopt inclusive, welcoming, and hospitable attitudes and behaviors. This "redirection" of attitudes and behaviors is both spiritual and justice-seeking. He concludes that attitudes of the heart play out in the way that people are treated. When one has the right spirit, bigotry and exclusion dissipate.

This section concludes with "Healing the 'Us versus Them' Divide," in which Enoch Sathiasatchi Charles addresses the problem of inter-group cooperation. Charles argues that exclusively naturalistic attempts to explain inter-group cooperation fail, leaving a "gap" which needs to be bridged or, as he says, healed. Assisted by Michael Palmer's pneumatological reading of Thomas Aquinas' account of theological virtues[5] coupled with a brief exegetical analysis of the Peter-Cornelius inter-ethnic encounter in the book of Acts, Charles advances the thesis that God offers an empowering friendship with humanity through the Holy Spirit. This Spirit-empowered friendship cultivates transformative virtues and enables human beings to open themselves to the other. According to Charles, "the pneumatological solution to the problem of inter-group cooperation is not only effective but also overcomes the inadequacies of the naturalistic alternative."

Section IV: Following the Spirit

The chapters in Section IV direct the conversation toward a re-visioning of God's ideal of justice. In "The Liberating Spirit," Anthony Roberts argues that the Spirit carries out its work within and through the human community, not apart from the community. And justice is the foundation of this community. Thus, for Roberts, the most important feature of the Acts 2 narrative is that the Church was established as a justice-making community empowered by the Holy

Spirit. To advance his thesis, Roberts examines the social thought of one of the fathers of the church, Basil the Great, fourth-century bishop of Caesarea. He concludes by constructing the basic points of the social evidence of the Spirit's presence. In his words, "a liberative Pentecostal pneumatology must center on the common life that comes into existence through God's power. By focusing on the social evidence of the Spirit's work, it is possible to avoid the mistake of simply seeing the work of the Spirit as an inward pietistic experience. Looking to the community created by the Spirit liberates pneumatology and makes it genuinely liberative."

John Moxen addresses the themes of the Holy Spirit and social justice from an Orthodox perspective. In "Orthodox Christian Spirituality and Social Justice," he advances the claim that anyone who follows Christ's mandate to serve impoverished, vulnerable, and destitute people is doing the work of the Spirit of God. (His exemplar of this claim is St. Basil.) "Social Justice," he says, "is an act of worship, connecting a person with Christ as well as his or her neighbor." That last word, "neighbor," is important for Moxen's *praxis*. He seeks to move beyond the practice of welcoming the stranger into our midst (which in some ways he views as a limiting concept) to the richer, fuller *praxis* of engaging people as "neighbors"—people who, because they bear the image of God, are already whole persons capable of establishing deep ties with us.

Richard E. Waldrop, in "Global Pentecostalism: A Spirit-Led Movement of, for, and by the Poor," explores the nuanced and complicated relationships between Pentecostalism(s) and the poor. He explains his purpose this way: "I see my objective as being able to communicate something of the disposition of the Pentecostal churches, leaders, and people in general toward the poor." In many ways, he explains, the relationships between Pentecostals and the poor are healthy and life-giving: "organic, symbiotic, and dynamic," as he puts it. But there are glaring exceptions, among them the tendency of North American Pentecostals to deliver to the rest of the world a message in which the gospel is too often "limited in scope to the spiritual dimension of human existence." Also, "North American missionaries and mission boards (Pentecostals and others) have been imperialistic in terms of their culture and politics as they have historically and uncritically sided with the policies of the U.S. government." In an important section entitled Recent Development and Challenges, Waldrop deals with two categories of challenges: (1) those which he regards as primarily internal to the Pentecostal movement and (2) the issue of the so-called "prosperity gospel." He concludes the chapter with what amounts to a benedictory prayer: "My hope and my prayer is that the global Pentecostal movement will continue to provide a home for the poor for many, many years to come and that we will all learn more and more how to embrace the poor and receive the gifts of the poor with dignity, love, and respect so that the Spirit of Life will continue to breathe in and through us."

This volume concludes with Herbert R. Marbury's homiletic essay entitled, "Write the Vision and Make it Plain!" This chapter brings the volume full circle. Preaching is the hallmark of theology. Also, it stirs-up the Holy Spirit in the midst of the congregation. Sermons meet the people where they are, in their lived situation – whether their "sin-sick souls" or the depredations of social life. The Word is made flesh as the Spirit moves with solutions that bring unspeakable "joy that the world can't give, and the world can't take away!"

Furthermore, Marbury continues a similar tradition of theologian Karl Barth who said, "Take your Bible and your newspaper, and read both. But interpret newspapers from your Bible."[6] Rev. Dr. Samuel D. Proctor calls this dialectical homiletics. Marbury holds Genesis 1 in one hand and contemporary concerns in the other. His dialectical sermon elucidates a biblical vision of hope from an ancient people who were living under Persian and Greek oppression. However, readers who expect the scholar side of Marbury to go down a rabbit trail of ancient history are mistaken. He puts ancient history in conversation with contemporary black history. In the tradition of black dialectical preaching, Marbury draws from the biblical text a message for those who live under the repressive force of white supremacy.

Contemporary experiences that are antithetical to beauty and hope mirror the conditions of the ancient world. Yet, true to the black preaching tradition, Marbury does not leave the reader without optimism. He ends the sermon with hope and something to do. First, the hope is that Genesis 1 envisages a God who creates beauty from decadence. Then, Marbury encourages believers to "write the vision and make it plain."

Too often, oppressed people merely react to isolated assaults upon their humanity. When emotions wane, they go back to the hustle and bustle of survival mode without a clear vision for what true freedom looks like. This was, however, not the case in antiquity. This article shows that Genesis 1 is a vision of hope and freedom written down. Marbury points out that the ancient priesthood wrote a vision and made it plain for their people, the new inhabitants of Jerusalem. When we write the vision of hope and plainly demand a better life for all oppressed people, we prophetically lift a broken world out of the ruins of our own metaphoric Babylonian devastation and point fragile humanity toward the freedom and fulfillment that God intended—in the beginning.

Bibliography

Anderson, A. H. *An Introduction to Pentecostalism: Global Charismatic Christianity*. Cambridge, UK: Cambridge University Press, 2013.

Barry, Brian. *Why Social Justice Matters*. Cambridge, UK: Polity Press, 2005.

Capeheart, Loretta and Dragan Milovanovic. *Social Justice: Theories, Issues and Movements*. New Brunswick, NJ: Rutgers University Press, 2007.

Clayton, Matthew and Andrew Williams, eds. *Social Justice*. Oxford, UK: Blackwell Publishing, 2004.

Dempster, Murray, Klaus, B. D., and Petersen, D., eds. *The globalization of Pentecostalism: a religion made to travel*. Eugene, OR: Wipf and Stock Publishers, 2011.

Fleischacker, Samuel. *A Short History of Distributive Justice*. Cambridge, Mass.: Harvard University Press, 2004.

Frankena, William. "The Concept of Social Justice," in Brandt, ed. *Social Justice*. Englewood Cliffs: NJ: Prentice Hall, 1964. 1-29.

Miller, David. *Principles of Social Justice*. Cambridge, MA: Harvard University Press, 1999.

Portier-Yong, Anathea E. and Gregory E. Sterling. Lanham, MD:
    Lexington Books/Fortress Academic, *Scripture and Social
    Justice.* 2018.

Vondey, Wolfgang. "The Unity and Diversity of Pentecostal
    Theology: A Brief **Account** for the Ecumenical Community in
    the West." *Ecclesiology* 10:1, May 9, 2014.

Westfall, Cynthia Lon and Bryan R. Dyer. *The Bible and Social
    Justice: Old Testament and New Testament Foundations for the
    Church's Urgent Call,* Eugene, OR: Pickwick Publications, 2016.

Chapter 1

Thinking Pneumatology and Social Justice

Néstor Medina

> Por lo mismo, una iglesia que no sea de los pobres siempre
> tendrá miedo de la libertad, y de luchar por la libertad. "Una
> teología del Espíritu Santo sólo puede proceder de la praxis
> de un pueblo cristiano libre."[1]

Can we; or, how do we discern the activity of the Spirit as it relates
to social justice? What are some insights one might glean from those
who organize and struggle against oppressive and discriminatory
social forces? What theological principles might one discover from
social justice movements? What are forces that provoke or inspire
people to want to work toward changing the social conditions of
inequality? These are challenging questions for many Christians. For
some, it is second nature to their Christian impulse; for them, it
appears self-evident that the Christian role and vocation includes
advocating for social justice. For others, including many Pentecostals
and Evangelicals, concerns about social justice are, at best, secondary
and, at worst, entirely absent. It seems that their central concern
laser focuses on issues pertaining to the *soul*.

The question often missing in these conversations has to do
with the role of the Spirit when it comes to social justice. Can we
imagine a) the Spirit involved in social justice struggles, and b) what
a Spirit-involvement in social justice might look like? As stated

above, Christians are also divided in their responses on the manner and degree to which the Spirit can be said to be (un)involved in social justice efforts. These questions are the central concern of this chapter. My goal is to reflect on how we can begin to imagine the activity of the Spirit in social justice movements and how we can theologize about it.

Holy Spirit, Social Justice and the Bible

Over the years, social justice movements have become fairly adept at quoting the biblical text to emphasize some of the material and social implications of the Gospel. Entire volumes have been dedicated to articulating and studying the multiple ways in which social inequality, in its multiple damaging expressions, is a crucial concern in the biblical text. Any person would be hard pressed to deny that the Hebrew Bible and the New Testament contain numerous passages concerning widows, migrants, the poor, the exploited, the socially disenfranchised, and the outright social responsibility of Christians toward others. We find in the Hebrew Bible evidence that spirituality and religious faith and devotion included measures akin to social transformation (Isaiah 48). The motifs of social transformation and responsibility appear in the New Testament as well. Jesus' teachings highlight our responsibility for the socially disenfranchised, the poor, the naked, the hungry, and the sick (e.g., Matt 25:36-40). This responsibility should not be postponed until the coming eschaton. Rather, struggles for social justice announce the eschaton prefigured in Jesus. Moreover, the biblical corpus teaches that this responsibility including the non-compromising principle of love, measured by how one responds in

25

the face of hunger and the social needs of other people (e.g., James 2:14-15; 1 John 3:16-18). I do not mean to enter into a proof-texting exercise. Instead, my intention is to show–in passing–how the biblical text itself does not leave much room for Christians to remain inactive in the face of social need. In addition, remembering what the Bible says can be an effective counter narrative to those who use the same Bible to justify forms and structures of injustice. In the words of Justo González,

> It is a well-known fact that the Bible has been used repeatedly in order to support repression and injustice. In Latin America, the Spanish conquest was justified on the basis of supposedly biblical teaching. In both North and South America, the Bible has been used to destroy significant cultures and civilizations. Again, in both continents, Paul's authority has been adduced in favor of slavery. In the United States, even after the abolition of slavery, and to this day, white supremacists claim that the Bible is on their side. Those--both men and women– who want to keep women subservient are constantly quoting the Pauline and Deutero-Pauline Epistles.[2]

Most people do not have a problem admitting that one ought to lend help to honest charitable organizations and causes when possible. But the questions we are considering are of a different nature. The biblical text, specifically the New Testament, shows a specific orientation toward a social restructuring in which the Holy Spirit seems to be directly involved. In Luke, Jesus' classic "The Spirit

26

of the Lord is upon me" speech (4: 18-20), which of course he borrows from the prophet Isaiah, announces the divine social jubilee for those most vulnerable in society. The same speech can be interpreted as the divine cry and commitment to correcting social ills. Also, the events narrated in the book of Acts demonstrate that the early church understood the *good news* as including a radical social reconfiguration, which undermined inherited social structures and ideas of hierarchies between ethnocultural groups (Peter and Cornelius in Acts 10). It also encouraged the empowerment and participation of women, as was the case with Paul and women like Lydia, Priscilla, and Phoebe (Acts 16, 18, and Rom 16:1-2 respectively). And it announced and embodied the creation of another social context where class-inspired social differences could be undone (they all had everything in common, Acts 4:32-35). By the time we arrive at the end of the New Testament, we encounter the disclosure of the fulfillment of the event of Pentecost as "a great multitude that no one could count, from every nation, tribe, people and language," are said to stand "before the throne and before the lamb." (Rev 7:9).

My point is that the biblical message moves beyond simple acts of charity, something else is afoot in the text. Inherent in the narratives one finds a divine impetus toward the restoration of creation and correction of social inequalities under the motif of justice. I propose that these two aspects are part of the original divine creative intent in which all of creation, including the social, cultural, political spheres, is being driven in the direction of full koinonia. It is not a romantic utopic vision of what we may "hope for" in the eschaton but a radical divine invitation to engage in struggles for social justice as ways of co-creating, participating in the continuation of the divine creative impetus. Understanding social justice movements as a way by which God continues the act of creating is particularly relevant today. It is an invitation for Christians, specifically Evangelical and Pentecostal churches, to change from remaining silent in the face of extreme racism, vitriol against immigrants, and discriminatory attitudes all of which run diametrically opposite to the divine invitation to love our neighbor. The rise of these movements begs the question of where the Spirit is engaged.

At the risk of sounding preachy, I must ask: if indeed poverty to the poor means death[3] and blackness and being Latina/o can guarantee police mistreatment sometimes to the point of death, longer incarceration, and greater under-employment and underpayment of wages, what is the responsibility of the churches, especially those that claim to be communities of the Spirit? What is our function in the presence of forms of government that stand diametrically opposed to the principles of life and human dignity which Christ espoused and which the Spirit continues to work toward?

Re-visiting the Question of Pneumatology and Social Justice

It is important to acknowledge that speaking of *social justice* to describe social inequality and advocate for social transformation and change is a relatively recent phenomenon. It is an even more recent shift to speak of social justice in connection with the Spirit. In the United States of America, Canada, and Western Europe the first half of the twentieth century witnessed the emergence of a wide range of social justice movements. It was the period of women's suffrage and temperance movements and the birth of the continuing struggles for women's participation in the political arena and social institutions. During the same period, social justice movements sprung up which included African descendants, Asians and Latinas/os in the Farm Labor Movements, civil rights movements and other social protest movements.[4] By the middle of the twentieth century, social justice struggles solidified and gained organizational momentum.

How do these movements translate into opportunities through which the church takes a stand on the side of the oppressed, marginalized, immigrant, discriminated against and racialized? It is common knowledge that the civil rights movement among African Americans emerged from and was deeply influenced by black churches. It is also common knowledge that many Latina/o Pentecostals were involved in the famous Farm Workers Union's Delano grape strike.[5]

But I argue that asking the romantic question, *what would Jesus do?* is not enough, I propose instead asking *what did Jesus do?* It better opens the possibilities for Christians to begin to reflect on the connections between the gospel message, the role of the Church, and God's activity in social movements. Moreover, discussing Jesus' life, ministry, His actions, and teachings only takes us halfway in addressing our question concerning the Spirit. We need to make the theological shift toward seeing Jesus' human existence and revelatory role as dependent on the work of the Spirit. The Biblical text says that much (Lk 1:35, 3:22, 4:18; Rom 8:11; Heb 9:14). Jesus' work, including His teachings about the poor, the widow, the incarcerated and hungry, were inspired and stemmed from His relationship and dependence on the Holy Spirit.

In other words, evangelization, which I understand as the extension of the proclamation of the *good news*, is a wholistic endeavor and reorientation to the fullness of life, including in the social realm. When the gospel is fulfilled, all people are deemed to be equal in social privileges and responsibilities; there is no one group which is entitled to more on the basis of their racialization or heritage. No-one goes hungry. All people from all ethnocultural backgrounds are welcome. The social, economic, political and cultural structures of society promote the dignity of all creation, including humanity. Pneumatologically speaking, can we say that the Spirit is more fully present and active—preferentially present and active—in those places and among those movements which seek to fulfill such objectives?

The Spirit and Social Justice Movements

Several theologians have reflected on the role and activity of the Spirit in social movements. However, an exhaustive analysis is too large for this short article. Here I offer a few examples to illustrate the range of how scholars have dealt with this most important theological question.

Seeking to build a bridge between religion and the cultural dimension, Paul Tillich argued for three cultures in a society: autonomous, heteronomous, and theonomous.[6] As he explained, autonomous cultures are those which function independently from religious concerns; these cultures do not exhibit any ultimate concerns and do not seem to be grounded in something unconditional or holy. Heteronomous cultures are those which emerge from and emphasize religious organizations. They can also be found in political movements which follow the patterns of religious institutions.[7] The third expression of the cultural, the theonomous, he identified as those cultures which provide the conditions for the reconciliation between the religious and cultural dimensions.[8]

Although Tillich found aspects of *ultimate concern* in the three groups, his discussion concerning autonomous cultures is pertinent here. He concluded that despite the fact that autonomous cultures function without any explicit religious concerns and do not explicitly express any ultimate concerns, they can still be said to be inspired by an ultimate concern. In specific reference to protest, revolutionary, and labor movements, he noted that "the Labor Movement, with the so-called de-christianized masses, showed me clearly that here too, within a humanistic framework, the Christian sub-stance was hidden, even though this humanism looked like a materialistic philosophy that had long since been discredited by art and science."[9] Echoed in other theologians' work, as in Karl Rahner's notion of anonymous Christians, Tillich finds in social justice movements a divine inspiration. But for our purposes, he goes only halfway in fully considering the activity of the Spirit.

Jürgen Moltmann is another theologian who has paid considerable attention to the connection between social justice and the Spirit.[10] In his theological understanding, the activity of the Spirit is manifest in the act of liberation for life. As he sees it, the Spirit is responsible for propelling believers to act in solidarity against forces of domination.[11] He claims the activity of the Spirit includes a social

31

dimension, where justification and sanctification relate to the restoration of communion and the construction of community. I would add that the activity of the Spirit must be understood as encompassing the church, which refers to the community of believers, but also extends beyond to encompass the whole created world. With Moltmann, we can conclude that the activity of the Spirit goes well beyond the confines of the institutional church.[12]

Resonating with Tillich, Moltmann also finds "Christian experiences of community" when people get together voluntarily and struggle against world problems and injustice, struggles which he credits to the Spirit.[13] This notion of the Spirit's involvement in creating community and fellowship is connected to experiencing God. In fact, it redirects individualist notions of relationship to God by affirming that God is most fully experienced in the encounter with others, and I would argue, with the different other.[14] By creating community, Moltmann argues, the Spirit "enters into fellowship with believers, and draws them into fellowship" with the divine.[15] As I see it, this perspective which views the Spirit's creation of community, both inside and outside the context of the church, has profound implications for viewing the Spirit as integral to social justice struggles and movements, including environ-mental justice.

Adopting a more church-centered approach, some Anabaptists see social justice as part of the church being a messianic community. For instance, John Driver argues that being a servant community is the concrete way in which the church can conform to and realize the messianic posture of Jesus in the world.[16] It is after Jesus—understood as the suffering servant—that Radical Anabaptists model them-selves.[17] The church—as servant community—adopts a non-resistant posture of non-conformity, refusing to reproduce the structures of oppression. The church is as sign or paradigm of the reign of God, according to Driver, and in the reign of God social justice is of necessity central.[18] Drawing on his own Anabaptist tradition of social disengagement, or put another way, engagement through service, he emphasizes that in the social struggle the church as messianic community distinguishes itself from other expressions of church in its willingness, or unwillingness, to "sacrifice persons in the interests of a just cause."[19] Crucial to Driver and the Anabaptists, then, is the realization that Christians are called to act in the face of injustice, and that a commitment to such action can bring with it negative effects against those who stand in solidarity with those who suffer injustice.

Latin American liberation theologians have dedicated much theological reflection to the question of social justice. Elsa Tamez, for instance, considers the connections between the notions of justification and social justice from the excluded.[20] She argues that justification means that God brings justice to those who do not have it; it denotes a type of justice that justifies and creates justice. At its heart, justification presupposes that God is on the side of justice and therefore on the side of those who suffer injustice.[21] In other words, justification, when viewed from the perspective of the excluded and marginalized, means in basic terms that God defends those who cannot do it themselves. God is integrally involved giving back to the oppressed the rights that until now have been withheld from them.[22] It is not just a question of justification for the sinner but the justification for those who have been sinned against.

Liberation theologians chastise traditional approaches to theology for not considering the social implications of the gospel or social contexts of oppression and discrimination as essential to the theological task. João Justino De Medeiros Silva, for example, insists that class interests and excesses are not supported by Christian spirituality. Using a Christological emphasis, he reasons that distributive equity and justice are diaphanously proclaimed in the gospel.[23] Meanwhile, Jorge Borán rejects individualist spiritualizing approaches. According to him, while personal change is fundamental, it cannot be separated from structural change. While the former leads to the improvement of individual social relations, the latter leads to social justice,[24] without which the former cannot take place. Liberation theologians insist that social justice must include an analysis of social structures including ecclesial structures and theological frames which preserve and reproduce forms of oppression.[25] At its roots, Leonardo Boff pointedly states that social justice is a struggle for life. Thinking about the implications of environmental justice, he writes that the church ought to seek for "the minimum social justice required to ensure that life has its basic dignity."[26]

Liberation theologians are not unfamiliar with the pneumatological implications of social justice. For example, thinking in terms of ethno-racial inclusiveness, José Comblin celebrates the creation of a new humanity summoned from all the nations of the world on the day of Pentecost. He writes that the activity of the Spirit is manifest in preventing the nations from losing their identity: "each speaks in its own language; the new humanity does not lose its diversity through being unified in Christ. The Spirit does not oblige the nations all to wear the same clothing."[27] In fact, "the Spirit is present in all human societies as a spur to point them in the direction of accepting liberation."[28]

In a similar vein, drawing on Vatican II, Comblin emphasizes that Christ is at work in the hearts of people through the energy of the Holy Spirit. It is the Spirit that is moving people to resist and to rise up against injustice. Movements of social justice, he claims, emerge from the presence of the Spirit among them. In other words, a life of faith and political life are, at this level, a single action. Faith, hope, charity, and political action are a single reality as people are moved by the Spirit.[29]

Comblin is critical of individualistic and spiritualizing views of the gospel often expressed among many Pentecostal-Evangelicals and many Catholics in Latin America. Concerning social justice movements, he argues that while in other times movements of change were viewed as being of the devil, today they are considered as stemming from the Spirit.[30] Not only is the Spirit active within the church but the Spirit also works outside ecclesial spaces.[31]

In fact, I would argue that the gap between the church and social movements is bridged by the very activity of the Spirit. For Comblin, the Spirit works toward social justice by making social miracles happen. He writes: "the Evangelical miracles that have greater success in Latin America are those which narrate that the paralytic walk, the deaf hear, the blind see, the dead are resurrected, those who did not act, are beginning to act.[32] But Comblin does not have physical miracles in mind. As he sees it, it is nothing short of miraculous when the people are able to see their own condition of oppression, poverty, discrimination, and marginalization. The poor

35

are healed when they take their destiny on their own hands. Blind people are healed when they can see their reality of oppression. The deaf are healed when they are willing to hear about their complicity in the oppression of others. And the dead are resurrected when the people rise up to become agents of social change. For Comblin, moving and inspiring people to resist and struggle against injustice must be credited to the activity of the Holy Spirit.

Other liberation scholars representing a variety of liberation currents have also reflected on the theological implications of social justice. They deserve a fuller analysis than is possible here. Briefly put, they are concerned about a wide range of issues which are viewed as constitutive of Christian living and action including the struggle for egalitarian social relations; inclusion and the celebration of racialized communities as equals; the construction of social conditions of equity, including preferential structures for minoritized communities; and efforts toward environmental justice. However, few of them have engaged in a sustained pneumatological reflection as it pertains to social justice.

Two important exceptions are worth noting, the Latina/o Pentecostals Eldín Villafañe and Samuel Solivan. Villafañe takes the socio-ethical and pneumatological implications of the gospel message seriously.[33] He invites Pentecostal believers to participate in the reign of God by challenging present social structures of evil and sin. Articulating an "ethics of pneumatology," he calls on Pentecostals to fulfill the prophetic and vocational role befitting those baptized by the Spirit.[34] He argues that love and justice are elements of the Spirit's strategy in the building of koinonia (manifest in our created connectivity with each other and with the divine) by

36

reimagining leitourgia (liturgy becomes people worshipping God by working with the poor and oppressed); announcing the kerygma (as fulfillment of the prophetic role against evil structures); and establishing diakonia (as geared to minister those in the periphery of society).[35] Put simply, for Villafañe, the empowerment of the Spirit must be shaped by love, justice and the praxis of liberation.[36]

A similar invitation to acknowledge the Spirit's activity in social justice can be found in Solivá n's proposal. He especially identifies the presence of the Spirit in diversity and inclusivity. So not surprisingly he views the event of Pentecost—the inclusion of diverse cultural communities—as a sign of the in-breaking of the reign of God. He argues that the outpouring of the Spirit was and continues to be a precondition for the possibility of diversity in the church today.[37] Solivá n sees the outpouring of the Spirit as breaking down walls designed to create barriers to fellowship across cultural and linguistic differences. For him, to be filled by the Spirit must provoke us to celebrate the cultural gifts of other ethnocultural groups. Not surprisingly, he states categorically that "any claim that one culture or racial group is superior to another is a direct assault on the justice and grace of God."[38] To be *Spirit-filled* therefore has social implications for Solivá n. It means to be *Spirit-led*, which is no easy task. It is a call and vocation to incarnate an ethic of love that directs us to love and "care for the stranger and the sojourner, and to extend hospitality to the foreigner and the sinner."[39] As the giver of faith, hope, and love, the Spirit also makes it possible for believers to "overcome the oppressive forces that seek to dehumanize us; the Spirit makes it possible for us to liberate our oppressors [also] because we can overcome the sinful tendency to oppress others."[40]

As I bring this section to a close, I wish to highlight decolonial thinking as the latest current which challenges the epistemological structures that created the conditions for the present social racialized hierarchical configuration in USA, Canada and the rest of the world. They argue that is important to acknowledge that there are social, political and economic structures that prevent minoritized and racialized communities from thriving, structures which are an essential part of the intellectual apparatus of colonization. Notions of racial superiority, of superior Eurocentric forms of knowledge, culture, and civilization, are all part of the ideological edifice which allowed Western Europeans and later Anglo North Americans (particularly the USA) to invade and colonize many places in the world.[41] That same edifice produced an intellectual tradition which systematically colonized and/or dismissed other forms of knowledge, cultural traditions and customs, and placed itself at the center of the present economic geopolitical configuration.[42] More importantly for our purposes here, such colonizing forces and intellectual tradition were supported theologically. It is this colonizing ethos; racialized dismissal of other communities and their cultural traditions and forms of knowledge as inferior; and the hierarchical organization of the world, society, and ideas, including theological ideas, and all systems and structures of domination that are encompassed in what these scholars call the colonial matrix of power.[43] The colonial power matrix in turn bolsters explicit and often violent expressions of racism or ethnic supremacy, racialized discrimination against immigrants, and sociopolitical structures that deprive minoritized communities from equity and fair opportunities even within the church. These scholars compel us to extend social justice efforts even to the intellectual and theological arena. Presently, theologians from minoritized cultural communities are colonized by the dominant ethos in academia which dismisses their theological contributions as not really dealing with the "real theological task," nor properly being "systematic." Yet, the task of systematic theology is Eurocentric because it stems from European concerns and contexts, asks European and Anglo North Atlantic theological questions, and draws on Eurocentric categories, all the while claiming to be universal.

Social Justice and the Being of the Spirit

As we have seen thus far, some thinkers have gone beyond charity frameworks by emphasizing that the Spirit actively moves the church and individual Christians in their social justice efforts. These thinkers insist that the church should strive to move beyond only helping the poor to stand in solidarity with poor and marginalized communities against forces of oppression. Liberation theologians have moved even further to remind us that standing with the poor and the oppressed also means to condemn structures that perpetuate social, political, and economic asymmetry—which they name structural sin even within the context of the church. They also emphasize that a key factor in the present configuration of forms of oppression, marginalization, and discrimination, is the idolatry behind profit, consumption, and the commodification of life itself embodied by capitalist systems. They argue that the Spirit is a central force acting against systems that have produced a global refuse whereby entire countries and their populations, as well as populations within richer countries, are seen as disposable.[44]

J. Kameron Carter and Grace Ji-Sun Kim articulate two other examples of dismantling the traditional theological apparatus, hinged, as it is, on Eurocentric categories and "whiteness." Their work tackles questions of social justice in sophisticated ways. Carter reclaims a traditional Christological position by emphasizing the relationship of the Spirit and Christ within the covenantal relationship of God with Israel, and in so doing critiques black liberation theology. His proposal argues for the disarticulation of inherited Eurocentric and white theological frames by rearticulating identity and culture in the Jewish Jesus.[45] Meanwhile, Kim draws from her Korean ethnocultural tradition to emphasize the concept of Chi and its parallels with the Holy Spirit. She envisions an ecological pneumatology where the Spirit is the force which animates Christians to take a critical stance for ecological justice.[46] She also reimagines the activity of the Spirit in relation to Euro-American expressions of racism and sexism.[47] In ways that resonate with Emmanuel Levinas' notion of transcendence,[48] Kim reconstructs the Spirit as the one who stands on the side of the marginalized. These two authors certainly invite us to rethink inherited expressions of theology and especially in relation to the Spirit and social justice in ever new ways. However, I suggest that their pneumatological perspective remains circumscribed because they only consider the activity of the Spirit and not the Spirit's being.

In fact, if we consider the contributions of each of the authors in the previous sections, one could also say that they focus exclusively on what the Spirit does and not on who the Spirit is. At the same time, each of them, in considering and affirming the activity of the Spirit, assumes certain characteristics of the Spirit without making them explicit. It is too easy to say that the Spirit does what the Spirit is. I want to suggest that such a stance only takes us half way. So then, what can we say about the identity, nature, and being of the Spirit in relation to social justice? What is it within the divine Spirit that moves, inspires and energizes social justice movements? A deep engagement with these questions is beyond the scope of this chapter. Let us nevertheless consider a few key points in order to begin to imagine the very being of the divine Spirit in relation to questions of social justice.

My first two points will be familiar to most, the biblical testimony of the prophetic tradition and the notion of koinonia, to which I alluded earlier. My third and fourth points are attempts to make explicit what other scholars have only implied: the continuation of creation in the very being of the Spirit and the effect of social violence and injustice on the Spirit. These four aspects have direct ecclesiological implications for us in the face of the present geopolitical and socioeconomic climate.

Rather than providing a series of biblical passages to bolster my first claim, instead, I allude to the content of the biblical corpus to emphasize the Spirit's role as part of the divine triune being. I am not saying anything new by asserting that the Spirit's desire for justice is consistent with God's own craving for what is right; God is by nature righteous and just. This divine longing for justice is the predicament with which the prophet Habakkuk was wrestling (1:13). The prophets certainly laid charges against those who exploited the poor and oppressed the alien and the widow,(e.g., Amos 4, Mal 3:5, Jer 22:13. Deut 24:14-15), and they did so on God's behalf. The Hebrew Bible reveals a spirit of justice that pushes prophets to incite

41

attitudes of justice in Israel for the society they were building. That is the very language that the prophet Isaiah uses (61:1) and which Jesus confirms to have been fulfilled in Him as He announced the divine jubilee for the poor, the blind, imprisoned, and the socially and economically oppressed (Lk 4: 18-19). In fact, Christians extend this prophetic cry for justice by claiming that what can be ascribed to God can be ascribed to the Spirit. As Jesus announced the "era" of the Spirit, he affirmed unequivocally the divine pneumatological impetus for justice which stems from the very being of a just God. In other words, the Spirit participates and inspires social justice because justice is consistent with the very being of the Triune God, after which the prophetic tradition was modelled. Justice is not an additional aspect but a constitutive characteristic of the righteousness and justice of the divine Spirit (Isa 28:6).

A second related characteristic of the Spirit is embodied in koinonia. I do not refer to the superficial and romantic notion of "community of love" which is often described by leaving structures of oppression and discrimination unchallenged. As we consider how the divine Spirit remains invested in the ongoing divine creative act, koinonia—fellowship-communion—stands out as a crucial justice-oriented mode in the Trinitarian economy. The breakup of this koinonia and its direct negative effect in all of creation (in terms of gender, ethno-racial, cultural, and ecological implications) is bemoaned by the theologian of Genesis (1-11). One could say that the rest of the Hebrew Bible narrates the after effects of the loss of that koinonia. Again, there is nothing new about stating that God's Spirit desires to restore koinonia in all of creation. It is, however, important to emphasize that the Spirit desires, inspires, and creates koinonia

42

because it is part of the very fabric of the divine. Restoring communion and fellowship with fellow humans and creation is a way by which the being of the Spirit as the creative power of God extends the intra-Trinitarian fellowship to all of creation.

The invitation to koinonia is a particular challenge for those communities who claim to be "of the Spirit." It is not just a question of the Spirit entering into fellowship with believers and drawing them into fellowship with the divine, as Moltmann would claim somewhat romantically.[49] Such an approach limits the Spirit's relationship building to the con-fines of the church, celebrating the koinonia that we have received but leaving unchallenged structures of oppression, discrimination, and racism. Rather, the very act of the Spirit in extending the divine triune koinonia is often forceful and prophetic, unmasking and unsettling forces of oppression and injustice which prevent koinonia from becoming a reality. Thus, the Spirit inspires and is active in movements of social justice because injustice in its multiple expressions stands in the way of achieving the quality of the koinonia proper to the divine triune being. In other words, the Spirit strives for social justice in order to restore this divine communion between God and humanity, between humans and other humans, and between humans and the rest of creation. This is another way of saying that the Spirit makes this kind of koinonia a necessary precondition for fellowship with the triune God because this type of koinonia is intrinsic to the very being of God, and a necessary precondition for constructing a society,[50] and because it is the divine desire for all of creation. To say otherwise would be tantamount to denying the entire saga of salvation.

Building on the second characteristic of the Spirit, my third point relates to the divine activity in creation. However, we may understand the nature, extent, and effects of what we call "sin", there is little doubt that sin not only disrupts and destroys human relations but also corrupts the human ability to distinguish good relations from relations of power and violence. With Comblin, I ague that it is the Spirit who moves humanity toward the continual restoration of the image of God.[51] For me, this restoration signals the investment of the Spirit in celebrating created life. The intentional energizing of the Spirit, therefore, guides individual humans and social justice movements toward struggling for life. The Spirit is also thus invested in denouncing and unmasking ideologies, organizations, sociopolitical structures, and theological ideas which run counter the divine Spirit's commitment for life in its colorful biological, sociopolitical and cultural expressions.

To clarify my point, the Spirit inspires and energizes social justice initiatives because they play a crucial collaborative role in the creative and recreative divine ordering for life. In and through social justice movements, the Spirit continues the creative process toward the full humanization of the population of the world. By definition, the Spirit spurs social justice movements forward and is preferentially present in the life of racialized communities who are threatened, incarcerated, and discriminated against, as well as commodified and cannibalized by structures of capitalism. The Spirit is also moving in contexts where people are prevented from representing their communities in society, politics, and church leadership. The Spirit is also present inspiring key individuals from the dominant culture to join social justice efforts in challenging dominant modes of white liberalism in which people make speeches which proclaim indignation against racism, discrimination, and structures of poverty, but are not willing to relinquish the power, privileges, good positions, and the wealth they receive from the structures of the dominant culture. When social justice takes place, we see yet another push forward in the Spirit's continuous act of creation.

My last point is that injustice impacts the being of the Spirit. Our proposed understanding of justice, koinonia, and the act of continuous creation as intrinsic to the Spirit gains new meaning when we understand that the Spirit is directly affected by injustice. Again, we find in the prophetic tradition the understanding that the Spirit feels indignation in the face of injustice and for this reason moves humans towards the restoration of relations, towards justice.

When one dies prematurely at the hands of racism; when experiences gender assault; when someone is discriminated against and prevented from obtaining a job because of the color of their skin, how their accent, or their customs and cultural traditions; when an immigrant is unwelcomed or even criminalized; or when someone is deemed a security threat because they are not Christian but Muslim, it pains the Spirit; such violent treatment affronts and assaults the Spirit's creative intent. It is in this vein that Paul asserts that the Spirit groans for the earth and for the disenfranchised, the homeless, and the exploited. Paul echoed this interpretation—albeit in more eschatological terms—when he wrote that the whole of creation groans and we groan (Rom 8:22-24) for justice. For me, this stance toward social justice means living justly, striving for koinonia, growing unto full maturity, and above all struggling against forces

45

that undermine the divine intent, that frustrate the celebration of human dignity, and that ravage and plunder the earth.

The imagination of creation as emerging from the womb of God suggests that evil, injustice, discrimination, sexism and all other forms of discrimination, in fact, inflict pain as assault on the divine Spirit. This understanding of the Spirit has implications as pertaining to eschatology. To adopt an eschatological stance that abandons human responsibility to the world on the basis of what is to come is both inconsistent with the divine Spirit as well as theologically irresponsible. In the words of Harvey Cox, to ignore the "threats of water and air pollution, resource exhaustion, and destruction of the atmosphere" because another better world awaits us, is both "morally irresponsible and patently unbiblical."[52] More to the point, for him, this type of eschatology also ends up denying the activity of the Spirit in the world and world history,[53] and I would add, God's very intention for humanity.

One Final Remark

The Spirit as interwoven fabric at Creation, or as intrinsic to divine creative intent means that all of Creation is tilted toward justice and, thereby, demands that the church champions a Spirit-inspired justice on behalf of all of Creation The church can draw on a Spirit-inspired sense of indignation, anger, and frustration against the very structures that preserve social and moral injustice, economic inequality, and political marginalization. Stated differently, when social injustice occurs, the church must not remain silent, inactive, or neutral. Inspired and energized by the Spirit, the church must stand on the side of those who experience injustice regardless of their moral condition. The preferential option here, does not mean that God is partial to some people against others. Rather, it means that God is partial for justice and against injustice.[54] The constructed divide between the social and the Spiritual realms must be broken down! I want to affirm that the social fall within the scope of the spiritual. In this truest sense I must struggle with and for my exploited, oppressed, and discriminated against neighbor (Gal 5:14).

Bibliography

Bedford, Nancy E. "Little Moves Against Destructiveness: Theology and Practice of Discernment," in Practicing Theology: Believes and Practices in Christian Life, ed. Miroslav Volf and Dorothy C. Bass. Grand Rapids, MI: Wm B. Eerdmans Publishing Company, 2002.

Carter, J. Kameron. *Race: A Theological Account* Oxford: Oxford University Press, 2008.

Comblin, José. "Espíritu Santo," in *Mysterium liberationis: Conceptos fundamentales de la teología de la liberación*, Ignacio Ellacuría, ed. Madrid: Editorial Trotta, 1990.

Cox, Harvey *Fire from Heaven: The Rise of Pentecostal Spirituality and the Reshaping of Religion in the Twenty-First Century.* Reading, MA: Perseus Books, 1995.

García, Matt. "A World of Its Own: Race, Labor, and Citrus." in the *Making of Greater Los Angeles, 1900–1970*. Chapel Hill, NC: University of North Carolina Press, 2002.

González, Mañana. *Christian Theology from a Hispanic Perspective.* Nashville: Abingdon Press, 1990.

Kim, Grace Ji-Sun. *Colonialism, Han, and the Transformative Spirit.* New York, NY: Palgrave Pivot, 2013.

_____. *Embracing the Other: The Transformative Spirit of Love* Grand Rapids, MI: Wm B. Eerdmans Publishing Co., 2015.

Licad, Abigail. "A Brief History of Political Collaborations Between Latinos and Asians in America," *Hyphen* (2014). Https://hyphenmagazine.com/blog/2014/11/4/brief-history-political-collaborations-between-latinos-and-asians-america.

Medina, Néstor. "Theological Musings Toward a Latina/o Pneumatology," in *Blackwell Companion to Latina/o Theology*, ed. Orlando Espín New York, NY: Blackwell, 2015, 173–89.

_____. "Transgressing Theological Shibboleths: Culture as Locus of Divine (Pneumatological) Activity," PNEUMA 36:3 (2014), 1–15.

Ortega-Aponte, Elías. "The Young Lords and the People's Church: Social Movement Theory, Telling of Brown Power Movements' Impact on Latino/a Religious History," *Perspectivas* (2016).

Romero, Roberto Chao. "The Spiritual Praxis of César Chávez," *Perspectivas* (2016).

Sobrino, Jon. "Poverty Means Death to the Poor," *Cross Currents* 36 (1986), 267–76.

Soliván, Samuel. "The Holy Spirit, A Pentecostal Perspective." In *Teología en Conjunto: A Collaborative Hispanic Protestant Perspective*, José David Rodríguez and Loida I. Martell-Otero, eds. Louisville, KY: Westminster John Knox, 1997.

Villafañe, Eldin. *The Liberating Spirit: Toward an Hispanic American Pentecostal Social Ethic*. Grand Rapids, MI: William B. Eerdmans Publishing Company, 1993.

_____. "The Socio-Cultural Matrix of Intergenerational Dynamics: An Agenda for the 90's." In *Apuntes: Reflexiones Teológicas Desde el Márgen Hispano* 12:1 (Spring 1992), 13–30.

Section One

The Holy Spirit in the Old Testament

Chapter 2

Elijah the Architect of the Spirit-Driven Prophetic Ministry

Jin H. Han

Ei m'offre la favella Io la *diffondo ai cor.*
"[The Creator] gives me the word; I make it known to the heart."
--Adriana Lecouvreur[1]

A story comes down the path of rabbinic tradition and is now immortalized in the Babylonian Talmud (b. Ketubot 105b-106a). It features Rav Anan, who had the privilege of conversing with Elijah the prophet regularly. One day, Elijah did not show up, and the rabbi started fasting and begging for mercy so that the prophet would return. Elijah did come back—but in forms that terrified the rabbi. It turns out that the prophet was punishing him by withholding his presence and now by instilling fear. The punitive measures had to do with a mistake that Rav Anan had made—the rabbi accepted a gift from a plaintiff. [2] Recognizing that he did what he was not supposed to do, he sent the plaintiff to Rav Nachman. The latter rabbi assumed that Rav Anan recused himself because it must have involved his relative. This compelled Rav Nachman to show great respect to the plaintiff, and the defendant was hopelessly disadvantaged in the proceeding. Elijah was horrified and refused to see Rav Anan, whose action facilitated injustice. Fasting and petitions for mercy finally brought back the prophet.[3]

Undoubtedly, this Talmudic tale sits well with the modern practice of associating prophetic ministry with justice and mercy. While these famous mandates can be lifted up as the morale of the story, the original context of the story in the Talmud underscores that the rabbis transmitted the story in pursuit of finding ways to fulfill what God required. In the contemporary world, which is conspicuously secular, modern theological discourses do not always make this important detail clear. The prophets of the Old Testament also lift up the banner of justice or mercy—within the framework of doing and saying what the Spirit tells them to do and say. In other words, the Spirit of God guides their prophetic activity.

Elijah's Commitment to God

The Old Testament yields enough grist to help us picture prophets as a distinct group, but they are easier to describe than to define. One may look up a lexicon, only to encounter disappointment, if not despair, for the famous Hebrew word *nabi'* "prophet" comes from a root whose meaning is unknown, and lexicographers state unapologetically that the Semitic root *n-b-'* represents what a *nabi'* does. Based on the use of the noun *nabi'* and its derivatives, it is commonly understood that the meaning of the word is to "announce" as God charges them. Of course, the literary context in which the word is used should not always be regarded as a definitive clue, for sometimes *nabi'* is also used to describe a mad person (see Hos 9:7). Even such a definition may not necessarily be far from the mark. Søren Kierkegaard has famously said, "To have faith is precisely to lose one's mind so as to win God."[4]

53

For Old Testament prophets, their historical context gives a distinct form to their ministry, and this observation has led a prominent biblical scholar to organize his study of the prophets by eras of empires.[5] It is important to point out, however, that historical situations do not determine what prophets do. Prophecy is a quintessentially Spirit-led phenomenon as amply attested to in the biblical and postbiblical rabbinic tradition.[6] Prophets come and go as the wind/Spirit blows (cf. Jn 3:8). To borrow from Kierkegaard, they lose their own minds so as to follow the mind of the Spirit.

Elijah too appears abruptly on the scene of history in 1 Kings 17, and very little is known of his provenance. He is introduced as the Tishbite and is further identified as someone from Tishbe in Gilead (v. 1). The precise location of Tishbe is debated, and the Hebrew text can also be construed as Elijah hailing "from among the settlers (*tishbe*) in Gilead," east of the Jordan river. The prophet shows affinity with the northern Israelite tradition, and in the Elijah cycle (1 Kgs 17-19, 21, and 2 Kgs 1, 2), the mountain of God is called Horeb instead of Sinai (as it is called in the southern traditions).[7] His prophetic activities are also located in the north, taking on the northern Kingdom of Israel while showing no clear contact with the Davidic dynasty of southern Judah.

Elijah is squarely located in the ninth century, showing engagements with two kings of Israel—mostly with Ahab (869-850 BCE) and briefly with Ahaziah (850-849 BCE), both in the Omri dynasty. Elijah's run-in with King Ahab centers on the major religious crisis Israel faces through Baalism, the traditional Canaanite fertility religion. The book of Judges indicates that this Canaanite religion poses a problem from the entry of Israelites into the land of Canaan, alluring the people of Israel into the Baal worship (Jdgs 2:11, 13 and so forth).

Baalism proves to be a strong attraction in that the people are obliged to perceive it not merely as a religious practice, but also as an agricultural technology, which Canaanites could cast as a time-proven method of securing rain for farming in Canaan where water resources are scarce. This topographical feature is instructively described in Moses' speech in Deuteronomy 11:10-11.

> For the land that you are about to enter to occupy is not like the land of Egypt, from which you have come, where you sow your seed and irrigate by foot like a vegetable garden. But the land that you are crossing over to occupy is a land of hills and valleys, watered by rain from the sky.

In this geographical description, it is not clear what it means to irrigate the land "by foot" (v. 10); however, it seems to refer to some type of irrigation. The picture of the landscape is otherwise clear. The land depends on rainfalls for the supply of water needed for farming. Israelites are compelled to choose whether or not they should resist the temptation of Baalism, which their Canaanite neighbors say is a sure way of getting water from the sky and ensuring bountiful crops.[8]

The threat of Baalism in the days of Elijah is further intensified through the state support for the Canaanite religion of King Omri. The king pursues a political alliance with the Phoenicians through the marriage of Ahab, his son, and Jezebel, daughter of Ethbaal, king of Sidon, a Canaanite state. Truthful to her origin, she acts as an active promoter of Baalism in Israel. The historian of 1 Kings makes this link clear by announcing Elijah immediately following the report of Ahab's marriage and the royal sponsorship of Baal worship (16:31-33). Elijah's prophetic service is urgently needed.

Elijah's first task is to declare the cessation of rain in a land that is already threatened by the scarcity of water, which would continue until another oracle lifts the ban on the rain. The ancient oath formula of "As the LORD[9] the God of Israel lives" that begins Elijah's oracle in 17:1 makes clear that this is not merely a meteorological prophecy. The drought is a divine intervention through the prophet.

What is at stake is made stark in the prophet's prayer on Mount Carmel (18:36-37):

> O LORD, God of Abraham, Isaac, and Israel, let it be known this day that you are God in Israel, that I am your servant, and that I have done all these things at your bidding. Answer me, O LORD, answer me, so that this people may know that you, O Yahweh, are God, and that you have turned their hearts back.

When Baal prophets' hectic rituals of extended howling and self-laceration fail to bring down the rain (vv. 26-29), Elijah's prayer results in the fire coming down from the heaven to consume the burnt offering and everything else set up around it (vv. 30-38), which leads to the people's statement of faith in verse 39: "The LORD is indeed God; The LORD indeed is God." The chapter ends with the end of the drought as Elijah predicted, establishing Yahweh is the God that provides rain. In this regard, Elijah's name is fitting, in that it means "My God is Yahweh," and it may well have been his nickname.

Elijah himself learns that God makes his ministry possible. When Jezebel's threat to kill the prophet instills fear in him, "he got up and fled for his life" (19:3). In his exhaustion under "a solitary broom tree," Elijah speaks of the state of exhausted spiritual resources, when he says, "It is enough now, O LORD, take away my life, for I am no better than my ancestors" (v. 4).[10]

In the account of his encounter with God at Horeb, Elijah is presented with a great wind, an earthquake, and fire, all of which turn out to be the precursors of God's appearance, including the wind, which often represents divine presence.[11] There follows "a sound of sheer silence" (v. 12 NRSV), widely known in the KJV's memorable translation of "still small voice." It is literally, "the sound of fine silence" and offers a grammatical form known as reduplication, which often conveys a repeated or sustained sense. In the midst of sustained delicate silence, God puts Elijah back on track. Elijah can sustain his ministry only through the strength God provides for him.

Elijah's Community

Prior to the showdown with the Baal prophets in chap 18 and the enabling presence of God in chap, 19, the ancient historian (commonly known as the Deuteronomistic Historian) reports how the prophet endures the drought that he started with his prophetic pronouncement (chap 17). The historian's realism depicts how the drought affects the prophet as much as the whole population. At first, God sends Elijah to the Wadi Cherith, east of the Jordan river, so that he can obtain drinking water from the wadi. A wadi by nature has a temporary supply of water, sometimes so full as to cause occasional flash floods. The lack of rain can make it dry up, and it did (v. 7). Ravens transport meals to the prophet, indicating that "he will be supported by creation."[12] The avian provision may simply be a feature of the storytelling; alternatively, the supply through unclean animals underscores the dire situation of the region. Unstable water supply and ravens' airdrop are minor issues in comparison with the whole nation that has started leaning to Baal and away from the worship of the Lord. Apparently, for Elijah, the potable water runs dry first before the ravens' supply stops.

As an emergency measure, God instructs the prophet to go to a widow in Zarephath located in Sidon, suggesting that God has sovereignty over all nations.[13] From an economic standpoint, God's direction makes less than clear sense, for widows usually are the most destitute part of the population. Upon his arrival, Elijah spots a widow gathering sticks, which must have been construed as a favorable sign for the hungry guest seeking food from a widow. Elijah first asks for something to drink, as if he wants to *test the water*. The widow's answer in 17:12 is a chilling one:

> As the LORD your God lives, I have nothing baked, only a handful of meal in a jar, and a little oil in a jug; I am now gathering a couple of sticks, so that I may go home and prepare it for myself and my son, that we may eat it, and die.

Why would God choose such a destitute family? There must be someone in town who would have more than she does. The initial instruction about seeking food from a widow who may have some resources turns out to be misguided. Elijah tells the widow to "do as you have said," making it unclear what he is referring to by "as you have said." As if sweeping aside the curious instruction, Elijah asks the destitute widow to prepare food for him first (v. 13). Elijah's request may invite the charge of *chutzpah*, but it makes sense under the premise that this dire situation will soon pass and that the drought and shortage of food are only temporary. It appears that Elijah asks the widow to practice hospitality as she would have done under ordinary circumstances. A Midrashic work of *Pirque de Rabbi Eliezer* points out that the widow did him honor by sharing the very little she had in her possession. Elijah becomes a companion to the family of the widow of Zarephath.[14]

Elijah's shared life is also made known in the subsequent passage, in which Elijah brings back to life the widow's son. When he becomes so ill that "there was no breath left in him" (v. 17), the mother blames herself and Elijah for the death of her son (v. 18).

> She then said to Elijah, "What have you against me, O man of God? You have come to me to bring my sin to remembrance, and to cause the death of my son!"

It was God who sent Elijah to stay with her, and it seems to be a cruel thing or an irresponsible thing to fail to spare the son of "the widow with whom I am staying" (v. 20). Elijah's prayer to God for her son in v. 20 offers another important clue to the nature of the prophet's relationship with God. It is precisely because God is totally in the picture that the prophet is obliged to lodge a complaint to God.

Elijah's Confrontation with the Power

Elijah's tender loving approach to the destitute family stands in stark contrast with the manner in which he stands up against the power that oppresses the poor.[15] In monarchic societies, protest against the throne either constitutes or borders on an act of treason. The king may not regard the prophet as patriotic; however, Elijah is following the directive of God, who calls him "to *criticize* in dismantling the dominant consciousness."[16]

Elijah's sense of justice is presented in Naboth's vine-yard in 1 Kings 21. The setup of the story features different approaches to governance. King Ahab approaches Naboth with a royal demand, which in ordinary Asiatic settings the subject of the Kingdom would willingly surrender the vineyard to the king. To the king's surprise, however, Naboth refuses, for "the Lord forbid that I should give you my ancestral inheritance" (v. 3). Ahab's later report suggests that he misconstrued it as Naboth's refusal to submit to the throne (v. 4). The conflict becomes tentatively resolved by the intervention of Jezebel, who finds Ahab's approach to the affairs of the state pathetic and devises a way to set up Naboth and seize his vineyard.

Ordinarily, this would be the end of the story. Naboth is a victim of royal violence in a situation in which the poor have no recourse. René Girard finds this to be the case in virtually all cultures. The powerful silence the poor. However, Girard observes that in the Bible "prophets began to view their history from the standpoint of God's concern for victims."[17] When there is a protest, violence usually targets the protester, who easily becomes a scapegoat. Gerard calls it the spiral of violence, but the Bible contains stories that defy this sequence of events. For example, the story of Jesus does not end with crucifixion. Christ is raised, and the victim of violence has a voice. In the Old Testament, Abel's blood cries out and refuse to be silenced. The prophets come forth and speak on behalf of the victim of royal violence. So, Elijah did for Naboth.[18]

The pericope of Naboth's vineyard provides a classic illustration of the ministry of justice. However, it would be a misleading eisegesis to declare that a sense of justice motivates the prophet to speak up against the injustice perpetrated by the palace. The passage makes it clear that Elijah gets involved in this case under God's direction (21:17-19):

> Then the word of the LORD came to Elijah the Tishbite, saying: Go down to meet King Ahab of Israel, who rules[a] in Samaria; he is now in the vineyard of Naboth, where he has gone to take possession. You shall say to him, "Thus says the LORD: Have you killed, and also taken possession?" You shall say to him, "Thus says the LORD: In the place where dogs licked up the blood of Naboth, dogs will also lick up your blood."

Elijah pursues justice on behalf of the victim of royal abuse. His notion of justice originates from his commitment to serve God in all circumstances. Elijah's righteous indignation is an external expression of the root of his ministry. He speaks as God's Spirit directs him. The Spirit will not permit Naboth to go away quietly into the night of oppression.

Conclusion: A Prophet Like Elijah

One finds justice highlighted in Amos of the eighth century, who is commonly known as the first classical prophet.[19] Hosea champions mercy that God offers for the sinful people.[20] Neither Hosea nor Amos serves mercy or justice as self-standing moral imperatives, however. Instead, they share in common the singlehearted service of God who calls each prophet for a particular historical situation. Like Elijah, later prophets are minted as servants who are committed to serving God, whether it is the proclamation of justice or the offer of divine mercy. Indeed, no other prophet ascends to heaven as Elijah did (2 Kgs 2:1-18), but Elijah's archetypal ministry is repeated by other prophets, who go forth and announce the message which God has entrusted with them. The prophets champion the cause of justice in the face of the powerful as God's fiery spokespersons.

The contemporary world is blessed with many proponents of justice, whose rhetorical style often resembles that of Elijah and other prophets. While humanity is indebted to those who have fought for justice and made sacrifices for the betterment of society, the origin of the advocacy of justice often serves as the touchstone that sets apart prophets from profit-seekers. Today the political utilization of justice or mercy can be a lucrative venture that taps into a sizable market of public discourses. It may even be an advantageous move for those who desire political fame or a career as an influence-monger that parades as a theological thinker. Such a self-serving approach is little different from the ideology of Baal worship that seeks abundance at the expense of the unconditional worship of God.

Justice is weighty, but for a prophet, its value resides in God who demands it. Mercy is precious, but as Hosea makes it clear, it directs attention to God, who is willing to forgive in spite of betrayals of the people. When Amos the prophet speaks for God in the name of justice (see chaps. 1-6) or protests to God based on mercy (see chaps. 7-9), neither justice nor mercy is placed on a par with God. Justice is God's to demand, and mercy, God's to deliver.

The epitaph of this article quotes from the Italian opera based on the life of Adriana Lecouvreur, the famous French singer who was among the first to advocate the use of normal speech (instead of *la déclamation*), simplicity in style, ordinary people's attire, and *le beau naturel*.[21] In the operatic scene, she attributes the excellence of her musical performance to the Creator, who provides her with the gift of gab. Her task is to receive the Creator's word and give it to the heart of audience. Likewise, the prophets of the Old Testament deliver God's message and engage themselves in the ministry of justice and mercy as God directs them—only as the Holy Spirit leads them. Perhaps, the present time is in critical need of such a prophet as Elijah, whose prophetic ministry can only be defined by his singlehearted service to God.

Bibliography

Aharoni, Yohanan. *The Land of the Bible: A Historical Geography*. Rev. and enlarged ed. Philadelphia: Westminster Press, 1979.

Brueggemann, Walter. *The Prophetic Imagination*. 2nd ed. Minneapolis: Fortress Press, 2001.

Dempsey, Carol J. *The Prophets: A Liberation-Critical Reading*. A Liberation-Critical Reading of the Old Testament. Minneapolis: Fortress Press, 2000.

Girard, René. "The Bible's Distinctiveness and the Gospel" in the *Girard Reader*, edited by James G. Williams. New York: Crossroad Publishing Co., 2000, 145-75.

Greenspahn, Frederick E. "Why Prophecy Ceased." *JBL* 108 (1989), 37-49.

Heschel, Abraham Joshua. *The Prophets*. New York: Harper & Row, 1962.

Kierkegaard, Søren. *The Sickness unto Death*. Translated by Walter Lowrie. Princeton: Princeton University Press, 1941.

Koch, Klaus. *The Prophets*. 2 vols. Translated by Margaret Kohn. Philadelphia: Fortress Press, 1983-1984.

Lindbeck, Kristen H. *Elijah and the Rabbis: Story and Theology*. New York: Columbia University Press, 2010.

McKenzie, Steven. *The Trouble with Kings: The Composition of the Book of Kings in the Deuteronomistic History*. Leiden: E. J. Brill, 1991.

Scott, Virginia. *Women on the Stage in Early Modern France: 1540-1750*. New York: Cambridge University Press, 2010.

Sweeney, Marvin. "The Prophets and Priests in the Deuteronomistic History: Elijah and Elisha." Pp. 35-49 in *Israelite Prophecy and the Deuteronomistic History: Portrait, Reality, and the Formation of a History*. Edited by Mignon R. Jacobs and Raymond F. Person Jr. Ancient Israel and Its Literature 14. Atlanta: Society of Biblical Literature, 2013.

Welker, Michael, *God the Spirit*. Translated by John F. Hoffmeyer. Minneapolis: Fortress Press, 1994.

Chapter 3

Social Justice in First Isaiah: A Pentecostal Perspective[1]

Jacqueline N. Grey

When the prophet Isaiah experienced his overwhelming vision of the thrice-holy God, he was changed by the encounter. Not only were his lips burnt but his vision altered. How does a religious experience transform people in the biblical text? In particular, how does that transformation impact the 'other'? This chapter will explore issues of social justice raised in Isaiah 1-39 (commonly referred to as 'First Isaiah') through the lens of a Pentecostal worldview. First, a framework will be developed that draws on values central to the Pentecostal community. This framework (or lens for reading) is based on the three elements of experience, empowerment, and eschatology.

Using this lens, the concerns for social justice in First Isaiah will be explored. This will include particular consideration of the original situation of eighth century Judah in which the prophet spoke his message. How does the prophet's experience of God (particularly his call to ministry in Isaiah 6) impact his message of social justice? In what ways is the prophet empowered to address the issues of injustice? What does Isaiah's vision for a just society look like? Finally, some implications for the contemporary Pentecostal community will be considered.

A Pentecostal Lens

There have developed in recent years a number of different and valuable approaches to reading the biblical text from a Pentecostal perspective. This includes Lee Roy Martin's development of an 'affective reading.'[2] In this approach, the reader (or what Martin calls the 'hearer' of Scripture) must be open and attentive to the emotional impact of the text. Another approach, developed by Rickie D. Moore is that of 'altar hermeneutics.'[3] Using a play on words, Moore reflects how interpretations get altered after an encounter on the figurative sacred space of the altar of the living God. This requires the reader to re-envision the context in which they approach and hear the biblical text.

To approach Scripture is to approach sacred space. On that sacred space of the altar, we encounter a text in the midst of our deeply felt desires, fears and hurts. It is on that altar that our full selves are exposed to God. The challenge is to allow a deep probing of ourselves by the Spirit and to allow ourselves to be read and thereby transformed by the text. It is this interest in the experience of encountering God through the biblical text that I wish to use as a foundation for developing a hermeneutical key, or lens, to read the prophets of the Old Testament. This framework is founded on three key values central to the Pentecostal community: the values of experience, Spirit empowerment, and eschatology. These three values create a lens through which we can approach the text. First, the lens of experience.

Much has already been written on the importance for Pentecostals of a dynamic experience of the Spirit, or encounter with God.[4] However, at the heart of the discussion is the idea of knowing

God in a relational and holistic way. The orientation towards and through experience can be understood as an epistemology in which religious truths are not objects of abstract belief (that is, belief as cognition). Instead, religious truth is comprehended through personal, first-hand know-ledge of a relational encounter. Yet, as Steven Land emphasizes, "the point of Pentecostal spirituality was not to have an experience or several experiences, though they spoke of discrete experiences.

The point was to experience life as part of a biblical drama of participation in God's history."[5] It is an experience that occurs in human temporality. Yet in that moment of time, the person encountering God is not a free-floating, ahistorical person. They draw from the wells of the past through the theology and traditions of their community and anticipate a future envisioned from their past and present understanding of God. The eighth century prophets of the Old Testament articulated their experience of God largely drawing from the treasury of language and symbols of covenant theology—such as God as holy, and God as King. In a similar fashion, Pentecostals encountering God have articulated their experience of God by drawing from the treasury of Scripture, often the prophets of the Old

Testament. The Pentecostal community often uses the words and experience from the biblical text to give voice to their own encounter with God (such as the prophet Isaiah in his call narrative of chapter 6).[6] This then grounds the individual Pentecostal experience in both the community of faith and the Scriptures they identify as their own. So, experience, or encounter with God, is a key value of the Pentecostal community as they seek to know God. It is a motivating factor in reading Scripture—to encounter the living God in the text. It is a lens through which the Pentecostal community then reads Scripture.

While the Pentecostal experience of the Spirit, or encounter with God, can be described and theologized, it can be difficult to explain to the broader academic community. It may also be perceived as problematic by scholars versed in historical-critical approaches to read contemporary Pentecostal experience back onto an Old Testament text (as though historical-critics are unimpeded by the risk of eisegesis). However, perhaps other disciplines can help us. Drawing on the broader study of religions, Luke Timothy Johnson in his work *Religious Experience in Earliest Christianity*, defines religious experience as "... a response to that which is perceived as ultimate, involving the whole person, characterized by a peculiar intensity, and issuing in action."[7]

While Johnson takes great pains to disassociate his definition from what he calls 'enthusiastic Christianity' his definition provides a connection point to define experience that can be helpful for Pentecostals and biblical scholars alike. This definition links religious experience to a response to a perceived Ultimate but also results in some kind of action or activity. To read the biblical text through the lens of experience is to ask: How, and what way (if any), is religious experience described? What do the responses to religious experience in the biblical text tell us about God? What action(s) result from the experience? This leads us to the second lens for a Pentecostal reading of Scripture: It is the resulting empowerment of believers through that same Spirit.

Central to the Pentecostal message is that the Spirit empowers believers to both witness to the message of Jesus Christ and serve the community of His body. As the definition of religious experience by Johnson highlights, religious experience is not contained to the interior, but flows out to the exterior of the person. There is both a response to the experience and an action that issues. The person cannot help but be changed by the encounter—or altered by the experience, to use the language of Rickie Moore. For the Pentecostal community, much of the response and issuing action can be defined under the category of empowerment. The altered believer is emboldened to witness, empowered to serve and enabled to love deeper. Spirit baptism has also been described as a baptism into divine love, by which the love of God is poured into the hearts of believers.[8]

Kim Alexander demonstrates that within early Pentecostalism this association of Spirit Baptism with love and the language of divine love[9] (such as "He baptized me with love"[10] – love for God, neighbor, and the world) was prevalent to describe the transformational experience of the Spirit. David Perry then goes on to write that, "This divine love, which has Spirit baptism as its source, then provides a strong rationale and functions effectively as a motivating force for both evangelism and social action."[11] So to read the biblical text through the lens of empowerment is to ask: How does a religious experience empower people in the biblical text? In particular, how is that expressed in concern for social justice?

A third value of the Pentecostal community is the anticipation of a new future. As Yongnan Jeon Ahn writes, "The role of the Spirit is to open the horizon of expectation about the future, in order for the believer to experience eschaton-logical reality in the present."[12] Religious experience for the Pentecostal is a foretaste of the coming Kingdom of God. It results in both an urgency and expectation of the soon-coming Christ, as well as a pragmatism that makes Pentecostalism more action-orientated than reflective.

So, to read the biblical text through the lens of eschatology is to ask: What vision for the future does the biblical text present? What does that future look like? Presently armed with this three-fold lens for reading Scripture (experience, empowerment, and eschatology), let us now turn to consider the text of First Isaiah. However, applying this lens, we should give particular consideration for the situation of eighth century Judah in which the message of the prophet is located. The religious experience of the prophet occurred in human temporality: Isaiah was not a free-floating, ahistorical person. So, to attempt to understand Isaiah's religious experience and resulting actions we need to consider the context as much as possible. In this way we honor the prophetic voice of the Spirit spoken to an earlier community.

Isaiah's Jerusalem

As the narrative sections of Isaiah 1-39 emphasize, Isaiah ministered during three main political crises[13] that occurred between approximately 735 and 701 BCE, during the reigns of Ahaz and Hezekiah. Within this greater international scene, the domestic politics of Judah played out. While the inter-national and domestic spheres are connected, the focus in this paper will be on the domestic issues raised in First Isaiah. The domestic issues raised by Isaiah center around governance and worship. The role of the king was to ensure proper governance in the nation, including oversight of legal, judicial and economic management of the Kingdom. This included the proper administration of justice. The litmus test for justice was in how the most vulnerable in their society were treated. It was a test that Judah was failing at that time. [14]

The concern for justice and righteousness is emphasized throughout the Old Testament. While justice is primarily a legal term,[15] it is found at the heart of the covenantal worldview of the pre-exilic community, best reflected in the Deuteronomistic writings. According to the covenant worldview, blessing will be the product of loving God, obeying Torah and doing justice. This worldview is reflected in the theology of First Isaiah. Despite the importance of this covenant world-view, arguably the most dominant theological construct in First Isaiah is Zion theology, or the Zion tradition.[16]

Zion theology builds on the covenantal worldview—that this same God who chose them and set them apart also chose David to be His earthly king and Jerusalem to be the place of his earthly dwelling. The descendants of David were expected to exercise their rule according to the covenantal worldview. That is, the Davidic rulers were required to be facilitators of God's justice. Yet, as John Goldingay points out, the idea of social justice in Isaiah (and the broader Old Testament) is quite different from our modern construct.

Modern definitions emphasize human rights and the equitable distribution of resources.[17] Instead, according to Goldingay, the broad meaning of *mišpāṭ* refers to governance and the exercise of authority, while *ṣĕdāqâ* is a relational term. He writes, 'It suggests the faithful exercise of power in the community.'[18] The actions of the kings and leaders were evaluated according to the criteria of the covenant. Their obligation was to ensure fairness in the legal system, integrity in their administration of the state economy, and faithfulness in worship.

However, here is the dilemma: the introduction of kingship also led to a stratified society. The management of the Kingdom introduced a class of people that were administrators and leaders of the nation. This stratification of the Judean society led to social and economic inequality. Although this was a period of increased wealth and flourishing international trade, the prosperity was not common to all but experienced only by the politically powerful elite. The leaders further increased their wealth and power by extracting bribes and financial incentives for favorable outcomes or prioritized legal hearings. Isaiah announces an indictment against these leaders for having oppressed their people in violation of the covenantal commandments. So, it is in this context that God first called Isaiah to be a prophet.

Prophet to the Poor

The role of the prophet was to communicate a message from Yahweh through the empowerment of the Spirit of Yahweh. The prophet was called to be a messenger. Because Isaiah functioned as Yahweh's spokesperson to the king and leader-ship, then it is no surprise that the prophet raises issues about social policy and social justice. The perpetuation of injustice in their community is inconsistent with true worship and covenantal faithfulness. This concern for justice will now be read in the light of the Pentecostal lens of experience, empowerment, and eschatology.

Experience

In considering the lens of experience, we can ask: How, and in what way (if any), is the religious experience of Isaiah described? What does the response of Isaiah to this religious experience tell us about God? What action(s) result from the experience? The central and dominant religious experience of the prophet in First Isaiah is the call narrative in chapter 6. Isaiah is overwhelmed by the encounter with God the King, who reigns over the whole earth despite the death of the earthly king, Uzziah.

The description of this religious experience is couched in language of the covenant. God is, in essence, holy. However, holiness does not simply mean 'completely good', as in an absolute moral attribute. Instead, as Rudolf Otto suggests in *The Idea of the Holy*, holiness is defined by the numinous; it so overwhelms the observer that they are submerged in their own nothingness in contrast to that which is supreme above all creatures.[19] This certainly fits the definition of Johnson that a religious experience is a response to that which is perceived as ultimate, involving the whole person, characterized by a peculiar intensity. Upon encountering the dangerous, thrice-holy God, Isaiah responds in stammering awe. He recognizes his own sinfulness and that of his people. However, Abernethy also notes that "holiness is active, not merely static."[20] So what action of Isaiah issues from this encounter? How did this religious experience impact his ministry?

Through this religious experience, Isaiah was able to grasp, in a non-rational way, essential truths about the nature of God and his requirements of his people.[21] From this encounter with the holy God, he discerned that the people were to reflect the nature and character of the God they served. A holy God required a holy community. Isaiah's community was to be different from other nations. They were to mirror the holiness and goodness of God. Despite the truth of the self-acknowledged sinfulness of the prophet, mercy was shown to him by the actions of God in provision for the purification of Isaiah's lips.

Justice, truth, and mercy were not simply abstract concepts; they were part of the nature and essence of God revealed to the prophet through this encounter.[22] As God is, so the people should be. Yet, who would be willing to be sent by God to speak this truth and call the people to account for their absence of justice, truth and mercy? The prophet volunteers and with purified lips is empowered to speak on behalf of God to his community. It is a call to action. Isaiah is told to 'go.' He is burdened with a message in 6:9-13 that judgement is looming. Yet, Isaiah's experience and subsequent empowerment give hope. His experience demonstrates that rebellious creatures can share the holy character of God for the sake of the world.[23] Even when he knows his message will be rejected by the obstinate people (Isa 6:9-13) he still speaks. So, at the core of Isaiah's ministry is this experience and encounter of the Holy One of Israel, on whose behalf he speaks. With what message is he empowered?

Empowerment

In what ways is the prophet empowered to address the issues of social and economic injustice? The prophet is empowered with speech to denounce the systemic exploitation of the vulnerable by the rich and powerful. There are three key texts in First Isaiah in which the prophet speaks on behalf of the voiceless condemning those that perpetuated injustice. He is empowered to speak on behalf of the vulnerable in society, symbolized by the widows and orphans. His empowerment is reflected in the transformation of the prophet from a stammering observer to a radical preacher[24] as he speaks authoritatively in the imperative form to the leaders of the Kingdom. In Isaiah 1:16-17 he demands for them to 'wash themselves', to 'seek justice, correct oppression.' This demand was part of a larger law-suit presented in chapter 1 that charged the people, specifically the leaders, with neglect of their covenant obligations. This neglect was not so much on the infringement of the minutiae of legal stipulations, rather the condemnation was on their general failure of "conduct unbefitting a member of the covenant community."[25]

As Isaiah 1:4 explains, this is because they have forsaken and despised the Holy One of Israel. Instead, the conduct expected was that they would embrace and mirror the Holy One of Israel in their obligation for caring for the vulnerable in society. This is just one symptom of a people that were rejecting their vocation as a holy and unique community, distinct from the other nations. The identification of the three-fold oppressed, the orphan, and the widow refers to "those in the community who are weak, vulnerable, without an advocate, and so subject to political exclusion and economic exploitation."[26] For example, because widows could not inherit the property of their deceased husbands there was an absence of legal protection for them, so the Deuteronomic law com-mended them to public charity as the 'social security' for their time.[27] However, instead of caring for the widows as the covenant law intended, Isaiah condemns the leaders for exploiting them. It is this group that the empowered prophet speaks on behalf of—for the sake of his community he identifies with and deeply cares for.

This same condemnation is reinforced, even stronger, in Isaiah 5 which commences with the Song of the Vineyard (5:1-6). His empowered speech is reflected in the stinging rebuke he directs to the leaders for their self-interested abuse of their power and governmental positions. While not necessarily acting illegally, their inequitable economic practice has caused an outcry among the vulnerable. So instead of producing a harvest of justice, the vineyard of the beloved has produced bloodshed. Instead of yielding righteousness, they have produced a cry of pain from the people who are being treated unfairly and oppressively (Isa 5:7).

As Goldingay notes, there is an irony that this same term (of outcry) is used to describe the crying out of Israel in Egypt, which is now used against one another.[28] The crying out of the vulnerable and poor is also an expression of a deep longing for justice. So, what were the leaders doing that is so offensive to the prophet? Using shifty economic practices, they were confiscating and then possessing the houses and fields belonging to the more economically exposed.[29] The prophet denounces them for these practices as the list of 'woes' continues from verse 8 to 24.

The powerful were taking advantage of the poor to procure their land for the building of great estates. The leaders of Judah, as verse 11 indicates, sought a hedonistic lifestyle. Roberts writes, "Judah's leaders in their intoxication with pleasure have lost the ability to discern God's work."[30] They exhibit little concern for the crying out of those they have oppressed. But what I want to highlight here, is both the empowerment of the prophet to speak and his passion to speak against social injustice. Again, this empowerment and passion flow from his encounter with the holy God at his call.[31] As God is holy, just and generous, so God's people should be. The prophet can speak such stinging rebuke and announce with authoritative certainty coming judgement because he knows they have rejected the holy God since he has seen and been in the presence of the holy God. His empowered speech is powerful, penetrating, and impressive.

Similarly, the empowered message of the prophet continues in Isaiah 10:1-2. This indictment strongly resembles that of Isaiah 5:8-24.[32] However, the perpetrators here are specifically the corrupt royal officials who were advancing legislation for their self-interest at the expense of the poor and needy. The prophet was condemning the structural weakness and systematic abuse by the government administrators that left no avenue for appeal for the oppressed. Just because an action was technically legal did not make it right. The prophet speaks boldly to condemn those that sought to increase their wealth at the expense of others. These descendants of David were not exercising their rule according to the covenantal worldview. However, the prophet does look forward to a future Davidic ruler that will ensure justice for the poor and share in God's concern for the needy. Isaiah lives in the liminal space between the real world and an ideal world. While justice may not be realized in the now, it will occur in the 'not yet.'

Eschatological

Finally, utilizing the third lens of eschatology, we can ask: What does Isaiah's vision for a just society look like? For Isaiah, the idea of a just

78

society could only be realized in an eschatological future.[33] In chapter 2 he presents a vision for humanity. That vision is part of the Zion tradition, centered around Jerusalem, the mountain of the Lord. To this mountain, the peoples will stream to learn of God. This transformed society will be anchored on the true *Torah* or way of the Lord. In this transformed society their weapons of destruction (swords and spears) will be re-purposed for harvest and construction (2:4). As Brueggemann notes, "There will be a cessation of political and economic oppression and threat."[34] This same Zion tradition is also reflected in the text of Isaiah 9:6-7 which presents the hope of a future ruler.

There is much to say about this text from a Christological perspective, however as a message of comfort to the poor and vulnerable of Isaiah's community it powerfully communicates the anticipation of a new future. The prophet opens the horizon of expectation about the future for those that are suffering in the present. The four names of the child express aspects of an ideal future ruler.[35] This coming Davidic ruler will bring peace, justice, and proper order.

This text also has a thematic connection to chapter 11:1-5, which further lists the characteristics of a just ruler. They will be empowered by the spirit of wisdom and counsel. The chapter continues in 6-9 with a vision of a peaceable Kingdom where the wolf and lamb will dwell in harmony together. As Andrew Davies writes, "Despite the fact that the poor, like widows and orphans, are denied due access to the legal system at present (10: 2), there is some comfort for them in the assurance that a predicted coming deliverer or 'messiah' will judge them righteously and 'decide with equity for the meek' (11:4)."[36] This future Davidic ruler will dwell in Zion, which will also be a place of refuge (14:32). This is also reflected in chapter 25:4, where the prophet praises God because of the great things he has done in this eschatological vision, which includes being a shelter to the poor and needy. This, again, is part of the Zion tradition as the poor find refuge in Zion, which has been established by God as the place of his dwelling.[37]

Finally, the eschatological future of Isaiah 26 holds great hope for the poor that their situation will be reversed. The prophet, having experienced the presence of the Heavenly King, is empowered to command the people with confidence and authority to trust in the Lord. He, again, speaks in imperatives as he charges them with certain instructions in 26:4-6. In a reversal of fortunes, the exalted, represented by the lofty city (perhaps Babylon or a Babylon-like city), will be brought low—so low, in fact, that the poor and needy can dance on its grave. The faithful community can trust the character and activity of Yahweh to "prevail over every pretentious, arrogant, self-sufficient, exploitative power."[38] So the prophet invites the reader (or hearer) to see their current situation with a new perspective—an eternal perspective. While the poor may be mistreated in the present, there is a future hope that God will transform the morally bankrupt community into one marked by peace and prosperity.

Conclusion: Application to the Pentecostal Community

In conclusion, what does this Old Testament text of First Isaiah offer the contemporary Pentecostal community as we navigate the moral dilemma of poverty and social injustice in a global society? I have two brief reflections on its application. First, I have been struck anew by the importance of this religious experience of Isaiah to his message. Of course, since this was a lens through which the text is read then it would obviously be prominent. However, it is not an experience that remained private. Isaiah's encounter with God transformed him—it produced an inner renewal that overflowed into his outer ministry and relationships. It also permeated his under-standing of the Deuteronomic covenant. Whether he viewed it differently prior to his call we cannot know. But certainly, after his call, he calls the people to renew their covenant obligations not with the minutiae of legalism but with a radical message of imitation— not to imitate the other nations, but to imitate the dangerous, thrice- holy God. His experience called him to a deeper love. For the contemporary Pentecostal community, renewal is not a return to legalism but a call towards the imitation of Christ.

Secondly, Isaiah lived in the liminal space between the real world and an ideal world. He preached a vision of the ideal community. He volunteered his lips and dedicated his life to see that ideal community realized. He was not ashamed of his vision but spoke powerfully to the powerful. However, from the outset, he knew his message would be rejected. Yet, even when he knows his message will be rejected by the obstinate people (Isa 6:9-13) he still speaks because he has a conviction. For the contemporary Pentecostal community in many locations, we have been moving from the disenfranchised to the mainstream. In many locations, we have shifted from being the poor and marginal to the powerful middle class with increased social and political capital. I hope that we are never too comfortable to speak the truth of our convictions or too self-interested to speak for the voiceless. I hope that we choose to continually associate with the disenfranchised. I hope that we do not passively allow injustice to continue, but speak up as a prophetic voice, even at the cost of our reputation and social standing. Instead, that like Isaiah, we volunteer our lips and dedicate our lives to see the ideal community realized: a community of peace and justice.

Bibliography

Alexander, Kimberly Ervin, "Boundless Love Divine: A Re-evaluation of Early Understandings of the Experience of Spirit Baptism," in Land, S. J., Moore, R.D., & Thomas. J.C., *Passover, Pentecost & Parousia: Studies in Celebration of the Life and Ministry of T. Hollis Gause,* JPT Supplement Series 35. Dorset, UK: Deo Publishing, 2010.

Abernethy, Andrew T. *The Book of Isaiah and God's Kingdom: A Thematic-Theological Approach*, NSBT Series. Downers Grove, IL: Intervarsity Press, 2016.

Althouse, Peter. "Toward a Theological Understanding of the Pentecostal Appeal to Experience," JES 38:4. Fall 2001.

Cross, Terry L. "Divine-Human Encounter Towards a Pentecostal Theology of Experience," *Pneuma* 31 (2009), 3:34.

Blenkinsopp, Joseph Isaiah 1-39, Anchor Bible. New York, NY: Doubleday, 2000.

Brueggemann, Walter Isaiah 1-39, Isaiah 1-39. Louisville, KY: Westminster John Knox Press, 1998.

Davies, Andrew Double Standards in Isaiah: Re-Evaluating Prophetic Ethics and Divine Justice, Biblical Interpretation Series. Leiden: Brill, 2000.

Davies, Eryl W. Prophecy and Ethics: Isaiah and the Ethical Tradition of Israel, JSOT Supp Series 16. Sheffield: JSOT Press, 1981.

Goldingay, John. *The Theology of the Book of Isaiah.* Downers Grove, IL: Intervarsity Press, 2014.

Gray, Mark. *Rhetoric and Social Justice in Isaiah.* New York-London: T & T Clark, 2006

Grey, Jacqueline. *Three's A Crowd: Pentecostalism, Hermeneutics and the Old Testament.* Eugene, OR: Pickwick Publications, 2011.

Johnson, Luke Timothy, *Religious Experience in Earliest Christianity: A Missing Dimension in New Testament Studies.* Minneapolis, MI: Fortress Press, 1998.

Land, Steven J., *Pentecostal Spirituality: A Passion for the Kingdom,* JPT Supp 1. Sheffield: Sheffield Academic Press, 1993.

Lewis, Paul W. "Towards a Pentecostal Epistemology: The Role of Experience in Pentecostal Hermeneutics." *The Church and Spirit* 2:1. 2000. 95-125.

Martin, Lee Roy "Oh give thanks to the Lord for he is good": Affective Hermeneutics, Psalm 107, and Pentecostal Spirituality," *Pneuma* 36. 2014. 355–378.

Martin, L R. 'Longing for God: Psalm 63 and Pentecostal Spirituality,' Journal of Pentecostal Theology, 22. 2013. 54-76.

Moore, Rickie D. "Altar Hermeneutics: Reflections on Pentecostal Biblical Interpretation," *Pneuma* 38:1-2 (2016), 148-59.

McKay, John "When the Veil is Taken Away: The impact of Prophetic Experience on Biblical Interpretation," *Journal of Pentecostal Theology* 5. 1994. 17-40.

Neumann, Peter D. *Pentecostal Experience: An Ecumenical Encounter,* Princeton Theological Monographs Series 187. Eugene, OR: Wipf and Stock Publishers, 2012.

Oswalt, John N. *The Holy One of Israel: Studies in the Book of Isaiah.* Eugene, OR: Wipf & Stock, 2014.

Otto, Rudolf, *The Idea of the Holy*. Oxford: OUP, 1982.

Perry, David "Spirit Baptism and Social Action: The Pentecostal Experience of Spirit Baptism as a Rationale for Social Action and Mission," *Australasian Pentecostal Studies* Issue 16. Online: [http://aps-journal.com/aps/index.php/ APS/article/ view/138/135].

Roberts, J. J. M., *First Isaiah: A Commentary*. Minneapolis, MN: Fortress Press, 2015.

Ahn, Yongnan Jeon. *Interpretation of Tongues and Prophecy in 1 Corinthians 12-14: With a Pentecostal Hermeneutics*, JPT Supp Series 41. Dorset, UK: Deo Publishing, 2013.

Chapter 4

"He raises the poor from the dust:" God, The Worshiping Community, and the Poor in the Book of Psalms

Lee Roy Martin

The Church loses its moral authority and its influence in the community when it fails to minister to the poor. While many churches are deeply and intentionally engaged in ministry to the poor, other churches are not responding to Scripture's call to care for those who are in need. This chapter argues that the book of Psalms challenges the Church to engage in redemptive activities that minister to the poor and the marginalized.

Issues of poverty and justice are often addressed by appealing to the Old Testament prophetic literature, but the book of Psalms is also a rich source of theology regarding economic concerns. According to the Psalms, poverty is a problem that involves God, the poor, and the broader worshiping community. The Psalter declares that God created Israel to be a community of justice and equity; therefore, God acts on behalf of the poor, and God makes the worshiping community accountable to care for the poor. The Psalms also encourage the poor to cry out to God whenever they experience oppression and injustice.

The book of Psalms is a song book that should inform our theology and practice of worship, and Pentecostals are known for their worship. However, as illustrated above, many Pentecostal churches claim to love God but show little evidence of loving their neighbors, particularly if those neighbors are poor. In addition to sinful bigotry, the individualistic and dualistic nature of American Evangelicalism is partly to blame for this disconnect. Our emphasis on saving the "soul" has caused us to downplay the suffering of the body, and our belief in personal responsibility requires every person to fend for themselves. The Psalter, however, is holistic and communal rather than individualistic and dualistic. It declares that love of one's neighbor (the poor) is a criterion for acceptable worship.

Although theology, social ethics, and worship are deeply and inextricably integrated in the Psalter,[1] modern study has too often divided these three areas into discrete, exclusive categories.[2] Don Saliers laments this separation:

> Communal praise, thanksgiving, remembrance, confession, and intercession are part of the matrix which forms intention and action ... But there has to date been a paucity of dialogue between liturgical studies and ethics, even though it seems obvious that there are significant links between liturgical life, the confession of faith, and the concrete works which flow from these. *How* we pray and worship is linked to *how* we live – to our desires, emotions, attitudes, beliefs and actions.[3]

Daniel Castelo points out that early Pentecostalism was an example of the kind of integration that Saliers calls for, the instinctive integration of all aspects of human existence into one redeemed and transformed life, which is a "living sacrifice" offered to God in worship (Rom 12:1). Castelo writes,

> For early Pentecostals, a conceptual divide did not exist between worship and ethics nor between private and public life; all of these subsequent distinctions and categories that compartmentalize life were incoherent to early Pentecostals, for they saw all of their life within an integrated scheme that originated in the context of God's altering and transforming presence.[4]

The Poor and Covenant Community

Both the love of God and the love of neighbor are covenantal responses and responsibilities. Therefore, the Psalter represents worship as a thoroughly ethical practice.[5] Inasmuch as it flows out of the covenantal relationship between Yahweh and Israel, worship both celebrates and promulgates the covenantal ethical commitments of Israel to Yahweh and to the community. Vigen Guroian insists that "ethics is possible because a new people has come into existence" by God's saving acts and is continually "nourished" by their liturgical life together before God.[6] This vital connection between worship and covenant is recognized by Eugene LaVerdiere, who observes that "the covenant penetrated and gave significance" to Israel's worship and that "the covenant is cast in a liturgical context from its very inception."[7] In its function as covenant renewal and remembering of Yahweh's acts, worship would "strengthen their moral life."[8]

Also, the above-mentioned function of worship in spiritual formation suggests that the moral life is shaped partially through the lifelong participation in the prescribed liturgy. Saliers describes the role of worship in forming the affections: *"the relations between liturgy and ethics are most adequately formulated by specifying how certain affections and virtues are formed and expressed in the modalities of communal prayer and ritual action. These modalities of prayer enter into the formation of the self in community."*[9] Gordon Wenham adds that it is the act of *participation* in prayer, praise, and confession that makes worship so effective in forming the moral life. He argues, for example, that "if you pray ethically, you commit yourself to a path of action."[10]

Furthermore, the book of Psalms aims for the "moral and ethical transformation of persons and society."[11] From the very beginning, the Psalter describes the ethical lives and destinies of the righteous and the wicked, because "the Lord knows the way of the righteous, but the way of the wicked will perish" (Psa 1:6).

Righteousness is more than an abstract quality—it includes ethical actions. Positively, the righteous are generous, lending to their neighbors, and they give "freely" to "the poor" (Psa 112:5-9). Negatively, the righteous "turn away from evil" (Psa 37:27). The wicked person, however, "plots destruction" and loves "evil more than good" (Psa 52:1-5). Therefore, because "Yahweh loves justice, he will not forsake his saints ... but the children of the wicked shall be cut off" (Psa 37:26-28).

Within this ethical world view, Yahweh takes up the cause of the oppressed. The psalmist warns the wicked, "You would confound the plans of the poor, but the LORD is his refuge" (Psa 14:6). Moreover, Yahweh "raises up the needy out of affliction and makes their families like flocks" (Psa 107:41). Yahweh's activity goes beyond compassion and concern; Yahweh's rule changes social hierarchies, toppling the powerful (107:40) and exalting the poor to positions of power and authority.[12]

The Poor in the Book of Psalms

Who are the poor people in the book of Psalms? The poor are most commonly designated by four Hebrew words: *ani* (עָנִי), which can be defined as "poor, wretched, in a needy condition,"[13] *evyon*, (אֶבְיוֹן), meaning "needy, poor,"[14] *dal*, (דַּל), which refers to the "low, poor … powerless,"[15] and *rush*, (רוּשׁ), defined as "be in want, poor."[16] These terms overlap in meaning; and combined they describe poverty from four perspectives: 1. Poverty is an economic state in which basic human needs are not being met. 2. Poverty produces a sense of lack – the poor are aware of their insufficient resources. 3. Poverty creates a social location – the poor are metaphorically "low." 4. The deficiency of resources causes genuine suffering and misery. The average citizen of ancient Israel would have lived very close to subsistence level, and they would often have been unable to provide their basic needs if they were among the orphans (יָתוֹם, appearing 8 times), the widows (אַלְמָנָה, appearing 5 times), or the aliens (גֵר, appearing 4 times). Altogether, these seven terms that refer to the poor occur 89 times within 150 psalms.

The poor are those who live in the lowest economic strata of society. Their poverty makes them powerless and, therefore, vulnerable to abuse[17] and oppression by wealthy property holders who control the bulk of the community's resources.[18] The poor are those who are alienated and marginalized because of their economic circumstances. Thus, the psalmist can plead with God: "Turn to me and be gracious to me, For I am alone and poor" (Psa 25:16). Poverty makes one subject to oppression, as illustrated in Psalm 37: "The wicked draw their swords and bend their bows to bring down the poor and the needy, to slaughter those whose way is right" (v. 14); and in Psalm 10: "In arrogance the wicked hotly pursue the poor; let them be caught in the schemes which they have devised" (v. 2).

Those who wield power sometimes continue to oppress the poor, believing all the while that they can do so with impunity because God does not intervene. Consider the example of the wicked in Psalm 94:

> How long will the wicked – oh, LORD!
> how long will the wicked win?
> They crush your own people, LORD!
> They abuse your very own possession.
> They kill widows and immigrants;
> they murder orphans,
> saying all the while, The LORD can't see it;
> Jacob's God doesn't know what's going on!
> (vv. 3-7 CEB)

God's Vindication of the Poor

The oppressors, however, will learn eventually that God *does* know what is going on. God cares for the poor, and God will arise to stand on the side of justice. "Because the poor are oppressed, because the needy groan, I will now arise, says the LORD; I will place him in the safety for which he longs" (Psa 12:5). The Psalmist insists that Yahweh "delivers the poor from him who is too strong for him, and the poor and the needy from him who robs him" (Psa 35:10).

Although sometimes overlooked, the concern for justice is a significant theme in the book of Psalms. We find in the book of Psalms 97 references to "justice" and 130 references to "righteousness."[19] Righteousness and justice are attributes of Yahweh,—"He loves righteousness and justice" (Psa 33:4-5)—and those attributes are also demanded in society. Israel is commanded, "Give justice to the weak and the fatherless; maintain the right of the afflicted and the destitute. Rescue the weak and the needy; deliver them from the hand of the wicked" (Psa 82:1-4). Worship, therefore, "plays a very special part in telling the story of what we "should be" if we could only see ourselves "truthfully" in its light."[20] In worship, the believer "makes a commitment to the service of others."[21]

In this just society envisioned by the Psalms, the weakest and most vulnerable members are afforded special consideration, and worship becomes a shaper of public policy. Therefore, "We may investigate worship as a motivator of moral behavior, or liturgy as a political act. Liturgy can be viewed as the promulgator of an ideology, or at least of specific moral and ethical policies."[22] In contemporary America, where the gap between the rich and the poor is growing ever wider, economic policies threaten to create a neo-feudalism in which the "land-owners" (market speculators, real estate moguls, CEO's, and the like) live in luxury while the remainder of the population struggles to survive.

Just as in other biblical texts and as we mentioned above, those weaker members are named as the alien, the fatherless, the widow, and the poor: "Yahweh watches over the alien; he upholds the widow and the fatherless" (Psa 14:9, cf. Psa 39:12; 94:6; 119:19). "Father of orphans and defender of widows is God in his holy habitation" (Psa 68:5). Regarding Yahweh's concern for the poor, the Psalmist writes, "Oh, Yahweh, who is like you, delivering the poor from him who is too strong for him, the poor and needy from him who robs him?" (Psa 35:10). God's care for the poor is generated by his holy attributes. The Psalmist explains, "In your goodness, God, you provided for the poor" (Psa 68:10).

As "father to the fatherless and protector of widows" (Psa 68:6), Yahweh not only cares about the weak, he requires that the community care as well. Israel is instructed, "Give justice to the weak and the fatherless; maintain the right of the afflicted and the destitute" (Psa 82:3). "Blessed is the one who considers the poor!" (Psa 41:1; cf. Psa 10:2, 9; 37:14; 72:4).

It would be incorrect to assume that the Psalms include the "poor" as a subcategory of the "righteous" and that God cares for the poor *because* they are righteous. First, the poor are never equated with the righteous. Second, God's care for the poor is based on God's commitment to justice and love of neighbor. As members of the covenant community, the poor deserve equitable treatment even if they are not "righteous." Regardless of their moral standing, the weak should not be abused and their rights should not be violated.

Worship and Justice

LaVerdiere observes that worship leads to the human "imitation" of Yahweh's righteousness, justice, goodness, and faithfulness.[23] "In theological terms, *tsedeq* ('justice') defines how God treats his people within the framework of the covenantal relationship and reveals how

God expects humans to treat one another."[24] "God stands right next to the poor, to save them from any who would condemn them" (Psa 109:31). In this imitation, the covenant faithfulness of Yahweh is brought together with the requirement for a just society. Yahweh's faithfulness is signified by the Hebrew term חסד (*hesed*), which can be translated "steadfast love." The חסד of Yahweh, therefore, inspires and shapes human חסד (cf. Psa 18:25-27; 32:5-6; 50:4-5). Don Saliers argues,

> Of God, the Psalmist continually sings: "for his love endures forever." From this, intense affectivity may flow; and, upon occasion, from a proleptic experience the dispositions for more enduring love may be laid down in a life. That is, from an overwhelming experience of being mercifully loved and accepted, a person may find new capacities for steadfast love suddenly in place.[25]

The maintenance of a just society is the responsibility of every member of the community, but a greater burden is placed upon those who are in positions of leadership and authority. The Psalms include prayers that the king may judge righteously, that he may ensure justice for the poor, that he may "defend the cause of the poor of the people, give deliverance to the children of the needy, and crush the oppressor" (Psa 72:1-4; cf. Pss. 72:11-14; 99:3-4).

> Let the king bring justice to people who are poor;
> let him save the children of those who are needy,
> but let him crush oppressors! ...
> Because he delivers the needy who cry out,

94

the poor, and those who have no helper.
Let him have compassion on the poor and the needy;
And let him save the lives of those who are in need
He will redeem their lives from oppression and violence;
their blood is precious in his sight
(Psa 72:4-14).

Today's polarized political climate begs for a renewed emphasis on the Psalms' demand for compassionate rulers who maintain justice and who prevent abuse and oppression. The privilege of leadership includes the weighty responsibility to care for those who are the weakest of society. Rulers must not take advantage of their positions of power to enrich themselves and their cronies. The Bible views the role of government as a safeguard against evildoers, but government does not work if the rulers are themselves the evildoers.

As a relational act, worship cannot be separated from the justice of Yahweh and the covenantal demand for justice within the community. Therefore, the genuineness or validity of worship is judged by ethical criteria that lies outside of the worship act itself. Yahweh accepts only worship that is offered in the context of a just and righteous community. Psalm 15:1-5 sets forth the ethical requirements for acceptable worship:

O Yahweh, who shall sojourn in your tent?
Who shall dwell on your holy hill?
He who walks blamelessly and does what is right
And speaks truth in his heart; ...
Who swears to his own hurt and does not change;

Who does not put out his money at interest

And does not take a bribe against the innocent.

He who does these things shall never be moved.[26]

Elias Brasil de Souza argues that "Psalm 15 establishes the inextricable relation between worship and conduct and thus highlights important characteristics of the true worshiper."[27] He adds, "Such a theology, without denying the value of formal adoration, brings ethics to the foreground of worship and makes appropriate relationships with the neighbor a prerequisite to communion with Yahweh."[28]

Walter Brueggemann insists that the ethical perspective of the Psalter is alien to the dominant culture of today. He states that the truth that we find in the Psalms, but which is absent from our present culture, is that Yahweh "is a real agent, a lively character, and an agent of firm resolve who brings transformative energy and emancipatory capacity to all our social transactions."[29] Brueggemann compares the ethical concerns of the Psalms to that of the Old Testament prophets, making clear that Brueggemann's characterization of the theology of the Psalms is in fact quite similar to his description of the fundamental message of the prophets, as we find it described in his book, *The Prophetic Imagination*.[30]

Brueggemann's insights help us to see that, in many places, Pentecostal worship imitates the dominant culture of American society when, instead, worship should imagine an alternative community and alternative way of life for God's people. Brueggemann's vision is echoed by Elizabeth Achtemeier:

I suppose only if a preacher has something of such a worldview – a view of human life and of a world from which God is never absent; a view of a world in which nothing is secular; of a life that is God-haunted and God-accompanied, do the psalms of praise and lament make much sense. For that is the context in which these songs occur.[31]

In the book of Psalms, the enactment of worship is a form of proclamation; and, as Patrick Miller has observed, we should recognize our worship as a similar witness to the world. Miller writes,

Praise and thanksgiving, therefore, turn prayer into proclamation. The very heart of the act of giving thanks and praise is a declaration of what I, or we, believe and have come to know about the Lord of life. It is a declaration that thus calls others to a response to that reality, to see, fear, and trust in the Lord who has taken away my fears and helped me.[32]

We find in the Psalms "the testimony by which those who sing, pray, and speak point beyond themselves, the 'kerygmatic intention' of their praise and confession, their prayers and teachings."[33] Pentecostals have always conceived of their preaching as prophetic speech, and they have practiced the prophetic charismata. I am suggesting, however, that we go even farther and recognize our entire liturgy as a prophetic witness to the transformative presence and power of God in this world. Our worship should point to the God who

97

"raises the poor from the dust; [and] lifts up the needy from the ash heap" (Psa 113:7).

Encouragement for the Poor

Poverty robs one of hope, but the psalms insist that the plight of the poor will someday be remedied: "Not forever will the needy be forgotten, and the hope of the poor shall not be lost forever" (Psa 9:18, cf. Psa 10:8-9). Despite their challenging status and circumstances, the poor are encouraged to worship God, trust God, and remain hopeful.[34] The Palmist declares, "The young lions suffer want and hunger; But they who seek the LORD shall not lack any good thing" (Psa 34:10).

Of course, the question of theodicy comes into play. The Psalter acknowledges the complexities of life and the evils of systemic abuse that continue while God apparently does not act. The paradox between God's care for the poor and the delay in God's action is embodied in the presence of both the Psalms of Orientation and the Psalms of Disorientation.[35] In Psalm 73, for example, the Psalmist complains that the wicked are prospering while everyone else is suffering. Moreover, inasmuch as the abuse of the poor is occurring within the covenant community, the blame for suffering is not entirely God's to bear. As mentioned above, the community, in God's name, must take responsibility for addressing injustice.

As a way of encouraging the poor to trust God, the book of Psalms includes many prayers of the poor, as they plead for God's assistance. Many of these prayers are in the form of a lament: "As for me, I am poor and needy, but the Lord takes thought for me. You are my help and my deliverer; do not delay, O my God!" (Psa 40:17). "But

98

I am poor and needy; hurry to me, O God! You are my help and my deliverer; O LORD, do not delay!" (Psa 70:5) "Incline your ear, O LORD, and answer me, for I am poor and needy" (Psa 86:1). (cf. 109:22). Other prayers of the poor come in the form of testimonies: "This poor man cried, and the LORD heard him and saved him out of all his troubles" (Psa 34:6).[36]

Conclusion

This study of the Psalms challenges the western worldview of individualism. It also challenges the theology of private spirituality that is detached from concrete communal ethics, in which believers can worship God on Sunday and oppress the poor on Monday, all with a good conscience because they are justified *Sola Fide*. Furthermore, it challenges recent trends that make participation in "worship" alone the highest expression of the Christian faith. While I agree that genuine worship of God is the Christian's ultimate goal, genuine worship is communal, which means that worship without ethics is not acceptable to God.

The obligation of a righteous community is to "Give justice to the lowly and the orphan; maintain the right of the poor and the destitute! Rescue the lowly and the needy. Deliver them from the power of the wicked!" (Psa 82:3-4). The duty to maintain justice rests most heavily upon leaders, who should exemplify the qualities of a "good king,"[37] but everyone in the community shares in that responsibility.

Bibliography

Achtemeier, Elizabeth. "Preaching the Praises and Laments," *Calvin Theological Journal* 36:1. 2001. 103-14

Brasil de Souza, Elias. "Worship and Ethics: A Reflection on Psalm 15," https://www. academia.edu /3089608/ Worship_and_Ethics_A_ Reflection_on_Psalm_15_A_short_study_on_ the_ inextricable_relation_between_worship_and_ conduct_in_Psalm_15, 4.

Bremer, Johannes. "'Doch den אֶבְיוֹן hob er aus dem עוֹנִי empor.' (Psa 107:41a)," *Biblische Notizen* 158. 2013. 57.

Brown, Francis, Samuel R. Driver, and Charles A. Briggs, *Enhanced Brown-Driver-Briggs Hebrew and English Lexicon*. Oxford: Clarendon Press, 1977.

Brueggemann, Walter. *The Prophetic Imagination*. Philadelphia: Fortress Press, 1978.

_____. *From Whom No Secrets Are Hid: Introducing the Psalms*. Louisville, KY: Westminster John Knox Press, 2014.

_____. *The Message of the Psalms: A Theological Commentary*. Augsburg Old Testament Studies; Minneapolis: Augsburg Pub. House, 1984.

Castelo, Daniel. "Tarrying on the Lord: Affections, Virtues and Theological Ethics in Pentecostal Perspective," *Journal of Pentecostal Theology* 13:1 (2004), 31-56 (50).

Charry, Ellen T. *Psalms 1-50*. Brazos Theological Commentary on the Bible; Grand Rapids, MI: Brazos Press, 2015.

Everett, William W. "Liturgy and Ethics: A Response to Saliers and Ramsey," *Journal of Religious Ethics* 7:2 (1979), 203-14.

Farley, Margaret A. "Beyond the Formal Principle: A Reply to Ramsey and Saliers," *Journal of Religious Ethics* 7:2. 1979.

Gerhard von Rad, *Old Testament Theology* (2 vols.; New York: Harper, 1962), I.

Gray, Donald. "Liturgy and Morality," *Worship* 39:1 (1965), 28-35 (30).

Guroian, Vigen. "Seeing Worship as Ethics: An Orthodox Perspective," *Journal of Religious Ethics*

Koernke, Theresa F. "Toward an Ethics of Liturgical Behavior," *Worship* 66:1. 1992.

Köhler, Ludwig. *The Hebrew and Aramaic Lexicon of the Old Testament* (Leiden: E. J. Brill, 1994–2000).

Kraus, Hans-Joachim. *Theology of the Psalms*, trans., K.R. Crim; Continental Commentaries; Minneapolis, MN: Augsburg Pub. House, 1986.

LaVerdiere, Eugene A. "Covenant Morality," *Worship* 38:5 (1964), 240-46 (240).

Macquarrie, John. *Dictionary of Christian Ethics* (Philadelphia: Westminster Press, 1967).

Rossi, Philip J. "Narrative, Worship, and Ethics: Empowering Images for the Shape of Christian Moral Life," *Journal of Religious Ethics* 7:2 (1979), 239-48 (244).

Saliers, Don. "Liturgy and Ethics: Some New Beginnings," *Journal of Religious Ethics* 7:2. 1979.

Wainwright, Geoffrey. "Eucharist and/as Ethics," *Worship* 62:2. 1988.

Wenham, Gordon J. "Reflections on Singing the Ethos of God,"
  European Journal of Theology 18:2, 2009.

Section Two

The Holy Spirit in the New Testament

Chapter 5

The Gospel and Racial Reconciliation[1]

Craig S. Keener

Glenn Usry is one of my former students at Hood, the African Methodist Episcopal Zion seminary; he was also my coauthor on *Black Man's Religion*. The two of us used to joke about whether the Nation of Islam or the Klan would try to kill us for that book first. In the 1990s it looked like Glenn would win the bet, since someone had warned him that he might need to be killed for challenging the Nation of Islam.

But the Nation of Islam isn't wrong on everything. Most of us disapprove when black Muslims call white people "devils" for the way they have treated black people.[2] Yet we Christians often read right past Jesus' words on a related topic. According to Scripture, all people are children of the devil, and bearers of his nature, until we are born again (Jn 8:44). True to what this might lead us to expect, individuals and groups throughout history have sought power over others and exploited that power once they achieved it, and White American slaveholders and racists have proved no exception. Yet granted that the racial history of our nation provides abundant illustrations of the biblical principle of human depravity, Christians also affirm the transforming power of the gospel. In other words, granted that the Nation of Islam is partly right in denouncing the White majority's general treatment of African-Americans, we might hope that history provides at least a few examples of individuals transformed by the gospel sacrificially crossing racial boundaries. Or, if history testifies only to human depravity and not to the transforming power of the gospel, we ought to be able to demonstrate that history indicts Christians' disobedience to the gospel, rather than the gospel itself.

But can the gospel genuinely prove relevant to contemporary racial questions? After all, the New Testament addressed a world quite different from ours, where differences in skin tone and other physical features were noticed but rarely understood in a prejudicial manner.[3] Nevertheless, "racism" in the sense of various cultures viewing themselves as superior was widespread. Greeks considered non-Greeks to be barbarians[4] and Jewish people correctly regarded the vast majority of non-Jews as idolatrous pagans. The historic barriers white oppression has created between black and white differ from the ancient barrier between Jew and Gentile, but if the gospel transcends a barrier that God Himself established in Israel's history, then how much more (to borrow a rabbinic line of argument) must it transcend all other human barriers we have erected among ourselves? Because Paul focuses most fully on the gospel of reconciliation, we will address Paul's teaching in most of the paper, and survey only briefly the perspectives of some of the other New Testament writers, at the conclusion of our examination of Paul. After that we will provide some brief examples from U.S. history of Christians who crossed racial barriers because of their commitment to Christ. Finally, we will include some remarks about some soteriological questions in the Bible and how part of the Church's ignoring them hampers the cause of racial reconciliation.

The Shattered Barrier

In Ephesians, Paul[5] seeks to bring unity to a church divided in part along Jewish-Gentile lines. He begins by assuring Gentile Christians that God has grafted them into the people of God, applying to the whole church many Old Testament designations concerning Israel (Eph 1:3-14: e.g., predestination; inheritance; possession).[6] As he prepares to discuss the new Temple comprised of both Jew and Gentile in 2:20-22,[7] he declares that Christ made both Jew and Gentile one (2:14). Especially when we consider Paul's social context, such a claim was entirely remarkable: not long after Paul dictated these words, riots broke out in Caesarea, the city of Paul's earlier imprisonment, with Jews and Syrians slaughtering one another.[8] Racial reconciliation sometimes demands saying what most of one's contemporaries do not wish to hear.

Paul goes on in Ephesians 2:14 to announce that Christ has shattered the dividing wall of partition between Jew and Gentile. He writes as if his hearers[9] will immediately understand the dividing wall to which Paul refers, and it does not take us long to imagine how Paul's hearers would have understood his point.

Tempting Tempers in the Temple

Paul's audience in the region around Ephesus would have known exactly why Paul was writing to them from prison; they were aware of the charge that he had transgressed a "dividing barrier" in the Temple. The Old Testament had welcomed Gentiles to the Temple alongside God's people (1 Kings 8:41-43), but by the first century, the Temple was a segregated institution. Because of new purity regulations,[10] the "outer court" had become the Court of Israel, limited to Jewish men; then, on a lower level and further from the priestly sanctuary, the Court of Women, beyond which Jewish women could not pass. Finally, still further from the sanctuary and on a lower level, was the new outer court, beyond which Gentile seekers of Israel's God could not pass. Signs posted at appropriate intervals between the outer court and the Court of Women announced to Gentiles that any Gentile passing beyond that point would bear responsibility for his or her own death.[11]

Some Jews who knew of Paul's interracial ministry in Ephesus recognized an Ephesian Gentile with Paul near Jerusalem's Temple and decided that Paul must have followed to its conclusion his ideal of breaking down ethnic barriers.[12] Paul had actually entered the Temple on an errand of racial reconciliation, affirming his Jewish identity for those who thought that he had accommodated the Gentiles too much (Acts 21:21-26).[13] Nevertheless, his opponents were wrongly convinced that Paul had brought a Gentile past the dividing wall into the Temple beyond which Gentiles could not pass. Once word spread, a riot quickly ensued (Acts 21:27-30).[14]

Once the guards atop the Fortress Antonia on the Temple Mount recognized that a riot was forming, soldiers from the Roman garrison rushed down the stairs into the outer court and seized Paul from the crowds (Acts 21:31-36).[15] In the racially tense situation, the Roman commander assumed that Paul was a notorious Egyptian Jew whom he wrongly associated with a group of "assassins" (21:38).[16] (Under cover of the crowds in the Temple, these "assassins" stabbed Jewish aristocrats, whom their attackers apparently viewed as the "Uncle Toms" of ancient Judaism.)[17]

But Paul makes use of all the cultural resources at his disposal. Most Palestinian Jews were probably bilingual, but few were proficient in a second language.[18] Thus when his interrogator hears his good Greek and learns that he is a citizen of a prominent city (21:37, 39),[19] he allows him to address the crowd—which Paul proceeds to address in Aramaic (21:40).[20] Impressed by his fluency in the nationalistic tongue of their ancestors, the crowd decides that the person addressing them deserves their hearing (22:2). In his speech, Paul emphasizes every possible point of identification with his nationalistic hearers, including having been raised in Jerusalem at the feet of Gamaliel and receiving ministry from a law-abiding Jewish Christian (22:3-5, 12).[21] Probably because the Jerusalem church had identified so effectively with their own culture, no one took offense as Paul narrated his encounter with the risen Christ (22:6-20); in contrast to earlier years (Acts 12:2-3), simply talking about Jesus no longer stirred much violence, just as talking about "salvation" does not in some segments of our culture today.

But then Paul said something that "lost" his audience, even though he was still expounding the *narratio*, the opening narration of his speech. Paul had earlier appealed to Stoic values in Acts 17, finding common ground with his hearers through much of his speech before the Areopagus (17:22-29). He had offended many members of his audience, however, when he pushed forward to an essential part of the gospel he could not accommodate to his hearers' worldview (17:30-32). Now Paul again loses his audience, but the essential part of the gospel to which he pushes – undoubtedly to the public embarrassment of the local Christians – is that it included the Gentile mission (22:21). On hearing this, his nationalistic hearers, who had suffered so much from the Romans and were so sure that God was on their side, resumed their riot (22:22-23). Paul ended up in prison, first in Caesarea and then in Rome, because he refused to compromise an opportunity to proclaim the full implications of the gospel.

When Paul wrote to Christian congregations around Ephesus about reconciliation between Jew and Gentile, they understood what he meant by a "dividing barrier." For Paul and for the Jewish and Gentile Christians of western Asia Minor, no greater symbol of the barrier between Jew and Gentile could exist than the dividing barrier in the Temple. Paul declares that in the new Temple of God's Spirit, the cross of Christ has abolished that barrier.

How to Have a Christian Riot

Paul was not the first New Testament person to pay a price for challenging nationalism in Jerusalem's Temple. Jesus did as well.[22]

The day the Rodney King verdict came back, and our streets erupted into violence, some members of our African-American Bible study group at Duke University questioned the Bible's relevance to this nation's racial problem. No one much felt like having a Bible study; the preferred option was joining a protest march (which some of us later did). But when I timidly suggested the possibility of staging a Christian riot, someone demanded incredulously, "How can you have a Christian riot?" The consensus was that we couldn't, but some of us did stay long enough to discover that the Bible does have something to say about a rather overt act of protest Jesus staged in the Temple courts.

Some scholars have traditionally doubted that Jesus could have foretold His death as the Gospels report, but the best historical evidence we have concerning Jesus indicts their skepticism. Jesus not only foretold His death; He deliberately provoked it. Some people threatened Jeremiah with death for merely prophesying against the Temple (Jer 26:8-9); in the first century, the Sadducean aristocracy urged the Roman procurator to execute Joshua ben Hananiah for prophesying against the Temple. Because Joshua was harmless the governor spared his life but had him scourged until his bones showed.[23] For Jesus to not only prophesy against the Temple but to march through the outer court overturning tables meant that from that day on He was a marked man.

Scholars have proposed various reasons for Jesus' act in the Temple, but Jesus provided at least a partial interpretation of His act in the Scriptures He cited. In Mark 11:17, He quotes two texts: Isaiah 56:7 and Jeremiah 7:11. The first text indicates God's ultimate purpose for the Temple: a house of prayer for all nations. The Herodian Temple, unlike Solomon's, segregated Gentiles from other worshipers.[24] Further, the outer court had become a site more for business transactions than for multiethnic prayer.[25] It is thus possible that Jesus was protesting the segregation of God's house. A biblical scholar would not dare venture to ask what the Lord might feel about many of our houses of worship today.

The second text refers to Jeremiah's diatribe against the Temple. God's people thought that the Temple would protect them (Jer 7:4), but Jeremiah warned that if they did not abandon their acts of injustice toward the poor, toward crime victims, toward their spouses and toward immigrants, God was going to destroy His house

(Jer 7:5-15). He would no longer allow His Temple to be their "robber's den" (Jer 7:11), the place where robbers gathered their loot assured of safety. He would make the Temple like Shiloh (Jer 7:14), where His ark had once been captured and the Tabernacle may have been destroyed (1 Sam 4:4, 11). Like Jeremiah, Jesus promised swift judgment on God's house where the religious leaders tolerated injustice; some forty years later, the Temple lay in ruins.[26] A biblical scholar would surely not want to guess what implications such a text might have for today.

Salvation by Grace or by Race?

When Paul first met Aquila and Priscilla, they had left Rome because the emperor Claudius had commanded Jews (or on some readings, Jewish Christians) to leave (Acts 18:2).[27] When he greets them at the end of his letter to the Roman Christians, however, they have returned to Rome (Rom 16:3-4), indicating that Claudius' edict is no longer in effect (presumably because he is dead). This greeting also suggests that what had been for some years an entirely Gentile church in Rome had experienced a fresh influx of Jewish Christians. The rest of Paul's letter suggests that these Jewish and Gentile Christians with their quite different customs were not getting along.

Carrying over the prevalent perspective of their own Roman culture, the Gentile Christians seem to have despised Jewish Christians' food laws and holy days (Rom 14:1-6).[28] Many of the Jewish Christians, conversely, probably questioned the orthodoxy of Gentile Christians who did not observe the laws God had established in the Bible. Thus Paul argues for the first eleven chapters of his letter that Jew and Gentile come to God on the same terms, and neither has an automatic preference regarding God's grace.

First, Paul establishes that all humanity is equally damned. In Romans 1:18-27, Paul proves what probably no one in the church was disputing: non-Christian Gentiles were lost. He focuses on the examples of idolatry and homosexual behavior, which Jewish people considered almost exclusively Gentile sins,[29] but quickly turns to a vice-list that includes sins which Jewish people also acknowledged as their own (1:28-32).[30] Romans 1 is ultimately a setup for Romans 2, in which Paul establishes that his own people are also damned, so that he may conclude in chapter 3 that all humanity is equally damned and in need of Christ (3:23-31).

Second, Paul shows that God has provided salvation for all people on the same terms. Jewish people commonly believed that they would be saved by virtue of their descent from Abraham, but Paul emphasizes that spiritual rather than merely physical descent from Abraham was what mattered (Rom 4). God had, after all, chosen Abraham when he was still a Gentile (4:10-12), as Paul's contemporaries also acknowledged.[31] But regardless of who was descended from Abraham, all of us have descended from Adam, and share Adam's sin and death (5:12-21). This, too, was an argument that should have carried weight with the Jewish Christians.[32]

Paul did not deny that the law was a special gift to Israel (3:2), or that the law was good (7:12, 14). But no one could be made righteous by observing the law because human nature was too sinful to keep the law adequately in its own strength. If approached through faith, the law could become God's gift of righteousness written in His people's hearts (3:27; 8:2; 9:30-32; cf. Jer 31:33; Ezk

36:27); but this was accomplished by grace, not by human merit. Paul depicts life under the law as a struggle resembling Greek depictions of reason versus one's passions,[33] or Jewish traditions concerning the good and evil impulse.[34] The law enabled one to know what was good but could not transform the human heart to be good. Thus, Israel's possession of Torah did not guarantee them salvation more easily than the Gentiles—a proposition that would have horrified his contemporaries.

Third, Paul closes his extended theological prologue by treating the relationship between Israel and the Gentiles more directly in chapters 9 through 11. Jewish people believed that God had chosen them in Abraham, but Paul establishes that not all descendants of Abraham in the Bible qualified for the promise (Rom 9:6-13). He argues that God is so sovereign that He can choose on any basis He pleases—in this context, not simply on the basis of one's ethnicity, but rather on the basis of one's response to His Christ (Rom 9:24-33).[35] Jewish people could not trust their ethnic Jewishness for salvation.

Neither should Gentile Christians trust their more recently adopted Gentile Christian subculture for salvation, either. (Such a warning might have relevance to some modern evangelicals who assume that they are saved by virtue of being evangelicals, rather than by being what evangelicals should be, i.e., followers of Christ.) Paul points out that Gentiles were saved by being grafted into the people of God, but if God could break off unbelieving Jewish branches who fit into that heritage more naturally, He could certainly break off the foreign Gentile branches (Rom 11:17-22). Further, Paul believed that someday God would bring a great harvest of Jewish branches back to the tree, preparing them for Christ's return (Rom 11:23-27).[36]

Finally, Paul worked out the practical implications for the Roman Christians. They must serve one another like one body with many diverse members (Rom 12), recognize that the epitome of the law is love (Rom 13:8-10), respect one another's customs so long as they are used to glorify God (Rom 14), and embrace models of ethnic reconciliation like Christ (Rom 15:8-12) and Paul himself (15:25-27). Paul's closing exhortation is to beware of those who sow division (16:17).

Reconciliation Elsewhere in the New Testament

Although our biblical focus has been Paul, we should mention in passing that ethnic reconciliation is not a solely Pauline agenda, but an issue which the ancient Mediterranean world frequently pressed upon the early Christians. The New Testament often addresses reconciliation between Jew and Gentile in the context of the Gentile mission. The Book of Acts testifies eloquently to the prejudices against Gentiles which had to be overcome to secure their evangelization (e.g., 10:28; 11:17-18).[37] Gentiles seem to fulfill the same function in Acts as "sinners" and other outcasts did in Luke's first volume, his Gospel. Acts opens where Luke closes, with a commission to evangelize the nations (Lk 24:47; Acts 1:8), and concludes with Paul in the heart of the Roman Empire, emphasizing the Gentile mission (Acts 28:28).

Matthew, writing to predominantly Jewish Christians, likewise lays a decisive emphasis on the Gentile mission (2:1-2; 3:9; 4:15; 8:11-12, 28; 10:15; 11:23-24; 12:40-42; 15:24-28; 16:13; 24:14; 25:32), beginning with four interracial marriages in Jesus' genealogy (1:3, 5-6) and concluding with Jesus' final commission (28:19).[38]

Because Jesus only rarely encountered Gentiles, sometimes the Gospel writers addressed the issue of reconciliation in terms of His encounters with Samaritans. Luke addresses one encounter in Luke 17:16 and through Jesus' parable about a Samaritan being one's neighbor that one ought to love (10:29-37). John likewise shows Jesus crossing three barriers with the Samaritan woman. Much to His disciples' astonishment (Jn 4:27), Jesus crossed a gender barrier: men were not supposed to be talking with women outside the home,[39] especially in an ambiguous social setting like a well.[40] He probably also crossed a moral barrier: that she came to the well alone (4:7) probably suggests that she was not welcome to accompany the other women – presumably because of her marital history (4:18).[41]

But most importantly for our purposes, Jesus clearly crossed a cultural barrier by talking with a Samaritan, as she herself recognized (4:9). Because strict Jewish pietists considered Samaritan women continually unclean,[42] drinking from her vessel would also communicate ritual impurity, yet Jesus requests a drink (4:7). The narrative probably includes some allusions to the history of conflict Jews and Samaritans shared: the woman reminds Jesus that Jacob was the Samaritans' father—as if to counter the Jewish notion that he was their own (4:12).[43] Later she speaks of her people's worship on Mount Gerizim in the past tense, presumably an allusion to its destruction by a Jewish ruler about two centuries earlier (4:20).[44] Although Jesus affirms Israel's priority in salvation history (4:22), He quickly transcends the ethnic issue and identifies her as someone the Father is seeking to worship Him in the Spirit (4:23-24). That John invites his audience to apply these principles to their own cross-cultural Christian relationships may be implicit in Jesus' prayer for unity among all who would believe through the apostolic witness (Jn 17:20-23).

Some Examples of Reconciliation in U.S. History[45]

Although racial division and white oppression of blacks is dominant in U.S. history, that history nevertheless provides abundant examples which demonstrate the transforming power of the gospel. Many early black churches were interracial, despite the persecution such ministry frequently invited. A White deacon may have also helped George Liele found the Silver Bluff Baptist Church in Savannah, though Liele became the leader.[46] In 1788 former slave Andrew Bryan joined a white and another black Baptist minister to start Savannah's "Ethiopian Church of Jesus Christ."[47] The white Baptist churches of Savannah praised Bryan for his work.[48] Other black Baptists in the South "participated in the rapid growth of legal biracial congregations," some of which belonged to local Baptist associations.[49] Slave-born African-American David George (1743-1810), who established the first Baptist church in West Africa, earlier faced persecution for baptizing a white woman.[50]

During the Great Awakening, the evangelical revival (especially among Baptists and Methodists) "fostered an inclusiveness which could border on egalitarianism," because it stressed conversion rather than a merely intellectual approach to Christianity.[51] In this period black preachers often preached to White as well as black audiences, sometimes even starting interracial churches.[52] In her first published poem, black poet Phillis Wheatley praised revivalist George Whitfield for the hope his message brought her people.[53] As Lerone Bennett, Jr., historian and senior editor of *Ebony* magazine, points out concerning the late 1700s, "Baptists and Methodists strongly condemned slavery," and blacks "like Joshua Bishop of Virginia and Lemuel Haynes of New England pastored white churches."[54]

> For the most part, northern black Christians adhered to the Protestant revivalist doctrines of the antebellum period. Those doctrines tended to brand slavery a sin, thereby making opposition to slavery a sign of holiness and a Christian duty...The American antislavery and reform movements were directly related to the evangelical movement of the early nineteenth century.[55]

Already in 1710, Anglican bishop William Fleetwood attacked American slaveholders for withholding Christianity from their slaves and went on to attack slavery itself.[56] Quakers like John Woolman (1720-1772) developed Christian antislavery arguments.[57] Wesley and all the other early Methodist leaders were committed foes of slavery.[58] Southern, as well as northern, Evangelicals supported the 1784 Methodist General Conference when it declared slavery "contrary to the golden laws of God."[59] The 1812 General Conference of the Methodist Church ruled that "no slaveholder should be eligible to the office of local elder."[60] By 1827, the Methodists and Friends were the most active antislavery denominations,[61] but many Baptists,[62] Presbyterians,[63] and others, also joined the cause.[64] The few minutes of Baptist meetings and letters of Baptist missionaries from the 1700s reveal considerable Baptist opposition to slavery.[65]

Some White Christians went further than nonviolent opposition to slavery. Both John Brown and George Boxley led slave revolts,[66] and northern African-Americans honored Brown.[67] As early as 1741 slaveholders suspected White missionaries of involvement with slave insurrections,[68] and the governor of Virginia in 1831 even blamed White Christian perspectives for influencing Nat Turner's revolt, although he and his contemporaries recognized that black biblical perspectives were still more critical.[69]

One could also list numerous examples of Whites who stood for justice after slavery. White statesman Thaddeus Stevens fought in Congress for Reconstruction and chose burial in a black cemetery. His gravestone includes the epitaph he chose for himself:

> I repose in this quiet and secluded spot,
> Not from any natural preference for solitude,
> But finding other cemeteries limited by charter rules as
> to race,
> I have chosen this that I might illustrate in my death
> The principles which I have advocated through a long
> life,
> Equality of Man before his Creator.[70]

In the Civil Rights era, Rev. Bruce Klunder, a white minister, laid himself in the path of a bulldozer to protest construction of a segregated school in Cleveland, Ohio and was crushed to death.[71]

Examples of interracial efforts for justice and reconciliation could be multiplied, but if we wished, we could list no fewer examples of Christians' failures to work for reconciliation. History testifies both to human depravity and to the gospel's transforming power, but in most periods, it testifies more to the former than to the latter, simply because few Christians express adequate commitment to Christ to stand fully for His values against those of their culture. Thus for example, while churches in the earliest period did not promote slavery and some actively opposed it, most failed to address the issue,[72] just as most people today, Christian and non-Christian, remain silent on most of the injustices practiced in various parts of the world (including the widespread practice of torture, extrajudicial executions, and massive slavery well-documented around the world, sometimes with our fellow-Christians as the victims).

Likewise, many of the Christian abolitionists feared taking a public stand for "amalgamation," mixing of whites and blacks in public meetings, lest they be viewed as too radical and thereby hurt the antislavery cause. Most of the male abolitionists counseled the Philadelphia Women's Antislavery Convention in 1838 not to provoke trouble by meeting together as a racially mixed group. The public outcry against the amalgamation was so severe that Philadelphians burned to the ground the place in which the women had met. Nevertheless, the black and white women met again the next day and courageously issued the following statement:

Resolved,
That prejudice against color is the very spirit of slavery, sinful in those who indulge in it, and is the fire which is

consuming the happiness and energies of the free people of color.

That it is, therefore, the duty of abolitionists to identify themselves with these oppressed Americans, by sitting with them in places of worship, by appearing with them in our streets...by visiting them at their homes and encouraging them to visit us, receiving them as we do our white fellow citizens.[73]

Such examples do reinforce hope for more courageous disciples today.

Other Soteriological Issues Relevant to Reconciliation

Much of the Black Church has escaped the dichotomy between prophetic concern for justice, on the one hand, and commitment to evangelism and personal piety, on the other, that has divided many of the white churches since the early part of this century.[74] Unlike most evangelicals today, most of the abolitionists had a fully evangelical theology that addressed both personal holiness and societal injustice.[75] While many of the white churches abandoned the fuller understanding of the gospel found in much of nineteenth century evangelicalism,[76] many African-American Christians never had that option.[77]

Some suppose that the prophetic concern for justice, while important, is not central to our faith as Christians; but they have read their traditions' soteriology into Scripture rather than heeding Scripture's full message. Consider texts like the following:[78]

'He pled the cause of the afflicted and needy; Then it was well. Is not that what it means to know Me?' Declares the LORD (Jer 22:16).

Learn to do good; Seek justice, Reprove the ruthless; Defend the orphan, Plead for the widow. "Come now, and let us reason together," Says the LORD, "Though your sins are as scarlet, They will be as white as snow; Though they are red like crimson, They will be like wool. If you consent and obey, You will eat the best of the land; but if you refuse and rebel, You will be devoured by the sword." (Is 1:17-20).

"What use is it, my brethren, if a man says he has faith, but he has no works? Can that faith save him? If a brother or sister is without clothing and in need of daily food, and one of you says to them, "Go in peace, be warmed and be filled," and yet you do not give them what is necessary for their body, what use is that? (James 2:14-16)

Luke is one writer who heavily emphasizes what we would call social concern. When people who have come for John's baptism of repentance ask him what they should do as the necessary fruit of repentance, John declares, "Let the person who has two shirts share one with the person who does not have any; and let the person who has food do the same" (Lk 3:11). Jesus announced, "In the same way, none of you can be My disciple without giving up everything that belongs to you" (Lk 14:33). Luke also reports the sacrificial lifestyle of the early Christians, who valued one another more highly than they valued their own possessions (Acts 2:44-45). The only clue for why the rich man in the story of Lazarus was damned is that he allowed Lazarus to starve to death at his doorstep (Lk 16:25). Of course, this could never happen to professed Christians in North America today; our society is too sophisticated to let starving people get near our doorsteps. Yet one wonders if knowledge of their need, rather than geographical proximity, is not the real point (2 Cor 8-9).

According to the biblical gospel, saving faith is something on which we stake our lives, not merely a fire escape. Biblical conversion involves salvation from sin's power, not only from hell. This transformation will ultimately produce the Spirit's fruit of love, and love demands a concern for justice once we understand the issues. Some thoroughly evangelical white ministers have told me of congregations they have served where professedly born-again Christians belonged to the Klan. Most black Christians I know have a problem with the idea that an active Klan member is genuinely converted. Which perspective better reveals a biblical soteriology?

For true dialogue to take place, many white churches must come to grips with their selective piety concerning social and political agendas. Dialogue does not mean that all of us will come to the same conclusions about methods to achieve justice or even the particular issues on which we lay our emphasis, but it does demand that we humbly listen to what our dialogue partners have to say. For the most part, white evangelicals have not listened to the perspectives of black church leaders on issues that often affect the black Church directly. Is the coercive power of a voting majority that ignores minority concerns less oppressive in *principle* than slaveholders who simply imposed their will on slaves? Can we act in such a manner and yet obey the example of Christ, who came to serve and counted not power a thing to be grasped?

Conclusion

Soteriology has important ramifications for ecclesiology—that is, how we understand the gospel affects how urgently we approach the unity of Christ's body. That biblical writers proclaimed racial reconciliation based on our common means of salvation has practical implications for us today. Because they together constitute a spiritual minority in workplaces and schools, Christians of different races and cultures often fulfill those implications, but the implications are more daunting, and more disturbing, for ministers, professors, or denominational leaders whose entire circle of fellowship exists in largely segregated religious institutions.

Many white conservative evangelicals invite dialogue only from black Christians who can speak conservative Evangelical language and become frustrated when many of even those black Christians turn out to be less "safe" than they had hoped. If I can extrapolate safely from the circles with which I am familiar, there are probably millions of born-again Christians in black Pentecostal, Baptist, and Methodist churches. In general, these churches are evangelical in theology and practice, yet most do not use the label "evangelical." Despite a number of notable exceptions, *most* white evangelicals who talk about reconciliation have not sacrificed the time or energy to explore relationships in those circles. By limiting the dialogue to African-American Christians who are willing to use "evangelical" labels, white conservative evangelicals essentially limit the dialogue to those African-American Christians who already have intentionally crossed the racial barrier.

If these observations are correct, the black evangelicals have born a much heavier part of the burden in seeking reconciliation than white evangelicals have, although many white evangelicals seem unaware of this situation. White Christians who are really serious about reconciliation must be ready to cross ecclesiastical as well as color boundaries, boundaries of longstanding cultural church traditions as well as boundaries of ethnicity. Such barriers can be crossed only if we unite on the basis of our common need before our Lord Jesus Christ, who has reconciled us all to the Father in one body by His cross. May we hear the pain of the one whose body we have dared rend asunder by our prejudices, and may we genuinely heed the truth of His gospel. In the name of the one we claim as Lord, amen.

Bibliography

Adams, Alice Dana. *The Neglected Period of Anti-Slavery in America (1808-1831)*. Gloucester, MA: Peter Smith, 1964

Bennett, Lerone Jr. *Before the Mayflower: A History of the Negro in America, 1619-1964*, Rev. ed. Baltimore, MD: Penguin, 1966.

Carmon, Efrat, ed. *Inscriptions Reveal: Documents from the Time of the Bible, the Mishna and the Talmud*, tr. R. Grafman. Jerusalem: Israel Museum, 1973.

Childs, John Brown. *The Political Black Minister: A Study in Afro-American Politics and Religion*. Boston: G. K. Hall, 1980.

Dupont, Jacques. *The Salvation of the Gentiles: Essays on the Acts of the Apostles*, tr. John R. Keating. New York: Paulist Press, 1979.

Fordham, Moroe. *Major Themes in Northern Black Religious Thought, 1800-1860*. Hicksville, NY: Exposition Press, 1975.

Gärtner, Bertril. *The Temple and the Community in Qumran and the NT*. Cambridge University, 1965.

Gordon, Grant. *From Slavery to Freedom: The Life of David George, Pioneer Black Baptist Minister*. Hantsport, Novia Scotia: Lancelot Press, 1993.

Josephus. The Jewish War, ed. Gaalya Cornfeld. Grand Rapids: Zondervan, 1982.

Klausner, Joseph. *Jesus: His Life, Times, and Teaching*. New York: Menorah, 1979.

Kirby, John C. *Ephesians: Baptism and Pentecost. An Enquiry into the Structure and Purpose of the Epistle to the Ephesians*. Montreal: McGill University Press, 1968.

Knox, Wilfred L. *St. Paul and the Church of the Gentiles*. Cambridge: Cambridge University Press, 1939.

Lane, Ann, ed. *The Debate Over Slavery*. Urbana, IL: University of Illinois, 1971.

Lincoln, Andrew T. Ephesians, WBC 42. Dallas: Word, 1990.

Mark Noll, *A History of Christianity in the United States and Canada*. Grand Rapids: Wm B. Eerdmans Publishing Co.,, 1992.

Mukenge, Ida Rousseau. *The Black Church in Urban America: A Case Study in Political Economy*. Lanham: University Press of America, 1983.

O'Brien, Peter T. "Ephesians I: An Unusual Introduction to a New Testament Letter," NTS 25. July 4, 1979: 504-16.

Raboteau, Albert J. *Slave Religion: The "Invisible Institution" in the Antebellum South*. New York: Oxford University, 1978.

Ripley, Peter C., ed. *Witness for Freedom: African American Voices on Race, Slavery, and Emancipation*. Chapel Hill, NC: The University of North Carolina Press, 1993.

Robinson, John A.T. *Redating the New Testament*. Philadelphia: The Westminster Press; London: SCM Press, 1976.

Sanneh, Lamin. *West African Christianity: The Religious Impact*. Maryknoll, NY: Orbis, 1983.

Snowden, Frank M. Jr. *Blacks in Antiquity: Ethiopians in the Greco-Roman Experience*. Cambridge, MA: The Belknap Press of Harvard University Press, 1970.

Unnik, W.C. Van. *Tarsus or Jerusalem: The City of Paul's Youth*. London: Epworth, 1962.

Usry, Glenn, and Craig Keener. *Black Man's Religion: Can Christianity be Afrocentric?* Downers Grove: InterVarsity, 1996.

Washington, James Melvin. *Frustrated Fellowship: The Black Baptist Quest for Social Power.* Macon, GA: Mercer University, 1986.

Wilmore, Gayraud S. *Black Religion and Black Radicalism: An Interpretation of the Religious History of Afro-American People,* 2nd rev. ed. Maryknoll, NY: Orbis, 1983.

Chapter 6

The Spirit of Christ, Identity and the Undocumented in Our Midst: Toward a Space-Making Theological Ethic

Tommy Cásarez

This chapter attends broadly to the issue of immigration, on the one hand. On the other hand, it specifically focuses on how followers of Christ must understand Christian identity in relation to the "other," in this case, the undocumented "other." This chapter investigates identity, Christian identity theologically understood – how Christ's identity shapes, defines, and determines not only our identity but also the shape and character of flourishing Christian life. It is from a theological understanding of identity that we will find resources for better understanding ourselves and the undocumented other in our midst. In the end, I hope to have pointed the way forward by proposing what I am calling a space-making theological ethic.

An important undocumented "other" of focus in this study refers to the 11.3 million undocumented Latino immigrants currently residing in the US with more than half of them of Mexican descent based on a PEW Study April 2017.[1] How we frame the conversation of the undocumented persons in our midst essentially guides the resulting attitudes, commitments and actions related to them.

In other words, what we see or how we see it determines what we do. How we see determines not only how we feel about it but also whether or not we will do anything positively or negatively. What we believe, shapes how we feel, and guides are actions. What we see or believe is essentially part of a story that we tell ourselves and one that we use to understand what is taking place. The story that we inhabit or participate in or abide by actually provides us with a lens for understanding the truth about the world and the way that it really is.

As Christians, there is a story that was meant not only to save us but to define, determine, change, and even transform us. As followers of Jesus Christ, the story of God serves not only as a reference point but essentially as the very background and horizon of our earthly existence. In the following, I focus primarily on the work of Yale University Theologian, Miroslav Volf, who also happens to be a pastor's kid born and raised in an Assemblies of God church in Croatia. Volf rightly focuses on the person and work of Christ on the cross as the key to who God is and the truth about who we are as God's creatures.

Imitatio: Made in the Image and Likeness Of God

Volf's theology of embrace or reconciliation is essentially rooted in three-fold advocacy of *imitatio trinitatis, cristi,* and *crucis.* In terms of a Christian worldview, this is where we find the answer to the questions: Who are we? What has gone wrong? and How are we to live? I intend to explicate Volf's description of each question (directly and indirectly) and the ethical grounds, warrants, and claims that his three-fold *imitatio* trinitatis, cristi, and crucis provides.

To begin, humans were created in the image of God with the image of God described in terms of human identity and with human identity in relation to God's identity. The goal of humanity then is to reflect the Trinitarian God or *imitatio trinitatis* with the imitation of the Trinity functioning as a social vision towards which human beings are oriented by virtue of being created in the image of God. Moreover, the creatures that God created are to strive to be like God or to be as God is in a perfect communion of love, so that the more God's creatures attain this communion, the more they image or reflect God. This striving towards imaging God, however, is done in humanly appropriate ways so as to consider human sin, historical limitations, and the spatial ramifications for doing so.

The rationale substantiating *imitatio* hinges in part upon a question to which the affirmative is the answer. The question goes something like this: Should not those who were created in the image of God and intended for communion with God also actually reflect the Triune God in whose image they were created?[2] Volf concludes the affirmative. He is helpful in pointing out that, according to Scripture, human beings were made to "image" God and "to be" as God is. Volf grounds his argument in Genesis 1: "Then God said, 'Let us make man in our image, in our likeness...So God created man in his own image, in the image of God he created him."[3] Human beings then were created in the image of God so that they were created to image God here on earth.[4] Imaging God ultimately comes in the form of existing or living in a communion of love in the same way that God is a God of love and exists in self-giving and other-receiving love. The doctrine of the Trinity then denotes a reality which human beings living in community "ought" to reflect.[5]

The doctrine of the Trinity in essence names a particular "social vision" in that it does contain "the contours of the ultimate normative end toward which all social programs should strive."[6] The social vision retains a final eschatological fulfillment, but it is also a goal that those created in the image of God should strive towards in creaturely appropriate ways. But the social vision does help to adjudicate between those social programs and ethical actions that better align themselves with this social vision and those that do not.

Furthermore, Volf directly points to the Biblical mandate to be like God and to the possibility of doing so when he discusses two complimentary sets of scripture that are compatible with the Genesis passage. In the first, Jesus explicitly commands his disciples to "Be perfect, therefore, as your heavenly Father is perfect (Matthew 5:48)."[7] Here human likeness and imitation of God—qualified as perfection—is given in the context of loving one's enemies as the preceding verses suggests, "But I tell you: Love your enemies and pray for those who persecute you, that you may be sons of your Father in heaven (Matt 5:44-45)." In another Biblical passage along the same lines, the Apostle Peter reminds Christians that those that God created are to be holy, "But just as he who called you is holy, so be holy in all you do; for it is written: 'Be holy, because I am holy'" (1 Peter 1:15-16 NIV). In both cases, Christians are called to (moral) perfection and to strive towards that perfection as the one who has called them is perfect. Jesus commands[8] his disciples to be prefect and the Apostle Peter also commands[9] the followers of Jesus Christ to perfection in their conduct. Taken together these two verses lead to the conclusion that human beings can in some way be perfect like God or at least strive to be so. Otherwise, why would Jesus give his disciples such a charge and why would Peter command Christians to be holy "as" God is holy. That perfection is framed in terms of being like God. But, being like God is understood to mean being as God is

131

in a creaturely manner. *Imitatio*, in the end, becomes a charge or command that one strives to fulfill not only an orientation and goal towards which human beings are purposed. The God who loves is also the God who demands or commands those whom God created to be like God.[10]

Volf makes an important distinction between God's identity and human identity so as to not make an exact one-to-one correlation between the two and so as to allow for human imaging of God without equating human beings with God. The closeness with proper distance and simultaneous distance with adequate similarity is expressed primarily in the way Volf describes God-likeness. The "like God" and God-likeness seem to be where Volf can maintain that human beings can image God and are created in the image of God without being God but properly image God in creaturely ways by being "like God." That human beings "ought" to image God is substantiated by the reasoning that human beings are created in the image of God (though they are not God) and that humans should, therefore, image God in ways that are humanly appropriate.

This suggests that human communities "can" image God and should image God in historically appropriate ways as well—meaning that though human beings will not be made perfect in every way here and now, they can nonetheless grow and strive towards that perfection despite the fact that "humans are inescapably marred by sin."[11] Perfection in the sense of a perfect agent, community, society, or social arrangement will never exist on this side of the eschaton. There will always be room for growing and bettering social agents, their relations, and structural arrangements.

The Trinitarian Shape of Human Identity

How we are, then, to image hinges upon our understanding of the Trinitarian God in whose image human beings were created. Accordingly, Miroslav Volf poses another question for which a social Trinitarian doctrine of God demonstrates the answer. The question goes something like this: If the Trinity and the life of the Trinity is the source of God's love, then what must the Trinity be like if God's love is visible through God's dealing with humankind as Father, Son, and Holy Spirit? The starting point here is that of the three in one rather than the one in three. The Trinitarian communion of persons is the key to God's Lordship and not the other way around. Volf primarily advocates Moltmann's thesis that one should think of the Trinity as "subjects of the one, common divine substance, with consciousness and will."[12] What we have in history then is an account of the interaction of these divine "subjects" with the world. Out of love God creates, redeems, and glorifies the world.

In his article, "The Trinity is Our Social Program: The Doctrine of the Trinity and the Shape of Social Engagement,"[13] Volf proposed a concept of humanity based upon a social model of the Trinity. That social Trinitarian model describes the identity of the triune Godhead as equal, mutually indwelling, irreducible, dynamic, and as existing in a communion of love.

What does it mean for us to be made in the image of God in light of the image of the Triune God? God's identity, essentially, is absolutely critical to human identity since human beings themselves were created in the image of God. In Volf's view of humanity, our human identity mirrors the identity of the Trinitarian God in whose image we have been created. In this sense, image refers not to "what"

133

we are as image bearers since the primary emphasis has more to do with image in terms of "who we are" (as opposed to what we are) as those creatures made to image God.

To start, as in the Trinitarian discussion above Volf relates the concept of equality to what it means to be human. So, for human beings, 'image of God' refers to their irreducible, equal, dynamic, interpenetrating identities that are oriented towards a communion of love but are also always striving towards that communion of love with the other because of the obstacle of sin in the world. Moreover, all human beings are equal and part of the human race. Thus, in reality, no individual is better than the other for all are equal in being and worthy of dignity, value, and respect; every human being bears the mark of what it means to be human and those whom God created.

Also, essential to our humanity is the fact that our identities are not "self-enclosed." The idea of "being-in-another," which is affirmed by the doctrine of appropriations as it relates to the Trinity, connotes the concept of mutual indwelling and assumes that the boundaries of each person in the Trinity are penetrable. Strictly speaking, to mutually indwell one another at the earthly level is impossible. However, there is a sense in which one is who one is because the "others are inscribed into us."[14] At the human level, there exists a situated self that is able to shape and be shaped by the inscription of others in their midst.

Inscription actually takes place through various modes of interaction and may take multiple forms. Inscription may, in fact, take place emotionally through one's memory as in the case of traumatic experiences in which the survivors struggle internally with the memory of their victimization and their victimizers. The victims' horrific memory of their traumatic experience has somehow been etched into the very soul so as to become a part of the sufferers' existence. Another example of the way in which inscription takes place concerns those closely involved in one's upbringing, whether individually, as in the case of a parental figure, or communally, as in the case of a tightly knit neighborhood. These primary care-givers or authoritative figures leave an imprint of their lives on others as is often seen in both the good and bad habits that are perpetuated by members of a specific family or community. Cycles of communal violence and hate towards those of another community are engendered and sustained through habits, practices, and beliefs that are subsequently enacted and passed on by older members of the community to its younger generation. Lastly, inscription takes place through personal narratives. One's story is grafted into the story that another uses to make sense of his or her own life. Personal and collective narratives provide resources which one selectively draws upon to narrate the story of one's own life in order to create one's personal identity.[15] The point is, essentially, that the possible means of human inscription are multiple. Basically, to varying degrees the identity of the other shapes our own identity positively or negatively degrees with the result that there in no way exists as an "unencumbered self."[16]

The concept of shaping and being able to be shaped by one another implies that identities in the Godhead, as in the identities of the creatures that God created, are dynamic. The active interchange between the Father, Son, and the Holy Spirit suggests that their identities are dynamic. The whole of John's Gospel, starting with the

Word's agency in the creation of "all things," (Jn 1:1) culminating in the Son's glorification of the Father, and ending with the Son's return to the Father and His sending of the Spirit narrates a history of engagement of divine persons with one another and the world.[17] Analogously, the identities of human beings are formed in part by their interaction and relationship to one another in the world as well. The history of human activity and relating to one another is one filled with potentiality and unlimited possibilities. Human identities are not set in stone but are dynamically shaped and reshaped as they engage one another in and through the world around them.

Not only are our identities equal and dynamic, and not only do they "interpenetrate" one another, but they are also irreducible.[18] There is a "self" present in each one of us that differentiates us from all others in the same way that there is something about the Father, the Son, and the Holy Spirit that belongs distinctly to each one If that is the case, then we are a situated self that is constituted by the other, but is not reducible to the identity or relations it has with the other.[19] However fluid the boundary of a self might be, there is still an "I" in each one of us. Yet, that "I" always exists in relation to another, even though it is able to stand on its own.[20] Our identity, therefore, is not bound to a well-defined self that only secondarily enters into relationship with other human beings. On the contrary, the existence of an "other" actively shapes our own identity, and that is exactly what it means to be human. Therefore, at all times the self that is present is an "interpenetrated" and irreducible self in relation to other human and non-human beings.

Furthermore, as human beings, we have a God-given orientation toward a "communion of love." In other words, we have a propensity toward loving communion with others. According to Volf, the phrase, "Let us make man in our image, in our likeness..." (Gen 1:26) points to the fact that God created us to be in communion with one another in a way similar to the divine communion present in the Trinity.[21] However, unlike the constant and continual reciprocity present in the Godhead, in this human existence, one must strive towards a communion of love because the human condition is such that a perfect communion of love is not possible. On the other hand, that orientation towards a communion of love is inherent to humanity's God-like design. The communion of love does not emerge from an encounter with the other exterior to another but through mutual indwelling of those who are different from one another and still internal to one another.[22] A communion of love presupposes the mutual indwelling, equal, non-reducible, and dynamic aspects of our human identity. But that communion of love also leads to their recognition and founding in situations where they are lacking.[23] On earth, human beings are to strive against the occlusion that sinful structures pose towards this communion of love. Wherever striving towards this communion of love is primary, both exclusion and assimilation of the other will cease. To this end, God created us in the likeness of the Trinitarian God.

The most significant aspect of Volf's notion of identity in terms of spatial ramifications is that this human identity is not only the condition for the possibility of making space for the other but already the orientation and goal of a space-making way of life. In the above, I have attempted to demonstrate the basis for Volf's understanding of human identity and the way in which it corresponds to God's own identity. This human identity describes what it means to be human in terms of equality, irreducibility, dynamic, interpenetrating, and striving toward a communion of love. In terms of identity, Volf argues for "making space" and the "social" construction of space through one's interaction with others and the environment around them. Yet, that space for Volf is also a spatially ontological way of being in the world that is essential to what it means to be human.

What it means to be human is to be made in the image of God and to be like God. Space and making space for the other is central to what it means to be human, I would argue, since it is so central to who God is as well. I would like to suggest that this implies that human beings strive to make space for their fellow human beings as part of a movement towards mirroring the communion of love present among the Trinitarian persons. That orientation towards this communion of love is the goal of humanity because it is part of the creaturely likeness to God. God-likeness then is the communal goal of humanity, male, female, immigrant, non-immigrant, documented and undocumented because God in God's self is also a communion of persons as Father, Son, and Spirit. The communion of love in the Godhead is the communion of love that human beings strive to achieve or mirror here on earth. Within the Godhead, divine love dances but here on earth the movement of God's love is more like a suffering love to which we will now turn.

The Cross of Christ and the Space-Making Power of the Spirit

The purpose of this section is, therefore, to show how Volf utilizes Christ's work on the cross as a space-making event which, I would add, ultimately embodies the work of the Spirit as the movement of God's love. This serves as the shape and character of the Christian way of life. In Christ's work on the cross, Volf sees the grounds and model for humanity to practice self-giving and other-receiving love. I would like to suggest that this self-giving and other-receiving love at work in the life of the believer is the work of the Spirit. It is, after all, the case that "...God's love has been poured out into our hearts through the Holy Spirit, who has been given to us".[24] The Spirit then empowers us to be space-making agents who embody this self-giving and other-receiving love by pouring out God's love into our hearts. As space-making agents filled with the Spirit we are able to make space for the other – materially, cognitively, and socially. The movement of God's love I would add makes space for our participation in the life of God by the Spirit. We are then empowered through the Spirit to make space for others on the road towards reconciliation, which ultimately restores human communion in a world of "non-innocence."

That God's love is space-making is demonstrated by the space that Christ makes for humanity to participate in the divine life through the Holy Spirit – in the relation that is the Father, Son, and Spirit. Volf understands Christ as opening up humanity to the very life of God, so as to allow for the life of God to pour forth or overflow onto humanity through the Holy Spirit. It is here by the presence and power of the Holy Spirit that humanity is made to participate in the life that God enjoys. Jesus, therefore, as fully human and fully God makes space for humanity's participation in the life of the triune God. However, I would like to specify that it is in and through the

Holy Spirit that we participate and become active space-making agents who embody God's self-giving and other-receiving love.

The focal point of Christ's space-making activity originates in the Incarnation and culminates in the crucifixion of Christ on the cross, but in my view, it is only realized and actualized for followers of Christ through the coming of the Spirit that Christ spoke of taking place after his departure (John 14,16). Just as Peter preached on the day of Pentecost, the fulfillment of Joel's prophecy ultimately makes space for humanity to be empowered by the Spirit since, "In the last days, God says, I will pour out my Spirit on all people."[25] The Holy Spirit makes our participation in the life of God possible, pours out the love God in our hearts, and empowers us to participate in the movement of God's of love as "space-making agents".

The central aim of the cross at Calvary was to restore communion between God and the creatures God made in God's own image.[26] The cross is what happened when the inner-Trinitarian love shared by the divine persons turned outward toward humanity and was met by a hostile community of human beings. Those human beings crucified the Son of God and executed Jesus of Nazareth on a wooden cross. In the Crucified, however, God refused to allow sin to serve as the reason for humanity's enmity with God and overcame it by sending His Son into the world (Jn 3:16). The distance that sin generates between God and God's own creatures was bridged in the incarnation of God and through Christ's suffering. The space that sin creates, the division that sin makes, and the fellowship that sin breaks between God and God's creation, were all overcome in the person and work of Jesus Christ. Christ, then, dealt with humanity's sin by taking it upon Christ's self, judging it as sin, and destroying it in His death. The distance between God and those creatures God created in God's own image was no longer a distance of separation due to guilt and a just condemnation, but a distance of differentiation and of an appropriate reclamation of the space that a reconciled relationship between God and God's creatures entails.

On the cross, Christ accomplishes forgiveness of sins, but forgiveness was not the "culmination of Christ's relation to the offending other," for forgiveness was the "passage leading to embrace."[27] In the Crucified, Christ makes space within Christ's self—and therefore also in the divine community of persons—for humanity to dwell "in the Spirit", "in Christ" and "in God," because it was there on the cross that Christ embraced the "beloved other" at its worst.[28] The life, death, and resurrection of Jesus Christ are all part of a movement of God's love to make space for that which is not God. God divinely loves that which God created and determines not to be God without God's creation.

In other words, I would argue that the Holy Spirit opens the door for humanity to participate in the space that God possesses, inhabits, and creates within God's self in the divine life, while the forgiveness of sins that Christ accomplishes on the cross keeps that open door permanently in place. The movement of God's love is the Spirit of God to humanity so that God is the one who opens the door leading to participation in the divine spatial life. From another angle, divine space is opened up by the Holy Spirit to human space in the crucified in such a way that it becomes a shared space only through the Holy Spirit. That shared space enters into human space through the Spirit and provides human space a point of entry into the divine space through the presence and work of the Holy Spirit. Ultimately,

141

God invites humanity to become a participant in the divine spatial existence of the triune God through the Holy Spirit.

Lastly, according to Volf, in Christ's death on the cross the wickedness of sin and wrongdoing were not overlooked or denied, for justice itself was affirmed. Yet, in affirming justice, justice was actually transcended by love so that God made space within God's self to receive the very creatures who detested God. On the cross, Christ ultimately embraced humanity at its worst. Volf writes:

> Instead of aping the enemy's act of violence and rejection, Christ, the victim who refuses to be defined by the perpetrator, forgives and makes space in Himself for the enemy. Hence, precisely as a victim, Christ is the true judge: by offering to embrace the offenders, he judges both the initial wrongdoing of the perpetrators and the reactive wrongdoing of many victims.[29]

As both God and man, Christ demonstrated divine self-giving and other-receiving love. Self-giving and other-receiving are part of the same movement of love. By giving His life on the cross, Jesus made space within the life of God for the perpetrator and the perpetrated as a victim who refused to imitate or repeat the victimizer's offense. According to Volf, on the cross, the God of love and justice received both the victim and the victimizer within God's self, and judged the wrongs committed by affirming justice when God transcended justice through love. God made space for the other by taking within God's self the perspective of the victim in allowing Christ to be victimized while simultaneously refraining from excluding the victimizer in making space for the victimizer within God's self through forgiveness.

Conclusion: Making Space for the Undocumented

More specifically, what does this means about how we should live, and the shape and character of the Christian life? In terms of *imitatio* and the particular character and shape of the Christian life, God-likeness is demonstrated for all through Christ's own self-giving and other-receiving love on the cross, which serves as the summation of Christ's life. In Christ, Volf finds the grounds to love another so that one loves others "because God loves" them and "as God loves" them. When we love others, we love them because they are the ones whom God loves and the ones whom God reconciled on the cross of Christ.[30] Because God loves them, therefore, Jesus followers do so as well.

In addition, followers of Jesus Christ are to imitate the kind of love that God demonstrates on the cross for those whom God loves. In this way, human beings are participating in that divine love, emulating God, and being most like God by striving towards that communion of love. *Imitatio Cristi* then involves self-giving love so that: "as God does not abandon the godless to their evil but gives the divine self for them in order to receive them into divine communion through atonement, so also should we – whoever our enemies and whoever we may be."[31] Human beings reflect God-likeness and that kind of love that God is when they love others as God loved humanity on the cross in Christ.

The key to God-likeness then does not primarily have to do with rules and regulations or commands. God-likeness has to do with

143

reflecting and imaging the same kind of love on earth that exists within the triune God as the Father, Son, and Holy Spirit. That self-giving and, other-receiving love, was demonstrated in the Crucified God. The source and origin of that self-giving and, other-receiving love, is ultimately the triune God. Christ's work on the cross makes possible our participation in the movement of God's love out of God's self towards humanity in order to bring humanity into communion with God and one another. The followers of Jesus Christ are moved and compelled by the love of God in Christ to love the other.

But, how are they supposed to love the other where a violation of a political law has occurred? By making space for the other, I suggest, because the love that God has called us to exemplify and model is a space-making love and we are space-making agents. It is not that we can and therefore we ought, but that we were created as such to be like the God who created us, and to go about doing so via the model of love that Christ demonstrates on the cross.

Remember that as both fully divine and fully human but without sin, Christ represents humanity in all its sinfulness as lawbreaker, overcomes the "wages of sin," and is raised from the dead. Thus, Christ confirmed the law of God and the impending judgment by affirming the law and transcending it through love. Christ modeled a self-giving and other-receiving love in which Christ gave of himself in order to make space for humanity to enjoy communion with God and with one another.

This kind of love invites the lawbreaker into communion without denying that a law has been broken. The act of forgiveness itself requires acknowledging justice while transcending it through love. It is love that opens the door and forgiveness that makes space to receive the other and to move toward a reconciled community.

While aiming at reconciliation, this generosity that is forgiveness also engenders in the other a mutuality that is essential to peaceful communion. Forgiveness entails fore-going all claims to revenge and retaliation as well as releasing the offender from a debt owed to the offended. That is exactly what Christ did for humanity on the cross. On the cross, Christ demonstrated that the requirements of justice had been fulfilled, removing from human beings the debt and guilt that humanity owed for its wrongdoings and placing it on the cross. On the cross, justice was affirmed, enacted, and transcended, which ultimately resulted in God's embrace of humanity.

Christian love astonishingly replaces the status of lawbreaker, illegal, criminal, perpetrator, invader or violator with that of "beloved other," "neighbor," or the "one for whom Christ died," because the other is also one who has been reconciled to God and other human beings in Christ. The other is no longer an "illegal," who does not belong to me or who is not a part of me, but someone who is intimately related to me in Christ. The other is one for whom Christ also died and one with whom God intended me to live in harmony. Christ died for the undocumented other that God also created and that God intended to enjoy fellowship with God and with all God's creatures. Viewed from a framework of love that leads to reconciliation, the other is one to whom I belong and with whom I am obliged to work to be reconciled. This does not deny justice or the need for justice, for it requires justice on the road to a reconciled community.

The categories of lawbreaker, illegal, invader tend to have the connotation of being somehow less human. When viewed solely from the category of lawbreaker or illegal, the other tends to be seen as one upon whom judgment is to be executed and not as a human being created by God for communion with God and others. When viewed from the framework of love, the categories of lawbreaker and invader become inaccurate and, on their own, are insufficient to fully identify the other, since the other is also one created by God for communion with God and with those whom God created. In that sense, the framework of love may require injustices to be named and rightfully so, but a framework of love also moves beyond injustices to remind both the citizen, documented and undocumented—regardless of legal status—that the two belong together as human beings and as those God created for peaceful communion.

The framework of love then shapes the way one views the other without foregoing justice and allows one to appropriately name the unjust actions of the other while also moving beyond that categorization to affirming the other as "beloved," "neighbor," or "the one for whom Christ also died."

As Christians, the shape and character of the Christian life is one that actively participates in the love that Christ exemplified on the cross. Moving towards the other in love requires one to do so with a measure of humility and a tremendous degree of the kind of hospitality that represents our participation in the movement of God's space-making love.

Bibliography

Passel, Jeffrey, and D'Vera Cohn. "As Mexican Share Declined, U.S.
Unauthorized Immigrant Population Fell in 2015 below
Recession Level." Pew Research Center. April 25, 2017.
http://www.Pewresearch. org/fact-tank/2017/04/25/as-
mexican-share-declined-u-s-unauthorized-immigrant-
population-fell-in-2015-below-recession-level/.

Taylor, Charles. "The Politics of Recognition," in *Multiculturalism:
Examining the Politics of Recognition*, ed. Amy Gutman
Princeton: Princeton University Press, 1994.

Volf, Miroslav. After Our Likeness: The Church as the Image of the
Trinity. Grand Rapids: Wm. B. Eerdmans Publishing Co., 1998.

_____. *Exclusion and Embrace: A Theological Exploration
of Identity, Otherness and Reconciliation*. Nashville: Abingdon,
1996.

_____. "The Trinity Is Our Social Program: The Doctrine of
the Trinity and the Shape of Social Engagement," *Modern
Theology* 14:3, July (1998).

_____. *Exclusion and Embrace: A Theological Exploration
of Identity, Otherness and Recon-ciliation* Nashville: Abingdon,
1996.

Chapter 7

God's Image and Likeness through Christ: Re-reading the Creation Narrative

Alaine Thomson Buchanan

Does the troubling claim that some people are "superior" to others, along gender or ethnic lines, find its roots in perspectives on Genesis 1-3? Or, does the claim find its roots in the later interpretation of the Hexameron narrative[1] of Genesis 1 and the Edenic Paradise narrative of Genesis 2-3? If people are still created in the "image" and "likeness" of God, how should this influence the way one relates to God, other human beings, and the rest of creation?

The "image" and "likeness" of God in the Hexameron of Genesis 1 and the decision of the man and woman in the Edenic paradise story of Genesis 2-3 have been interpreted in a variety of ways in Second Temple Jewish and New Testament literature. The ramifications of these interpretations have impacted the way certain expressions of the Church have authorized division and inequality. Some Christians continue to use Scripture to rationalize unequal treatment of human persons: treating some as "greater" or "better than" or "less" or "worse than" others along the lines of gender, race, socio-economic status, ability, disability, and age. Some examples are American slavery, South African Apartheid, and the oppression of women across so-called Christian societies.[2] This chapter argues that a greater understanding of the context of the Hexameron and

Edenic Paradise narratives and key elements in their history of interpretation in Second Temple Jewish writings and Pauline letters in the New Testament are important for tracing the trajectory of scriptural interpretation that lends to the authorizations of unequal treatment. Notwithstanding, a closer look at Jesus' life and teachings jolt His follower's consciousness to the life and work of the Spirit that empowers them to live into the fullness of what God intends to be an equal human reflection of divine image and likeness.

In order to accomplish this task, I will offer a basic synopsis of the Hexameron and Edenic stories. Next, I briefly examine interpretations of the narratives within selected Second Temple Literature and then assess how Pauline literature employed early chapters in Genesis to explain how human beings should relate to God and each other. This chapter's main objective is first to scrutinize interpretations of the Hexameron and Edenic Paradise narratives that have purported "isms" and consequently became the driving force for unequal treatment of human persons and people groups. Secondly, this chapter explains that Jesus's interpretive framework and practice of ministry as presented in the canonical Gospels defy human partiality as influenced by certain Hexameron and Edenic interpretations. Thus, a Christian interpretation of the Genesis narratives requires a Jesus hermeneutic, a vision of creation through the lens of the internal norms of the gospel. Any such reconsideration renders a more equalized treatment of all human beings, regardless of gender, age, nationality or social location.

Ground Zero: A look at the Hexameron in Genesis 1-3

The Hexameron in Genesis 1 is one of several stories from the Ancient Near East that addresses how the world and humanity came into being.[3] Genesis 1:26-27 is unique in that both the masculine gender (זָכָר) and feminine gender (נְקֵבָה) are made in the image and likeness of God and serve as descriptors of the collective אָדָם.[4] The word "image" (צֶלֶם) occurs three times in these two verses and suggests a visual appearance of something or someone, a resemblance, a shadow or a replica. "Likeness" (דְּמוּת) in Genesis 1:26 suggests similarity in appearance, character or nature between persons or things. Although the meaning of these words within this context are abstract, the text itself suggests that humanity was made as a visual resemblance that points to its Creator and is embedded with part of the character of God, which can be cultivated to align more closely with various attributes of God. In Genesis 1:28, humanity is commanded by God to 1) be fruitful and multiply, 2) fill the earth and subdue it, and 3) have dominion or exercise authority over the fish of the sea, the birds of the air and over every living thing that moves on the earth in a similar way to the way God does it, with love, care and concern.

Scholars have varying insights into what it means to be made in the "image" and "likeness" of God. For example, Douglas John Hall addresses two different ways to understand *imago Dei*: substantial (embodied within humans as a physical, emotional or spiritual attribute, such as physical appearance, rationality, freedom) and relational (outward actions of justice, peace, love, righteousness).[5] Richard S. Briggs explains that being made in the image of God means that humanity is meant to rule over God's creation in the place of God and as God's representatives. Characteristics such as rationality, compassion, concern for others and reflectiveness, rather than the physical appearance, suggest what it means to be made in the image of God.[6]

Andreas Schüle adds that within the Ancient Near East, an image or object represents the presence of the referent and functions as an extension of the referent; therefore, humans represent the presence of the Creator.[7] W. Sibley Towner believes that being created in the "image of God" directly relates to nurturing and stewarding relationships with God, each other, and all of God's creation.[8] Humanity has dominion over animals and the earth and is expected to act or function as a representative of God within this capacity.[9] At the same time, the presence of the deity is believed to reside within humanity in such a way that humanity is a representative of the divine for each other and to the rest of God's creation. Humanity is expected to "exercise their kingly rule within the ecosphere in God's manner, the way God would do it."[10] Ellen F. Davis suggests the abstract meaning and connection of צֶלֶם and דְּמוּת is best explained through storytelling and providing examples of those who functioned well (and not so well) as God's emissaries in the rest of Genesis 1-11 and the Old Testament as a whole.[11]

By giving human beings "dominion" over the earth, God installs humanity as his representatives on earth to care for all of creation in a similar manner to how God has cared for them. By doing so, God invites human beings into a divine relationship; also, God intends for all of humanity to live in community with each other and to be in harmony with the rest of creation.

Genesis 2-3: The Edenic Paradise Narrative

Ellen van Wolde points out that Genesis 1 presents the totality and broader perspective of the creation of heaven and earth; whereas Genesis 2-3 hones in on the relationship among God, human beings and the earth.[12] Genesis 2, the groundling (אָדָם) is closely connected to the ground (אֲדָמָה), which is different terminology than that of the "image of God" in Genesis 1. The verbal linking between "ground" and "groundling" in Genesis 2 emphasizes that humanity is closely related to and made from the ground.[13] John H. Sailhamer agrees that the description of the creation of humanity "in the image of God" in Gen 1:26-27 shifts to man being made "from the dust of the ground" in Genesis 2 and that what Genesis 1 expresses as a simple statement of creation regarding humanity becomes an explained and developed narrative in Genesis 2.[14]

In Genesis 2:7-8, man is created from the dust of the ground, and God breathes into his nostrils the breath of life, and he becomes a living being. God commands אָדָם to till and keep the garden, which is God's sacred space and is where God comes to meet with him. God explains that אָדָם can eat of every tree in the garden but not the tree of the knowledge of good and evil because the consequences will result in death. God knows what is good (טוֹב) and what is not good or evil (רַע) for human beings. "To enjoy the 'good,' man must trust God and obey him. If man disobeys, he will have to decide for himself what is good (טוֹב) and what is not good (רַע)."[15]

In Genesis 2:18-24, God notices that it is not good for man to be alone, so God creates a helper (עֵזֶר), a succor, a support, one who assists or is compatible with him *and* who is an equal partner (נֶגֶד) with him, being similar in appearance, character and nature. Every animal that was created was brought to Adam, and he named them...yet none could be an equal partner with him. God caused a deep sleep to fall upon the man, and God took one of man's sides (צֵלָע) and closed (סגר) his flesh back up. God built (בנה) woman from the man's side and flesh, and God brought her to him. The man (אִישׁ) proclaimed that she has flesh and bones, just like he does, and he called her "woman" (אִשָּׁה) because part of him was taken by God to create her. John H. Sailhamer writes, "It appears, then, that in the mention of the rib from which the woman was created, no particular meaning is to be attached to the rib as such but rather to 'the rib and the flesh' as showing the woman to be in substance the same as the man."[16] He states that the "likeness" that the man and the woman share with God in chapter 1 finds an analogy in the "likeness" between the man and his wife in chapter 2.[17]

Phyllis Trible contends that the creation of woman is the culmination of creation because she is not created from the ground like the man is.[18] In this way, the creation of the man first (before the animals) and the woman last suggests an egalitarian status of women in the creation order.

Mark S. Smith rightly argues that humanity was created with a capacity for desire,[19] which takes center stage in Genesis 2-3. In Genesis 3:1-8, the serpent tests the woman and tempts her to eat from the tree of the knowledge of good and evil. The woman saw that the tree was good for food, a delight (תַּאֲוָה) or a craving or longing, to the eyes, and to be desired (חמד), to be worth having in order to make one wise. She took of the tree's fruit, ate and gave some to her husband, who was with her, and he ate.

The eyes of both the man and woman were opened, and they were able to cognitively perceive, experience and understand both good (טוֹב) and evil (רַע). They were cognizant and understood (ידע) they were naked, and they sewed fig leaves together and made loincloths for themselves. They heard God walking in the garden at the time of the evening breeze, and they hid from his presence (פָּנֶה). Smith correctly asserts that as a result of her deception and his disobedience, fear is the first emotion expressed in the story.²⁰ Fear then gives way to sin in Genesis 4 when Cain kills his brother, Abel.

Genesis 3:9-12 relays that when God called out to the man, the man explained that he heard the sound of God in the garden and was afraid because he was naked, so he hid. God asked who told the man he was naked and asked if he had eaten from the tree that God commended him not to eat. The man evades the first question and blames the woman in answer to the second question.

In Genesis 3:13-16, God asks the woman what she did, and she tells the truth. After God curses the serpent, God tells the woman that He will greatly increase her pains in childbearing, yet her longing (תְּשׁוּקָה) for her husband, her desire to have sexual union with her husband, will overrule this pain she experiences. The man will exercise authority (משׁל) over her, which indicates that he has the ability to decide whether or not and how to fulfill her longing. Joseph Abraham asserts, "The text does not intimate that the man will rule over the woman other than in the area of sex."²¹

Genesis 3:17-21 relays that because the man listened and adhered to the voice of his wife rather than heeding God's command to refrain from eating from this specific tree, the ground will be cursed, which will make it toilsome to harvest food throughout the rest of his life. When the time comes for the man to die, he will return to the ground and the dust from which he came. At this point, the man names the woman, Eve, because she was the mother of all living. God made garments of skin for the man and his wife and clothed them. Mark Smith observes "...common to both the man and woman is 'difficulty.' The woman will suffer pain or difficulty (בְּעֶצֶב) in childbirth in 3:16, and the man will suffer the difficulty (בְּעִצָּבוֹן) posed by the now cursed ground in 3:17. Their shared destiny is one of difficulty."[22]

God acknowledges that human beings now have the cognitive ability to perceive, know, understand, and experience both good (טוֹב) and evil (רַע). In order that the man and woman refrain from eating from the tree of life, God sent the man and woman away from the Garden of Eden and placed the cherubim and a flaming sword to guard the way to the tree of life in Genesis 3:22-23.

After this, Adam and Eve continued fulfilling the initial commands God gave to humanity in Genesis 1, but they now have more knowledge, more understanding, and more difficulty, and the struggle for intimacy with God and with each other becomes more real. From this point onward in Genesis, one reads about this struggle for relationship with God, with each other and with God's creation, such that one could potentially assume that the decisions of Adam and Eve initiated a struggle that continues to this day. The struggle to understand, believe and practice the reality of what it means to be made in the image and likeness of God.

Walter Vogels writes, "God created the human being as a partner with whom he enters into communication. God does not completely dominate the human being but leaves him free. God runs the risk of experiencing not only joy and harmony but also anguish and disharmony in his relationship with the human being."[23] Richard S. Briggs rightly states that there is no Hebrew term for "fall" in the Edenic story of Genesis 2-3, and the word "sin" is not addressed until Genesis 4:7, when sin is lurking at the door of Cain, and he chooses to kill his brother Abel anyway.[24] He rightly states that "Genesis 3 presents the beginning of the downward spiral in which humanity moves towards sin, death and distrust,"[25] which affirms that the world is caught between being a "good" creation of God and being fractured.

What it means for human beings to be made in the "image" and "likeness" of God in the Hexameron and the consequences of the Edenic Paradise are not directly addressed again throughout the rest of the Old Testament, with the exception of Genesis 5:1-3 and 9:6. Adam, Eve, and the Edenic Paradise story resurfaced in the midst of the Second Temple Period (515 BCE-70 CE).

Inequity Rooted in Edenic Paradise in Second Temple Jewish Literature

The Second Temple Period begins with the building of the second temple in 515 BCE while still under Persian rule and ends with the destruction of this temple in 70 CE.[26] Writings that were written during this time period or are closely connected with this time frame are considered part of Second Temple Literature. Examples include the Old Testament Pseudepigrapha, Old Testament Apocrypha, Dead Sea Scrolls, and the writings of Philo and Josephus. Because of circumstances surrounding events such as the Maccabean Revolt in the second century BCE, questions surrounding where evil came from and how it began as well as hopes and desires for how God would right the consequences of evil and diminish or destroy evil became increasingly important. Stories of Adam, Eve and Eden are then brought back into focus as an explanation of how and why humanity struggles with sin and in relationships with God, each other, and all of God's creation.

Lyn M. Bechtel asserts that Adam and Eve and the Paradise of Eden narratives are not used elsewhere in the Hebrew Bible/Jewish Scriptures/Old Testament in relation to sin, the fall, and punishment, even though there are plenty of opportunities to do so.[27] Rather, conceptions of the "sin" and "fall" of Adam and Eve begin to come to the fore beginning in the second century BCE around the time of the Maccabees, which is also a time of Hellenistic influence.[28]

Old Testament Pseudepigraphal books addressing Adam, Eve, and the Edenic Paradise narrative include Jubilees, 2 Enoch, 4 Ezra, 2 Baruch, and the Life of Adam and Eve. Jubilees was written in the second century BCE and is connected to Moses during his forty days on Mount Sinai. According to Jubilees, Adam and Eve spent seven years in Eden, and then the serpent tempted the woman. Eve ate first and covered her shame with a fig leaf. Then, she gave it to Adam and he ate, his eyes were opened, and he understood that he was naked. He took a fig leaf, sewed it, and made an apron to cover his shame. Consequences of this decision include all living creatures being expelled from Eden and the common language used among people and the animals being dismantled.[29]

2 Enoch and the rest of the writings connected to the Old Testament Pseudepigrapha in this section are believed to have been written near the end of the first century CE, within a generation after the Temple was destroyed in 70 CE. The Creation story and Edenic Paradise story are recounted in 2 Enoch 30-31 with details regarding how God's wisdom created man out of the seven components: flesh—earth, blood—dew and sun, eyes—sea, bones—stone, reason—mobility of angels and from clouds, veins and hair—grass of the earth, and spirit—from God's spirit and from the wind.[30] God also gave humanity seven properties: hearing—flesh, sight—eyes, smell—spirit, touch—veins, taste—blood, endurance—bones, and sweetness—reason.[31] Humanity received the designated responsibility of being a king of sorts, to reign on earth with the wisdom of God and was given a name based on the four directions and components: East (A), West (D), North (A), and South (M).[32] God allotted Adam free will and explained the way of light (what is good) and the way of darkness (what is bad) to him so that God would know if Adam loved or abhorred him.[33] When God caused Adam to fall into a deep sleep, God took one of his ribs and created a wife for him, in order that death might come to him by his wife. Adam called his wife "Mother," which is another name for Eve.[34]

In 2 Enoch 31, God gave Adam control over the Edenic Paradise.[35] According to the author, God intended to create another world for Adam to rule over; however, the devil became aware of demonic condemnation and previous sin, which is why the devil thought up a scheme to come against Adam via Eve. Because of Eve's decision to eat from the Tree of Knowledge, God cursed both Adam and Eve's evil fruit-bearing, which is also why the fruit of doing good is a result of sweat and exertion.[36] In 2 Enoch 32, God expels Adam out of Eden and to the earth from which he was taken, yet God does not wish to destroy him in the Age to Come.

In 4 Ezra 3:21-26, Adam was burdened with an evil heart, transgressed, and was overcome, as are all who descend from him. 4 Ezra 7:116-18 is a lament that the earth produced Adam and could not stop him from sinning. The "fall" is not limited to Adam. It is for all his descendants: therefore, what was initially "good" departed and what was "evil" took root. Sin is then passed down from Adam to all future generations.

In 2 Baruch 54:15-22, Adam was the first person to sin and brought death upon all future generations, but each person is responsible for the choices they make, Thus, each and every person is their own Adam and can choose to live a life of either torment or glory. The Life of Adam and Eve is a text comprised of a Greek (Apocalypse) text and Latin (Vita) text that explain what happens to Adam and Eve upon their exit from Eden. In the LAE (Vita) 9-11, Eve succumbs to another temptation from Satan. In LAE (Apocalypse) 15-30, Eve tells her offspring that the snake sprinkled the poison of covetousness on the fruit before she ate it. She then offered some to the man, knowing that it had already been poisoned. Adam blames her, and she blames herself, for eating the poisoned fruit.

Old Testament Apocryphal books that address Adam, Eve, and the Edenic Paradise include Sirach, which was written in the early second century BCE during Hellenistic rule and close to the time of the Maccabean Revolt, and *Wisdom of Solomon,* which was composed in the late first century BCE or first half of the first century CE. The writer of Sirach, Ben Sira, places all the blame for the entrance of sin into the world on the woman. He writes "from a woman sin had its beginning, and because of her, we all die"[37] and also writes that a wicked man is better than a good woman because a woman brings shame and disgrace.[38] The author of the Wisdom of Solomon writes, "For God created us for incorruption, and made us in the image of [God's] own eternity, but through the devil's envy death entered the world, and those who belong to [the devil's] company experience it."[39] In other words, God is the creator of life and does not delight in the death of the living.[40] On the other hand, the devil is the serpent in Genesis 3 who was jealous because of humanity's incorruptible relationship with God, and in the devil's envy, tempted humanity, and they succumbed. Because of this, death became a reality for humanity.

Within the Dead Sea Scrolls, there is an emphasis on desiring to return to the glory of Adam.[41] At the same time, there are a couple of instances where the decision of Adam in the Edenic Paradise story is addressed. 1QH[a] ix.26 expresses that knowledge and all works of justice and the foundation of truth belong to God, while Adam's descendants are filled with the service of iniquity and the deeds of deception. God shows compassion and kindness to humanity by strengthening them in the midst of affliction and purifying iniquities so that they can recount the glory of God. 4Q504 Frag. 8 recto (*Words of the Luminaries*)—recounts that Adam was fashioned in the image of God's glory. God breathed intelligence and knowledge into his nostril when giving him the breath of life. God also caused humanity to govern and imposed on him not to turn away; however, he is flesh and will return to dust (because of his decision).

Philo argues that Genesis 1 describes the "heavenly man" while Genesis 2 describes the "earthly man."[42] He claims the "image of God" in humanity resides in the mind, and "in our likeness" refers to resemblance in form.[43] He argues that the first human being is superior to all humans who come later and is ideal in body and soul.[44] Philo regards the decision of the man and woman to eat from the Tree of the Knowledge of Good and Evil as an allegory about the character of the soul. For him, sexual intimacy is the beginning of iniquity and transgression.[45] Philo further claims that the man is occupied with the mind while the woman is occupied with sensation. Pleasure associates first with sensations, and then the mind follows. In other words, pleasure (or sin) begins with the sensations of the woman, and the mind/man becomes a slave to sensation.[46]

Josephus interprets Genesis 1-3 in *Antiquities* 1.1.1-4 par. 32-51. He explains that God commanded Adam and his wife to refrain from eating from the Tree of Knowledge and that if they touched it, it would bring about destruction. The serpent told Eve that she would have a happy life if she ate from the Tree of Knowledge. She believed the serpent, touched and ate the fruit, and gave some to Adam. When God returned to Eden and entered into a discussion with Adam and his wife, Adam asked God not to be angry with his decision to listen and adhere to the instructions of his wife. He claimed that Eve was the offender and blamed her for his decision.[47] The story implies that per their disobedience to God's command concerning the prohibited fruit, Adam and Eve forfeited their good life in Eden.

With the desire to explain humanity's part in bringing evil into the world, the decisions of Adam and Eve played an important role for a few Second Temple writers. Not only was Eve deemed to be responsible for tempting Adam and introducing evil to the human race, in some cases, she was actually created to be subordinate to Adam and thus usurped Adam's authority when she handed him the fruit, which also creates a platform for believing that some people are created as "less than" others due to their gender, religious/cultural background, color of skin, ability or disability and on and on from there.

Paul's Perspective: Caught Between Two Interpretive Worlds

Letters attributed to Paul that address Adam and/or Eve include Romans 5:12-21, 1 Corinthians 15:21-22 and 45-49, 2 Corinthians 11:3, and 1 Timothy 2:13, all of which connect with various Greco-Roman people and communities within the first century CE. Paul interprets who Christ is through images from the Genesis 2-3 narrative and turns the Edenic Paradise story into something different than what it previously was because it becomes the "primordial account of the fall of humanity."[48] Peter Bouteneff points out that Paul never addresses Adam as being made in the image of God. Rather, Adam is only mentioned in relation to sin in juxtaposition to Jesus, who "is the image of God (Col 1:15; Heb 1:3) and to whose image humanity must conform (Rom 8:29).[49]"

James Barr writes, "To [Paul] the total and unqualified gift of salvation through Jesus Christ was the reversed image of the equally total and unqualified disaster brought about by Adam and through

Adam transmitted to the entire human race."[36] In this way, Adam, as the first transgressor, serves as the theological and rhetorical juxtaposition of Christ, the redeemer.[50] While Adam becomes the prototype for all humanity in Genesis 2-3, Christ redeems humanity and makes it so that a "new person" replaces the old, according to Romans 5:12-19. In doing so, Adam's choice is identified by Paul as "sin," which in turn became the starting point for humanity's rebellion and disobedience to God.[51] For Paul, the "old man" is represented by Adam and Eve; whereas the "new man" is represented by the person who has been transformed by Jesus.

In 1 Corinthians 11:7-8, Paul teaches that man is made in the image and reflection of God (Gen 1:26); but woman is the reflection of and a derivative of man. He also argues that man was not made from woman, but woman from man (Gen 2). In doing so, Paul brings both the Hexameron and Edenic paradise stories together, making them united into one functional narrative. In 1 Corinthians 15:21-22 and 45-49, death comes through Adam, who was a living being, and resurrection of the dead comes through Jesus, who is a living spirit from heaven. In 2 Corinthians 11:3, Paul is metaphorically describing the Corinthians as being "married" to Christ. Eve is used to describe the potential for the Corinthian Christians to be deceived by their thoughts and their desire to be led away from their devotion to Christ.

In 1 Timothy 2:13-15a, the author uses part of the Edenic Paradise narrative to create an analogy between Eve and at least one Ephesian woman who was spreading heretical teachings throughout the church. The author of 1 Timothy likely refers to the creation narrative of Genesis 2 and 3 to refute the popular viewpoint of

Ephesian Artemis worshippers who believed that Artemis (the Ephesian fertility goddess) appeared first and then created her male consort. The author corrects this perspective by explaining that Scripture relays that Adam was created first, then Eve. He also uses this creation story to serve as an analogy between Eve and the unnamed Ephesian woman or women. Both women listened to a voice of false teaching, both were deceived, and both spread that false teaching to others (to Adam in Genesis and to various members of the Ephesian church in 1 Timothy).

There does seem to be a bit of an internal struggle in that Paul also writes that the Spirit makes all believers are part of the body of the Christ, dependent upon each other, and equally valued and needed, regardless of their ethnicity or socio-economic background in 1 Corinthians 12:13. He writes something similar in Galatians 3:28, where he claims that there is no longer Jew nor Greek, slave nor free, male and female, because all have been made one in Jesus Christ, which suggests that the socio-cultural concepts of patron and client relationships and honor and shame disintegrate because of who Jesus is and what Jesus has done. All are equal, and all are needed in the body of Christ.

Could it be that Paul, as an early apostle within the Jesus movement, struggled between traditional Jewish readings of male dominance and what he had discovered in Christ to be an equalizing of people groups? Perhaps, Paul is the pivot between the struggle with the 2nd Temple interpretation of Creation and the new-found Christ-interpretation of God's intended world as expressed in his common "in Christ" theology. Paul's writings at times send mixed messages in his pursuit to fully understand the concrete reality of what it means to be "in Christ." Perhaps this is why 1 Corinthians 11 seems to send one message and 1 Corinthians 12:13 seems to send another.

However, Paul defies cultural norms of his day in that he has a vision of the new reality of being "in Christ" as divine regard for the equality of all of humanity. This is the distinctive identification with God through Christ to which New Testament scholar Craig S. Keener points. In *Mind of the Spirit,* Keener explains that Paul's notion of being "in Christ" is a particular notion that sets his idea of human-deity relations apart from any Greco-Roman or even Egyptian analogies.[52] Keener explains that "Given the reality in Christ... Both instrumental and local, as well as personal and corporate, uses of 'in Christ' appear in various contexts."[53]

Paul struggles, moreover, to appropriate the narrative of Adam and Eve to help the churches understand how being "in Christ" (or their relationships with Jesus) should work into relationships with each other and the community-at-large. He seems to direct his focus on questions as pertaining to what the church needs to know, to be reminded of, or to believe in order to continue growing in their relationships with God and on how the divine-human relationship works itself out in daily life within Paul's context. However, Paul's understanding of Christ, what it means to be "in Christ," and God's continued work through the Spirit is helpful in his theological resolve regarding a history of bifurcated human existence. 1 Corinthians 12:13-14 states, "Christ redeemed us from the curse of the law ... He redeemed us in order that the blessing given to Abraham might come to the Gentiles through Christ Jesus so that by faith we might receive the promise of the Spirit." Also, in a highly patriarchal society, Paul reasons, in Galatians 3:26-28, "So in Christ Jesus, you are all children of God through faith, for all of you who were baptized into Christ have clothed yourselves with Christ. There is neither Jew nor Gentile, neither slave nor free, nor is there male and female, for you are all one in Christ Jesus." In Christ, we discover the great equalizer.

Experiencing Christ affords His followers the insight of God's intentions for gender, racial and/or ethnic equality. Keener comments that "the experiential aspect is accomplished through the Spirit."[54] It is through the experience, life, and work of the Holy Spirit that believers exist in Christ. Being Spirit-filled is eye-opening for those who would allow. The Spirit reveals to the believer that everyone is equally part of the Image of God and empowers them to continue Christ's work to reform human inequalities.

In addition, several women connected to Paul were known for their leadership within the church: For example, Priscilla was a teacher/preacher and tent maker (Acts 18:2, 18, 24-26; Rom 16:3, 1 Cor 16:19; and 2 Tim 4:19). The four daughters of Philip were prophetesses/preachers (Acts 21:8-9). Phoebe was a deaconess (Rom 16:1-2). Junia was an apostle (Rom 16:7). These examples seem to contradict the claim that Paul was anti-women. Such accusation is largely based on proof texting the letters attributed to Paul.

Jesus Reveals Divine Equity

In the canonical Gospels, Jesus does not mention the creation of the man and woman, the decision to eat from the Tree of Knowledge of Good and Evil or the ensuing consequences. Notwithstanding, the tenor of Jesus' life, ministry, death, and resurrection challenge

166

prejudicial ideology that was deeply embedded within Jewish and Greco-Roman culture. For example, many women were included in his ministry, including Mary and Martha, the two sisters of Lazarus in Luke 10:38-42 and John 11:1-6, 17-44 and 12:1-8, and the Samaritan woman at Jacob's well in John 4:7-42. Mary from Magdala (Aramaic) or Migdal (Hebrew), Joanna, and Susanna and other unnamed women are disciples who accompanied Jesus on his travels (along with the twelve disciples), according to Luke 8:2-3. In Mark 15:40-41, the author includes Mary, the mother of James and Joses and Salome, along with Mary of Migdal, and other women as providers and followers of Jesus during his Galilean ministry who were also present at his crucifixion and burial site.

Foreigners, immigrants, people from various national origins (such as the Samaritan in the Parable of the Good Samaritan in Luke 10:25-37, the demoniac of the Gadara in Luke 8:26-39, and the Syrophoenician woman who approaches Jesus on behalf of her daughter in Mark 7:24-30), abilities, disabilities, sicknesses, illnesses (such as the woman with a twelve-year hemorrhage in Mark 5:25-34, the raising of Jairus' daughter in Mark 5:22-23 and 35-43, the ten lepers who were healed in Luke 17:11-19, and the blind man healed at the Siloam pool in John 9:1-11), social statuses (such as children in Matthew 19:13-15, Peter's mother-in-law whom Jesus heals in Matthew 8:14, eating with Levi the tax collector in Mark 2:13-17, the widow who gives two copper coins in Mark 12:41-44, the widow of Nain whose son had died and Jesus brought back to life in Luke 7:11-17, the parable of Lazarus and the Rich man in Luke 16:19-31, Zacchaeus the tax collector in Luke 19:1-10, and the woman who anoints Jesus in Mark 14:3-9), and "sinners" were all included in his life's work.[55]

Rather than viewing some as "better than" or "less than" others, Jesus sought to bring all people to the realization that each and every one of them was created in the image and likeness of God and each and every one of them has equal value and importance within the Kingdom of God.[56] In doing so, He provided opportunities for others to join together with Him or to reject Him.

Conclusion: The Holy Spirit Continues Christ's Work of Justice

We now return to our initial questions: Does the idea that some people are "superior" to others find its roots in Genesis 1-3? Or, does it have roots in the later interpretation of the creation and Edenic stories? If people are still created in the "image" and "likeness" of God, how should this influence the way one treats and interacts with God, other human beings, and the world at large? Old Testament Scholar Derek Kidner writes,

> After the fall, man is still said to be in God's image (Gen 9:6) and likeness (Jas 3:9); nonetheless he requires to be 'renewed ... after the image of him that created him' (Col 3:10; cf. Eph 4:24). As long as we are human beings, we are, by definition, in the image of God. But spiritual likeness—in a single word, love—can be present only where God and man are in fellowship; hence the fall destroyed it, and our redemption recreates and perfects it."[57]

In the narrative of Genesis 1, people (both male and female) were created in the likeness and image of God. They were created to take care of God's sacred space (the earth and all its inhabitants), to be co-creators and multipliers of humanity, and to have intimate communion with God and with each other. The male and female were given equal responsibilities, gifts, and authority to respond to and continue caring for creation in God's stead. The second Creation story proceeds with the creation of man and woman and the deception of the woman and the disobedience of man in Genesis 2-3, which in turn has prompted a variety of interpretations regarding 1) what it means to be made in the likeness and image of God after the Edenic Paradise narrative concludes, 2) what relationships between God, people, and the earth initially looked like and 3) how this deception and disobedience affects and influences one's viewpoint on relationships with God, each other and all of God's creation.

Worldview, in a Judeo-Christian sense, is largely shaped and formed by Scripture, tradition, reason, and experience,[58] which means that every interpretation of the Hexameron narrative of Genesis 1 and the Edenic Paradise narrative of Genesis 2-3 we have encountered in this chapter is coming from a particular person or group of people with a variety of understandings of Scripture, a variety of traditions, a variety of perspectives regarding what is reasonable and unreasonable, and a variety of experiences. Our interpretations of Genesis 1-3 are shaped and formed in a similar manner. With a Second Temple influenced theological training, Paul struggled both fully to understand and to articulate a clear and consistent manifesto of God's intended equality in Christ; however, he points to the Christ-focused vision of equality. The fundamentals of Paul's understanding of Christ and the Spirit's work, moreover, lay the foundation for a theology of human equality for the contemporary Church.

Will we choose to let the Spirit guide us in our understanding and interpretation of Scripture? The way we choose to interact with God matters. The way we choose to interact with each other matters. The way we choose to interact with all of God's creation matters. The way we choose to approach and interact with Scripture matters too, and we must keep these four elements in mind (Scripture, tradition, reason, and experience) and in check as the Spirit guides and empowers us to live out what it means to be created in the image and likeness of God.

Due to a variety of interpretations of the story of Genesis 1-3 in Second Temple Jewish literature, including the Pauline literature in the canonical New Testament, what was once meant to bring hope, peace, and assurance in explaining how relationships worked before and after the Garden of Eden had become tainted to serve as impetus for deeming the "other" to be less than and subordinate to one's self. Many people misuse responsibility and authority to cause damage, heartache, and pain to God's creation, those who are also created in the image and likeness of God. Historically speaking, far too many societies have used Scripture to authorize treating others 'greater than' or 'less than.' Prejudice, discrimination, pride, envy, jealously, assault, and sexism emerge and persist as common. In response, the Spirit of God who was and is active in the process of creation calls out to the church to remember and advocate for every single person because she and he are created in the image and likeness of God.

Christian theology teaches that the work of God in Christ makes restoration of relationship a possibility, hope and goal. Although struggle and strife continue to be integral relationships, the more enduring truth persists that God loves all of creation and that every human being is created with equal standing within God's image and likeness. This enduring truth undergirds God's continued invitation to all of humanity to be in relationship with God. God continues to hold human beings accountable for the divine responsibility given for us to care for creation. The Spirit empowers the human community to keep this charge. The choice is ours.

Bibliography

Abraham, Joseph. *Eve: Accused or Acquitted?: An Analysis of Feminist Readings of the Creation Narrative Texts in Genesis 1–3.* Eugene, OR: Wipf & Stock Publishers, 2006.

Barr, James. *The Garden of Eden and the Hope of Immortality.* Minneapolis: Fortress Press, 1993.

Bouteneff, Peter C. *Beginnings: Ancient Christian Readings of the Biblical Creation Narratives.* Grand Rapids: Baker Academic, 2008.

Briggs, Richard S. "Humans in the Image of God and Other Things Genesis Does Not Make Clear." *Journal of Theological Interpretation* 4:1 (2010), 111-26.

Brink, CB. "The fundamental Principles of the Mission Policy of the "Nederduitse Gereformeerde" Churches in South Africa." In FJ Van Wyk, ed. *Christian Principles in Multi-Racial South Africa.* Johannesburg: Voortrekkerpers, 1954, 33.

Davis, Ellen F. *Scripture, Culture, and Agriculture: An Agrarian Reading of the Bible.* Cambridge: Cambridge University Press, 2009.

Hall, Douglas John. "Two Historical Conceptions of Imago Dei." In *Imaging God: Dominion as Stewardship.* Grand Rapids: 2004, 88-112.

Herring, Stephen L "A 'Transubstantiated' Humanity: The Relationship between the Divine Image and the Presence of God in Genesis I 26f. *Vetus Testamentum* 58 (2008), 480-94.

Keener, Craig S. *The Mind of the Spirit.* Grand Rapids: Baker, 2016.

Kidner, Derek. *Genesis: An Introduction and Commentary* vol. 1. Tyndale Old Testament Commentaries. Downers Grove, IL: InterVarsity Press, 2008.

Lombard, Christo. 2009. "Does contextual exegesis require an affirming Bible? Lessons from 'apartheid' and 'Africa' as narcissistic hermeneutical keys." *Scriptura* 101, 276.

Matthews, Victor and Don C. Benjamin, *Old Testament Parallels*. 4th ed. New York: Paulist Press, 2000.

Oseik, Carolyn and Margaret Y. MacDonald with Janet M. Tulloch. *A Woman's Place: House Churches in Earliest Christianity*. Minneapolis: Augsburg Fortress Press, 2005.

Rause, Deborak. "Keeping It Real: The Image of God in the New Testament." *Interpretation* (October 2005), 358-68.

Saler, Robert. "The Transformation of Reason in Genesis 2-3: Two Options for Theological Interpretation," *Currents in Theology and Mission* 36:4 (August 2009), 275-86.

Schottroff, Luise. *Lydia's Impatient Sisters: A Feminist Social History of Early Christianity*. Louisville: Westminster/John Knox, 1995.

Schüle, Andreas. "Made in the Image of God: The concepts of Divine Images in Gen 1-3," *Zeitschrift für die alttestamentliche Wissenschaft* 117:1 (2005), 1-20.

Stone, Howard W. Stone & James O. Duke. *How to Think Theologically*. 3rd ed. Minneapolis: Augsburg Fortress Press, 2013.

Tamez, Elsa and Matthew J. O'Connell (trans.). *Bible of the Oppressed*. Eugene: Wipf & Stock, 2006.

Towner, W. Sibley. "Clones of God: Genesis 1:26-28 and the Image of God in the Hebrew Bible." *Interpretation: A Journal of Bible & Theology* 59:4 (October 2005), 341-56.

Walton, John H. *Genesis 1 as Ancient Cosmology*. Winona Lake, IN: Eisenbrauns, 2011.

Weems, Renita. *Just a Sister Away*. San Diego: Lura Media, 1988.

Wells, Shaniqua Janeè. "A Basis of the Civil War: The Theological Views of Nineteenth Century Christians on the Justification of Slavery." Honors Thesis: The University of Southern Mississippi, 2015. https://aquila.usm.edu/cgi/viewcontent.cgi?article=1319&context=honors_theses.

Chapter 8

Waiting for a Hero:
Will Someone Do the Right Thing?

William L. Lyons and Jordan M. Way

There is universal appeal in the story of Ruth, the Moabite woman who despite devastating loss ended up at the center of ancient Israelite society, becoming an important person in the lineage of King David and, later, Jesus. The story is unforgettable, and like other compelling stories has a complicated plot full of surprises. Although centuries have passed since it was penned, it still commands a huge following and is the object of ongoing scholarly scrutiny. Like all great literature, it is open to differing interpretations.

Scholars are not alone in their attention to Ruth; literary and visual artists have captured diverse interpretations of the book in their work. Laffey and Leonard-Fleckman offer an expansive summary of artistic interpretations of the story of Ruth's story in the *Wisdom Commentary* series.[1] Three books offer a visual history and narrative of notable artistic depictions of the story: *Great Couples of the Bible* (Haag and Söelle); *Listen to Her Voice: Women of the Hebrew Bible* (Raver); and *Great Women of the Bible in Art and Literature* (Söelle).[2]

The Story of Ruth

Chapter 1 begins with famine and bereavement, "In the days when the Judges ruled there was a famine in the land" (1:1). In response,

Elimelech, Naomi, and their family were driven by famine from Bethlehem[3] to Moab in search of food. While there, Mahlon and Chilion, their sons, took Moabite wives (Ruth and Orpah).[4] As the story progresses, all the men of the family died, and the three widows[5] were left to fend for themselves.[6]

When Naomi heard that the famine had ended and that there was food in Bethlehem, she began the journey home—a sensible thing to do. Yet, what of her Moabite daughters-in-law? Should they return to Israel with her or remain in the land? She suggested that the women remain in their homeland, Moab (1:8, 11–13, 15), and the narrative overflows with deep sadness as the difficulties of their situation compound. Sometimes life isn't fair. With great hesitation, Orpah chose what most ancient readers would expect; she followed Naomi's suggestion and remained in her homeland.[7] Ruth, however, did the unexpected, and her actions are expressed with unforgettable words:

> [16] Ruth replied [to Naomi], "Don't urge me to leave you or to turn back from you. Where you go I will go, and where you stay I will stay. Your people will be my people and your God my God.[17] Where you die I will die, and there I will be buried. May the LORD deal with me, be it ever so severely, if anything but death separates you and me."[8]

Adele Reinhartz has called this "the most well-developed and positive portrayal of women's relationships in biblical literature" (1:16–18).[9] The passage hints at the beginning of deep-seated change for Ruth. There would be no community of expatriate Moabite women in Bethlehem, and readers wonder what would happen next.

In contrast to Ruth, Naomi is anything but hopeful. When the two returned to Bethlehem she laments that her life is "bitter" and "empty" (1:20–21). Despite the end of the famine in Bethlehem (note the beginning of the barley harvest, 1:22), Naomi's demeanor here is at polar opposites to the beginning of the story where she appeared to be happy that "the LORD had considered his people and given them food" (in Moab). Now without men in their lives, how would the women survive in a patriarchal society?

As the story progresses, it seems that Ruth met Boaz by happenstance, but there is more to the casual meeting than meets the eye. Boaz saw her gleaning[10] in the fields and asked about her identity (2:5–7). He had heard that she made a favorable impression on the foreman and he could see that she was a hard worker. Moreover, Boaz had heard that Ruth decided to remain with Naomi after the death of her husband and return to Israel with her mother-in-law. He then summarized what she had done with Naomi in Abrahamic terms: "May the LORD reward you [Ruth] for your deeds, and may you have a full reward from the LORD, the God of Israel, under whose wings you have come for refuge!" (2:12). In response, Boaz allowed Ruth to glean *unharvested* grain (the "standing sheaves") behind the harvesters without fear of harassment, and the workers were to "pull out some bundles" from the harvested grain and share them with her (2:15–16).[11] Moreover, she could drink from their water and eventually eat with them and Boaz. These actions are unprecedented.

Ruth's report to Naomi about what happened elicits another blessing from Naomi, "Blessed be he by the LORD, whose kindness has not forsaken the living or the dead! (2:20). Then, surprisingly, Naomi shares an important insight into the interchange between Boaz and Ruth—Boaz is a close family member.[12] This portion of the story (Ch. 2) ends with the close of the barley harvest. About seven weeks have ensued since the initial meeting between Ruth and Boaz. He was kind to them, but the story says little more.

At the beginning of chapter 3, readers learn of Naomi's concern about a "resting-place" ("some security," NRSV) for her daughter-in-law, and she proposed a brazen plan. She directed Ruth to wash and anoint herself and put on her best clothes. After discovering where Boaz would be sleeping, Naomi told Ruth to "uncover his feet" and lie down with him. Although lost to modern readers, this phrase in Hebrew carries distinct, unmistakable sexual overtones.[13] It was an audacious and risky proposal because Ruth's overture could have just as easily been rejected as accepted.

Ruth complied with Naomi's plan, and her first words to Boaz when he awoke with a start while she was sitting on his bed are a turning point in the larger narrative. By answering Boaz's query, "Who are you" (3:12) with "I am Ruth your handmaid" (instead of "your servant" as we read in 2:13), she directly asserted her availability for marriage. In the NRSV, we read that she then said, "Spread your cloak over your servant" (3:9) but in Hebrew the phrase reads, "spread your *wing*" (an unmistakable reference to Boaz's initial blessing, "May the LORD reward you, ... the God of Israel, under whose *wings* you have come for refuge," 2:12). Thus, the interchange carries much more than sexual overtones.[14] As Boaz initially asked the God of Israel to reward Ruth for her deeds (2:12), Ruth was now asking Boaz to act as God would do and take care of her. It is a powerful moment in the story. Would he do it? Would he do the right thing?

Boaz did choose to do the right thing and responded with yet another blessing acknowledging her actions as an expression of loyalty (*hesed,* 3:10).[15] Although he would be happy to be her "redeeming kinsman," in an unexpected twist, Ruth and readers learn that another person who was a closer relative to Ruth than Boaz had the first right of refusal (3:12). Naomi's carefully devised plan could still go awry. Nevertheless, Ruth's report of the night's events to Naomi (3:16–18) was hopeful; the plan might succeed, but all the women could do was wait to see what would happen.

The final chapter of the narrative offers important insights into how legal agreements were negotiated in ancient Israel. The unnamed family member was interested in Naomi's land (which we learn about for the first time here), but not in the woman. Since the women are bound to the land in this negotiation, this kinsman declined, and Boaz accepted both land and the woman.[16]

The story ends with Boaz taking Ruth as his wife, and more blessings follow in rapid succession:

1. The townspeople[17] bless Ruth in 4:11–12 ("May the LORD make this woman who is coming into your house like Rachel and Leah" 4:11). She is thus installed as one of the "mothers of Israel."
2. While Ruth eventually bore a child, *Naomi* was blessed by the women of the town (4:14–15). Naomi

nursed the child and the women of Bethlehem named him Obed, and he was the father of Jesse and the grandfather of David. A son was born to Naomi... and finally, she was anything but empty!

3. Surprisingly, Ruth is not even mentioned at this point, and readers discover that this small story is much bigger than Ruth; it is about fidelity and loyalty.

4. The book ends with a genealogy (4:18–22) that traces the line of Obed back to Perez (son of Judah and Tamar; Gen 38) and forward to King David. Although the genealogy is traced via the fathers, "the people of Bethlehem remind us that it was the mothers who made sure that the continuity of the family line remained unbroken."[18]

Matters of Interpretation

Modern readers may be surprised to learn that the Book of Ruth is found in different places in the Jewish Bible (Hebrew Bible) and the Catholic/Protestant Bibles (Old Testament)—and placement influences interpretation. Where do we "place" Ruth? Is one position better than the other? Essentially, there are two choices:

1. Locate Ruth within the later part of the Hebrew Bible in a section called "the Writings."[19] If Ruth is placed here, then it would have been written ca. 586–500 BCE (during the Babylonian exile or shortly following the return from exile). The story is well-suited here as Ruth resonates with the virtuous woman in Proverbs (Prov 31) or the

woman who pursues her lover during the night in the Song of Songs (3:14; 5:6–7), both later biblical books. Like Ezra-Nehemiah, also located during this time, Ruth addressed the difficulties of repatriation back to Israel following the Babylonian Exile and the problems of marriage to non-Israelites. Similarly, like Jonah, which some scholars place within the post-exilic period (after 536 BCE), Ruth presents a favorable perspective on foreigners. There is much to ponder here. Taken together, these books offer an extended discussion of what it means to be a part of a covenant community, serve as a model of covenant fidelity, and ponder how to live in increasingly multi-cultural communities or among people of diverse backgrounds.[20]

2. Alternatively, Ruth is placed much earlier in Christian Bibles, between Judges and 1 Samuel the Historical Books.[21] Here, it serves as a counterpoint to the moral decline and chaos of the last chapters of Judges and especially the final verse of the book: "all people did what was right in their own eyes" (21:25 NRSV).[22] The story is set in the period of the Judges (1:1) and ends with a genealogy of King David (4:18–22), and thus Ruth serves a pivotal role in simultaneously recalling the mistakes of the past and peering forward with hope for the future.[23]

Both textual locations carry ancient meaning, and we will not argue for the prominence of one over the other. Rather, it should be noted that even ancient hermeneuts hundreds of years before the establishment of the Jewish or Christian canons (the formally accepted and approved order of biblical books) did not agree on where to place Ruth. The problem is ancient, but also simple: Ruth fits well into both biblical locations, and we will demonstrate that the message of the book complements both locations in the Bible.

By focusing on "the world of Israelite women," which is only occasionally visible elsewhere in the HB/OT, Ruth makes readers aware of a narrative line that although untold, is nevertheless moving forward parallel to the men's stories. Although the story is about ancient Israelite women, it is still told through a patriarchal lens, or as Phyllis Trible reminds readers, "a man's world tells a woman's story."[24] Modern readers can read Ruth as a champion for women's issues working within the confines of her sociohistorical framework. Indeed, some would argue that Naomi and Ruth are "trapped in a patriarchal system that does not always respect the dignity of women."[25] Here, female happiness is defined through masculine eyes: being married to a wealthy man; giving birth to a son; being the great-grandmother of a king. Although the book ends with a masculine genealogy, women are the primary actors.

Modern biblical hermeneuts read Ruth variously, either as subversive or liberating literature.[26] Leila Bronner and Esther Fuchs see Ruth as the paradigm of submission and obedience in support of the patriarchal hierarchy.[27] Sarojini Nadar, however, employs a different perspective with the ingenious technique of reading Ruth from the role of "dedifferentiation" (or role reversals).[28] In the narrative, Ruth consistently challenges the dogmatisms of ethnicity and gender by taking command of her and Naomi's plight. In the narrative, Ruth's first role switch appears early in the text as she shifts from being Mahlon's wife to Naomi's daughter-in-law. She is thus identified with another woman instead of her husband.[29] With the death of the initial male characters, the story moves from being a man's tale to a woman's (or women's) story.[30] Ruth then assumes a traditionally masculine role by "clinging" to Naomi (a phrase never applied to women),[31] or as Trible puts it, Ruth "reverses sexual allegiance. A young woman commits herself to an old woman in a world where life depends on men."[32]. Additionally, by dismissing Naomi's unambiguous commands to leave her, Ruth becomes the leading member of the relationship. Her role of dedifferentiation reaches an apex in Ruth's daring initiation of the kinsman-redeemer rights, which results in the continuation of Naomi's family line. For her courageous act, she secures a lineage for Naomi and ensures the security necessary for both women in a patriarchal society.

A problem with the story of Ruth that modern readers easily overlook is the issue of "the Moabites." These people were prohibited from entering the "assembly" of Israel (Deut 23:3–6) and they could not become full members of Israelite society. Thus, Ruth is repeatedly referred to as a "Moabitess."[33] Hostilities grew between the peoples east of the Jordan River valley (including the Dead Sea) when the Amalekites and perhaps the Moabites and the Ammonites attacked the Israelites as they travelled from Egypt to the Promised Land (Ex 17:8–16; Deut 25:17–18) and Moab became "one of Israel's most hated enemies."[34] Thereafter, these peoples were frequently depicted negatively. Moabites, in particular, play a significant role in the historical accounts of Genesis–2 Kings,[35] and Bible readers first meet them in the story of Lot's sexual encounter with his two daughters following the destruction of Sodom and Gomorrah (19:30–

38). Each daughter bore a son: Moab and ben-Ammi, the progenitors of the Moabites and the Ammonites. In light of the strong Deuteronomic prohibition against anyone entering the assembly of the LORD who is "born of an illicit sexual union," it is shocking to see Ruth, the Moabitess on center stage of the story.[36] As if to highlight her "otherness," she is never referred to as an "Israelite." Sometimes she is simply called "Ruth" and at other times she is called "Ruth the Moabitess,"[37] and in the final chapter of the story, she is called "the Moabitess" twice (4:4, 10). Her identity never changes. Nevertheless, at a time when Israel was doing anything but deepening its covenantal bonds to their God, as the narrative depicts in the final chapters of Judges, ironically, a Gentile, Moabite woman proves utterly committed to her grieving mother-in-law, her mother-in-law's people, and her mother-in-law's God. For this, she is included in the royal lineage extending to David, and in the New Testament, to Jesus (Matt 1:5). The story is at once a rebuke to the shallow covenant fidelity of the people of Israel at that time and an example of hope to those who were outside the biblical covenant. Hereafter, true covenantal community membership would not be achieved by physical lineage alone.

Direct divine interaction in Ruth is surprisingly rare. Early in the story, the Lord "considered" his people and gave them food (1:6); and then as a concluding bracket to the narrative, the Lord "made [Ruth] conceive, and she bore a son" (4:13). Although the leading characters mention the LORD repeatedly (e.g. "the LORD bless you" [2:4]), beyond the beginning and end of the story, events are never directly connected to the Lord. This continues the story of Judges where, following chapter 10, readers look in vain for direct divine intervention in the narrative. Later, in 1 Samuel 3 readers observe that "the word of the LORD was rare in those days," even with Eli the priest. However, divine silence does not equal absence, and careful readers discover that the Lord was on the sidelines of the narrative,[38] acting on behalf of those who remained committed to him and waiting for someone to "do the right thing." The book demonstrates how the God of ancient Israel blessed the people when they organized their lives as a committed covenantal community; conversely, by demonstrating *hesed*, Ruth acted as a covenant community member even though she is never completely nationalized. The book calls later readers to do the same.

As a woman living in a patriarchal society, Ruth resorted to alternative methods to achieve her goals. This has been called *tricksterism*, and it appears in the biblical narrative when there is no other means to affect change.[39] If Ruth is a trickster, what is her primary goal? Is she interested in self-promotion or self-preservation? Does she promote the patriarchy or is she supporting a subversive counter-cultural movement? Ruth is an amalgamation of purposes. She is a widow seeking self-preservation, and unlike her sister-in-law (Orpah, the other Moabitess in the story), she aligns herself with a woman instead of a man. She thus combines trickster methods with loyalty for Naomi so that the two may survive.

As a trickster, Ruth is responsible for creating a strategy that accomplishes her own intended outcome. This becomes very clear early in the narrative. First, Ruth defies Naomi's directives to return to her homeland and find another man (1:6–22). The initial step of her plan is successful as Naomi relents, and the two become allies in poverty. The strategy becomes clearer as Ruth is the first to suggest a plan of action, "I would like to go to the fields and glean among the ears of grain, behind someone who may show me kindness" (2:2). While elements of power and personal connections belong to Naomi and Boaz, Ruth remains the initiator of the unfolding events. Ruth then shifts role from instigator to obedient servant of Naomi and Boaz as she follows their instructions. Her chameleonic ability to shift roles according to circumstance allows her to concoct a plan while simultaneously playing the submissive role in others' manufactured designs. In other words, she is in charge, but not technically, and this is a masterful plan.

One of the high points of the story occurs during the night at the threshing floor in chapter 3. Instead of waiting for a directive from Boaz as Naomi told her to do, Ruth acted and appealed to his sense of duty, "you are a redeeming kinsman" (3:9).[40] Here, readers see her most polished skill as trickster: subtle manipulation of a direct order. Ruth's trickster techniques carry divine approval, perhaps because of the purity of her intentions. She was seeking the well-being and security of her mother-in-law, and her methods were rewarded by Boaz, who responded with a blessing. Johana Bos summarizes Ruth's trickster approach well, "Although Ruth's act does not involve deception, there is a motif of hiding and cleverness."[41] Ruth is not the typical trickster; she is the trickster reformed. It is her initiative that sets the plan in motion and her loyalty that brings it to fruition. She is a trickster that God can use: the conscientious manipulator. Ruth forms an alliance of "weakness to weakness,"[42] but in doing so, she extends a lineage of faithfulness that reaches its pinnacle in King David. The fidelity of a trickster secured a legacy of faith.

Conclusion

This study has demonstrated that readers, scholars, and artists of the Book of Ruth have interpreted it variously through the ages. Even the earliest hermeneuts (as early as 250 BCE) did not agree on the historical locus of the narrative, and the matrix of the book remains uncertain. It simply fits well into two different canonical locations. Perhaps this is what the earliest readers saw in the book, a story that could address more than one context.

One of the overlooked foci of the story is social justice. As widows in a patriarchal society, Naomi, Ruth, and Orpah develop different strategies to face the hard times ahead. Orpah chose to return to her family, a sensible thing to do by any standard of measure. Her role in the story ends here. Ruth, on the other hand, "clung" to her mother-in-law, and together they returned to Israel in great need. Readers wonder, "who would help them"?

The story fronts the needs of the disenfranchised and marginalized peoples in antiquity, and this is its lasting appeal today. It addresses the universal human need for social justice through individuals who act with integrity. At great risk, Naomi and Ruth began to do what they could to find help. Boaz, in turn, responded, and his actions set an example for all Bible readers. He would do the right thing. Ulterior motives aside, Ruth and Boaz take non-compulsory initiative (they did not have to do what they did) to care for those in need: Ruth with Naomi and Boaz with Ruth. Thus, they exemplify the height of human character by intentionally engaging the lives of the marginalized and powerless with fairness and equity, regardless of societal demands that at times can be cold and uncompassionate. The heroes and heroines of this book set an enduring example of social justice for future generations by opposing oppression and standing for righteousness. Ruth meets us right where we are, at the intersection of precept and principle, and shows us that justice prevails if only someone will "do the right thing."

Bibliography

Baldwin, J. B. "Ruth." *The New Bible Commentary: Revised*, edited by D. Guthrie, et al. Grand Rapids: Wm B. Eerdmans Publishing Co., 1970, 277–83.

Berlin, Adele, and Marc Zvi Brettler, eds. *The Jewish Study Bible*, 2nd ed. Oxford, UK: Oxford University Press, 2014.

Berquist, J. L. "Role Dedifferentiation in the Book of Ruth." *JSOT* 18 (1993), 23–37.

Bos, Johana W. H. "Out of the Shadows: Genesis 38; Judges 4:17–22; Ruth 3." In *Semeia* 42, edited by J. Cheryl Exum and Johana W. H. Bos, 37–67. Atlanta: SBL, 1988.

Brenner, Athalya. "Introduction" in *A Feminist Companion to Ruth*, edited by Athalya Brenner, 9–18. *FCB* 3. Sheffield: SAP, 1993 [reprinted 2001].

_____. "Introduction." In *Ruth and Esther*, edited by Athalya Brenner, 13–19. *FCB* 3, 2nd Series Sheffield: SAP, 1999.

_____. "Ruth as a Foreign Worker and the Politics of Exogamy." In *A Feminist Companion to Ruth*, edited by Athalya Brenner 158–62. *FCB* 3, 2nd Series. Sheffield: SAP, 1999.

_____. "Ruth and Naomi" in *A Feminist Companion to Ruth*, edited by Athalya Brenner, 70–84. *FCB* 3. Sheffield: SAP, 1993 [reprinted 2001].

_____. "Ruth and Naomi: Further Reflections" in *A Feminist Companion to Ruth*, edited by Athalya Brenner, 140–44. *FCB* 3. Sheffield: SAP, 1993 [reprinted 2001].

Bronner, L. L. "A Thematic Approach to Ruth in Rabbinic Literature," in *A Feminist Companion to Ruth*, edited by Athalya Brenner, 146–169. Sheffield: SAP, 1993.

Claassens, L. Julianna M., "Resisting Dehumanization: Ruth, Tamar, and the Quest for Human Dignity." *CBQ* 74:4 (2012), 659–74.

Donaldson, Laura E. "The Sign of Orpah: Reading Ruth Through Native Eyes." in *Ruth and Esther*, edited by Athalya Brenner, 130–44. *FCB* 3, 2nd Series. Sheffield: SAP, 1999.

Farmer, Kathleen R. "Ruth." In *NISB*, edited by Walter J. Harrelson, 387–88. Nashville: Abingdon Press Harper Collins, 2003.

Fewell, Danna Nolan. "Space for Moral Agency in the Book of Ruth." JSOT 40:1 (2015), 79–96. https://doi.org/10.1177/0309089215605796.

Freedman, David N., ed. *Anchor Bible Dictionary 5 Vols*. New York: Doubleday, 1992.

Fuchs, Esther. "The History of Women in Ancient Israel: Theory, Method, and the Book of Ruth." In *Her Master's Tools: Feminist and Postcolonial Engagements of Historical-Critical Discourse,* edited by Caroline Vander Stichele and Todd Penner, 211–32. Atlanta: SBL Press, 2005.

Haag, Herbert, and Dorothée Söelle, eds., et al. *Great Couples of the Bible*. Translated by Brian McNeil. Minneapolis: Fortress Press, 2006.

LaCocque, André. *The Feminine Unconventional: Four Subversive Figures in Israel's Tradition*. Minneapolis: Fortress Press, 1990.

Laffey, Alice L., and Mahri Leonard-Fleckman. *Ruth*, edited by Amy-Jill Levine. Vol 8 of *Wisdom Commentary*, edited by Barbara Reid. Collegeville, MN: Liturgical Press, 2017.

Lau, Peter H. W. "Another Postcolonial Reading of the Book of Ruth." In *Reading Ruth in Asia*, edited by Jione Havea and Peter H. W. Lau, 15–34. Atlanta: SBL Press, 2015.

Lau, Peter H. W., and Gregory Goswell. *Unceasing Kindness: A Biblical Theology of Ruth*. Downers Grove, IL: IVP Academic, 2016.

Legaspi, Marnie. "Ruth: The So-Called Scandal" in *Vindicating the Vixens: Revisiting Sexualized, Vilified, and Marginalized Women of the Bible*, edited by Sandra Glahn, 59–80. Grand Rapids: Kregel Academic, 2017.

Nadar, Sarojini. "A South African Indian Womanist Reading of the Character of Ruth" in *Other Ways of Reading: South African Women and the Bible*, edited by Musa W. Dube, 158–75. Atlanta: SBL Press, 2001.

Raskas, Jennifer. "The Book of Ruth: A Contrast to the End of Judges." *JBQ* 43:4 (2015), 223–232.

Reinhartz, Adele. Introduction to "Ruth" in *The Jewish Study Bible*, 2nd ed., edited by Adele Berlin and Marc Zvi Brettler, 1573–74. Oxford: Oxford University Press, 2014.

Rowell, Gillian M. "Ruth." In *The IVP Women's Bible Commentary: An Indispensable Resource for All Who to View Scripture Through Different Eyes,* edited by Catherine Clark

Kroeger and Mary J. Evans, 146–53. Downers Grove: IVP, 2002.

Sakenfeld, Katherine Dobb. *Just Wives? Stories of Power and Survival in the Old Testament and Today.* Louisville: WJKP, 2003.

Söelle, Dorothée, et al. *Great Women of the Bible in Art and Literature.* Grand Rapids: Wm. B. Eerdmans Publishing Co., 1994.

Trible, Phyllis. "Book of Ruth." In Vol. 5 of *The Anchor Bible Dictionary*, edited by David Noel Freedman, 846. New York: Doubleday, 1992.

_____. "Ruth" in *Women in Scripture: A Dictionary of Named and Unnamed Women in the Hebrew Bible, the Apocryphal/Deuterocanonical Books, and the New Testament,* edited by Carol Meyers, 146–47. Grand Rapids: Wm, B. Eerdmans Publishing Co., 2000.

Walsh, Carey. "Women on the Edge" in *Imagining the Other and Constructing Israelite Identity in the Early Second Temple Period*, edited by Ehud ben Zvi and Diana V. Edleman, 122–43. London: Bloomsbury, 2016.

Weisberg, Dvora E. "The Widow of Our Discontent: Levirate Marriage in the Bible and the Ancient Near East." *JSOT* 28 (2004), 403–29.

Chapter 9

God Chose the Poor: Recapturing the Radical Vision of Early Pentecostalism and the Original Pauline Communities

Adam White

From its inception, Pentecostalism was a movement that brought with it social and cultural upheaval. The Azusa Mission defied race, gender, class, and nationality norms. In a time that called for segregation, multi-racialism was a feature of the early Azusa Mission meetings.[1] In regard to gender, likewise, Pentecostalism has always recognised that the outpouring of the Spirit came equally to men and women and that charismatic gifts operated freely in both;[2] it has thus been a powerful voice and active proponent of women in ministry.[3] In terms of culture, Pentecostalism has always had an ability to enculturate its message and experiences in diverse cultural contexts. While other forms of Christianity have a tendency to be tied to specific ethnic groups, such and Russian Orthodox and German Lutheran, Pentecostalism has been much more effective in crossing these divides.[4]

Pentecostalism has also been a movement that transcends social classes. Against the long prevailing idea that early Pentecostalism was a sect of poorly educated, immigrant, rural lower-class workers, it has been shown instead that the social status of early Pentecostals reflected a cross section of American life. "While some Pentecostals were at the lower end of the socioeconomic strata, others were well-to-do ... most Pentecostals, however, were firmly planted in the middle classes."[5] Pentecostal churches had a slightly higher ratio of women to men and, while predominately white, had a representation of African-Americans that was twice the percentage of the American population and two-thirds the population in the south. Pentecostals were concerned to work out the biblical worldview found in Galatians 3:28 that seeks to create racial equality and integration, where there is neither Greek nor Jew, male nor female, slave nor free.[6] Its spiritual ideals of empowering all of its members for ministry irrespective of their education or social status, likewise, its prioritising of a person's gift and calling over against their gender or ethnicity are some of its great strengths. Moreover, as we will see, these ideals also firmly align it with the radical vision of the original Christian communities.

In this paper, we will see that Pentecostalism, at its heart, reflects the same values that Paul attempted to establish in his own communities. We will also see, however, that Pentecostalism, like the early Pauline communities such as in Corinth, quickly lost sight of their egalitarian mooring. Despite both beginning as movements that transcended social divides, Pentecostalism, as well as the early Pauline communities, soon gave way to pressures to conform to the broader culture's values. Equality and commonality quickly gave way to divisions along traditional social lines. The Pentecostal community, in other words, lost sight of its original ideals and continues in many ways to do so today. For us, therefore, the challenge remains to recapture this original vision.

This chapter will begin with a survey of the first-century society followed by a close reading of 1 Corinthians 1:20-28, a passage in which Paul reminds the Corinthian Christians of the radical nature of the community of which they are a part. It will then proceed to highlight some of the challenges we face—challenges not unlike those faced by the Corinthians—to maintain or even regain this identity.

The Ancient Economy

Scholars have long noted that the Roman economy was underdeveloped, meaning that the mass of the population lived at or near subsistence level. The majority of the labour force (about 80–90 per cent of the population) in the ancient world was employed in agriculture, which also accounted for 70–80 per cent of the value of production.[7] Investment in manufacturing industries was low. Most resources that could be invested in growth production were consumed and demand for manufactured goods was low; most needs were met locally with goods made by small craftsmen or at home.

> In ancient Rome, small-scale handicraft industry was predominant. Some goods were made in quantity, notably pottery and textiles. But little technical expertise or accumulation of capital was required for their production. They were in constant demand as basic and inexpensive consumer goods. However, no one producer or group of producers could be sure of a steady or expanding non-local market.[8]

By the period of the New Testament, the Augustan regime had inaugurated an era of relatively stable government, dedicated to the cause of civil peace and the pacification of Rome's enemies. As in any culture, this peace and stability was the basic ingredient for economic recovery and expansion. Augustus' success was instrumental in creating internal economic development, as well as expanding the economic horizons of the empire through expansion of Rome's territories.[9] Nevertheless, despite the Empire's stability and potential for economic growth, the disparity of wealth was stark. Whatever economic growth there was took place amongst the already rich, who simply became richer. For the majority of ancient people, their existence was one of subsistence.[10]

In the ancient world, everyone lived near the level of subsistence, only a very small, wealthy elite controlled commerce and politics. In between the masses and the elite, there was no economic middle class as we might find today. The reason was that in a preindustrial society such as ancient Rome, there are few economic mechanisms for gaining significant wealth. However, some people did manage to achieve moderate surplus income through various means. These people occupied the large gap between the elite and the masses.[11] Friesen has attempted to give more detailed definition to this category of "poor" in the ancient world. He offers the following "Poverty Scale" (PS) as a categorical breakdown of the various socio-economic stations of the population:[12]

PS 1 Imperial Elite: imperial dynasty, Roman senatorial families, some retainers, local royalty, some freedpersons (0.04%)

PS 2 Regional or Provincial Elite: equestrian families, provincial officials, some retainers, some decurial families, some freedpersons, some retired military officers (1%)

PS 3 Municipal Elite: most decurial families, wealthy men and women who do not hold office, some freedpersons, some retainers, some veterans, some merchants (1.76%)

PS 4 Moderate Surplus Resources: some merchants, some traders, some freedpersons, some artisans (especially those who employ others), military veterans (7%)

PS 5 Near Subsistence Level: many merchants and traders, regular wage earners, artisans, large shop owners, freedpersons, some farm families (22%)

PS 6 At Subsistence Level: small farm families, laborers (skilled and unskilled), artisans (especially those employed by others), wage earners, most merchants and traders, small shop/tavern owners (40%)

PS 7 Below Subsistence Level: some farm families, unattached widows, orphans, beggars, disabled persons, unskilled day laborers, prisoners (28%)

Friesen's analysis makes clear the point that the vast majority of the population (some 90%) of the ancient world lived at or near subsistence level, while even the majority of those who had some sort of surplus only had moderately more than they needed. The point of all this is to remind us that, when we look at the typical Christian community of the first century, we must remember that they would have represented a cross section of this society. Put another way: almost every Christian in the first century would have lived at subsistence level with a handful of members that possessed moderate surplus resources. These few families living above subsistence, Friesen argues, would have been the leaders of the communities.[13] Martin has summarized the situation well when he states:

> Almost all New Testament scholars admit that although we have evidence that some early Christians enjoyed a high status relative to manual laborers, artisans, the destitute—the majority of the inhabitants of the Roman Empire—probably none of them could be called members of the highest class of the Empire. The official ruling class of the Roman Empire was a minute fraction of the population, made up of members of the highest Roman *ordines* ('orders')—senators, equestrians, and decurions—along with local aristocracies in the provinces. Below them were the *humiliores*, an economically wide-ranging category that included people who controlled considerable amounts of money (for example, many merchants) and both freedmen and freed, all of whom

depended upon the labor of others for their livelihood. Below that were 'poor': artisans, construction workers, and owners of small business establishments like bars, baths, and brothels. And further down still were the destitute poor: unskilled laborers, those who made do with the occasional day job, and the unemployed.[14]

The stark disparity of relative wealth between the few and the many within the early Christian communities is universally agreed in New Testament scholarship; only a small handful of Christians would have come from the wealthier levels of society.[15] Martin suggests that these more affluent members of Paul's churches fell into the middle area between true elite and poor. They would have had households that included freed persons and slaves and would have made their living from the surplus labor value of their dependents.[16] However, there appears to be an exception to this rule in the Corinthian community.

The Corinthian Economic Situation

Recent archaeological and epigraphical studies in Corinth have demonstrated that, in the time of the New Testament, the city of Corinth presented an economic situation quite unlike other ancient cities. Corinth had been re-founded by Caesar in 44 BCE, only a century before Paul's arrival, and had grown rapidly into a major centre of commerce within the empire. Its rise was meteoric. It began as a settlement with a large population of subsistence farmers. Within a generation, it had become a market city and some of the original subsistence farmers had become solidly established with business interests and were supportive of other poorer agricultural families.[17] By the beginning of the first century, Corinth had probably doubled in population and had developed a vital economy that attracted immigrants from all over the region and from afar. It had become a town of regional significance and had a fully developed social hierarchy. By the period of the New Testament, Sanders argues, "Corinth was a city of empire-wide significance with two dependant harbour towns acting as both entrepôts and emporia. At the time of Paul's visit, international commerce was of major significance to the city."[18]

The Roman colony also presented many commercial attractions that would have drawn to it both Roman and Greek *negotiatores*—investors who made wealth through money lending and large-scale wholesale trading. These *negotiatores* were often wealthy enough upon arrival in the city to establish themselves and their dependents as leading families and hold the highest magistracies. Others would be moneylenders attracted by the prospect of making profitable (what Spawforth calls) "pump-priming" loans.[19] This commercial success was most clearly seen in the impact of Corinth's two harbors on its economy.

In an ancient city, the urban centre itself typically acted as the centre of trade in the region, with the urban markets functioning as mechanisms for the redistribution of goods to rural dwellers and visitors.[20] While Corinth certainly had different kinds of markets, its main source of wealth was its harbours, which formed a major *emporion* for maritime trade through the Isthmus. These two harbours, Kenchreai and Lechaion, were places of large-scale trade in the territory. Harbours like these would create manifest commercial activities such as "money lenders and merchants negotiating loans, merchants buying up craft in the town for exporting abroad, land owners seeking markets for their surplus olive oil and wine, and retailers and peddlers redistributing imported goods in the city's more specialised markets, fora, and fairs."[21] The harbours also created space for a wide range of individuals linked to trade such as wholesale dealers, financiers, ship owners, traders, landowners, middle men, retailers, craft specialists, sailors and rowers, and many others. Pettegrew notes:

> The commercial activities occurring during sailing season likewise employed a myriad of workers at the sea front. Hundreds of people were needed to manage the arrival of ships and movement of goods at the quays and storehouses: stevedores and porters, customs officials and clerks, inspectors, crane operators, lightermen, shipwrights, ballast handlers, and divers and dredgers. Transferring goods from farm estates to harbours and from harbours to towns demanded many muleteers and wagon drivers. And the services provided to arriving merchants, sailors, and passengers put to work retailers, shopkeepers, tavern and bar owners, innkeepers, craftsmen, and prostitutes. In the varied economic activities that occurred at harbours, there was a large demand for seasonal labourers both skilled and unskilled.[22]

The numerous studies of first century Corinth present us with an image of a city with a sizable population consisting of an elite, freedman base, as well as landholders, laborers, itinerant merchants, as well as a share of urban destitution.[23] It was a city that drew to itself wealthy business people and families seeking to capitalize on the city's exceptional trade opportunities. Furthermore, its status as the provincial capital and esteemed status in the region would make it the logical place to be for those with ambitions for Roman offices. It was, in other words, a new and fast-growing city that defied the typical pattern found within an ancient city.

This uniqueness is shown by Sanders. He argues that the typical ratios of rank and inequality in an ancient city (per 100 citizens) resembled 89 cultivators: 10 managers: 1 administrator. In this picture, cultivators lived at a survival level while the managers and administrators had incomes also of subsistence levels. Corinth in Paul's time, however, resembled something more like 60 cultivators: 30 tradesmen and managers: 1 administrator with a much larger gap between the poorest and the richest elements. He suggests that Corinth may have had quite a substantial consumer class, especially when compared with the average income distribution of the Roman Empire.[24] In other words, compared to a typical ancient city, Corinth seemed to contain a slightly larger "middle class"; something more akin to a mid 18th-century England and Wales.[25]

The city of Corinth, in other words, appears to present a higher proportion of wealthy members by comparison to other cities. In the same way, the Christian community appears to contain a significantly greater number of wealthy members compared to Paul's other churches. In some instances, these members likely possessed substantial wealth.²⁶ It is precisely this group of wealthier members who are at the heart of the issues that Paul addresses in 1 Corinthians. When we look at the problems that Paul is addressing in his letters to them, what we find are divisions between those who controlled their economic destiny and those who did not.²⁷

God Chose the Poor

1 Corinthians is a letter that, for the most part, addresses issues that are undergirded by distinctions in social status. In chapters 1–4, Paul deals with divisions that have occurred because some of the elite members have taken preference to Apollos on account of his superior style and perceived status in comparison to Paul.²⁸ In chapters 5–6, we find issues such as an elite member in an incestuous (and illegal) relationship with his step-mother, while the rest of the congregation is powerless to deal with him.²⁹ We also see certain wealthy members taking one another to court over trivial lawsuits. In chapters 8–10, we find wealthier members laying claim to their rights to attend pagan festivals, even at the expense of the consciences of the poorer members.³⁰ In chapter 11, the social issues are most evident with poor treatment of the "Have nots" by the "Haves".³¹ In chapters 12–14, we see the arrogant behaviour of the elites in their abuse of the gifts as a way of demonstrating their superior status.³² All in all, it is a community that has lost its egalitarian moorings and has resorted back to the way things always were. External social pressures and the arrogance of some of the wealthier elite have driven a wedge between the rich and the poor in the community.³³ In addressing this division, Paul opens the letters with a blunt reminder of the type of community to which they belong. More pointedly, he reminds them

of the type of person that God is looking for and the type of person that God will honour. He does this with the use of three rhetorical triads found in 1 Corinthians 1:20–28.

Triad 1 (1 Cor 1:20)

The first triad is found in 1:20, where Paul asks rhetorically "Where is the one who is wise? Where is the scribe? Where is the debater of this age?" These three terms (*sophos*, *grammateus*, and *suzētētēs*) refer to the three main types of tertiary scholars in the Graeco-Roman world. Specifically, the rationalistic philosopher, the Jewish legal expert, and the rhetorician, respectively.[34] All three of these public figures were drawn from the highest levels of society, for the simple reason that only the wealthiest families could afford the necessary education to achieve this status.[35] In highlighting the fact that none of these figures are present in the community, Paul wants to remind the Corinthians that the teachers and those who hold authority in the Christian community are not to be found amongst the elite *sophoi*; in fact, a closer inspection will reveal that such men are virtually nowhere to be seen. Quite the opposite, the wealthy and elite of that world would have been repelled by what they saw in the Christian community. As Paul goes on to demonstrate, those of significance are an inversion of the world's expectations. The "elite" of the Christian community are the poor, the humble, and the fools of the world.

Triad 2 (1 Cor 1:26)

The second triad is found in 1 Corinthians 1:26. Here, Paul reminds them of their calling, pointing out that not many of them were wise (*sophoi*) according to worldly standards, nor were they powerful (*dynatoi*), nor were many of noble birth (*eugeneis*). These three terms (*sophos, dynatos,* and *eugenēs*) were all used to describe the members of the upper class, those who are distinguished by education, wealth, and birth.[36] The term *dynatos* in this passage had an economic sense and most likely referred to wealth and its associated power.[37] For example, Ps-Plutarch lists the various attributes that are honored by the society

> Good birth is a fine thing, but it is an advantage which must be credited to one's ancestors. Wealth is held in esteem, but it is a chattel of fortune. Repute is imposing, but unstable. Beauty is highly prized, but short-lived. Health is a valued possession, but inconstant. Strength is much admired, but it falls easy prey to disease and old age. But learning, of all things in this world, is alone immortal and divine. (*Lib. ed.* 5C–D)[38]

As we saw above, the *sophos* was the product of the highest levels of education. The financial means needed to achieve this were only available to the most-wealthy members of society. To be "powerful" (*dynatos*) was to have influence that resulted from wealth. One's "power" was the ability and privilege in society—typically in the form of political power—afforded to those of significant means.[39] Finally, those of noble birth (*eugeneis*) are those born into the most elite and powerful families.[40] Paul's use of the three terms here, in conjunction with "not many of you" (*ou polloi*), would seem to indicate the presence of at least a few of these wealthy and powerful elites in the church.[41] Nevertheless, Paul's point is that only very few of the Corinthians could lay claim to such titles. Put in opposite terms: "effectively, all but a few of you are poor." But, Paul goes on to tell them, it is precisely because of this humble station that God chose you.

Triad 3 (1 Cor 1:27–28)

The third triad is found in 1 Corinthians 1:27–28. The centrality of this passage and its importance in Paul's thinking is indicated by its clearly intentional composition.[42] The text contains three identical structures that create a paradox of low/high status with God and His purposes as the immediate center (following the Greek word order):[43]

> But the foolish (*ta mōra*) things of the world God chose,
> in order to shame the wise
> And the weak things (*ta asthenē*) of the world God chose,
> in order to shame the strong
> And the lowborn things (*ta agene*)
> And the despised things (*ta exouthenēmena*) God chose,
> The things that are not, in order to nullify the things that
> are

Paul first states that God chose the fools (*ta mōra*) of the world. In Classical Greek, the term *moros* denoted "a physical or intellectual deficiency in animals or men, in their conduct and actions, also in things. The word can refer to physical sloth or dullness, but its main reference is to the intellectual life."[44] The *moros* was the product of an absence of education and wealth and was deemed morally inferior and weak. Quintilian says that no one can concede intelligence to someone unless he is a good man. Since, then, "a bad man is necessarily a fool ... the fool will most assuredly never become an orator" (*Inst.* 12.1.4).[45] In other words, Paul says that God has chosen those of the most-humble social and economic stations; those of virtually zero standing in society.

He then says that God chose the weak things (*ta asthenē*) of the world. The term in classical Greek was typically non-ethical and had a broad range of usages, referring to physical, social or even metaphysical weakness; it was also a frequently used antonym to *dynamis*.[46] Weakness was a direct result of a lack of wealth, and, resulting from that, education. Epictetus suggests that every faculty acquired by the uneducated and the weak (*asthenēs*) is dangerous for them since it is prone to make them conceited and puffed up over it.[47]

Finally, Paul refers to those that are lowborn (*ta agene*). We have seen above the reference to the well-born as being a reference to those from the wealthiest families. The term also implies things that are base and insignificant.[48] He says that God has chosen the things that have been rejected (*ta exouthenēmena*). And, finally, refers to the majority with the catch-all term "those that are not" (*ta mē onta*), things that are to be regarded as if they do not exist.[49] The sum total of these terms corresponds to the "sharpest form of discrimination".[50]

In summary, the Christian community was called to be one that transcended social distinctions. It was meant to be a community that not only made space for the "Have nots" to participate, but it also went so far as to esteem them with honor and even empower them with equal status as the "Haves". It was a radical vision that was meant to overturn—at least in a localized setting—the typical values of its time. However, as we have seen, this vision—if it was ever fully realized at all—quickly bowed to social pressures and the community reverted to merely a microcosm of the broader society. In a similar manner, the radical, social upheaval of early Pentecostalism—if, as with the Christian community in Corinth, it ever fully realized the ideal—soon gave way to social pressures of its time. As Althouse and Waddell have noted

> The social reforms of Azusa were short lived. Cultural pressures of racism, sexism, classism, and nationalism impinged on the community from both secular sources and (unfortunately) from their fellow Pentecostals. The failure to maintain this newfound diversity resulted in racial segregation, the marginalization of women, and populist xenophobia and suspicion of multiculturalism, all of which continue to plague the global movement.[51]

Like the Corinthians, we Pentecostals face the constant challenge of keeping in view the radical ideals upon which we were established. The external cultural pressure to define ourselves along social, gender, and class lines are ever-present, as is the vulnerability to cultural blindness.

Cultural blindness

Discussing the way in which Pentecostalism within any particular country can reflect and be shaped by its own national concerns, Grey has recently challenged us of the blindness that comes through our cultural embeddedness. She reminds us that the concerns and fears that inform, in this context, our scholarship, are often localised and relevant only to the particular culture and geography of our location.[52] Our values as Pentecostals are often informed by concerns that have no relevance in any other place but our own.

This cultural blindness is also found at the local church level. This is particularly the case in smaller congregations, which tend to reflect the social profile of their immediate suburban location. To offer a personal example, I, like many Christians in a western country such as Australia, attend a church that is—for the most part—socially and economically homogenous. In my particular church, there is very little ethnic diversity (predominantly Anglo-Saxon) and probably all of the members fall into a middle-income bracket. Each of us lives in almost identical suburbs and own similar size and style of houses and cars. But this homogeneity is not due to some sort of intentional exclusivity. It is simply that our church is a cross section of the community in which we live.

This homogeneity would be the same in most smaller, local churches, ones in which the attendees all live within a short distance of the meeting place. The congregation would be a reflection of the local suburb in which it is found. Put another way, in my (our) daily lives, including church life, there is a tendency to be surrounded by those of similar social status. In this context, it is easy to lose sight of the radical effect that Pentecostalism can have on a community.

This cultural blindness can also take the form of historical blindness. That is, we too easily fall into the Ricardo-Malthusian Trap. We forget that in any given time, everywhere, except in parts of Europe and North America after the Industrial Revolution, the great majority of humanity has lived at a level at or near subsistence. Subsistence is the state where a family has only sufficient resources to pay taxes, to feed itself, and to replace such necessities as livestock and tools. Before the Industrial Revolution their material culture was ephemeral: their houses may not have had proper foundations or solid walls, they did not eat off delicate ceramic plates but durable wooden platters, and storage bins were more likely to have been mud plastered wicker than expensive ceramic jars.[53]

We (especially in the western world) can too easily imagine ancient communities and people as something like ourselves. At the very least, we have little understanding of what daily life was like for the people in the New Testament communities.

We have already seen the economic situation of the ancient world. Almost all of the citizens of that time existed at or near subsistence level. A typical family lived in a small dwelling of simple construction (often of perishable material such as timber or even grass) that functioned as both a place of residence and trade.[54] There was also no geographical separation of rich and poor. There were no "rich" suburbs and "poor" suburbs. What there were instead were communities in which the majority poor coexisted with the very few rich on whom they were completely dependent in patron-client relationships. This is what we need to picture when we think of the early Christian communities. That is, small gatherings of rich and poor in often cramped dwellings attempting to live out the ideals of this radical new community. For them, the issue was not that the rich and the poor were part of the same community; the issue, rather, was that the poor in this community held the same status as the rich. When Paul addressed his congregations, he addressed them as a single body or *ekklēsia* in which every part had equal standing.[55] Something that often proved impossible to live out.

This image of the ancient (Christian) community is more or less foreign to most of us in a western setting. It is therefore easy for us to view the New Testament Christians through the lens of our own culture. But in doing so, we lose sight of the reality and the radicalness of what they were called to be.

Conclusion

In summary, the radical transformation of communities and upheaval of social boundaries is at the heart of Pentecostalism. This vision of creating communities that are not defined by social status, ethnicity, or gender is one of the great features of our movement— at least at an ideological level. And as we have seen, it is something that closely aligns us with the earliest Christian communities that Paul envisioned. At the same time, it is also something that is easily forgotten or something we too easily lose sight of. Early Pentecostals, as with the first Christians, too quickly lost sight of this foundational value. Pressure to conform to societal norms and, in the case of Pentecostals, an overall cultural and historical blindness, has resulted in a drifting away from this original and radical ideal. The challenge for us is to always keep in view our origins as we seek to bring God's Kingdom to the world.

Bibliography

Althouse, Peter. "Waxing and Waning of Social Deprivation as a Model for Understanding the Class Composition of Early American Pentecostalism: A Theological Assessment." In *A Liberating Spirit: Pentecostals and Social Action in North America*, ed. Michael Wilkinson and Steven M. Studebaker. Eugene, Or: Wipf & Stock, 2010.

Althouse, Peter, and Robby Waddell. "The Transformation of Pentecostalism: Migration, Globalization, and Ethic Identity." In *Pneuma* 39:1–2. 2017.

Conzelmann, *First Corinthians*, 51; Dieter Sänger, "Die 'Dynatoí' in 1 Kor 1:26," *ZNW* 76 (1985), 290.

Downs, David J. "Economics, Taxes, and Tithes." In *the World of the New Testament: Cultural, Social, and Historical Contexts*, ed. Joel B Green and Lee Martin McDonald. Grand Rapids, MI.: Baker Academic, 2017.

Forbes, Christopher. *Prophecy and Inspired Speech: In Early Christianity and Its Hellenistic Environment*. Peabody, MA: Hendrickson, 1997.

Friesen, Steven J. "Prospects for the Demography of the Pauline Mission: Corinth among the Churches." In *Urban Religion in Roman Corinth: Interdisciplinary Approaches*, ed. Daniel N. Schowalter and Steven J. Friesen, HTS 53. Cambridge, MA: Harvard University Press, 2005.

Garland, David E. *1 Corinthians*, BECNT. Grand Rapids: Baker, 2003.

Garnsey, Peter, and Richard Saller, *The Roman Empire: Economy, Society and Culture*. London & New York: Bloomsbury, 2014.

Hock, Ronald F. "Paul and Greco Roman Education," in *Paul in the Greco-Roman World: A Handbook*, ed. J. Paul Sampley. Harrisburg, PA: Trinity Press, 2003.

Kay, William K. *Pentecostalism*. London: SCM Press, 2009.

Martin, Dale B. *The Corinthian Body*. New Haven: Yale University Press, 1999.

Millis, Benjamin W. "The Social and Ethnic Origins of the Colonists on Early Roman Corinth." In *Corinth in Context*, ed. James C. Walters, et al. Leiden: Brill, 2010.

Pettegrew, David K. "The Diolkos and the Emporion: How a Land Bridge Framed the Commercial Economy of Roman Corinth." In *Corinth in Contrast: Studies in Inequality*, ed. Steven J Friesen, et al. Leiden: Brill, 2014.

Sanders, G. D. R. "Landlords and Tenants: Sharecroppers and Subsistence Farming in Corinthian Historical Context." In *Corinth in Contrast: Studies in Inequality*, ed. Steven J. Friesen, et al. Leiden: Brill, 2014.

Stephenson, Lisa P. "Made in the Image of God: A Theological Reflection for Women Preachers." In *Toward a Pentecostal Theology of Preaching*, ed. Lee Roy Martin. Cleveland, TN: CPT Press, 2015.

Thiselton, Anthony C. *The First Epistle to the Corinthians*, NIGTC. Grand Rapids: Wm. B. Eerdmans Publishing Co., 2000.

Thomas, Christopher John. "Biblical Reflections on Women in Ministry." In *Toward a Pentecostal Theology of Preaching*, ed. Lee Roy Martin. Cleveland, TN: CPT Press, 2015.

White, Adam. *Where Is the Wise Man? Graeco-Roman Education as a Background to the Division in 1 Corinthians 1-4*, LNTS 536. London: Bloomsbury T & T Clark, 2015.

Winter, Bruce W. *After Paul Left Corinth: The Influence of Secular Ethics and Social Change*. Grand Rapids: Wm. B. Eerdmans Publishing Co., 2001.

Section Three

Living in the Spirit

Chapter 10

Spirit-Shift: Paul, the Poor, and The Holy Spirit's Ethic of Love and Impartiality in the Eucharist Celebration

Lisa Bowens

There is evidence of congregational division throughout 1 Corinthians. The members divided over issues such as apostolic personalities (1:12), the use of spiritual gifts (12:1-14:40), and weak and strong (8:7-13). Also, 1 Corinthians indicates that there were divisions among them around economic status—rich and poor—and that this split manifested during the observance of the Lord's Supper. Yet, Paul observes that the believers in Corinth were zealous about their spirituality.

The following questions are relevant: how could a Spirit-filled congregation like the Corinthian one be so full of divisions? How does Paul's admonitions to the Corinthians in their observance of the Lord's Supper speak to us today about the Spirit and issues of social justice, especially that of economic justice? This chapter will answer these questions by 1) providing a brief history of the city of Corinth; 2) reviewing Paul's "Spirit-speech"; 3) engaging in exegetical analysis of 1 Corinthians 11:17-26; and 4) delineating some contemporary reflections upon this exegetical analysis. It will conclude with some final thoughts on the meaning of Paul's words for the church today.

Corinth: An Urban Center

Corinth, located about forty to fifty miles from Athens, was a busy urban center in Paul's time. As a crossroads to the world, its wealth derived from goods and services to sailors, merchants, bankers, artisans, soldiers, and visitors to the Isthmian games. Corinth was, as S. J. Hafeman states, an "economic boomtown."[1] Despite its prosperity, however, the vast majority of the Corinthian population remained poor while a minority stayed wealthy. In this regard, the Corinthian congregation mirrored the city, for Paul writes in 1 Corinthians 1:26 that *not many were powerful, not many were of noble birth*," statements which provide insight into the makeup of the congregation.[2] Not many in this *ekklēsia* were wealthy or held high societal status; only a few could claim such a résumé. Along with a sizeable poor population, Corinth had a reputation for abuse of the poor by the rich. Indeed, the pericope 11:17-26 indicates that the wealthy believers in the Corinthian congregation continued this accepted societal practice of abusing the poor in their observance of the Lord's Supper. Yet Paul rebukes such actions and seeks to reframe the meaning of the Lord's Supper for his audience. He proclaims to them that God in the Christ event has liberated and transformed the world, and that the cross signifies a transformation of relationships and perception of the other, including those who are "not powerful" and not of "noble birth."

Paul's "Spirit-Speech"

Spirit speech permeates the epistle from the beginning of the letter to the end. Paul describes his preaching as not with eloquent words of wisdom but in demonstration of the Spirit (2:4), and how God reveals divine mysteries to believers through the Spirit (2:6-16). In

219

addition, he reminds the Corinthians that the Spirit lives in them asking, "Do you not know that you are God's temple and that God's Spirit dwells in you (3:16)?" Since the Spirit dwells in them Paul expects them to act like it and to cease following the ways of the world. The Spirit's advent makes a difference in the believer's life transforming the way they think, act, and perceive the world around them. We find that in this letter Paul narrates for the Corinthians what a life led by the Spirit is and is not. It is not a life led by the wisdom of this age (3:18), led by allegiance to apostolic personalities (3:4), or a life led by societal dictates, but rather a Spirit-led life speaks God's wisdom (2:7), realizes the inappropriateness of pitting human personalities against one another when God is the one who gives the increase (3:6-7), and views societal standards as not the same as God's expectations (1:20-29). As an apostle, Paul understands that just because the Corinthians have the Spirit and operate in the *charismata* of the Spirit (12:1-14:40) does not mean they know how to live out their Spirit experience on a daily basis, especially in light of the culture around them (e.g., 3:1-23). As his correspondence to them demonstrates, Spirit-filled people still need instruction, and Paul attempts to instruct them in this letter, revealing to them what a Spirit-possessed life looks like.

The Spirit's advent through the Christ event is part of God's divine invasion of the cosmos in which God liberates the world from the enslaving powers of Satan, Sin, and Death. Alexandra Brown observes, "That this invasion is inaugurated by the crucifixion of God's Son is cause for scandal, for it contradicts what the world recognizes as a powerful, saving gesture. Yet it is also the occasion for a transforming perceptual shift: in the cross one sees the love of

God entering into real battle with the 'rulers of this world (2:6)' for the sake of human beings."[3] As recipients of God's Spirit, the Corinthians are to bear witness to God's redemptive act in Christ and to reveal that a new creation now exists in the midst of the old age order, for this new creation follows a different vision than the world around them.

The "transforming perceptual shift" that Brown highlights has import for the Corinthians' behavior during the Eucharist. The abuses taking place during the Lord's Supper are symptomatic of the Corinthians not understanding who they are, not fully comprehending the transforming perceptual shift that has taken place in their lives and how they are to exhibit and live out this "Spirit-shift." They are no longer just Corinthians who live in Corinth, an "economic boomtown" but believers, part of the "church of God (1:2)" which means their identity as "saints" and "sanctified in Christ Jesus (1:2)" surpasses their societal status because such status remains tied to old age distinctions such as those predicated on wealth, personality, and human wisdom. Paul proclaims to them that these distinctions become null and void in the Corinthian assembly, for their identity as the temple of God (3:16), one body with many members reigns (12:12-31). In 11:17-26 Paul attempts to remind the Corinthians of who they are and the kind of people God and God's Spirit calls them to be and display to the world.

Exegetical Analysis: Abuse During the Eucharist

The pericope 11:17-26 begins with Paul's refusal to praise the Corinthians for their actions, for they do not adhere to the tradition that the apostle received and passes on to them. In fact, his statement that their coming together is for the worse and not the better emphasizes the harmful consequences of their behavior. Paul uses the term *synerchomai* ("come together," "assemble," "be united") in v. 17 and reuses the term 4 additional times in vv. 18 and 20. His repeated use of the word indicates his desire for a unified gathering, not a divided one. Richard Hays paraphrases what is taking place: "When [the Corinthians] come together as a church, they paradoxically do not 'come together' in unity and peace. Rather, their coming together merely makes things worse..."[4] In other words, they are assembling together in one place, but the assembly is anything but a cohesive one. Consequently, Paul's repetition of *synerchomai* censures such divisive behavior.

The fact that there are divisions when the Corinthians gather as an *ekklēsia* has great significance. The presence of *synerchomai* ("come together," "assemble," "be united"), *ekklēsia*, and *schismata* ("divisions") in v. 18 illustrate the great contrast between what the Corinthians are doing and what they are called to be. They are called to be the "church of God (1:2)," but due to their contentious behavior, they are not acting like it and so are not living out their true identity. The term *haireseis* ("factions") in v. 19 along with Paul's other statements in vv. 21-22 indicates that the *schismata* ("divisions") in v. 18 derive from social demarcations in which the community's economic disparities became particularly evident when they celebrate the Lord's Supper. Although they believe they are eating the Lord's Supper, Paul informs them in v. 20 that as a result of their divisiveness, they are not. For Paul, when the Corinthian assembly is full of factions, the meal that they eat is not a meal belonging to the

Lord because they destroy the character of the meal through their conduct.[5]

In v. 21 Paul gives his audience more information as to why he cannot praise them. Key words in v. 21 "each one" (*hekastos*), "take beforehand/consume" (*prolambanō*), combined with Paul's use of the verb "wait for" (*ekdechomai*; v. 33) allows for a probable reconstruction of what is taking place at Corinth. In Paul's day, the Eucharist celebration consisted of a communal meal, the blessing, and then the Lord's Supper. In Corinth, the wealthy, when gathering for the Lord's Supper, eat their own extravagant meals before the poor members arrive. Such behavior emphasizes the status issues of the congregation because only the wealthy members have the greater opportunity of arriving early or on time because they are not under restrictions from owners and employers like the members who are slaves and poor. In addition, when the poor do arrive two things are happening: a) they are being served smaller portions of lesser quality or b) they are not receiving anything at all because the food is gone by the time they get to the assembly. More than likely, some combination of the two is taking place, and it seems from Paul's words that (b) is becoming the norm since many are going hungry (v. 21). In addition, the phrases "each of you" (*hekastos*) and "own supper" (*to idion deipnon*) accents the individualistic nature of the rich Corinthians' behavior. Hence, Paul makes a striking contrast between the "Lord's Supper" and "one's own supper."[6]

It is also important to note that during this time sitting at the same table during meals did not automatically result in receiving the same food. In Greco-Roman society, it was customary for wealthy guests to receive better and larger portions than others sitting at the same table with them. While well-to-do guests have meals of higher quality, the poorer guests receive meager portions and food of lesser quality.[7] From Paul's censure, we can deduce that all of these Greco-Roman practices spilled over into the Corinthian *ekklēsia* where the wealthy make their status known by making sure they receive the best and largest portions and consume all the food. The apostle's statement that some are hungry may indicate that the only meal the "hungry" receive consists of the bread and wine belonging to the Lord.[8] As gentiles who have become believers, the Corinthians are treating the Eucharistic gathering just like any other Greco-Roman dinner party.[9] Such behavior, however, does not celebrate that in Christ all are one, regardless of social standing, but rather, continues divisions inherent in the old age. The wealthy's inconsiderate behavior results from not realizing that the church of God involves new practices, new customs, and a new way of being in the world.

Throughout the letter, Paul continues to remind the Corinthians of their new identity since they repeatedly engage in "pre-baptismal behavior."[10] Like the larger Greco-Roman society the Corinthians sue each other (6:1-11), accept the practice of seeing prostitutes (6:12-20), and sanction the eating of idol meat (8:1-13). The cultural norms that influence their behavior in these instances influence the Corinthians' behavior at the Lord's Supper. They follow old ways, which died in baptism and should no longer govern their actions.[11] Equally important is that Paul remained in Corinth for eighteen months which makes the possibility that he did not deal with such discordant issues around the celebration of the Eucharist during his time there highly unlikely (v. 23). He passes on a tradition to the Corinthians as he states in v 23, but unfortunately, as the reports he hears indicate, they no longer follow it. Stephen Barton sums up well the situation in Corinth:

> In relation to the common meal, it is clear that what should have been a ritual of incorporation and group solidarity as members together of the "one body of Christ" has degenerated into a ritual of social rivalry and competition threatening to split the fellowship apart (11:17-22). The rich householders distinguish themselves from the poor by the timing of their meal—they eat first and without waiting for the others to arrive (11:21, 33); by its quantity and quality (11:21); and by their refusal to share (11:21). In this way, the rich may be seen also as attempting to extend their influence in the church. Their eating practices are a demonstration of social status and an attempt to dominate by imposing shame (11:22).[12]

As indicated by the wealthy Corinthians' behavior, they continue to live by the values of the old age, where wealth and status become the preeminent markers of identity. Barton's comments also point out that the affluent members attempt to dominate the gathering, so Paul reminds them and the rest of the congregation that believers' identities do not derive from material possessions but the cross, which the Lord's Supper commemorates.

In v. 22 Paul poses a series of rhetorical questions aimed at the "haves"—those who have their own houses.[13] The first question expects a positive answer—of course, they have houses to eat and drink in. Why, then, do they come to an assembly whose purpose

225

involves unity, fellowship, and sharing if they are not going to do any of these things? Paul surmises that their actions are meant to despise the church of God, a charge he reveals in his second question. Paul utilizes the term *kataphroneō*, which means despise, a vivid term that indicates how strongly inappropriate Paul views these actions. For those Corinthians who really think nothing is wrong with their behavior and that they are in fact eating the Lord's Supper, Paul's language serves as a sharp rebuke.[14] Through their actions, they illustrate that the community God calls into being means nothing to them, for their willingness to continue divisions reveals that they value their social status more than God's plan of bringing all to unity in Christ.

Paul makes clear that the shame they bring upon the poor (the have-nots) is evidence of their contempt for God's church.[15] Those who "have nothing" stand in stark contrast to those who "have houses" and echoes the popular divide in Greco-Roman culture where distinctions between the wealthy and the poor appear in every facet of societal life.[16] Paul views the old age distinctions between bond/free, Jew/Greek, male/female, rich/poor as not decisive for those baptized in the Spirit (12:13; cf. Gal 3:28). Therefore, through his rhetorical questions and direct language, Paul reveals to the Corinthians that by shaming their brothers and sisters they are in fact shaming God.

The final two questions of v. 22 (cf. v. 34) evoke the relationship between Paul and the community. As their father (1 Cor 4:15; cf.; 2 Cor 11:2) he informs them that they are to share a communal meal, and if the rich have problems waiting for other members to arrive because they are hungry, then they should eat a meal at home to stave off their appetite before they gather together. In addition, if they feel that there may not be enough food to satisfy them fully once it is divided equally among all the members, then they should also eat something before they come. In this regard, when Paul admonishes them in v. 33 to wait (*ekdechomai*) for one another, he expects them to wait until all members of the *ekklēsia* have arrived and then to eat a common meal as a body of believers.

Paul faces the serious challenge of transforming the thinking of the Corinthian congregation. Hays calls Paul's assignment a "massive task of resocialization seeking to reshape the Corinthians moral imaginations."[17] The Corinthians' minds must be renewed to perceive and understand the new way of being that they are called to in this new age inaugurated by Christ. As believers, their identity is found in the cross by which the world is crucified to them and they have been crucified to the world (Gal 6:14). This is the tradition that Paul passes on to them, and this is the tradition he turns to in v. 23.

By recalling what he passes on to them, Paul endeavors to make the Corinthians recognize and understand the meaning of Jesus's death for the community and the difference his death makes for their fellowship. The two technical terms, *paralambanō* (receiving) and *paradidōmi* (handing over) form a dyad in Paul's admonition of the Corinthians (v. 23). By emphasizing that he received the tradition of the Lord's Supper from the Lord, Paul reminds the Corinthians that what he hands on to them does not originate with him and is therefore not his own directive, but a tradition that derives from the highest power— "the Lord."[18]

The verb *paradidōmi* (handing over) appears twice in v. 23 and can be translated as handed over or delivered, but most translations do not indicate that Paul repeats this verb. As a result, an important nuance is lost. In the first appearance of the word most translations use one of these phrases, "handed over" or "delivered." However, in the second occurrence of the term most translations read "betrayed," which tends to restrict the meaning to Judas's betrayal of Jesus.[19] Yet the way Paul uses this term in other instances indicates that more than Judas's action is meant here. In Rom 4:25 Paul employs the word to signify that Jesus was "handed over" to death by God for the sin of humanity and in Rom 8:32 he utilizes the word to illustrate that God handed Jesus over for all of us.[20] In light of these other occurrences, Hays' translation is appropriate: "On the night when God handed the Lord Jesus over to death for our sake he took a loaf of bread..."[21] Such an interpretation coheres with Paul's continuous depiction of Jesus's death as an act of obedience to God and not just an act perpetrated by Judas.[22]

Moreover, by incorporating this meaning into the passage, one glimpses echoes of Isaiah, "And the Lord gave him up for our sins" (53:6 LXX) and "On account of their iniquities, he was handed over" (53:12b LXX). And so, the Lord's Supper commemorates God handing Jesus over and Jesus's self-sacrifice. Thus, when the Corinthians observe the Eucharist, they partake in something bigger than themselves, God's liberating plan of salvation for humanity and the world foretold centuries earlier.

In vv. 24-25 Paul continues the narration begun in v. 23 in which Jesus takes bread and the cup while gathered with his disciples. Through the sharing of bread and cup, the supper confirms to the members that Christ's body is for all believers and that Christians have their primary identity as members of Christ's body.

228

Every time the Corinthians "do this in remembrance" of Christ, that is, taking the bread and cup, blessing it, breaking it, passing it, eating it, drinking it, and repeating what Jesus said during his last meal, they are, in fact, immersing themselves into Jesus's life and death. When the Corinthians tell the story of the Lord's Supper by participating in it, it becomes their own story by which they are transformed and renewed.[23]

Verse 26 demonstrates Paul's perspective that the nature of the Corinthians' communal life offers a mighty proclamation to the world concerning the purpose of Jesus's death. Through Jesus's death unity becomes possible among people whose economic and social circumstances differ. The verb *kataggellō* means "to proclaim" and is often used when describing a verbal proclamation toward outsiders. Paul uses it in this sense in Rom 1:8. Yet Paul's decision to use this word here speaks volumes. When the Corinthians observe the Eucharist they proclaim the message of the cross (2:1-2; cf.; 1:18, 23) through their actions and behavior. Again Hays:

> The proclamation of the Lord's death occurs not just in preaching that accompanies the meal; rather, the community's sharing in the broken bread and the outpoured wine is itself an act of proclamation, an enacted parable that figures forth the death of Jesus 'for us' and the community's common participation in the benefits of that death... The problem is not that they are failing to say the right words but that their enactment of the word is deficient: their self-serving actions obscure

the meaning of the Supper so thoroughly that it no longer points to Christ's death.[24]

The Corinthians' celebration of the Lord's Supper should have been the remembrance of a selfless act: Christ's death on behalf of others. Instead, the Lord's Supper becomes a means of promoting their own agenda. They are more concerned with affirming their status roles and positions than proclaiming the Lord's death. Only by loving and caring for each other, do the participants in the Eucharist really eat the Lord's Supper (v. 20) thereby proclaiming and honoring the salvation bestowed by Christ.[25]

The Holy Spirit's Ethic of Love and Impartiality: Contemporary Implications

This brief examination of the Corinthians' actions during the Eucharist and Paul's address of this situation has serious ramifications for today's church with regard to the Spirit's ethic of love and impartiality. Although the Corinthian congregation experienced dynamic *charismata*, such as speaking in tongues, prophecy, interpretation of tongues, and gifts of healing (12:1-14:40), the members still followed cultural customs where status based upon wealth was the norm. Believers today have to guard against similar tendencies to follow a culture that often contradicts God's call to live out the new creation. Likewise, the existence of Spirit gifts in a congregation does not automatically mean that a Spirit-led life follows such demonstrations of these gifts. A Spirit-led life, as Paul demonstrates in his harsh words to the Corinthians, includes acting justly and refraining from discriminatory acts. Indeed, Paul reminds the Corinthians repeatedly throughout the Corinthian correspondence to align their actions with their identity as Spirit-filled people (e.g., 2:6-15; 6:11-19; 2 Cor 1:22; 3:17-18).

Similarly, the existence of *charismata* in a congregation and the presence of members who can operate in these gifts do not mean that these gifts *replace* God's call to act justly. Spirit-filled believers need to exemplify actions and behavior aimed at justice and in their own lives exhibit the Spirit's concern for the least of these. Thus, those that speak in tongues utilize those tongues to speak out against injustice, those that prophesy, prophesy against prejudice, and those that have the gifts of healing employ those gifts to heal the many who suffer hurt and pain because of unjust systems. After all, the powers of Sin, Death, and Satan, which Christ defeated in the cross, are the sources of such injustices, and when Spirit-filled believers intentionally act against prejudice and discrimination they bear witness to the fact that the powers of darkness do not win.

As discussed above, it was normal in Greco-Roman society to abuse the poor and so the wealthy Corinthians may not have seen their behavior as problematic. After all, this was how Greco-Roman meals were often carried out. In our own society, how does the abuse of the poor take place? The perpetuation of inadequate housing, low wages, and poor education opportunities are only a few of the many ways in which abuse of the poor occurs. In addition, the common rhetoric regarding the poor such as labeling them as criminals, lazy, or dumb is another way in which abuse takes place. The church has to be mindful that it does not adopt the "normalized" ways of the world in its demonization of those "who have nothing" to use Paul's language. The church can advocate for better housing, fairer wages, and better education. It can also speak out against systemic practices that tend toward keeping the poor in poverty. Paul's censure of the Corinthians' behavior demonstrates that the poor matter to God and that they are just as important to God as those who have wealth. Since this is the case, then those led by God's Spirit need to embody this reality as well.

Interestingly, Paul appeals to tradition to speak out against the abuse taking place in Corinth. In our time when tradition is often under fire for being outdated and irrelevant, Paul provides an example of how traditions matter and how to use them to advocate for justice. His appeal to Jesus's words and to what was handed down to him, which he in turn hands down to the Corinthians, illustrates that the church has a legacy in its history to deal with injustice and to protest wrongs within and beyond the believing community. The church needs to learn about and then lift up these moments in our history so that we can employ the tools that are prevalent in our own faith.

God's invasion of the cosmos through the Christ event brings about a people filled with the Spirit, a body of people whose members are rich, poor, black, brown, white, Jew, Gentile, female, male, young, and old. Paul writes in 12:13: "For in the one Spirit we were all baptized into one body—Jews or Greeks, slaves or free—and we were all made to drink of one Spirit." As indicated in this verse, Paul often admonishes the Corinthians concerning unity whether through the imagery of the body or in his directives in 11:33 to wait (*ekdechomai*) for one another. The word "wait" (*ekdechomai*) can also mean welcome or accept. The semantic density of the term suggests that Paul has all of these meanings in mind. The wealthy

Corinthians are to wait, welcome, and accept the poorer members of the *ekklēsia* which will illustrate their preference for God's agenda not their own agenda of status and superiority. In addition, the *ekklēsia* should be the one place where its poorer members can feel welcomed, affirmed, and accepted. Although they may face abuse and neglect on the outside from the larger society, such an atmosphere should not exist in their gatherings with other believers. Likewise, when believers today come together, they too should be more concerned with God's agenda and not their own. God's concern for the poor, as Paul knew, filled the Old Testament prophetic literature and here too the apostle aligns his admonitions with his prophetic predecessors. In doing so, he reveals to the Corinthians and us the need to be aware that not just in words but in actions we demonstrate God's liberative call to the world. Proclamation is about oral preaching *and* actions.

When reading Paul's rebuke of the Corinthians' observance of the Eucharist, one may remark that the apostle's reprimand is quite harsh toward the wealthier members of the assembly. Yet Paul strives to instill a sense of solidarity within these members of the church. Because of their privilege, they can arrive at the gathering early and/or on time, whereas those who are poor or slaves cannot. The wealthy Corinthians, then, should use their status that affords them such privilege to wait, welcome, and accept their sisters and brothers, not shame them. Paul refocuses the Corinthians' vision from society's vision for them to God's vision for them. Whereas society divides them between rich and poor, emphasizing their differences, he endeavors to show them that they are deeply connected to one another regardless of status. Discerning the Lord's body (11:29) includes discerning the body and blood of Jesus in the Eucharistic meal, but it also includes discerning Jesus's body, which consists of the members of the *ekklēsia*. Jesus's body *and* the individual members that make up the body of Christ are intricately linked.

Paul's effort to instill solidarity in the assembly appears in 11:29,33 but occurs again in 12:23-26 and sums up his focus in 11:17-26:

> And those members of the body that we think less honorable we clothe with greater honor, and our less respectable members are treated with greater respect; whereas our more respectable members do not need this. But God has so arranged the body, giving the greater honor to the inferior member, that there may be no dissension within the body, but the members may have the same care for one another. If one member suffers, all suffer together with it; if one member is honored, all rejoice together with it.

Paul reminds the Corinthians and us that every time we celebrate the Eucharist we remember the Lord's solidarity with humanity and creation in its subjection to Sin and Death and so it follows that we too should have solidarity with those who need it most.

Reflections

This chapter demonstrates through an exegetical analysis of 1 Corinthians 11:17-26 the implications of the Corinthians' behavior during the Lord's Supper for their time and ours. Such an analysis underscores the strategic necessity of today's church to be intentional about its care for the poor and its refusal to blame the victim.

Julia Foote, famous for her Spirit empowered sermons and one of the few nineteenth century black female preachers, relates in her autobiography the treatment of her parents and other black Christians by the church. This excerpt, particularly because of its focus on the Lord's Supper, is worth noting:

> [My parents] made a public profession of religion and united with the M[ethodist] E[piscopal] Church. They were not treated as Christian believers, but as poor lepers. They were obliged to occupy certain seats in one corner of the gallery, and dared not come down to partake of the Holy Communion until the last white communicant had left the table...How many at the present day profess great spirituality, and even holiness, and yet are deluded by a spirit of error, which leads them to say to the poor and the colored ones among them, 'Stand back a little—I am holier than thou.'[26]

Foote's account of blacks' unjust treatment during worship and the Eucharist in which they had to sit in certain sections of the church and could not receive communion until all the white believers had been served, provides another illustration of how churches throughout history often capitulate to the prevailing cultural norms. In Corinth, the divisions at the Lord's table occurred between rich and poor, but here in this American congregation, divisions occurred around black and white. In every age and in every generation, believers face the recurring challenge of either rejecting society's polarities or adopting them. Both Corinth and Julia Foote's church demonstrate what happens when the church fails this challenge, when it neglects its call to be God's new creation, the witness to the divine inbreaking of God. Yet if the church is to remain true to its calling, to God's mission and purpose in the world, it will embrace the Spirit's ethic of love and impartiality and illustrate to the world the true power of the gospel to destroy divisions, to eradicate hate, to bring justice to the oppressed, and to impart God's love and healing. May God grant us a fresh outpouring of His Spirit and the courage to follow the Spirit's lead.

Bibliography

Barclay, John. "I Corinthians." Pages 1108-1127 in *The Oxford Bible Commentary*. eds., John Barton and John Muddiman. Oxford: University Press, 2001.

Brown, Alexandra. "The Gospel Takes Place: Paul's Theology of Power-in-Weakness in 2 Corinthians. *Interpretation* 52 (1998) 271-285.

Campbell, R. Alastair. "Does Paul Acquiesce in Divisions at the Lord's Supper?" *Novum Testamentum* 33 (1991), 61-70.

Collins, Raymond. *First Corinthians*. Sacra Pagina 7. Collegeville, Minnesota: Liturgical Press, 1999.

Conzelman, Hans. *1 Corinthians: A Commentary on the First Epistle to the Corinthians*. Hermenia. Trans. James Leitch. Philadelphia: Fortress Press, 1975.

Fee, Gordon. *The First Epistle to the Corinthians*. NICNT. Grand Rapids: Wm. B. Eerdmans Publishing Co., 1987.

Foote, Julia. "A Brand Plucked from the Fire: An Autobiographical Sketch by Mrs. Julia A. J. Foote" Cleveland, Ohio: W. F. Schneider, 1879. Repr. 161-234 in *Sisters of the Spirit: Three Black Women's Autobiographies of the Nineteenth Century*, ed. William L. Andrews. Bloomington: Indiana University Press, 1986.

Fowl, Stephen. "The New Testament, Theology, and Ethics." Pages 397-413 in *Hearing the New Testament: Strategies for Interpretation*, 2nd ed. Edited by Joel Green. Grand Rapids, MI: Wm. B. Eerdmans Publishing Co, 2010.

Gaventa, Beverly. *Our Mother Saint Paul*. Louisville, KY: Westminster John Knox Press, 2007.

Hafemann, S. J. "Letters to the Corinthians," Pages 164-179 in *Dictionary of Paul and His Letters*, Gerald Hawthorne and Ralph P. Martin, eds. Downers Grove, IL: InterVarsity Press, 1993.

Hays, Richard. *First Corinthians*. Interpretation: A Bible Commentary for Teaching and Preaching. Louisville: John Knox Press, 1997.

Lampe, Peter. "The Eucharist: Identifying with Christ on the Cross." *Interpretation* 48 (January 2001), 36-49.

Lowery, David K. "The Head Covering and the Lord's Supper in 1 Corinthians 11:2-34." *Bibliotheca Sacra* 143 (May 2001), 155-163.

Sampley, J. Paul. *First Letter to the Corinthians*. New Interpreter's Bible Commentary 10. Nashville: Abingdon Press, 2001.

Thiessen, Gerd. *The Social Setting of Pauline Christianity*. Edinburgh, 1983.

Chapter 11

Indictment of Partiality and Redirection (James 2:1-13)

J. Lyle Story

A few years ago, prior to the start of a class I was teaching, I sat with two adult learners and sought to engage them in conversation about their lives and their aspirations. They didn't know at that point that I was the professor of the course; I didn't want to approach them as such. One was fully engaged with me and warmly shared something about what had brought him to school and the other was cold and distant. I said to him, "Hi, I'm Lyle, what's your name?" and he mumbled his name, and never made eye contact with me. When I would ask a question, he either failed to answer or gave a blunt "yes" or "no," while he shuffled his papers and textbook, waiting for the professor to arrive. His eye was on the door and lectern so that he would be fully ready to be the model student when the professor should walk through the door to his station in the classroom. In many ways, I was treated as a non-person. When I stood up and introduced myself, welcomed the learners to the course, and began to lead in worship, this man's face whitened as he began to realize what he had done and not done in his initial encounter with me. I can only hope that this was a powerful teaching moment for him. Acts of favoritism emerge in countless ways.

James indicts his faith-community, Christians of the diaspora, for sins of partialities (plural) and redirects his audience to a new way of life, whether he addresses an unnamed community or several assemblies of Christian Jews living outside of Palestine (ταὶς ἐν τῇ διασπορᾷ 1:1); the word family, "partiality" occurs in both 2:1 and 2:9. Whether the actual setting is that of a worship service or a judicial setting within their meeting, the message remains the same, then and now.

I use socio-rhetorical criticism,[1] inter-textuality, and structure to suggest how James seeks to influence the communities to new attitudes and behavior that are inclusive. Special treatment of the rich is fundamentally wrong and James takes special care to substantiate why such attitudes and behavior are antithetical to the very nature of God, God's choice, Jesus' trust, the unitary role of Scripture, logic, experience, their own Christian identity and the royal law of love. James' community thinks, speaks and acts in ways that are contrary to their very identity.

Thus, James redirects his community, "thus continue to speak and act" (2:12) in an inclusive manner, supported through the Torah and Jesus' application of the Torah that brings genuine freedom. Since James' letter is intensively practical in nature, I include some real-life stories, both negative and positive, since "partiality" is expressed through innumerable faces in our day, whether seen through the lens of culture, achievement, education, position, race, gender, politics, or spheres of power. This is an important text, since the tension of the rich and poor is front and center in the Book of James. Our Evangelical and Pentecostal faith-communities need direction and training in how people must be treated in our communities. Every person, no matter what their condition, is of inestimable worth and needs to be treated as such with genuine inclusion and hospitality.

The Indictment (Theme[2] 2:1)

The initial charge is forceful, "My brothers (and sisters), stop holding the trust of[3] our glorious[4] Lord Jesus Christ with acts of favoritism" (James 2:1). The present imperative that is negated, "stop holding" (μὴ ... ἔχετε) suggests the cessation of some act that is already in progress.[5] This is both a statement of fact and also a statement of something that should not occur in James' community.

In the language of socio-rhetorical criticism, influence is central; James' negative imperative is intended to influence his readers to make a change, for, in the imperative, one will address another will.[6] James' discourse is community-based[7] and seeks to address "sins of partialities" to affect his readers, and most importantly to correct the core issue of special treatment for the powerful rich. The more general, "with acts of favoritism" (ἐν προσωπολημψίαις), is followed by one specific case of special treatment accorded to the rich at the expense of the poor (2:2). Such special treatment is antithetical to Jesus' trust in God and his will, which he consistently expressed through his faithful obedience. In particular, his impartial treatment of others is surely evident, whatever their condition might be, "a challenge that echoes the ministry of Jesus as recounted by the Synoptic Gospels."[8]

The singular noun, "act of favoritism" (προσωπολημψία 2:1) and the verb, "I show favoritism" (προσωπολημτέω 2:9) are not found in secular Greek but are based upon the compound from the LXX, "to receive/lift the face" (πρόσωπον λαμβάνειν), from the Hebrew,

נְשָׂא פָנִים. The Old Testament expressions can refer to respectful greetings or granting a request (Gen 19:21) but more frequently in negative contexts of favoritism. Such partiality contradicts the very nature of God, who is "impartial" (Deut 10:17— "he accepts no bribes"; (2 Chr 19:7)—"for with the Lord our God there is no injustice or partiality or bribery"). God calls upon his people to mirror his impartiality (Lev 19:15; Job 13:8, 10) with numerous prohibitions that are framed in judicial contexts (Deut 1:17; 16:19), especially in the Middle-Eastern language and culture of the "bribe" (Prov 6:35).

In accord with Old Testament thought, the writings of the New Testament and Apostolic Fathers underscore the gravity of this sin since God's very nature and actions are impartial: "God judges *impartially*" (ἀπροσωπολήμπτως 1 Pet 1:17); "for there is no *partiality* (προσωπολημψία) with God" (Rom 2:11); "for there is no *partiality* (προσωπολημψία) with him" (Eph 6:9); "there is no *partiality*" (προσωπολημψία Col. 3:25); "God is not *partial*" (προσωπολήμτης Acts 10:34); "you shall not *lift the face*, i.e. be *partial*" (οὐ λήμψῃ πρόσωπον Did 4:3; Barn 19:4); "keeping away from all ... *partiality*" (προσωπολημψίας Pol 6:1); "do all things *without partiality* (ἀπροσωπολήμτως 1 Clem 1:3); "the Lord judges the earth *without partiality*" (ἀπροσωπολήμτως Barn 4:12).

Indeed, in Jesus' person, words, and works, he is fully inclusive in his approach with all people in their countless stations and life conditions. Even his opponents, who to try to entrap Jesus, affirm, "You are not influenced by others for you do not look at the face of men" (οὐ γὰρ βλέπεις εἰς πρόσωπον ἀνθρώπον Matt 22:16; par. Mark 12:14; Luke 20:21). Although the term "partiality" is not used in the Sermon on the Mount, the idea of God's impartiality is implicit in Matt 5:43-48, for "God causes the sun to shine on the evil and good and sends rain upon the righteous and unrighteous alike" (Matt 5:45). Jesus says that the people of God are to mirror God's impartial attitude and behavior. Impartiality is the way that they can become sons and daughters of your heavenly Father (Matt 5:45) and can become "complete" (τέλειοι) as your heavenly father is "complete" (Matt 5:48). The same paragraph dealing with God's impartiality in Luke's Sermon on the Plain concludes with, "Be merciful (οἰκτίρμονες) as your Father is merciful" (Lk 6:36).

For James, acts of favoritism, special treatment, or partiality are totally contradictory to Jesus' trust in God, expressed in his countless impartial encounters with others in terms of ethnicity, gender, socio-economic condition, power, politics, station, religious condition, or status within the community. For Jesus, these conditions and labels don't matter as he personally interacts with individuals and groups. James' "theme ... introduces contraries, two incompatible courses of action: one honorable, the other honorable."[9]

Central Figures in the Indictment

The more general indictment of "acts of favoritism" is followed by one case that substantiates the censure. In his argument, James draws attention to both individuals and groups and what they do in a social setting; communal relationships are central:[10]

The Community (the Elect Poor)
- "your gathering" (συναγωγὴν ὑμῶν 2:2)
- "My brothers" (Ἀδελφοί μου 2:1)

- "my beloved brothers" (Ἀδελφοί μου ἀγαπητοί 2:5)
- "the poor" (ὁ πτωχός 2:5)
- "God chose the poor in the eyes of the world" (ὁ θεὸς ἐξελέξατο τοὺς πτωχοὺς τῷ κόσμῳ 2:5)
- "rich in trust" (πλουσίους ἐν πίστει 2:5)
- "heirs of the Kingdom" (κληρονόμους τῆς βασιλείας 2:5)
- recipients of the promised Kingdom (ἧς ἐπηγγείλατο 2:5)
- "they love him (God)" (τοῖς ἀγαπῶσιν αὐτὸν 2:5)
- "the excellent name, which is invoked over you" (τὸ καλὸν ὄνομα τὸ ἐπικληθὲν ἐφ᾽ ὑμᾶς 2:7).[11]

James underscores their real identity in a pastoral manner ("beloved brothers"). Like the poor, they are recipients of God's choice and manifold blessings. Wachob comments, "the audience elicited here are persons who are capable of becoming mediators of change by not 'showing partiality' 2:1, 9; 2:8, 13)."[12] James doesn't want them to forget all of the benefits, which have been accorded to them by God in a context of love and divine ownership. They are not to overlook whose they are and their privileged condition (present and future) even in the midst of poverty and oppression.

Dibelius is correct when he says, "The more piety was understood as humbling oneself before God's will, the more poverty could function as intrinsically fertile soil for poverty. As a result, 'poor' and 'pious' appear as parallel concepts (Psa 86:1f; 132; 15f), and the typical enemy of the poor is also the enemy of God (Psa 109:31)."[13]

Bruce Malina, with others, contextualize James' argument in the cultural codes and social scripts (both verbal and non-verbal) in the era of the New Testament world. These cultural-social scripts include honor, limited goods, and patron-client relationships.[14] Honor and its opposite, shame, are deeply embedded in the culture, and are spelled out in terms of goods one possesses or doesn't possess, and how patrons and clients relate. The idea of limited goods relates to the poor, who lack the bare necessities of life or who live a "hand-to-mouth" existence and are dependent upon daily wages for survival ("Do not hold back the wages of hired hand till morning" (Lev 19:13b); "Look, the wages you failed to pay the workmen who mowed your fields are crying out against you ..." James 5:4b).

The poor also include the imprisoned, blind, deaf, lame, those who hunger and thirst, and society's vulnerable people, such as widows and orphans (1:27). "These adjacent descriptions of the poor point to the 'poor' as one who has undergone some unfortunate personal history or circumstance."[15] They are non-elites and powerless. As Wachob states, the patron-client relationship was in one sense a way of dealing with limited goods... in networks of individuals characterized by inequality and asymmetry in power and status."[16] Thus, in James' paragraph, special honor is accorded to the gold-fingered man with splendid clothing as a patron, with the implicit script of reciprocity that he might bestow on the community, either with goods or services. Accorded honor to a patron by the client (the Elect Poor) belongs to the social script of the New Testament world. In some way, the clients would stand to benefit by the patron's special treatment. This social structure and ethos were accepted, normal, and presupposed. Although the Book of James is Jewish Christian, the argument counters the Greco-

Roman culture with its explicit and implicit codes and scripts for both patrons and clients.

To be sure, James' readers are economically poor, "poor in the eyes of the world"; they are the non-elites, but James adjusts the perspective to the Jewish piety of the poor. Through the full paragraph, James assumes that his readers, for the most part, are poor, and can be collectively labeled as the Elect Poor, which includes the gold-fingered man dressed in shining clothes[17]; he is not given the title, "the rich." Thus, the poor community is rich in trust, loves God, has been chosen by God, and enjoys God's promise of the Kingdom of God. James wants his readers to hear the voice of Jesus, which parallels God's voice. From James' perspective, the poor are known by their true identity.

The Rich

- "the rich exploit you (beloved brothers)" (οἱ πλούσιοι καταδυναστεύουσιν ὑμῶν 2:6)
- "they themselves haul you into court" (αὐτοὶ ἕλκουσιν ὑμᾶς εἰς κρητήρια 2:6)
- "they themselves blaspheme the excellent name invoked over you" (αὐτοὶ βλασφημοῦσιν τὸ καλὸν ὄνομα τὸ ἐπικληθὲν ἐφ' ὑμᾶς 2:7).

Clearly the rich are socially aggressive and abusive to the beloved brothers and religiously hostile to God in their blasphemy against the excellent name. They are characterized by their antagonistic behavior both to the Elect Poor and to God; contrary to the poor, the rich are known here by their aggressive behavior—not their identity.

As a category, the term, "rich," means more than their simple economic status, but the term conveys an elite status, governed by excess, greed, a defensive posture of maintaining or furthering their wealth—at the expense of the poor, since goods are limited.[18] In Middle Eastern culture, honor belongs to "the rich." Rich is a moral term—not simply an economic statement, for in James 5:1-7, James goes to great length to narrate the depravity of the rich in moral terms: trust in perishable items (clothing, gold, silver); hoarding wealth; holding back wages; luxury; self-indulgence; condemning and killing innocent people. The language of 5:1-7 more fully describes the aggressive attitudes and behavior of the rich, which James expresses in 2:6.

Divine Persons
- "our glorious Lord Jesus Christ" (τοῦ κυρίου ἡμῶν Ἰησοῦ Χριστοῦ τῆς δόξης 2:1)
- "God chose" (ὁ θεὸς ἐξελέξατο 2:5)
- "he (God) promised" (ἐπηγγείλατο 2:5)
- "him (God)" (αὐτόν 2:5)
- God is the own who invokes (τὸ ἐπικληθὲν) the excellent name over the beloved brothers (2:7)
- God is the one who prohibited adultery and murder (ὁ γὰρ εἰπών 2:11)
- God is the one who will judge (κρίνεσθαι 2:12)
- Divine retribution (ἀνέλεος) falls on the one without mercy (2:13).

God, paired with the glorious Lord Jesus Christ, chooses the poor, promises and bequeaths his Kingdom, invokes his excellent name over them in the context of a loving relationship. At the same time, God is a judge who makes demands on his people and possesses the right to judge law-breakers. He is the real Patron.

A Specific Case of Partiality (Reason or Ratio[19] 2:2-4))

James singles out one particular case of partiality that is dominated by extreme contrasts in a lengthy conditional sentence. This rationale provides the reason for the indictment in 2:1. The protasis (if-clause) is found in 2:2-3 with the stinging apodosis (then-clause) in 2:4:

Protasis

[2] For if a man

    wearing a gold ring

        and

    splendid clothing

                comes into your assembly,[20]

        and

    a poor man

    in filthy clothing

              also comes in,

               [3] and

if you pay attention[21]

    to the one who wears the splendid clothing

      and say,

        "You sit here in a good place,"

while you say to the poor man,

"You stand over there,"

or,

"Sit down at my feet,"

Apodosis

⁴ have you not then become divided²² among yourselves

and

become criminally minded judges²³?

The conditional sentence is rhetorical, for the question with the Greek negative ("not") οὐ in 2:4 assumes the positive answer, "Of course! You have become divided and are regarded as criminally minded judges." It is important that the key verbs in the conditional sentence are plural; the community as a whole is indicted in a social setting.²⁴

The stark contrasts are initiated by the entrance of two people in the gathering. Initially, there is the contrast in apparel: a gold ring/splendid clothing²⁵—poor man with filthy clothing; paying special attention—no attention; two forms of saying: "You sit in a good place—here"—"You stand over there" or "Sit down at my feet." James contrasts their clothing, their appearance, and their treatment by the poor community; even the disparities between seating arrangements and the adverbs, "here" and "there," are telling.²⁶

Some scholars view this event as: "an example and not a special case ... without any concern for its reality;"²⁷ "a hypothetical example of the kind of behavior he warns against;"²⁸ "an imaginary situation"²⁹; "an artificially contrived picture."³⁰ However, there are several indications in the paragraph that point to a familiar scene that troubles James: 1) the strong language throughout the paragraph; 2) the frequent present indicative verbs (2:4, 6, 7)—"an iterative case in the present time"[31]; 3) the gnomic aorists, "you have become divided" (διεκρίθητε 2:4), "you have become" (ἐγένεσθε 2:4), "you dishonored" (ἠτιμάσατε). Martin states, "The ... situation ... where the rich oppress and insult the poor—surely depicts an actual happening in James' church, and it makes little sense to combine reality (vss. 4-7) with a hypothetical example."[32]

What is the specific scene in question? Traditionally, the paragraph has been understood to refer to a worship service in which partiality would be expressed through someone one, e.g. an "usher," with tacit approval from a leader, who directs the two visitors (perhaps new converts) to a particular seating arrangement within the worshipping community.[33] The explanation for the choice of "visitors" would then be based upon the need to direct the two people to places within the gathered community. Why would frequent participants in the gathered community need to be told where to be seated?

On the other hand, Roy Bowen Ward has produced a compelling article, with substantial evidence from rabbinic texts that point to partiality in judicial proceedings.[34] The many references that Ward provides "indicate a concern lest the difference in apparel should lead to partiality and hence unjust judging, and it condemns the practice of having one litigant stand and the other sit as an instance of unjust judging and partiality."[35] This would then mean that these are two regular persons of James' community who are at legal odds and the Christian "synagogue/gathering" (συναγωγή 2:2) weighs their respective cases. Ward's approach has been followed by

251

many scholars, noting parallels with Matthew 18:15-20; 1 Cor 6:1-6.[36] Still, others have given extensive investigation into the man with the "gold ring," as an allusion to Roman senators and equestrians, of the ruling elite.[37]

In terms of the actual charge, the indictment of partiality remains the same whatever the setting. As Keck observes about the poor in this setting, "Their weakness is not a wistful recollection of previous wealth which they gave up when they became "the Poor" but their tendency to honor the rich more than is really warranted or proper."[38] Preferential treatment of the powerful rich at the expense of the poor is wrong, for it is the antithesis of Jesus' trust (2:1); His trust in God was fully hospitable to all people in all walks of life. James takes up the important issue of hospitality with the example of the prostitute Rahab, who was fully hospitable to the two Jewish spies (2:25); her trust was expressed in her hospitable reception and protection of them.

Substantiation for Why Partiality is Wrong (2:5-11 Probatio)

Proof 1: God's choice (2:5). Through more rhetorical questions, James provides further reasons why preferential treatment is wrong. "Of course, God chose the poor in the eyes of the world[39] to be rich in trust and heirs of the Kingdom, which God promised to those who love him" (2:5). James prefaces his rhetorical question with winsome language, "My beloved brothers." In terms of the rhetorical setting, James says that partiality flies in the face of God's choice[40] of the poor; that is what James wants his readers and community to see. They contradict God's very nature of impartiality; James intends that his readers appreciate God's activity of choosing the poor, by making them rich in trust, heirs of the Kingdom (both present and future) and recipients of God's promise in a loving relationship.

The two aorist verbs, "he chose" (ἐξελέξατο) and "he promised" (ἐπηγγείλατο) are in the middle voice and suggest God's own personal volition. He involves himself in the new relationship with people. The combination of the two verbs implies that God is both the initiator ("chose") and the guarantor ("promised") of the new relationship in a context of love.

Inter-textuality is important in that James alludes to Jesus' sayings without direct literary dependence, for five Christian quotes connect "the poor" (οἱ πτωχοί) with "the Kingdom" (ἡ βασιλεία), four of which are framed as beatitudes (μακάριος Matt 5:3; Luke 6:20b; Pol. *Phil.* 2:3; Gos. Thom. 54). Within a rhetorical culture, Vernon Robbins argues that the "repetition of words and phrases in a document regularly is the result of 'recitation composition' rather than 'copying.'"[41] All combined, the sayings affirm the promise of the "Kingdom" to the "poor."[42] Thus, the saying echoes the voice of Jesus and Jesus' trust that aligns with God's attitude and will for the poor.[43] Wachob suggests, "It is reasonable to believe that the author assumes that the Christians he addresses knew (in some form or other) the saying of Jesus he exploits in James 2:5."[44] Further, the promised Kingdom is not simply relegated to the future, but a present reality, "yours is the Kingdom of God (heaven)."[45]

Before further proof for why partiality is wrong, James again indicts the community, "But you (emphatic) have dishonored/insulted the poor" (ὑμεῖς δὲ ἠτιμάσατε τὸν πτῶχον 2:6), the very ones that God chose, who are rich in trust, and are recipients of the Kingdom, and live in a loving relationship with God. James' community has bought into the world's system by according honor bestowed upon the patrons—not the clients (the community).

Rose started Columbia Road Health Services (CRHS), a free clinic for the homeless, unemployed, and working poor in Washington DC, and later the Washington DC ministry for Health Care for the Homeless (HCH). After years of working with the homeless, the entire staff felt the need for a place where homeless men could recover. As Rose walked to the CRHS, she passed an abandoned home that had become a crack-house and a haven for the addicted. Every day for three years, she and her fellow nuns stopped in front of the house to pray, convinced that a respite care facility would replace the crack-house.

Soon a few thousand dollars came in and was earmarked for the purchase and restoration of the house. One day Rose's pastor, Gordon Cosby, called concerning a lady wanting to donate in person. Rose asked Gordon to thank the lady, accept the donation, and inform her that she was too busy to come. But Gordon insisted, and Rose came to his office to meet her. They chatted for a bit and Rose wondered how long the discussion would continue. Then the woman said she wanted to offer a donation and hoped it would help fund the project. The two-million-dollar check was enough for the purchase price, extensive renovation, and operating expenses for six months! It became Christ House, a respite care facility for homeless men, offering a warm, clean, and safe place while they recover from serious illness and prepare for employment.

Commitment, compassion, and prayer by Rose and the nuns were effective. However, we note a silent partiality concerning the woman's begrudging welcome; surely the reception would have been markedly different if Rose knew the dollar amount of the gift.[46]

Proof 2: Experience and Logic (2:6). The rhetorical questions in 2:6 also expect a positive answer in terms of what the rich do, "Of course, this is the way that they (emphatic) treat you." James appeals to the community's experience and expresses his argument with three strong present verbs, used in the iterative sense, "they exploit" (καταδυναστεύουσιν ὑμῶν), "they themselves haul" (αὐτοὶ ἕλκουσιν), "they themselves blaspheme (αὐτοὶ βλασφημοῦσιν 2:6). From their experience, James appeals to the illogical nature of what the community is doing by providing special treatment of their very oppressors. Perhaps the forceful appeal to experience might be expressed in our current idioms, "Why would you even think to act in this way? It makes no sense."

Proof 3: The Torah and the love-commandment (2:8-9). In his rhetoric, James then appeals to the royal law (νόμος βασιλικός), which broadly applies to the Torah, through two contrasting conditional sentences:

"If you really keep the royal law   you are doing well.

But if you show partiality   you sin" (2:8-9).[47]

In the context of 2:1-13, the first conditional sentence is not true in James' community; it is adversatively noted through the contrasting conjunctions, "really" (μέντοι) and "but" (δέ). Yes, both commandments are true, but in James' community, the first conditional sentence is not true; perhaps the language is sarcastic, for they are guilty of partiality and are indicted as such.[48] At the same time, the conditional sentence can be hopeful, for this is where James seeks to convert his community—to practice the royal law, and consequently, do well. He reverses the patron-client network of relationships. Wachob states, "the conflict between the powerful and the powerless is not merely between insiders and outsiders. It is being replicated in the interpersonal relationships of the elect community itself."[49] This prepares for the important conclusion in 2:12; by being impartial, his community will do well.

The law is royal, "so called probably not because of its transcending significance ... but because it is given by the king (of the Kingdom of God 2:8)."[50] Thus, "obedience to the 'love commandment' fulfills the royal law, which refers to the entire will of God, especially as revealed in the teaching of Jesus."[51] Moo's argument is similar, "James' suggestion that the love command stands at the heart of the New Testament ethical code goes back, of course, to Jesus' teaching."[52]

Intertextuality emerges again as James appeals to the quote from Lev 19:18, "You shall love your neighbor as yourself."[53] This quote is from a paragraph in Leviticus that also contains the prohibition against partiality, specifically in a similar contrast of treatment in a judicial setting. Partiality equals injustice and stands as the opposite of judging fairly:

"Do not pervert justice;
Do not show   partiality against   the poor (οὐ λήμψῃ
                                                πρόσωπον πτῶχου)

              Or
              favoritism to   the powerful
                                                (θαυμάσεις πρόσωπον
                                                δυνάτου)

              but
judge your   neighbor
              fairly" (Lev 19:15)

In both imperatival futures, the term "face" is used for partiality, special treatment, or favoritism in a judicial setting— judging, the very attitude and behavior that James later decries (James 3:11-12), for there is only one lawgiver and judge. Luke Timothy Johnson argues, "Where we can show a cluster of allusions from one document to another, it is easier to argue for the probable presence of other allusions in passages which, considered alone, might seem at first unlikely candidates."[54] James' allusion here to Lev 19:15 falls in line with the mention of law and judgment in James 2 (4 occurrences in James 2:8, 9, 11, 12, 13).[55]

257

Leviticus 19 follows the holiness code (Lev 11-18) with relational and financial concerns (19:11-18); that is to say that holiness is not simply a matter of ritual holiness but relational holiness that is expressed in social contexts in this paragraph. We discover the use of neighbor 5X, vulnerable (hired hand, deaf, blind, poor) 5X, brother 1X, sons of your people 1X. The paragraph is punctuated by the expression, "I am the Lord your God" 4X and the divine name 2X.

Although Michael D. Fiorelli argues for the centrality of holiness in the Book of James, holiness per se doesn't dominate James' argument. Fiorelli does make the important point that "the purity laws in Leviticus 19 have the effect of broadening the concerns of holiness to every level of relationship. The mandate to love one's neighbor is situated in the middle of a chapter addressing communal holiness."[56] There can be no holiness without love. In Matthew's paragraph about the greatest commandment, Jesus says that the dual love commandment is the commandment upon which all of the other commandments "hang/depend/find their fulcrum" (κρεμάννυμι), "as a door hangs on its hinges, so the whole Old Testament hangs upon these two commandments."[57]

The antithesis of the love commandment is expressed as a social partiality, which renders the community[58] as sinners and its natural consequence, "being convicted by the law as law breakers" (ἐλεγχόμενοι ὑπὸ τοῦ νόμου ὡς παραβάται 2:9b). By adopting the patron-client relationship, the community has adopted the world's system. Thus, James argues that the adverse of partiality is the central love commandment.

Through his indictments of his community and his proofs, James seeks to shame his readers to influence, change, alter, and convert them to the new way of life of equal treatment of all, each of whom "has been made in God's likeness" (τοὺς καθ᾿ ὁμοίωσιν θεοῦ γεγονότας 3:9); each person, whether rich or poor, is of inestimable worth.

Proof 4: The unitary aspect of God's law (2:10-11). The opening conjunction, "for" (γάρ) explains why a partial community can be labeled as "lawbreakers/lawbreaker" (παραβάται 2:9; παράβητης 2:11). In short, James' readers cannot pick and choose which commandment they cherry-pick to follow, for the royal law is a whole and expresses the way of life for the people of God.[59]

Intertextuality surfaces again as James appeals to the Decalogue with the two prohibitions of adultery and murder (Ex 20:13-14; Deut 5:17-18), topics taken up by Jesus and internalized as he addresses the people of God (Matt 5:21-22, 27-30). James explains ("for" γάρ) to his readers that these prohibitions are not simply texts to observe and notice, but that God (and Jesus) stand behind these prohibitions, "for he who said ... said" (ὁ γὰρ εἰπών ... εἶπεν 2:11). While Martin raises the possibility of actual murder,[60] it is more likely that James appeals to assumptions already accepted by his community that both murder and adultery are wrong. His readers would already know that they cannot pick and choose which of these two commandments can be kept and which mandate they can break and be innocent; for his readers, this is nothing new—the argument is self-evident. James says that stumbling with one commandment is tantamount to breaking the entire law, for the law is unitary (Deut 27:26) and is given by one lawgiver. Again, the voice of Jesus echoes from the Sermon on the Mount, "smallest letter ... least stroke

...anyone who breaks one of the least of these commandments" (Matt 5:17-20).

James forces his readers to grapple with the reality that favoritism to the rich and powerful at the expense of the poor is equally reprehensible to God and Jesus' trust as murder and adultery. No one can say, "I haven't murdered or committed adultery and demonstrate partiality and be innocent." Such persons are "guilty of all" (πάντων ἔνοχος 2:10), "convicted by the law" (ἐλεγχόμενοι ὑπὸ τοῦ νόμου 2:9), "law-breakers/a law breaker" (παραβάται 2:9; παραβάτης νόμου 2:11), "judgment without mercy" (2:13). By pointing the finger at special treatment in a social setting, James underscores the severity of favoritism. His readers cannot play fast and loose with this prohibition.

Although James approaches his community in a pastoral manner, he is thoroughly honest in his indictment, for the Elect Poor possess attitudes and behave in ways that are contrary to their real identity. He piles on numerous negative statements throughout the paragraph in the hope that his people will convert to true piety: "stop combining acts of partiality that stand counter to Jesus' trust" (2:1); a particular case of partiality in the community—expressed through graphic contrasts (2:2-3); "you have become divided against yourselves" 2:4a; "you have become criminally minded judges" (2:4b); "you have dishonored/insulted the poor" (2:5); a muted doubt that his readers actually fulfill the royal law (2:8); "if you show favoritism" (2:9a); "you commit sin" (2:9a); "convicted by the law" (2:9b); "law breakers" (2:9b); practicing a part of the law (2:10-11); "a law breaker" (2:11); "without mercy" (2:13).

All of these statements build with cumulative force, exposing his Elect Poor to the fact that they are thinking and acting in ways that are contrary to their true identity as "my brothers" (2:1), "my beloved brothers" (2:5), "chosen by God" (2:5), "rich in trust" (2:5), "heirs of the Kingdom" (2:5); recipients of the promise (2:5); they live in a loving relationship with God (2:5).

By their preferential treatment of the powerful rich, they have adopted the world's standards (2:5), and sided with the rich who oppress, haul them into court, and blaspheme the excellent name by which they are called. They are owned by God and yet, their attitudes and behavior are antithetical to that very name.[61] These things really concern James and he wants his readers to be concerned about the same attitudes and action. He wants to influence his readers to avoid selling-out to the world's system and be genuinely Christian in thought and action.

Conclusion (conclusio 2:12-13)

James brings his community-oriented rhetoric to his central exhortation:

"Thus   continue to speak

                    and

thus continue to act

                    as

those who are about to be judged

                              through the law

                                        that brings freedom" (2:12).

The repeated adverb, "thus" (οὕτως)[62] looks back to the central thrust of James' argument about favoritism. Since partiality is so wrong, thus "continue to speak" (λαλεῖτε) and "continue to act" (ποιεῖτε) without special treatment accorded to the powerful rich; the present imperatives are significant. This is the redirection that James intends that his readers adopt, internalize, and practice; the entire argument builds with cumulative force to this exhortation. Anything short of this leads to breaking the law. Previous shaming of his community must lead to social reform and corporate solidarity that includes both the wealthy and the poor. This is to be the ongoing lifestyle of the people of God. Speaking and acting reveal deep-seated attitudes of the heart. In the previous indictment and case, partiality had been expressed by both speaking and acting in contrary ways to the gold-fingered man and the poor man. Simply put, they cannot speak in contrasting ways to people in their community based upon appearance and status.

James intends that his readers reverse their attitudes, speech, and behavior and convert to a new way of life; his message is counter-cultural[63] and subversive. Thus, the new way of life must cohere with their very identity as the people of God, which he has clearly accentuated. John H. Elliot views the previous contrasts as "the rhetorical mechanism for combining a description and diagnosis of the negative situation with positive teaching concerning its reversal."[64]

To underscore the importance of continued attitudes, speaking, and acting, James counter-balances judgment with freedom. The participle with the passive infinitive, "about to be judged" (μέλλοντες κρίνεσθαι) points to a certain future action in view. Judgment relative to partiality/impartiality that occurs through the law also leads to genuine freedom. Earlier, James argued for "the perfect law (νόμον τέλειον) that gives freedom" that leads to blessedness (1:25).[65] The community possesses freedom but not a selective freedom with God's commandments. Words and deeds matter, which "suggests that the quality of that judgment corresponds to the quality of one's actions, a suggestion that verse 13 confirms."[66]

In 2:13, the conjunction, "for" (γάρ) explains more specifically the dual mention of judgment and freedom, "For judgment is merciless to the one who has shown no mercy, yet mercy triumphs over judgment."[67] In the context, a "lack of mercy" is equated with favoritism to the powerful rich at the expense of the vulnerable poor and leads to its consequence—a merciless judgment. Such divine judgment may be both present and eschatological.

At the same time, James concludes with a hopeful note, "yet mercy (impartiality) triumphs over judgment." Again, the voice of Jesus is heard through James, "Blessed are the merciful for they shall receive mercy (by God)" (Matt 5:7). As Dyrness says, "Mercy boasts, glories, or triumphs over judgment. That is, mercy does not merely vindicate itself, it is able to triumph."[68] James is thoroughly pastoral and encouraging even in the midst of shedding light on the community's behavior, indicting them for acts of partiality, and proving to his readers why they are acting in ways that are contrary to the trust of Jesus (2:1). James believes in their best, desires that they think, speak, and act in ways that are consistent with their true identity, and concludes with a hopeful note.

As a whole, this paragraph prepares for the next paragraph, in which James contrasts genuine trust with a practical atheism in the case of a hungry brother and sister without clothes (2:14-26). For James, genuine trust and action are inseparable, "faith without works is dead" (2:17). Mercy (2:13), surely includes a compassionate response to those in need.

Implications

For Evangelical and Pentecostal communities, the implications are far reaching. To be sure, our faith communities must fight against the hiatus between the rich and poor in community life and lifestyle. At what point does contentment with necessities spill over into excess? How hospitable are faith-communities to a homeless prostitute? How do our faith communities respond to the urban poor? David P. Nystrom applies James' message to the ghetto, "Drug dealers ... are people of 'substance' because they have money, women, and material goods ... 'props' that in this corner of America the 'props,' the incidentals, have become the markers and symbols of 'substance,' even though there is no 'substance' underneath."[69] "Props" that symbolize success appear in countless ways as if the "image" embodies a person. In an age of consumerism, television programs, and advertisement, there is the consistent message that the acquisition of products are status markers, e.g. vehicles that we drive or brand names that we wear. In community life, how are we socially aware of how we "size-up" a person based upon their clothing and appearance and fail to look upon each person through the lens of inestimable worth, made in the likeness and image of God (James 3:10) and a brother or sister "for whom Christ died" (1 Cor 8:11)?

With the rise of some televangelists and mega-churches, the frequent message is that of consumerism as if God is a cosmic Santa Claus, who can bestow excess. Material goods are not inherently evil as long as there is spiritual substance undergirding community life. Yes, churches require money; salaries need to be paid to pastors and staff-persons, insurance is important, church facilities require funding, programs require resources, but at what point does functionality spill over into excess? When churches plan for building sanctuaries, what are the guiding motives and principles? Most certainly, our faith-communities are not immune to the peril of consumerism. At what point do technological displays in church services become an end and not a means to an end? Wealth, power, and technology are heady intoxicants. At the same time, wealthy members of churches so frequently use their wealth in life-giving ways for the Kingdom of God, e.g. funding for vans, missions trips, new ventures for faith-communities to be involved with the urban poor and global outreach. Money is not the core issue, but rather, it is the attitudes and behavior of both the poor and rich.

Since the setting of James 2:1-13 appears to be in a judicial setting, the Church needs to ponder long and hard on social justice issues where money, influence, and appearance often prejudice the police, judges, and juries, at the expense of the poor and people of color. Consistent with James' language, a Spirit-empowered Church can speak out against violent and greedy aggressors of those involved in subprime mortgages and foreclosures, wherein powerful rich lenders victimize people through corrupt loans, balloon-payments, rising interest rates, and qualifying people whom they know cannot repay them. Violent aggressors live as God's enemies, including the powerful rich who display riches, exact dishonest repayments, are greedy landlords, and foreclose on poor homeowners with a callous disregard for the vulnerable weak. Greed and aggression are portrayed through numerous faces in the global economic world.

The need for social justice reflects itself in the high proportion of people living in poverty in the U.S. and the broader global community that is rich and prosperous. Although the poor in America live better than the global poor, manifestations of abject poverty call into question the Christian commitment to help the poor in our midst (local and global). The existence of widespread abject poverty in the world's poorest nations must also be met with practical help to relieve suffering and to empower the poor to help themselves.[70]

James targets his Jewish Christian community and does not address societal or institutional reform directly. Yes, his people live in the world and carry on their business pursuits within the world (3:13), but they must not allow the dominant culture's values to contaminate their community (4:4). James does not advocate an isolationist withdrawal from the world.

In our day, James' message includes the issue of race and the genuine welcome of people of color and different cultures. He intends that his community be fully inclusive and hospitable to the stranger with authenticity. A welcome must be genuine; so much is conveyed through a perfunctory glance or a genuine look. The eyes, "the windows of the soul," communicate so very much. James is certainly committed to a theology of social justice that in our day would also include a theology of racial justice. He would say that Jesus' trust is the total contradiction of attitudes and behavior that discriminate against others. Discrimination is based on prejudice, which is an internal negative judgment based upon individuals and groups, deemed to be inferior. James attacks such prejudices that are deeply ingrained within the Greco-Roman culture. Attitudes of the heart play out in the way that people are treated.

In Jesus' inaugural address (Luke 4:18-19; Isa 61:1-2; 58:6), he makes it clear that his agenda reflects the truth that God's lot has always been cast with "society's broken victims" (NEB), the marginalized, the other, those who lie below a subsistence level. James' message is counter-cultural and reinforces the very identity of the Elect Poor and what they mean to God and he seeks to align their priority with Jesus' focus upon the marginalized, for they are high on God's agenda. James is both honest about what his community has done in his indictment but also pastoral in that he seeks to influence them to think, speak, and act in ways that are consistent with their identity. Church leaders need to be empowered by the same Pentecostal power of Jesus and need to be trained to put on the glasses of Jesus through which people are seen through the lens of inestimable worth, no matter how they appear or what they might bring to the community. Further, leaders need to mentor their faith communities to really "see" others in the same way.

For James, the poor are both elect and vulnerable. Joe is one such person of the vulnerable poor.

Joe was a thirty-year old crack addict, with a long history of entering treatment, dropping out, or relapsing within weeks after completing programs. His attendance at Alcoholics Anonymous or Narcotics Anonymous meetings was spotty at best. The social worker that worked with me helped Joe get a job as a stock person in a neighborhood grocery. He completed an outpatient program and remained clean for many months.

Joe had two children who lived with their maternal grandparents, since their mother, also an addict, was of no help. In his recovery, the grandparents agreed to share and eventually relinquish custody of their grandchildren to Joe. The court specified that he needed a solid residence for them. The social worker helped him to get SSI assistance. Along with his salary, Joe obtained approval for a publicly subsidized apartment. As part of the final approval for his apartment, a physical exam was required. I did his physical and the required lab-testing, which was then analyzed by the lab. He passed in all areas except that he tested positive for HIV. He was devastated. Then, it was believed that HIV positive people would develop AIDS and die within 2-4 years. He was denied approval for his apartment and in a few days committed suicide. A week later, the public hospital, which analysed the lab-test for free, wrote me a letter and informed me that a lab-mistake resulted in a false positive for Joe and that he was not indeed HIV positive.

Community groups in larger churches are wonderful and are opportunities for Spirit-empowerment, genuine sharing, encouragement, instruction, and transformation. At the same time, favoritism is often expressed on Sunday mornings when community group members gravitate towards each other, with absolutely no notice of others who visit the service. Why is it that a person may visit the church gathering for four consecutive Sundays and not be really noticed or really welcomed, aside from a perfunctory "Good morning" by an usher who hands out the Sunday bulletin? Frequently, community group members only notice members of their group on Sunday morning.

Partiality in our faith-communities is often expressed through professions and educational levels, with preference given to those who are higher on the professional or educational scale. Often, people with advanced degrees assume church "offices" based upon their educational achievement at the expense of uneducated church members who may be more spiritually mature and wise. "Lord Acton, the man who said that 'power tends to corrupt and absolute power tends to corrupt absolutely,' also said, 'There is no worse heresy than that the office sanctifies the holder of it.'"[71] When honor is accorded to people with "higher" professions and advanced degrees, faith communities contradict Jesus' trust and the supreme worth of people with "lower-level" jobs and lesser educational background. Sins of partiality are also evident in our faith communities when special treatment is accorded to people with more spectacular spiritual gifts of the Spirit at the expense of people who have been gifted with service or administration.

The issue of favoritism also extends to gender, for preference is so frequently given to men at the expense of women in terms of leadership and church office. The Pentecostal message from Peter and Joel is fully inclusive in terms of gender. Baptism in the Spirit will mean the power (empowerment) to both speak and act for God. Joel's prophecy of visions and dreams plays a substantive role in the Book of Acts. Such charismatic experiences and expressions are the direct result of God's "pouring out" (ἐκχέω) of his Spirit, stated three times in Peter's Pentecostal address; two of the occurrences are found in Joel's text:

- *"I will pour out my Spirit"* (ἐκχεῶ ἀπὸ τοῦ πνεύματός μου Acts 2:17),
- *"I will pour out my Spirit"* (ἐκχεῶ ἀπὸ τοῦ πνεύματός μου Acts 2:18),
- "He has received from the Father the promised *Holy Spirit* and *has poured out* what you now see and hear" (τῇ δεξιᾷ οὖν τοῦ θεοῦ ὑψωθεὶς τήν τε ἐπαγγελίαν τοῦ πνεύματος τοῦ ἁγίου λαβὼν παρὰ τοῦ πατρὸς ἐξέχεεν τοῦτο ὃ ὑμεῖς καὶ βλέπετε καὶ ἀκούετε Acts 2:33)

Joel's prophecy is certainly inclusive in nature, "I will pour out my Spirit on *all flesh*" (Acts 2:17, which incorporates both genders (twice) and different age and socio-economic groups. It also advances the list of language groups of Acts 2:9-11. Mention of "all flesh" corresponds to the Baptist's words, *"All flesh* shall see the salvation of our God" (Luke 3:6 taken from Isa. 40:5).[72] In the Book of Acts, Luke notes the inclusive nature of God's Spirit when the good news advances from the Jewish Jerusalem into the Gentile world, including the African Ethiopian eunuch and the Gentile Cornelius (Acts 10-11). Much progress has been made in terms of Pentecostal and Charismatic churches with the full inclusion of women, and yet, it is true that so many churches show favoritism to men—at the expense of women, whether it be the choice for deacons, elders, pastors, and bishops, etc.

I experienced the privilege from 2000-2002 of working with Sean and Linda, two elderly people of minimal means, who experienced a radical transformation of life, leading to their grateful response through a significant ministry. Initially, they targeted various blocks in Norfolk, Virginia, where they lived, by passing out free loaves of bread to countless households. Their influence widened as they worked in partnership with local food banks and numerous grocery and convenience stores. With their limited funds, they purchased several vans and daily collected and distributed food to numerous low-income facilities. In addition, they opened the church's fellowship center three times a week for food-distribution (not cash) after a short service for people who were homeless, poor, and addicted. While the poor had every opportunity for a decision to begin the Christian life, their Christian experience never became the basis for their privilege of receiving food. Over twenty years, thousands of people made life-changing decisions through gifts of bountiful compassion. Their reward consisted in helping others in the vicious cycles of poverty.

"The posture of James with respect to the community is that of a broker. Is it possible that the text is here setting up James of Jerusalem as the broker for God and Jesus, and the benefits they espoused (wisdom, justice, social status, self-status)?"[73] He desires to influence his readers. Consistent with James' thrust, we need to be reminded and remind others of real Christian identity and to live out that identity through inclusive attitudes, accepting behavior, and language that is winsome—the very opposites of what had plagued James' readers. James drives his audience, then and now, to the only acceptable conclusion, "Continue to speak and continue to act as those who are about to be judged by the law that brings genuine freedom" (2:12). He appeals to a radical willingness to live in a consistent new way of life.

Bibliography

Adamson, James B. *The Epistle of James* Grand Rapids: Wm. B. Eerdmans Publishing Co., 1976.

Bauckham, Richard. *James*, London: Routledge, 1999.

Coker, K. Jason "Identifying the Imperial Presence," in Identifying the Imperial Presence Augsburg, Fortress Publishers, 2015.

Daney, H. E. and Julius R. Mantey, *A Manual Grammar of the Greek New Testament*. Toronto: The Macmillan Company, 1927.

Davids, Peter H. *The Epistle of James*. Grand Rapids: Wm. B. Eerdmans Publishing Co., 1982.

Dibelius, Martin. *James*. (ed. Helmut Koester; trans. Michael A. Williams. Philadelphia: Fortress Press,

Dyrness, William. "Mercy Triumphs over Justice: James 2:13 and the Theology of Faith and Works," *Themelios* 6:3 (1981).

Eichler, J. "Inheritance," *New International Dictionary of New Testament Theology*. Grand Rapids: Zondervan Publishing House, 1975).

Elliot, John H. "The Epistle of James in Rhetorical and Social-Scientific Perspective," *BTB* 23:2.

Fiorello, Michael D. "The Ethical Implication of Holiness in James 2," *JETS* 55:3.

Johnson, Luke Timothy. "The Use of Leviticus 19 in the Letter of James," *HTR* 101 (1982).

Keck, Leander E. "The Poor Among the Saints in the New Testament, ZNW 56 (1966).

Kennedy, G. A. "Aristotle" *"On Rhetoric": A Theory of Civic Discourse*. Oxford, UK: Oxford University Press, 1991.

Kistemaker, Simon J. "The Theological Message of James," *JETS* 29:1 (1986).

Laws, Sophie. *A Commentary on the Epistle of James.* San Francisco: Harper & Row Publishers, 1980.

Lockett, Darian R. *Purity and Worldview in the Epistle of James.* New York: T & T Clark, 2008.

_____. "Structure or Communicative Strategy? The 'Two Ways' Motif in James' Theological Instruction," *Neotestamentica* 42:2 (2008).

Mack, B. L. *Rhetoric in the New Testament.* Minneapolis: Fortress Press, 1990.

Malina, Bruce J. "Wealth and Poverty in the New Testament and Its World," Interpretation 41:4 (1987.

Mayor, Joseph B. *The Epistle of St. James.* Grand Rapids: Baker Book House, 1978.

Moo, Douglas J. *The Letter of James.* Grand Rapids: Wm. B. Eerdmans Publishing Co., 2000.

Moule, C. F. D. *An Idiom Book of New Testament Greek,* 2nd Edition. Cambridge, UK : University Press, 1963.

Nystrom, David P. *James: The NIV Application Commentary.* Grand Rapids: Zondervan Publishing House, 1997.

Perdue, Leo G. "Paraenesis and the Epistle of James" ZNW 72 (1981).

Robinson, Vernon K. "Writing as a Rhetorical Act in Plutarch and the Gospels," in Persuasive Artistry: *Studies in New Testament Rhetoric in Honor of George A Kennedy* ed., D. F. Watson; Sheffield, JSOT Press, 1991).

James Hardy Ropes, *A Critical and Exegetical Commentary on the Epistle of St. James.* Edinburgh: T & T Clark, 1978.

Schrenk, "ἐκλέγομαι", *Theological Dictionary of the New Testament* IV, ed, by Gerhard Kittel and Gerhard Friedrich. Grand Rapids: Wm. B. Eerdmans Publishing Co, 1965.

Stulac, George M. *James.* Downers Grove: InterVarsity Press, 1993.

Wachob, Wesley Hiram. *The Voice of Jesus in the Social Rhetoric of James.* Cambridge: University Press, 2000.

Wallwork, Ernest. "Thou Shalt Love Thy Neighbor as Thyself: The Freudian Critique," *The Journal of Religious Ethics* 10:2 (1982).

Ward, Roy Bowen. "Partiality in the Assembly," *HTR*, 62 (1969).

Chapter 12

Healing the "Us" vs. "Them" Divide: The Holy Spirit, Naturalistic Ethics, and Inter-group Cooperation[1]

Enoch Sathiasatchi Charles

The philosophically trained experimental psychologist and neuroscientist, Joshua Greene, argues that humanity is challenged by the "Us"–vs.–"Them" divide or the problem of inter-group cooperation.[2] In attempting to bridge this divide, Greene offers a naturalistic solution while ignoring or minimizing the role of God and religion.[3] This chapter, however, building on the work of John Hare and Craig Boyd, probes the effectiveness of Greene's solution and highlights some deficiencies in his naturalistic proposal.[4] Then, helped by Michael Palmer's pneumatological reading of Thomas Aquinas' theory on theological virtues[5] coupled with a brief exegetical analysis of the Peter-Cornelius inter-ethnic encounter in the book of Acts, this chapter proposes that God offers an empowering friendship with humanity through the Holy Spirit, thereby cultivating transformative virtues and graciously enabling the human nature to open itself to the other. Fundamentally, this research contends that the pneumatological solution to the problem of inter-group cooperation is not only effective, but also overcomes the inadequacies of the naturalistic alternative.

Methodologically, this chapter draws inspiration from the approach of the moral philosopher, Alasdair MacIntyre, as it unfolds in his, *After Virtue*. Here, MacIntyre engages two rival moral traditions (Aristotelian virtue tradition and modern moral philosophical tradition), but ultimately argues that one is better than the other without appealing to any neutral or universal standard for judgment.[6] Therefore, in the spirit of MacIntyre's approach, this chapter sees naturalistic ethics and Renewal[7] ethics as two rival traditions of morality, and argues that through this process of shared moral inquiry into this issue of inter-group cooperation, the inherent soundness, coherence, beauty, and rational superiority of Renewal ethics would emerge. Moreover, Palmer's take on Aquinas and virtue serves as a vital link in aligning the pneumatological solution to the problem of inter-group cooperation closer to the Aristotelian-Thomistic virtue tradition.[8]

The argument of this chapter unfolds in two major sections. The first section defines and deals with the problem of inter-group cooperation from a naturalistic perspective while also offering an assessment of the naturalistic solution. The second section approaches the problem of inter-group cooperation from a pneumatological perspective and evaluates its effectiveness in comparison to the naturalistic alternatives.

Naturalistic Ethics and Inter-Group Cooperation

Joshua Greene argues that morality evolved as a solution to the problem of cooperation. He writes: "Morality is a set of psychological adaptations that allow otherwise selfish individuals to reap the benefits of cooperation" and "the essence of morality is altruism, unselfishness, a willingness to pay a personal cost to benefit others."[9]

For Greene, however, there is a caveat to this understanding of morality:

> Biologically speaking, humans were designed for cooperation, *but only with some people*. Our moral brains evolved for cooperation *within groups*, and perhaps only within the context of personal relationships. Our moral brains did not evolve for cooperation *between groups* (at least not *all* groups). How do we know this? Why couldn't morality have evolved to promote cooperation in a more general way? Because universal cooperation is inconsistent with the principles governing evolution by natural selection.[10]

According to Greene, human morality has only evolved to solve the problem of in-group cooperation, which he calls the "Me"–vs.–"Us" problem or the "Tragedy of the Commons." But what is still unresolved by evolutionary morality is the "Us"–vs.–"Them" problem or the "Tragedy of the Commonsense Morality." Because the evolutionary moral conditioning "that enabled cooperation within groups is undermining cooperation between groups." Therefore, "morality evolved to avert the Tragedy of the Commons, but it did not evolve to avert the Tragedy of Commonsense Morality."[11] Now, the moral problem that needs to be solved is the "Us"–vs.–"Them," and for Greene, natural selection has not helped in solving this problem or meeting this moral demand—the need to get along with others outside one's group.

This understanding of morality is also supported by other naturalistic thinkers, who take an evolutionary approach to ethics. For example, the social psychologist, Jonathan Haidt, argues that humans are not designed to love everyone unconditionally. Only "parochial love—love within groups—amplified by similarity, a sense of shared fate, and the suppression of free riders, may be the most we can accomplish."[12] The leading primatologist, Frans de Waal, asserts that "morality is very much an in-group phenomenon. Universally, humans treat outsiders far worse than members of their own community: in fact, moral rules hardly seem to apply to the outside."[13] For de Waal, "in the course of human evolution, out-group hostility enhanced in-group solidarity to the point that morality emerged."[14] Thus, for Greene and these naturalists, the contemporary problem of inter-group cooperation is due to the evolved nature of human morality that renders humanity groupish and tribal.

Greene's Solution to Heal the "Us"–vs.–"Them" Divide

Unlike some naturalistic solutions that tend to lower the moral demand for inter-group cooperation,[15] Greene's proposal tries to meet this demand through a pragmatic solution. He seeks to develop a type of "thinking that enables groups with conflicting moralities to live together and prosper... a moral system that can resolve disagreements among groups with different moral ideals, just as ordinary, first order morality resolves disagreements among individuals with different selfish interests."[16] Greene writes that the inter-group cooperation problem remains unresolved because humans are trying to fix it primarily through moral instincts conditioned by evolution. For him, the emotions or feelings that worked well to promote in-group cooperation ("Me"–vs.–"Us"), can no longer be trusted for achieving inter-group cooperation ("Us"–vs.–"Them"). "What feels right may be what works at the lower level (within a group) but not at the higher level (between groups)."[17] He, therefore, needs a metamorality and turns to utilitarianism (what he calls "deep pragmatism").[18]

Greene recommends this solution based on his neuroscientific research and study of the human brain and its moral decision making. When moral decisions are made, one can observe in the brain emotional activity in the ventromedial prefrontal cortex, and rational activity in the dorsolateral prefrontal cortex. When people are asked to solve complex moral dilemmas such as the Trolley problem,[19] as they contemplate footbridge-type cases (throwing off a person over the bridge and killing him to save more lives) there is increased activity in the ventromedial prefrontal cortex. The ventromedial prefrontal cortex is a part of the brain associated with emotion (indicating feelings of moral disgust). Dealing with switch-type cases (just clicking a switch that allows the trolley's direction to be changed to kill one person for saving more people's lives) elicits increased activity in the dorsolateral prefrontal cortex (indicating more calculated reasoning to decide the best moral outcome). The dorsolateral prefrontal cortex is a part of the brain associated with rational thinking. For Greene, this means that our brain—like a dual-mode camera that operates with both automatic and manual settings—has two different ways of making moral judgments: (1) the automatic mode of moral decision making based on emotions; and (2) the manual, more deliberative mode of making decisions based on reason and calculation.

On encountering these moral problems, more people preferred to use the switch option than the footbridge option. On the other hand, people with damage to their ventromedial prefrontal cortex, who lack normal emotions, were five times more likely than others to approve of pushing the fat man over the bridge.[20] From his analysis of the Trolley problem, Greene points out that a hypothetical action that is seemingly good and useful—at least in the utilitarian sense, one that involves pushing and killing a person to save more lives—seems "terribly, horribly wrong" because it pushes human moral buttons (rightly so). At the same time, a moral action of equal consequence (flipping a switch to kill a person to save more lives) does not seem that repugnant as the rational brain weighs in while the emotions seem to disappear into the background. While Greene does not recommend one action over the other, he uses this moral dilemma to illustrate his point that human "moral intuitions are generally sensible, but not infallible."[21]

Now since Greene has already pointed out that a human being's automatic moral settings (emotional part) cannot be trusted for solving the problem of inter-group cooperation, he wants to tap into the manual, calculative part of the brain. This could be done only by switching to the rational, utilitarian mode of moral reasoning in order to adjudicate inter-group moral disputes and achieve cooperation. Therefore, while facing a moral problem that links to inter-group cooperation, one has to transcend their tribal moral emotions and rationally decide using utilitarian logic. Though Greene understands that deep pragmatism is not a perfect ethical system, he nevertheless contends that it is the best possible solution to solve this problem of inter-group cooperation in contemporary human society. For Greene, deep pragmatism is impartial since it cares for everyone's happiness and tries to maximize happiness for everyone on a neutral and unbiased standpoint. Therefore, utilitarianism alone has a common moral currency in today's polarized and divided world.

On the other hand, for Greene, religion, which has done well to promote tribal and in-group morality and solve the "Me"–vs.–"Us" or the "Tragedy of the Commons," fails to achieve any common currency and therefore is unable to solve the "Us"–vs.–"Them" or the 'Tragedy of the Commonsense Morality."[22] The religions of the world "exacerbate, rather than ease, conflicts between the values of 'Us' and the values of 'Them.'"[23]

Assessment of the Naturalistic Solution

Moral philosopher and Kant scholar, John Hare, disagrees with Greene's quick dismissal of religion for achieving inter-group cooperation. As a divine command ethicist, Hare reasons that within a theistic framework, God's commands help humans to transcend their groupish tendencies, enabling them to do what is right rather than merely care about our reputation or other selfish interests.[24] He argues that the "the God of Abraham not only includes us in community, but pushes out beyond community, to meet the needs of the poor and the marginalized who are objects of God's care just as much as we are."[25] Hare thus disagrees with the conclusion of Greene that religion only promotes in-group solidarity.

Further, Hare highlights some philosophical incoherencies in Greene's "deep pragmatism" and exposes some of his unwarranted optimism in utilitarian moral reasoning to adjudicate inter-group moral disputes. Hare points out that Greene's naturalistic bent conveniently stripped off the theistic roots of utilitarianism (found in Francis Hutcheson, William Paley, and John Stuart Mill), rendering it inadequate for ensuring the consistency between personal happiness and the maximum happiness to the greatest number of people.[26] Greene is desperate to achieve this consistency because he does not want to sacrifice his personal commitments to his family for the sake of an impartial, rational utilitarian moral agenda. Therefore, Greene seems realistic in his "impartial utilitarianism" and advocates accommodation (meaning one may decide with self-interested emotions that promote personal happiness whenever necessary). He contends that "it's not reasonable to expect actual humans to put aside nearly everything they love for the sake of the greater good." [27] He also argues that "as with selfish causes and personal relationships, when it comes to noble causes, there's no formula for drawing the line between reasonable and indulgent uses of our resources."[28] The claim may seem fair, but it only reinforces John Hare's point that Greene's theory lacks consistency between personal happiness and the greater good that is happiness for all.[29]

For Hare, this consistency is ensured by trusting in God and in the divine providential role in ensuring the real possibility of the highest good for all—a union of virtue and happiness. God has infinite resources at his disposal for coordinating the many different and competing human ends, duly rewarding anyone's life of virtue with happiness proportional to that virtue.[30] On the other hand, for Greene, this idea of virtue seems to get muddled as he excuses himself in saying, "I'm only human! But I'd rather be a human who knows that he's a hypocrite, and who tries to be less so, than one who mistakes his species-typical moral limitations for ideal values."[31] In the naturalistic framework, therefore, it seems that the motivation for pursuing virtue for its own sake is lacking; whereas in the theistic framework, belief in divine providence provides the rationale and moral faith, undergirding the desire to pursue both virtue and happiness together—coherently and consistently.

Another question that Greene's theory faces is how one knows when to switch from an automatic mode to a manual mode of moral reasoning, especially in solving inter-group moral disputes. If human moral conditioning is groupish, how does one transcend such deep-rooted moral sentiments on one's own and subscribe to a pure, neutral utilitarian and rational logic to adjudicate moral disputes? This seems to suggest that humans need assistance.[32] If evolution has not produced such virtues (or moral dispositions) to cooperate with outside groups, on what basis could humans transcend these moral intuitions for these deliberate out-group pursuits based on reason? Also, would it be fair to put more trust on the rational side of the brain to solve the inter-group cooperation issues? This means that Greene seems to think that human reasoning is somehow unscathed and unaffected by the evolutionary history of morality that has promoted tribal behavior and rendered emotions groupish. This thinking leads one to assume an emotion-reason divide in the brain.

The moral philosopher, Craig Boyd, critiques Greene from the point of view of an Aristotelian virtue ethic. For Boyd, *both* the affective (emotional) and the intellectual (rational) centers of the brain are important for every moral judgment. Drawing on William Casebeer, Boyd argues that in every "virtuous" moral decision there is a "synthesis of affect and intellect" in the brain. It is not only that one knows that it was the right action, but she also feels that it is the right thing to do. This picture of moral reasoning seems to offer a better explanation of one's experience of moral decision making than Greene's, who seems to prefer the intellectual at the cost of ignoring the affective in many moral decisions involving inter-group issues.[33]

The moral consequences of Greene's affect-intellect dualism and rational utilitarian reasoning to solve inter-group disputes could become disastrous, especially if humans are holistic beings with reason and emotion bundled together as Boyd and Casebeer argue. Repeated, calculative, rational, utilitarian moral reasoning for solving human moral problems while ignoring the moral sentiments (as Greene suggests) could render the emotional and affective moral apparatus of the human brain weak and underdeveloped. In a theological sense, one can say that the human conscience becomes seared. Such a condition may result in dysfunctional moral emotions (even for a vital in-group situation like parental care for a child). Thus, Boyd makes sense when he states that "a rational calculus devoid of affective insight seems to deny the truly human element in moral deliberation."[34]

Moreover, Boyd probes Greene's use of the Trolley Problem (discussed earlier) for his moral reasoning:

Does a utilitarian approach based as it is on "net utility" or the "greatest happiness"—adequately account for the narrative nature of existence? How do the people who are on the track come to be there? Why am I here? Do I stand in any particular relationship to the people on the track that might alter my decision-making process? It would seem that if I am the father of a small child on the track there are five convicted murderers doing manual labor on the other track, this could possibly alter my views in decidedly nonutilitarian ways.[35]

Boyd draws attention to the "narrative history of relationships to the agents involved in the moral action" to which Greene's utilitarianism is blind. Greene focuses only on the particular type of moral action at stake and its consequences. But Boyd argues that "the narrative structure of the moral life requires that we understand not merely how to act in a particular situation (e.g., The trolley problem), but also how to determine what we should do in the ongoing narrative of our—and others'—lives."[36] It seems that the rational utilitarian cannot account for this level of maturity in moral decision making. In giving importance to the whole person (affect and intellect) and the narrative history of relationships behind the moral action, one cannot help but think of the need for moral formation and cultivation of virtue that enables one to take the right ethical decision.

For Greene, humans are groupish, so their moral sentiments are fallible when it comes to inter-group cooperation and hence, the need to transcend emotions to achieve cooperation outside one's group. But what about the presence of out-group altruistic and sacrificial behavior that occurs among humans from time to time?

Could one explain these behaviors from an evolutionary sociobiological perspective? Christian theologians and ethicists such as Stephen Pope and Thomas Jay Oord do not think so. Oord argues that "Darwin and contemporary biology offer no plausible explanation for why a creature might act self-sacrificially for an outsider, stranger, or enemy."[37] Pope avers, "The entire sociobiological project of attempting to 'explain' human behavior in strictly behavioral terms, then, cripples its analysis of genuinely human altruism. The key factor in interpreting the meaning of an act lies in the agent's intention."[38] Motives always matter in morality and sociobiology that studies behavior (external) has no proper access to the heart and motivation of a moral action. In a similar fashion, the philosopher, William FitzPatrick, argues that the moral reasoning internal to the human agent is not under the investigation of empirical (evolutionary) science. Because the science itself "does not deal with such things as moral truths, truth makers, and right- or wrong-making features of actions, and instead sees only empirically accessible causes."[39]

Also, though out-group altruism is indeed rare and there is plenty of empirical support to Greene's and Haidt's claims regarding humanity's groupish tendencies, the inability of sociobiology to explain real altruistic behavior leads one to question this dualism between the "Me"–vs.–"Us" and "Us"–vs.–"Them" situations and the underlying claim that our morality evolved to promote only in-group cooperation. On the other hand, contrary to Haidt's and Greene's claims, evolution may not have convincingly solved the "Me"–vs.– "Us" problem by developing robust, adaptive moral sentiments for "groupish righteousness." Even if in-group cooperative behavior is advantageous for survival and flourishing, humans falter many times. Within the same family, there is divorce, adultery, cheating, murder, abuse, and rape. There are deep-seated and unresolved issues and differences between likeminded people. Jealousy, anger, envy and so many other vices still rage within same ethnic or religious group. Close friends sometimes turn against each other and resort to violence against their partners. Even couples, perhaps best friends and lovers for many years, sometimes separate on bitter terms and go their separate ways. Therefore, the claim that humans have morally evolved to solve the "Me"–vs.–"Us" problem and only the "Us"–vs.–"Them" issue remains unresolved seems dubious and too simplistic. Further, the unexplained examples of out-group altruism, however rare, seem to point out the need for human nature to acquire necessary virtues in order to take the right moral judgments for solving both "Me"–vs.–"Us" and "Us"–vs.–"Them" problems.[40]

Moreover, as per Alvin Plantinga's Evolutionary Argument Against Naturalism (EAAN), evolution, if true, is altogether incompatible with naturalism but compatible with theism.[41] For the analytical philosopher, Plantinga, if naturalism is true, the probability that human cognitive faculties (that evolved through the process of natural selection) are reliable is low. If that is the case, given the fact that Greene trusts in human cognitive and rational capabilities to solve moral problems implies that human cognitive faculties are indeed reliable. So, for Plantinga, this reliability of cognitive faculties is only because theism is true and evolution, if true, is divinely guided. The very fact that cognitive faculties are reliable due to divine causation means that humans need no longer to persist on naturalistic options for resolving inter-group hostilities. Also, as argued in the preceding paragraphs, if there is indeed a God, who ensures the real possibility of the highest good (union of happiness and virtue) and the consistency of personal happiness and virtue along with happiness and virtue for all, why could not this divine being help humans achieve inter-group cooperation? What if human nature, which is already capable of both selfish as well as altruistic behavior, is understood as "fallen" and needs the grace of God to be forgiven, healed, and elevated to acquire virtues that enable one to co-operate better both within and outside the group?[42] Why would not God's transformative grace work in and through us to "love our neighbor as ourselves" including someone, who is not in one's own group? Why could not the virtue of hospitality that is usually practiced among insiders of a group be transformed for the out-group context as well? This leads one to ask specifically, is there a way to solve this problem of inter-group cooperation without subscribing to Greene's affect-intellect divide or his dualism between "Me"–vs.–"Us" and "Us"–vs.–"Them" or the nagging inconsistency between personal happiness (and virtue) and the happiness (and virtue) of all? The following section explores these questions further.

The Holy Spirit and Inter-Group Cooperation

Through a theological-exegetical analysis of the inter-ethnic Peter-Cornelius encounter sketched in Acts 10, 11:1–18, and 15:7–11, this section explicates how the Holy Spirit, by cultivating of the virtue of hospitality in Peter and other Jewish believers, resolved the problem of inter-group cooperation exacerbated by the Jew-Gentile divide of the first century C.E. For this task, Renewal philosopher Michael

Palmer's explication of the moral theory of the highly influential medieval scholastic thinker, Thomas Aquinas, is foundational. Palmer helps one to understand the role of theological or grace-given virtues (faith, hope, and charity) in shaping moral character. He also unpacks the relationship between the theological (infused) virtues and the naturally acquired virtues that include the four cardinal virtues (prudence, justice, temperance, and courage) as well as habits such as truthfulness, generosity, and loyalty.[43] He points out that for Aquinas, the "grace-given virtues do not invalidate or destroy the naturally acquired virtues. Rather, they build on and extend the scope of these virtues, which are already present and operational." In short, for the believer, "the infused virtues inform, orient, and perfect the naturally acquired virtues."[44] Also, "the person who is touched by the grace of God undergoes a shift in vision and values, and this shift shows up in the way the person experiences and embodies the moral virtues."[45]

Palmer also brings to light how Aquinas explains the role of the Holy Spirit in facilitating the human-divine friendship (as a form of participation in the divine) in this process of moral formation and cultivation of virtue.[46] Aquinas basically sees the grace-given virtue of charity as a type of fellowship (*communicatio*) in which one shares in the divine life. "Christian life is a kind of fellowship (*communicatio vitae*) with God. This fellowship underlies and establishes the friendship between God and human beings. The name for this special friendship is charity."[47] For Aquinas, it is clear that the Holy Spirit is the one who facilitates this friendship.[48]

Now helped by this pneumatological reading of Aquinas, this section offers an exegesis of the Peter-Cornelius narrative in Acts and gleans a "pneumatological theology of inter-group cooperation." The central argument is that the Holy Spirit's empowering friendship with Peter (that Aquinas would term, "charity") orchestrated Peter's holistic moral development and exercise of the virtue of inter-group hospitality, eventually leading to the eradication of the Jew-Gentile divide in the early church. Peter and the Jewish believers already practiced the virtue of hospitality within their own group, but the Spirit of God transformed their vision and practice elevating it to a whole new level to include the Gentiles, a notion almost unthinkable in those times. First, from the Peter-Cornelius encounter recorded in Acts, this section offers a pneumatological solution for the "Us"–vs.–"Them" problem. Second, it assesses whether this "pneumatological theology of inter-group cooperation" can overcome the inadequacies encountered in the naturalistic solution of Joshua Greene seen earlier.

The Spirit-empowered Solution to the "Us"–vs.–"Them" Problem in Acts

The Acts 10 record of the meeting between Peter, the Jew, and Cornelius, the Gentile, is a classic case for inter-group cooperation. It demonstrates how the Holy Spirit breaks down dividing walls of hostility between two different ethnic groups. At the beginning of chapter 10, an angel appears to Cornelius, the pious Gentile (God-fearer), instructing him to invite Peter to his household. The experience of the Angelic visitation (vv. 3-6) at first terrifies Cornelius, but soon it becomes reassuring for him to know that God has remembered his prayers and good works (v. 4). This Angelic visitation reiterates John Hare's point made earlier that it is God who acts providentially and duly rewards one's life of virtue with happiness proportional to that virtue. Cornelius readily obeys the heavenly messenger and sends for Peter (v. 7). It is Peter who would need more spiritual-moral transformation than Cornelius for this inter-group encounter. Though a disciple and apostle of Jesus Christ, Peter's Jewish heritage and religious understanding prevented communion with the Gentiles (especially going to a Gentile's house and eating with them). So, the Spirit of God worked in Peter in order to bring them together.

First, through the vision recorded in Acts 10:10–17, the Holy Spirit prepares Peter to receive the men sent by Cornelius. Peter's imagination gets stirred by this interesting vision as the Holy Spirit "uses the symbolism of clean and unclean food."[49] This vision meets Peter at the point of his bodily hunger, and captures his imagination in a powerful way.[50] The vision also disturbs his psychological makeup and deeply-rooted moral sentiments because God instructs him to eat everything that God has provided and not discriminate between clean and unclean (vv. 13–16). Moreover, this experience seems to trigger the reasoning part of Peter's brain and changes the posture of his heart to receive the word from the Spirit instructing him to go without hesitation with the men coming to meet him (vv. 19, 20). Peter cannot discriminate or show no distinction (v. 20; cf. Acts 11:12; 15:8, 9). The Spirit of God, through this vision and direct instruction, touched Peter's imagination, affections, and intellect. The Holy Spirit works a moral transformation to cultivate within Peter the virtue of hospitality necessary for this important inter-group encounter. Peter, in obedience to the Spirit, then hosts his Gentile guests at the place he is staying. He then becomes their guest and travels with them on the next day to Cornelius's household in Caesarea.

Cornelius greets Peter with great reverence (v. 25). Peter's words to Cornelius and his household portray the gravity of the situation: "You yourselves know that it is unlawful for a Jew to associate with or to visit a Gentile; but God has shown me that I should not call anyone profane or unclean" (v. 28). The transformation in Peter has thus begun the healing of the "Us"–vs.–"Them" divide. The Spirit's empowering work in Peter involves his whole person—appealing to his imagination and desires, triggering of his rational mind, and instructing him directly with clarity. With both his emotional biases and moral reasoning touched and transformed by the Spirit, Peter is ready for the next part.

After seeing Cornelius, and hearing his side of the story, Peter declares: "I truly understand that God shows no partiality, but in every nation anyone who fears him and does what is right is acceptable to him" (vv. 34–35). Now Peter is convinced that God is impartial, always hearing the prayers and remembering the good works of the Gentiles. While Peter is still sharing the gospel of Jesus Christ to the household of Cornelius, the Spirit of God falls "upon all who heard the word" and the Gentiles begin to speak in tongues and praise God (vv. 44–46). Touched and transformed by the whole experience, Peter exercises his intellect and offers his own constructive moral reasoning, saying, "Can anyone withhold the water for baptizing these people who have received the Holy Spirit just as we have?" (v. 47). The Gentiles are baptized in water and Peter and his Jewish friends stay with the Cornelius clan for several days (v. 48)—a new era of Jew-Gentile hospitality and friendship begins.

In the next chapter, Peter stands up and justifies his extraordinary visit to the Gentiles before the Jewish believers who question the legitimacy of his table fellowship with the Gentiles (Acts 11:1–18). Luke also records Peter's recounting of the same incident at the Jerusalem council (Acts 15:7–11). Here, Peter says, "And God, who knows the human heart, testified to them by giving them the Holy Spirit, just as he did to us; and in cleansing their hearts by faith he has made *no distinction between them and us*" (vv. 8–9, emphasis mine). For Peter, the Gentiles' receiving of the gift of the Spirit settles the issue. Peter is fully clear that God does not show partiality and he himself cannot, therefore, discriminate between *us and them*.

Assessment of the Spirit-Empowered Solution to the "Us"– vs.–"Them" Divide

The Holy Spirit's friendship with Peter is the central point of this reflection. The Spirit of God "walks alongside"[51] Peter step-by-step and enables him to see the value of his inter-group encounter and table fellowship with the Gentiles. As Palmer points out, Thomas Aquinas calls this Spirit-enabled divine-human friendship, "charity." This friendship is a "mutual indwelling" since "by the Holy Spirit not only is God in us, but we also are in God."[52]

The Spirit gently guides Peter through the vision, instructing and directing him to get to know the people from Cornelius and to go with them to Caesarea. Peter risked rejection from his own group and boldly obeyed the voice of the Spirit because he was convinced that the Spirit's "divine power has given [him] everything needed for life and godliness" as he became a "participant of the divine nature" (2 Peter 1:3–4). The Spirit's empowerment gave Peter the impetus to sacrifice his personal happiness and act on behalf of the common good. Only the Spirit's constant guiding and assuring presence on Peter could give him the courage and confidence in stepping out to have table fellowship with Gentiles, which was unthinkable during those times.

Moreover, in this friendship with humanity, the Holy Spirit leads by example with an outpouring of kenotic love. Pentecostal theologian, Frank Macchia, sees the Spirit's coming on the believer as an act of divine self-giving, which in turn "fills us with the love of God so that we transcend ourselves and cross boundaries."[53] Therefore, it makes more sense to see why the Spirit's pouring out on Peter and other Jewish believers on the Day of Pentecost (Acts 2) and the Spirit's continual guidance and empowerment enabled Peter and his friends to transcend their biases and socio-cultural barriers for this Gentile encounter. After the Spirit's coming on the Gentile believers (Acts 10:44–46), the Spirit-baptized Jew and the Spirit-baptized Gentile, both having tasted the pure, self-giving love of God through the Holy Spirit (Rom 5:5), were able to work together. They opened themselves to each other, forming the multi-ethnic and multi-cultural *koinōnia* of God in Christ. This Spirit-empowered self-transcendence and accepting of the other as one's own seems to account for the consistency between personal happiness and another's happiness that Greene's rational-utilitarian theory struggled with (see the previous section). Consistency is only achieved by the common currency of the Holy Spirit who, with a life-long friendship that shows no discrimination, empowers both "Us" and "Them" with the same altruistic divine love for everyone. For the Pentecostal theologian and missiologist, Amos Yong, this divinely infused love is "not just a predisposition toward others but expresses a deeply rooted sensibility that our success, comfort, and happiness are intimately intertwined with that of others."[54]

As Craig Boyd argued earlier, human beings make moral judgments with emotion and reason together. In order to make the right judgment, both the affection and intellect need transformation. To cultivate the virtue of inter-group hospitality, the Spirit of God worked in and through Peter in a holistic fashion, transforming his imagination and affections, helping him to transcend his in-group biases, instructing and provoking him to think and arrive at the right moral judgment and action. Peter is fully convinced (affectively and intellectually) that what he did was right and he passionately defends his decision to have fellowship with the Gentiles (Acts 11:1–18; 15:7–11). As with Peter, the Spirit of God can work within the believer, touching both intellect and affections, leading her to make the right moral judgements in order to bridge the "Us"–vs.–"Them" divide. Without the Spirit, there is no bridge within to bring affections and intellect together and move one as an integral whole toward the right moral direction. Yong sums this up beautifully, writing, "When the Spirit shows up ... (people's) bodies are touched, their emotions healed and liberated, their affections reoriented, and their ways of life transformed."[55]

The Spirit-led Peter-Cornelius encounter, while healing the "Us"–vs.–"Them" divide, also brought a huge shift to the identity and language of the early church. New Testament scholar, Aaron Kuecker, points out that, prior to Acts 15, no non-Israelite had ever been called a "brother" to the Israelites. Of the 96 times the word *adelphoi* (meaning "brothers") appears in all the Gospels, it refers to no non-Israelites until Acts 15:23.[56] Acts 15:23, in the opening words of the letter from the Jewish apostles and elders regarding the non-imposition of Jewish circumcision and other food laws on the believing Gentiles, specifically, addresses those Gentile believers as *adelphoi*. This language clearly implies that those Gentile believers were considered part of the same community of the Jewish believers of Jesus.[57] And Kuecker shows that Luke's usage of *adelphoi* after Acts 15:23 revealed a profound shift in the identity of the early Christian community in relation to ethnicity. After Acts 15, Luke employed *adelphoi* for one of two reasons: "(1) to express ongoing ethnic solidarity with fellow Israelites or (2) *to describe the Jesus group, irrespective of the ethnic identities of its members.*"[58] For Luke, the Spirit of God is indeed the go-to person for removing the ethnic divides and creating this new identity. Acts 10:1–11:18, the section in Acts that deals with the erasing of ethnic boundaries, contains the densest cluster of references (eight in all) to the Holy Spirit. Acts 10:44–47 and 11:12–16 contain three references each. [59] These portions of Scripture represent some of the most transformative moments for the early church.

In fact, the Spirit of God enhances both the in-group bonding as well as the out-group friendships, thereby overcoming the dualism between the "Me"–vs.–"Us" and "Us"–vs.–"Them" that is witnessed in Greene's utilitarian approach. Pentecostal ethicist, Murray Dempster, traces through the Lucan narrative of Spirit baptism and points out in Acts 2, value discriminations based on gender and status (vv. 17–18) are broken. In Acts 4 and 5, economic *koinonia* broke rich-poor distinctions. As discussed earlier, in the Peter-Cornelius narrative in Acts 10, the Jew-Gentile divide is overcome as the Holy Spirit instructs and guides the Spirit-baptized Peter not to distinguish between us (Jews) and them (Gentiles). The Spirit also commands Peter to have fellowship with the Gentiles without hesitation (Acts 10:20; 11:12; 15:8–9).[60]

As a Pentecostal, Dempster is keen to emphasize the significance of Spirit baptism and glossolalia while highlighting the Spirit's role of bringing the community of God together in the Acts narratives. For him, "glossolalia functioned in Acts 2 and in Acts 10 to signal the coming of the Spirit to overpower deeply entrenched moral biases; it played this apologetic function for Luke again in Acts 19."[61] He says:

> "As the Spirit came—accompanied by glossolalia—Luke detailed how the apostolic community was empowered to overcome the moral biases and social prejudices resident in the value demarcations of the old social order between male and female, rich and poor, Jew and Gentile, and even prejudices tied to differences of religious backgrounds within the Christian community itself. The power of the Spirit transformed the apostolic fellowship into an inclusive community of men, women, rich, poor, Jew, Gentile, the Baptist's disciples and the disciples who had personally followed Jesus. That all the members of the believing community were regarded as possessing equal value and worth Luke attributed to the creative power of the Spirit."[62]

It is the same Spirit's gracious and transformative empowerment that brought unity between groups (Acts 10) as well as between believers from different traditions (Acts 19) and between people of the same community (Acts 2). In a sense, the Spirit's coming in Acts is the solution to both the problems—the "Me"–vs.–"Us" and "Us"–vs.–"Them". There is no dualism here. It is one solution what fallen humanity needs: receive the Holy Spirit!

Thus, it is the Holy Spirit, and not utilitarianism, that seems to be the common currency that Joshua Greene is looking for. As seen in the Acts narratives, the Spirit of God, by means of a life-long, empowering, and transformational friendship with human beings, cultivates the necessary virtues for inter-group cooperation by overcoming the affect-intellect divide, ensuring the consistency between personal and group happiness, and also removing the dualism between the "Me"–vs.–"Us" and "Us"–vs.–"Them". This leads us to conclude that this "pneumatological theology of inter-group cooperation" that emerged from the Acts narratives has better explanatory power or "empirical fit" in solving the actual issue of "Us"–vs.–"Them" when compared with the naturalistic solution of Greene.

Conclusion

While naturalistic ethicists such as Greene are keen to throw God out of the picture in addressing the problem of inter-group cooperation, their solutions to the problem of inter-group cooperation are seen as inadequate. It has been pointed out that Greene's "deep pragmatism" creates an affect-intellect gap, an unnecessary dualism between "Me"–vs.–"Us" and "Us"–vs.–"Them", and inconsistency between personal happiness and happiness for everyone. At the same time, a "pneumatological theology of inter-group cooperation" through a Spirit-baptized and virtue-oriented reading of the Acts narratives offers a counter explanation, and help us understand how God, through the power of the Holy Spirit, befriends humanity and acts on us in a holistic fashion, cultivating transformative virtues and solving the problem of inter-group cooperation by graciously enabling human nature to open itself to the other. It has been argued from the Acts narratives that the Spirit-empowered solution to the problem of inter-group cooperation is not only effective, but also overcomes the inadequacies of the naturalistic solution studied earlier. This chapter forms a part of a larger research project that seeks to forge an apologetic dialogue between naturalistic ethics and Renewal ethics.[63] Moreover, further work is required especially in fleshing out the theme of Spirit-empowered hospitality in Luke-Acts while building on some significant scholarly contributions in this area.[64] Also, this chapter has just started to explore the connections between Aquinas's notion of friendship with the divine through the Spirit and the Pentecostal understanding of Spirit baptism (both as a source of cultivation of virtue). There is potential for further work in this regard.

Bibliography

Aquinas, Thomas. *Summa Theologiae.*

Augustine, Daniela. "Pentecost and the Hospitality of God as Justice for the Others." in *Brethren Life and Thought* 57:1 (Spring 2012), 17–26.

————. *Pentecost, Hospitality, and Transfiguration: Toward a Spirit-Inspired Vision of Social* Transformation. Cleveland, TN: CPT Press, 2012.

Boyd, Craig A. "Neuroscience, the Trolley Problem, and Moral Virtue." In *Theology and the Science of Moral Action: Virtue Ethics, Exemplarity, and Cognitive Neuroscience*, edited by James A. Van Slyke, Gregory R. Peterson, Kevin S. Reimer, Michael L. Spezio, and Warren S. Brown, 130–47. New York: Routledge, 2013.

Bruce, F. F. *The Book of Acts.* rev. ed. Grand Rapids, MI: Wm. Eerdmans Publishing Co., 1988.

Byrne, Brendan. *The Hospitality of God: A Reading of Luke's Gospel.* rev. ed. Collegeville, MN: Liturgical Press, 2015.

Cartledge, Mark J. "Spirit-Empowered 'Walking Alongside': Toward a Renewal Theology of Public Life." *Journal of Pentecostal Theology* 27:1 (2018), 14–36.

Casebeer, William D. "Moral Cognition and Its Neural Constituents," *Nature Reviews Neuroscience* 4 (2003), 841–47.

Castelo, Daniel. *Revisioning Pentecostal Ethics: The Epicletic Community.* Cleveland, TN: CPT Press, 2012.

————. "Tarrying on the Lord: Affections, Virtues, and Theological Ethics in a Pentecostal Perspective." *Journal of Pentecostal Theology* 13:1 (2004), 31–56.

Charles, Enoch S. "Toward a Pneumatological-Participatory Theology of Divine Moral Assistance: An Apologetic Dialogue with Naturalistic Ethics and Kantian Ethics of John Hare." PhD diss., Regent University, 2018.

Clark, Kelly James. "Naturalism and Its Discontents." In *The Blackwell Companion to Naturalism*, edited by Kelly James Clark, 1–15. Chichester, West Sussex, UK: Wiley Blackwell, 2016.

Dempster, Murray. "The Church's Moral Witness: A Study of Glossolalia in Luke's Theology of Acts" *Paraclete* 23 (Winter 1989), 1–7.

Dennett, Daniel C., and Alvin Plantinga. *Science and Religion: Are They Compatible?* New York: Oxford University Press, 2011.

Fitzmeyer, Joseph A. *The Acts of the Apostles: A New Translation with Introduction and Commentary*. The Anchor Bible. New York: Doubleday, 1997.

FitzPatrick, William. "Why Darwinism Does Not Debunk Objective Morality?" In *Cambridge Companion to Evolutionary Ethics*, edited by Michael Ruse and Robert J. Richards, 188–201. Cambridge, UK: Cambridge University Press, 2017.

Greene, Joshua. *Moral Tribes*. New York: Penguin, 2013.

Haidt, Jonathan. *The Righteous Mind*. New York: Vintage Books, 2012. Paperback.

Hare, John E. "Evolutionary Theory and Theological Ethics." *Studies in Christian Ethics* 25:2 (2012), 244–54.

———. *God's Command*. Oxford, UK: Oxford University Press, 2015.

———. *The Moral Gap*. New York: Oxford University Press, 1996.

Kuecker, Aaron J. *The Spirit and the 'Other': Social Identity, Ethnicity, and Intergroup Reconciliation in Luke-Acts*. London: T & T Clark, 2011.

Lewis, Paul W. "A Pneumatological Approach to Virtue Ethics." *Asian Journal of Pentecostal Studies* 1:1 (1998), 42–61.

———. "Value Formation and the Role of the Holy Spirit in the Writings of J. Rodman Williams." *Asian Journal of Pentecostal Studies* 14:2 (2011), 272–309.

Macchia, Frank. *Baptized in the Spirit: A Global Pentecostal Theology*. Grand Rapids, MI: Zondervan, 2006.

MacIntyre, Alasdair. *After Virtue*. 3rd ed. Notre Dame, IN: University of Notre Dame Press, 2007.

Mittelstadt, Martin. *Reading Luke-Acts in the Pentecostal Tradition*. Cleveland, TN: CPT Press, 2010.

Ober, Josiah, and Stephen Macedo, eds. *Primates and Philosophers: How Morality Evolved*. Princeton, NJ: Princeton University Press, 2006.

Oord, Thomas Jay. *Defining Love: A Philosophical, Scientific, and Theological Engagement*. Grand Rapids, MI: Brazos Press, 2010.

Palmer, Michael D. "Ethical Formation: The Theological Virtues," In *The Holy Spirit and Christian Formation: Multidisciplinary Perspectives*, edited by Diane J. Chandler, 107–26. New York: Palgrave MacMillan, 2016.

Plantinga, Alvin. *Where the Conflict Really Lies: Science, Religion, and Naturalism*. New York: Oxford University Press, 2011.

————. "The Evolutionary Argument against Naturalism." In *Blackwell Companion to Science and Christianity*, edited. J. B. Stump and Alan G. Padgett, 103–15. Hoboken, GB: Wiley-Blackwell, 2012.

Pope, Stephen J. *Human Evolution and Christian Ethics*. Cambridge: Cambridge University Press, 2007.

Volf, Miroslav. *Exclusion and Embrace: A Theological Exploration of Identity, Otherness, and Reconciliation*. Nashville, TN: Abingdon Press, 1996.

Wariboko, Nimi. *The Charismatic City and the Public Resurgence of Religion: A Pentecostal Social Ethics of Cosmopolitan Urban Life*. New York: Palgrave Macmillan, 2014.

Yong, Amos. *Hospitality and the Other: Pentecost, Christian Practices, and the Neighbor*. Maryknoll, NY: Orbis Books, 2008.

_____. *Spirit of Love: A Trinitarian Theology of Grace*. Waco, TX: Baylor University Press, 2012.

Section Four

Following the Spirit

Chapter 13

Liberating Pneumatology: Basil the Great in Conversation with Pentecostal Pneumatics

Anthony Roberts

A brief survey of contemporary Pentecostal theologies allows us to discern a common thread regarding the continuing work of the Spirit of Christ in drawing creation to God the Father.[1] In *Pentecostal Spirituality: A Passion for the Kingdom*, Steven Jack Land constructs a thesis emphasizing the cultivation of "distinctive apocalyptic affections" rooted in Christ and drawn out by the power of God (the Spirit) that moves the world towards the eschatological horizon.[2] Amos Yong's *The Spirit Poured Out on All Flesh: Pentecostalism and the Possibility of Global Theology* envisions a way of doing God-thought that is suited to grapple with the deep complexities of the modern/postmodern world through a biblically-rooted, Jesus-centered, and Spirt-filled framework.[3] In his *Baptized in the Spirit: A Global Pentecostal Theology*, Frank D. Macchia argues that Spirit baptism is "an eschatological gift that functions as an outpouring of divine love" towards God and others.

Importantly, these Pentecostal theologies flesh out the connection between *what* the Spirit is doing in the world and *where* the Spirit carries out its work: within and through the human community. What I am calling *Pentecostal pneumatics*—whether this be sanctification, holy living, Spirit-baptism, the giving of supernatural gifts, divine love, standing against injustice, and other observable acts carried out by the Spirit—are meant to unfold in *connection* with other believers rather than in seclusion. Luke's narrative in Acts 2 points to the foundation of divine speech and the other charismatic gifts: a justice-making community empowered by the Spirit. Rather than emphasizing *forensic physical evidence* (though one could argue that this was present), the heart of Luke's recounting of the day of Pentecostal seems to rest on *social evidence* of the Spirit's presence in the first Christian community.[4] Though there are indeed miraculous signs and wonders taking place on the day of Pentecost, what is most miraculous—and particularly crucial in ascertaining the Spirit's presence in the believing community—is the justice-making community that comes into existence. This rereading of Acts 2 stands as a critique of any theology that limits its search for evidence of the Spirit's work in spiritual gifts—though these are still critically important. *Liberative possibilities* arise out of Pentecostal pneumatology by freeing up space to include social evidence of the Spirit alongside others.

In this chapter, I will argue that Pentecostal pneumatics can be seen in a liberative fashion by emphasizing the *social evidence* of the Spirit's presence, observable in the ecclesial community where the multiplicity of poverties is addressed by tangible graciousness and justice-making. Out of a true Wesleyan Pentecostal-Holiness approach to theology, I want to do this in conversation with the larger Christian tradition. In order to do this work, I will examine the social-theological thought of Basil the Great (perhaps the most well-

307

known of the Cappadocian Fathers), outline some openings in existing theologies of the Spirit, and conclude by constructing the basic points of the social evidence of the Spirit's presence. Rather than trying to give a comprehensive survey of Basil's theology—perhaps this could be done in a larger project—I will give special attention to his social thought through his pneumatology. Another important limitation of this chapter is that the section on current liberative pneumatologies does make intentional inclusions and exclusions. The absence of certain voices should not be taken to mean they are inadequate nor is the inclusion of others meant to imply that they are without their problems. With this in mind, it is possible to turn to Basil the Great's socio-theological thought.

Basil the Great's Social-Theological Framework

Basil's pedigree is chalked full of *privilege*: he was born into a prominent Christian family and he had access to some of the best education in his day (even spending a few years in Athens).[5] Despite his deep connection to privilege, Basil is remembered for his commitment to addressing poverty and famine, and using his resources—even at the risk of losing them—to address the real needs of his community. In certain ways, Basil's socio-theological commitments very much led him to divest himself of his to create a more just existence for others. Demetrios Constantelos notes that Basil was able to make "monasticism a redeeming social force and the Church an influential organization in several aspects of society—education, welfare, health, and Church and state relations."[6] The power in Basil's thought is found in his attention to alleviating oppressions on the soul *and* body.

In his homily, "To the Rich," Basil argues that "those who love their neighbor as themselves *possess nothing more than their neighbor* [emphasis added]..."[7] Holy affection is inclusive of the interiority of the human, but it cannot stop there. Love has a *concrete* sense to it. Rather than being a mere interior feeling, holy affection must *externalize* itself. The externalizing of the inward experience of divine love may (and probably should) prove costly; it may require believers to give up much so the basic needs of others can be met. This commitment must be seen against Basil's own backdrop of privilege and his *reorientation* to that privilege by giving it away in order to work towards the creation of different social realities. In his own words, holy love means being willing to "divest" oneself of wealth in order to make that love tangible and felt.[8] The divestment Basil speaks of is a critique of hoarding one's temporal things—the very definition of guarded wealth. The wealth that persists in the face of suffering and injustice stands in contrast to God who graciously scatters benefits to all of creation.[9] To hoard one's wealth is to distrust God's abundance from which "comes everything beneficial."[10]

The mechanism that is empowered to create a different society—where everyone has as they need—is the church. Again, Basil's context is important at this juncture. At this point in history, modern categorizations of the religious and the secular have not arrived on the scene. To a greater or lesser extent, there is not a clear line where church and political authority are delineated. It is no surprise that Basil's social thought works on a macro level in his community, shaping the social commitments of both the church and the political structure. However, Basil is clear: the church is the community empowered to address social injustice.

In a sermon given at a time when there was famine in the land, Basil argues that it has been brought about by having and willingly overlooking those who lack. He notes that "we do not share what we [those who have] receive with others...Though we have a God who is generous and lacks nothing, *we have become grudging and unsociable towards the poor* [emphasis added]."[11] It is important to note who Basil is addressing: *wealthy, privileged believers*— probably from a background similar to his own—who see the suffering around them and do nothing in order to protect their pockets. In an alarming way, the love of wealth is coming before the love of the Other. Basil proposes a radical solution: it is necessary to return to the common life of that first Christian community "where everything was held in *common* [emphasis added]—life, soul, concord, a common table, indivisible kinship—while unfeigned love constituted many bodies as one and joined many souls into *a single harmonious whole* [emphasis added]."[12] He points to nothing other than the first Christian community that is brought into common life by the Spirit. Importantly, the common life of the first Christians is both spiritual and practical. Indeed, there are miraculous signs and wonders. However, there is simultaneously a *divine leveling of existence* in the world in order to create just conditions for others. Here is where we can begin to see an opening into the pneumatological themes in Basil's social theological thought.

Basil's *On the Spirit* is an important contribution to patristic theology, particularly because the pneumatology tends to be a secondary matter or peripheral in much of the literature from this intellectual period. Fighting against those who claim the Spirit is a creature or simply God's power (not a person), Basil argues that "God works the differences of operations, and the Lord the diversities of administrations, but all the while the Holy Spirit is present too of His own will, dispensing distribution of the gifts according to each recipient's worth."[13] At the heart of Basil's pneumatology is the sense that one can be assured of the Spirit's status because its actions are reflective of the work of the Father and Son. Commenting on Cappadocian pneumatology—which is deeply indebted to Basil— William J. Abraham argues that "it is precisely from the *effects* [emphasis added] of the Holy Spirit in a host of actions that we in part know that the Holy Spirit is divine and must be regarded as a full Person in the Trinity."[14] Out of the Spirit's place in the holy community of Father, Son, and Spirit, The Spirit acts in the world and does God's work since it is God. Importantly, the Spirit is the one who *completes* the love of God and the work of the Son in humanity. Lewis Ayres notes that this move within the larger Cappadocian framework points to their understanding of the Spirit as one who perfects and completes the work of the triune God.[15] The Spirit is no passive divine presence or emanation; it is God who *continues* and *completes* the Son's reconciling of the world to the Father.

As I conclude this section on Basil's socio-theological framework, there are a few points of his thought that are important to reiterate at this point. First, the holy affection that plays a central role in Basil's thought demands externalization towards others even to the point of divesting oneself of wealth in order to address the needs of others. Second, the community that is called to make this change in society is the church that is empowered by the Spirit to live out a common life that is both spiritual and practical. The concreteness of this common life manifests itself in a divine leveling of human existence in order to address the multiplicities of lack that create an unjust existence for so many. Finally, Basil's socio-theological framework is pneumatologically rich. The Spirit is the continuer and completer of God's action. It is of no little consequence that Basil considers the community in Acts 2 as the natural outcome of the Spirit's work. The church formed out of Pentecost exemplifies the new social order brought into existence by the Spirit. Underneath his socio-theological perspective is a pneumatological vision that makes possible the restructuring and reordering of human relationships in the world. With this in mind, it is helpful to look to the work of a recent constructive theology where liberation and Spirit are intimately connected.

A Liberative Opening for Pneumatology

A pneumatological vision for liberation is found in Dwight N. Hopkins's *Being Human: Race, Culture, and Religion*. In his discussion of various models of theological anthropology and the concrete ways humans separate themselves from one another—the obsession with the self in Western thinking is called out at this point and closely identified with the many manifestations of poverty in the world—he suggests a Spirit-driven way forward. He argues that "co-laboring with God's spirit [we could say Holy Spirit at this point], liberation becomes a move *beyond harmful restrictions on the self and the poor* [emphasis added]."[16] God's activity in the world through the Spirit works to enhance human life by drawing people into *common life* (the essence of community) by moving them away from hoarding resources and prioritizing things above the Other. A deep Pentecostal vision for human life must take seriously this *Spirit-created common life*. There are two important guides that Hopkins's argument will provide for the constructive section that will conclude this chapter.

First, the freedom arising out of the Spirit's activity is one that realizes *love in community with others*.[17] Hopkins notes that one of the basic problems with Western ideas about wealth and the accumulation of wealth is that it necessarily privatizes what God has given *collectively* to humanity. The fall of humanity is *the failure of community*. Hopkins notes that "the greatest Fall or sin in human history was the individual's choice to accumulate personal capital (in contradiction to God's gift to all) as private ownership (the primordial wickedness of Adam in the Garden)."[18] Many of the ideas about wealth in Western society—private land ownership, unequal access to natural resources, systems of capital that privilege a small elite section of society, and other ideas that are justified through a particular theological-philosophical perspective—replicate Adam's sin by attempting to privatize things that God has given in abundance to creation for its collective good. The Spirit's work in humanity moves believers towards a collective love that releases humans to become who God calls them to be, but not through

313

existing as a mere individual who is unaffected by the needs of others. Rather, the community in the Spirit is one where the needs of others are fundamental to how resources are used and distributed.

Second, the liberating work of the Spirit always works towards the *missio dei*—God's mission in the world—by deconstructing unjust structures of power and privation that diminish the humanity of the multitudes. Importantly, there is a connection between the community and the individual at this point. Hopkins argues that the community uses the resources God has given to the earth in order to help the individual develop.[19] It is not as if one's uniqueness is done away because the community controls how resources are used. Rather, the individual is always responsible to the larger human collective for its use of God's resources in the world.[20] God's mission in the world is disrupting unhealthy forms of being a unique self and privation that creates poverty.

As I conclude this section, it is important to reiterate that the Spirit's work is *liberative*. God the Spirit is bringing about freedom in the world, but in a way that subverts many ideas about Western individualism and disrupts privatizing access to resources that come out of God's own abundance. Love in community is at the heart of the Spirit's work in the world; this is the only way to deal with the brokenness of human relationally that manifests through the failure of community. God's mission in the world is creating a return to this first love, a love that is never meant to be had in seclusion but in connection with others. Hopkins's discussion of the Spirit of liberation and Basil's socio-theological framework have something to offer a theory of Pentecostal pneumatics: the language of a social

314

pneumatology that looks for the evidence of divine love in the sort of community that comes into existence. It is now possible to engage in a bit of constructive work.

Toward a Pentecostal Social Pneumatology

As a global movement, Pentecostalism is defined more by its *diversity* of discourses around similar themes than by its conformity to narrow doctrines. While there are ways in which groups and individuals who identify as Pentecostal share common theological language, what is actually meant by this language can be wide ranging and even in conflict. Therefore, this brief constructive section does not attempt to speak for all Pentecostals or suggest that there is such a thing as a singular Pentecostal theology. Pentecostal from here forward is used loosely to forms of God-thought and speech that emphasize God's continuing work in the world.

First, it will be helpful to see a Pentecostal social pneumatology in the framework of the Fivefold Gospel. The Fivefold Gospel—an accessible theological affirmation within many Classical Pentecostal circles—affirms that Jesus is Savior, Sanctifier, Spirit-Baptizer, Healer, and Soon-Coming King. All of these functions of Jesus continue through the Spirit's work in the context of the local church that is called into the world and to be for the world. Following on Basil's socio-theological framework, it is appropriate to see Jesus as *Unifier* of humanity since the Spirit of Christ draws humans together; this seems to be at the heart of the Acts 2 narrative. The Spirit's drawing together of humanity is one that moves fluidly across lines of radical difference that separate communities in violent and deeply felt ways. In real ways, the Spirit problematizes the harmful ways in which human difference is constructed and marked. The Spirit's unifying power is *a transgressive* power because it cannot be co-opted into the demonic systems of power that divide humanity and categorize some human bodies as "less-than." Rather, the transgression of the Spirit is bringing together what is so often kept a part.

Second, a constructive Pentecostal social pneumatology will take seriously the *leveling-power* of the Spirit—this work is emphasized in Basil's work. Since the Spirit is a transgressive power—one that is not formed and coerced by the trends of the world—it does not bring people together without working towards the removal of those things and powers that separate. If the church goes along with the structures that create lack so that some can become wealthy, deny access to life-giving resources so that some can commodify God's collective gift to humanity, or other forms of systemic oppression, one has to question whether the Spirit is at work there. The Spirit of Jesus the Unifier does not achieve His work by maintaining the status quo. Rather, the Spirit empowers the people of God to challenge and dismantle the systems that are responsible for the many forms of injustice in the world. If need be, the Spirit empowers war against these systems.

Finally, a Pentecostal social pneumatology will see justice-making as the *continuing* and *completing* work of the Spirit in the world. Perhaps the most significant contribution to and in connection with Pentecostal thought that Basil the Great has, is his sense that Spirit's role as *continuer-completer*. Part of the reason why Basil is convinced that the Spirit should be fully recognized as divine is that the Spirit carries out what is in the Father's heart and in Jesus's good news to the world. It is true that charismatic gifts are a significant part of the first Christian community; they point to the presence of God in the ecclesial community. However, the work of the Spirit is not reducible to these charismas. Rather—and inclusive of the charismatic gifts—the Spirit is pushing the people of God towards a common life where no one goes without. This common life demands that we make the wrongs right. It requires the people of God to use their powers to make sure that no one goes hungry or is denied access to the resources that God has collectively given to humanity. Furthermore, it empowers believers to seek out gracious common life by directly addressing those systems and principalities that deny it. The unifying work of the Spirit of Christ is necessarily *justifying* work.

Conclusion

As I conclude this section and the chapter, I want to reiterate that a liberative opening is found in Pentecostal pneumatics when the work of the Spirit is evidenced in the formation of a gracious community where there is a holy common life where all needs are met. Importantly, this thesis does not dismiss the importance of the charismatic gifts that are often key to theorizing the work of the Spirt. However, a liberative Pentecostal pneumatological must center on the common life that comes into existence through God's power. By focusing on the social evidence of the Spirit's work, it is possible to avoid the mistake of simply seeing the work of the Spirit as an inward pietistic experience. Looking to the community created

by the Spirit liberates pneumatology and makes it genuinely
liberative.

Bibliography

Abraham, William J. "Divine Action and Pneumatology in the Cappadocians." In *Divine Agency and Divine Action, Volume II: Soundings in the Christian Tradition*, 62-79. Oxford, UK: Oxford University Press, 2017.

Ayers, Lewis. "Basil of Caesarea and the Development of Pro-Nicene Theology." In *Nicaea and its Legacy: An Approach to Fourth-Century Trinitarian Theology*, 187-221. Oxford, UK: Oxford University Press, 2004.

Basil the Great. *On Social Justice: St. Basil the Great*. Translated by C. Paul Schroeder. Crestwood, New York: St. Vladimir's Press, 2009.

_____. *On the Spirit*. S.l.: Beloved Publishing, 2015.

Constantelos, Demetrios. "Basil the Great's Social Thought and Involvement." *The Greek Theological Review* 26 (1981), 81-86.

Hopkins, Dwight N. *Being Human: Race, Culture, and Religion*. Minneapolis, MN: Fortress Press, 2005.

Land, Steven Jack. *Pentecostal Spirituality: A Passion for the Kingdom*. Cleveland, TN: CPT Press, 2010.

Macchia, Frank D. *Baptized in the Spirit: A Global Pentecostal Theology*. Grand Rapids, MI: Zondervan, 2006.

Yong, Amos. *The Spirt Poured Out on All Flesh: Pentecostalism and the Possibility of Global Theology*. Grand Rapid, MI: Baker Academic, 2005.

Chapter 14

Orthodox Christian Spirituality and Social Justice

John Moxen

Justice for individuals within a society is an idea that has been practiced in the Orthodox Church since the time of the Apostles. Principles of Orthodox social justice are as biblical as they are historical. Understanding social justice from an Orthodox Christian perspective requires one to move beyond teaching to understand that fighting for a just society means confronting the status quo within a culture from a pastoral perspective. After all, it is people who enact and receive justice. Justice is an act of true worship, based on love for God as well as one's neighbor.

It is only when a person sees Christ in another that he or she is able to minister as agents of Christ to that person. Demonstrating justice not only connects a person closer to Christ, but more closely connects him or her with fellow brothers and sisters, providing a glimpse of the Kingdom of God. While observing that the movement of the Spirit of God is not always an explicit action, like the projects and programs accomplished through robust social ministry, the work of the Spirit continually takes place, implicitly, anytime a person or group pursues the teachings of Christ, passed down through His Apostles, through the Church. What one says about one Person of the Trinity never negates that the work is being accomplished by the community of all its members. The Holy Spirit cannot be separated from Christ. While the Spirit is distinct, the essential nature is not different. Therefore, when a person elects to follow the teachings of Christ to care for the least of these, per Matthew 25:40, remaining sensitive to the problems that occur within society, he or she pursues the work of the Spirit, Who seeks to build a more just society through the Church.

Social Justice and the Spirit of God within Orthodox History: A Treatment of St. Basil

Social Justice has become a hot-button phrase in American culture. It is a notion that seems to either cause a listener to inch closer in anticipation of agreement or immediately turn away from the discourser in dissent. But what this phrase is not is a new idea. In fact, one of the Orthodox Church's most revered saints wrote extensively on the subject in the fourth century and his writings continue to influence Orthodox Spirituality within a context of social ministry amongst the poor today. St. Basil lived a life of notable privilege[1], which is worth considering when reading about his views toward wealth and affluent people in his later writings. In his homily, "To the Rich", St. Basil writes how "care for the needy requires the expenditure of wealth: when all share alike, disbursing their possessions amongst themselves, they each receive a small portion for their individual needs."[2] To those with wealth and means, he says, "If you had truly loved your neighbor, it would have occurred to you long ago to divest yourself of this wealth."[3]

Along with all of the benefits that society affords to a person of noble status and means, St. Basil's position at birth afforded him many freedoms that were otherwise unavailable to those who were sold and enslaved at birth or capture, or who simply did not have access to such social and financial insurances as he did. St. Basil notes in his homily, "Against Those Who Lend at Interest", that borrowers, who render involuntary service to the profit of another, are enslaved to their lenders.[4] And, in "I Will Tear Down My Barns", St. Basil warns lenders not to traffic "in the needs of others"[5] because scourging another person where it hurts the most—their pocketbook—has a way of binding them to the person who controls their money, which strips them of their freedom, and the lender becomes one who doles out human misery.

Another privilege afforded to St. Basil because of his family's wealth and status was his access to a good education. This concept is no different today for people who are able to afford housing that places them in neighborhoods with the best public schools or in proximity to the best private schools money can buy. St. Basil noticed a difference in the way the world in which he grew up operated in contrast to what he read in the Gospels. He "saw there that a great means of reaching perfection was the selling of one's goods, sharing them with the poor, giving up all care for this life, and the refusal to allow the soul to be turned by any sympathy to earthly things."[6]

Eventually, St. Basil would leave his home in Caesarea to travel through monastic communities in Palestine, Syria, and Egypt, where he witnessed cenobitic monks living a communal life where they all held their goods in common so that there was no private property. He decided that this was the new society that Christ had wanted to establish through his Apostles, and so St. Basil made it his effort to continue these efforts back home. The idea that underpins St. Basil's actions, which does not need to remain in the past, but can be applied even today, is the notion that all material things are not our own. Everything belongs to God. If Christians are willing to view everything as a gift from God, it is far easier to accept the fact that material possessions are to simply pass through one's hands so that others may receive care. This kind of social order is not one that is based on competition and private ownership, but on simplicity and sharing[7]—these ideas appear to be foreign in the modern, Western context, but they are ideas that must be recovered in order to fulfill the vision of Christ for His Kingdom.

St. Basil's conversion was like the conversion of other Christians—it came about as a result of reading the Gospels. But, he interpreted the message more literally than some, especially the mandate to go and sell one's goods and share them with the poor. St. Basil identified with the Rich Young Ruler in the gospels and determined that it was worth letting go of all of his earthly possessions to become perfect. Similarly, St. Clement of Alexandria noted the Rich Young Ruler's unhealthy, even sinful, attachment to worldly possessions, but saw Christ's mandate as a plea to break free from one's fondness for them. When Christians see injustice in today's world, it is often economic injustice. St. Clement believed that a person is not truly free if he or she is attached to the things of this world—like money or material goods.[8] It stands to reason that a person who refuses to let go of what he or she has amassed might feel the need to extend this sense of vassalage toward others. Economic injustice can be observed in any place where there is a wide disparity of wealth. But the people who hold the money, as well as the people who have none, are often in different kinds of subjection. A wealthy man has created for himself a prison of the goods and money he has amassed, which may mean more to him than the people he has taken advantage of in order to create his wealth. And, the man who has less, experiences a lack of financial freedom which keeps him from fully participating in all that God has created for him.

In the writings of the monastic periods of Orthodox Christian history, the poor were always referenced anonymously. Poor people did not have names or faces but were seen as things to whom one could give extra stuff.[9] The problem with this notion is that people who are materially poor are not anonymous. These are real people with real names and real faces. These people are you, the reader, and I, the writer. These people are Christ, the Savior, and Sustainer of all creation. This notion informs the Orthodox understanding of Justice. Schroeder observes that St. Clement's figurative approach and St. Basil's literal approach to the Gospel mandate to sell his possessions, to share with the poor, came to be contextualized by how a person chooses to live out his or her vocation. Monks and nuns would fulfill this commandment by renouncing their worldly possessions in favor of pursuing a cenobitic life in devotion to Christ while others who choose to realize their vocation in the world, do so by breaking free from their attachment to that which had previously bound them— an activity, which is accomplished by the grace provided by Christ.

This two-tiered distinction of pursuing economic freedom by precept vs. counsel has been, and continues to be, widely understood, even if implicitly, by Orthodox Christians, especially in the West. But it is this two-tiered approach that St. Basil rejects, and he does so out of practicality as well as compassion. In "To The Rich", he writes how "care for the needy requires the expenditure of wealth:

when all share alike, disbursing their possessions amongst themselves, they each receive a small portion for their individual needs. Thus, those who love their neighbor as themselves possess nothing more than their neighbor."[10] And, "In Time of Famine and Drought," St. Basil offers the question to people who have great wealth, which, like today, referred to people who held positions of influence and power, whether they have preferred their own enjoyment to the consolation of many others. The more one abounds in wealth, the more they lack in love. If someone has great wealth while another person lacks, the wealthy one has violated the law of love, which applies to everyone—not just monks and nuns.[11] Likewise, a person who allows another to live beneath his means while he enjoys a luxurious life is committing a social and economic injustice against his brother, whereby he expressly rejects the opportunity to show him love. In doing so, the wealthy person distances himself away from his brother, which, in turn, creates a chasm between himself and Christ. Only when a person is willing to see the value in every human life will he recognize that material possessions are not what signals a person's standing with Christ. Rather, this inverse relationship only serves to create greater opportunities for further injustice.

So, when articulating an ethic of justice, in relation to the Spirit of God, from an Orthodox Christian perspective, with St. Basil's ideas in mind, Schroeder rightly explains that justice must be sustainable, distributive, and sociable. From a paradigm that sees resources as limited, St. Basil believes that God has provided a sufficient quantity of materials, land, and food to satisfy every person's needs. However, because the resources are quantitatively limited, they must be dispersed out to be shared equitably. Only when resources are ceaselessly circulating, as opposed to being hoarded by a few wealthy individuals, can an economy be perceived as healthy and just.[12] St. Basil interprets the parable in the Gospel where the rich man decides to tear down his barn in order to build a bigger one so that he can store his enormous harvest as a sign that wealth concentrated in the hands of a few who refuse to adequately disperse what's been given to them by God, will necessarily mean that there will be less for others. This zero-sum approach to economic justice seems to be perceived, by St. Basil, as unsustainable.[13]

A consequence to understanding justice as a sustainable ethic is what Schroeder describes as a distributive mandate, which he receives from St. Basil's teaching to give away whatever extra is left after a person takes care of his or her immediate needs. The Greek word, "επανίσουν" literally translates, "to restore the balance", which describes the process whereby a person responsibly observes the commandment to love one another by sharing with those who are hungry, naked, sick, and needy.[14] However, at the risk of sounding anachronistic, modern society is not very different from the socio-economic context in which St. Basil found himself. The reason people may offer the notion that they have nothing left to share with others is that when they find themselves with a surplus, their definition of need adjusts to fit their new economic situation. But, St. John Chrysostom states that any person who refuses to help another in need is guilty of theft.[15] St. Basil echoes this thought when he asks, "Is not the person who strips another of clothing called a thief? And those who do not clothe the naked when they have the power to do so, should they not be called the same?[16] And, "In Time of Famine and Drought", St. Basil forthcomingly proclaims that "whoever has the ability to remedy the suffering of others, but chooses rather to withhold aid out of selfish motives, may properly be judged, the equivalent of a murderer."[17] What is equally important to St. Basil, which should be equally as important to any Christian, Orthodox or otherwise, concerning justice, is not simply looking to ameliorate the plight of the poor, but to also identify and reform the "structures that create and reinforce the cycle of poverty."[18] This includes, but is not limited to, any kind of scheme that targets the poor, such as predatory lenders, which, anecdotally, seem to be found in abundance in lower-income neighborhoods, or economic deserts. Any attempt to monetize the injustice experienced by the poor is an act of supreme inhumanity. While St. Basil warns the poor to live within their means, he also admonishes those who take advantage of people who borrow money in order to cover their most basic needs for survival. Any society where this takes place provides the appearance of being plagued with moral disability.

In addition to an ethic of justice being sustainable and distributive, Schroeder further suggests that sociability is equally as critical. He notes St. Basil's frequent use of the word, "κοινός", which translates, "common" or "shared", which comes from "κοινωνία", from where we get the English word, "communion." The world was created and is sustained by God for the shared and common benefit of all creation. Humanity has been given many gifts in order that they may be shared with everyone. Sharing and cultivating these gifts is part of what it means to be a good steward of the talents given to us by God, per Matthew 25. While this notion seems to be at odds within the natural order, which appears to promote competition within species, humans seem to be the best at taking more than they actually need for survival, depriving others of their basic needs to live. People who compete with others to continuously expand their catalogue of private ownership are what St. Basil would describe as, "ακοινώνητοι", which means, "unsocial" or "unsociable". God, rather, calls everyone to be social people (κοινωνικός άνθρωπος), which means a person recognizes his or her obligation to the collective order of society and lives in proper relationship with his neighbor.[19] Only when a person is in right relationship with his neighbor can he been seen as one who strives toward creating a just society.

This just society is what St. Basil saw as the purpose of his episcopal ministry. His "New City" is a continuous reconfiguration of the social order, which came to be known as the Basilead. At St. Basil's funeral, St. Gregory of Nazianzus, a contemporary of St. Basil, described his philanthropic legacy as one, which created a "storehouse of piety, the common treasure of the wealthy...where disease is regarded in a religious light, and disaster is thought a blessing, and sympathy put to the test."[20] St. Basil's goal was for these societies to populate the earth. In the United States, there are organizations, like FOCUS North America[21] who seek to participate in St. Basil's vision for taking care of the poor by providing food, resources for job placement, clothing, understanding, shelter, and medical treatment, free of charge.

This social vision for a more humane order is predicated upon an Orthodox notion of justice that requires a full buy-in on principals of sharing. Jesus instructed His disciples to give their extra coat to somebody who did not have one. For St. Basil, selling one's possessions and distributing them to the poor is how one becomes spiritually just. But this way of life is not simply an avenue to help the poor. It is an act of worship amongst the people of God, who are committed to the common good, which is demonstrated through a life of service.[22] This is exactly what the Church is supposed to look like—it is the Kingdom of God, present on earth. St. Basil encourages those willing to participate in this life to imitate the early Christian communities who held all of their material possessions in common to be distributed to each, according to his or her need. They shared meals at a common table and their sense of loving kinship could not be divided or feigned.[23] Wherever people are living with regard for the welfare of the collective whole, there remains the pursuit of justice, which is an idea that is as Biblical as it is historical.

A Biblical Hermeneutic on Social Justice is a Pastoral One

Jesus Christ issued a blueprint on how to live a just life. St. Matthew records in his gospel account, the parable of the sheep and the goats. According to St. Matthew, these two groups will be separated during the eschaton to be positioned at the King's right and left hand, respectively. The sheep, Jesus calls, "blessed" because they are the recipients of His inheritance, which Jesus notes as the "Kingdom prepared for you since the creation of the world" (Matthew 25:34). What sets this group on the right apart from the group on the left is their actions. When Jesus details His prescription, which includes feeding the hungry, satiating the thirsty, welcoming the stranger, clothing the naked, healing the sick, and visiting the imprisoned, the just group is invited to think about how taking care of each kind of person described by Jesus is the same as caring for Jesus, Himself. The King suggests to this group that taking care of the most vulnerable and disenfranchised members of society is what makes one just.

Conversely, the King speaks to the group on his left—the goats. This group has effectively removed themselves from the presence of God by the nature of their actions. Jesus notes how this group failed to feed the hungry, satiate the thirsty, give attention to the stranger, to clothe the naked, to visit the imprisoned, and look after the sick. When this group, likewise, asked Jesus when they saw Him suffer these things, He responded in kind: whatever one fails to do for the most vulnerable and disenfranchised members of society, fails to do for Christ. Mistreating the people who need the most attention and care is an injustice that curses a person to the point of self-removal from the presence of God. This pericope concludes with the reminder that those who refuse to pursue justice for their society's poor will face a judgment, ad infinitum, while those who pursued social justice are rewarded by participating in Divine Life.

What Can We Do?

The beauty of the parable is that it communicates a truth, which transcends first century Palestine. The wisdom contained therein can also be applied today. There are opportunities to pursue social justice in a modern, western context that doesn't require a person to look outside what has been suggested in St. Matthew's recorded account. More than 16% of Americans face hunger (one in six).[24] These people often lack basic access to enough food to feed all of their household members. The USDA refers to this notion as, "food insecurity" and it is a problem that faces homes with children at an 8.6% higher rate than households without children.[25] This problem is not necessarily concentrated, either. A person is able to find food insecure families in every single county across the United States. Only five years after the 2008 recession hit the US, as many as 17.5 million households were labeled, "food insecure." The number of Americans who struggle to find enough food on their table is even higher; close to 50 million.[26] This injustice is not due to a scarcity of food. Forty percent of all purchased food is thrown out, which is worth approximately $165 Billion.[27] This uneaten food could feed twenty-five million Americans. Rather, food insecurity is due to the pervasiveness of poverty.[28]

When one begins to examine a more granular breakdown into some of the United States' disaffected communities, the evidence presents an even bleaker picture.[29] While one in five children are at risk for hunger, the number of Latinos and African-Americans is actually one in three.[30] Food insecurity, which is a result of poverty, which is a consequence of wastefulness, is inherently sinful. Only when a person consciously decides to be a good steward with the plentiful natural resources that exist in the United States can he or she be considered acting according to a Spirit of Justice. A sense of urgency must be shared and spread amongst all people who care to pursue justice for the most vulnerable members of society, especially children who are suffering. Prior to the parable about the separation of the sheep and goats, Jesus gave the example of what behaving like a good steward looks like in Matthew 25:14-30, which describes the cultivation of talents that have been given to a person for the sake of multiplication. God rewards these individuals because

331

they have behaved justly with the talents they have been given. Conversely, to be a poor steward of God's creation could be seen as a disregard for the Spirit of God's pursuit for justice. But, pursuing justice for society is not an impossible task. If one wishes to take seriously the urgency that Christ has given His followers, he or she must look for ways to feed Christ in his or her own community. Donating money or volunteering time at a local food bank or food pantry is one of the easiest ways to feed Christ in one's neighbor, which doesn't require a person to tirelessly search for him. Meeting a person's physical need for nourishment is, at the same time, an act of true worship toward God and participation in the Spirit of God's orientation towards justice with one's neighbor.

Who is My Neighbor?

The Orthodox Churches are against racial segregation and believe in the full equality of all races and people. The Greek Orthodox Archdiocese of America said as much in their statement on Racial Equality in 1963.[31] Regardless of skin color or religion, all people deserve access to equal advantages and benefits afforded to the public. Orthodoxy calls upon people of all faiths who pursue truth and justice to oppose any expression and action of intolerance toward other people. The notion of Christian love is not meant to only be a rhetorical symbol. Rather, it is a commandment, which requires that Christians conform their actions to God's will, which was expressed by [God's] Son, Jesus Christ in John 13:34 when He said that "you must love each other." Equality, peace, and justice aren't just righteous words. They are essential and operational ideas for humanity, and all of creation, that help us grow and develop a deeper sense of respect and love for one another.[32]

The immediate context of the Orthodox leadership for writing this statement had Americans of color in mind. The Greek Orthodox Church made this statement amidst the Civil Rights Movement and were considered thought-leaders amongst other ecclesial groups. While these words are just as true today as they were thirty-five years ago, the audience can certainly be expanded. Not only are Orthodox Christians commanded to regard people of all racial backgrounds within their country, they are also required to treat people beyond invisible boarders respectfully. Whether a person is an immigrant, a refugee, an asylum-seeker, or a citizen, the not-so-radical notion of justice means that every person deserves fair treatment.

Ethnophyletism and Nationalism are an Abdication of Justice

In the ancient Orthodox Church, cities and small towns had their own bishops who exercised ecclesiastical authority over the churches within their territories. Major Christian capitals were called Patriarchates, which are only geographically significant, today. "They are not ethnophyletic, cultural, liturgical or anything else of the sort, and were defined by Ecumenical Synods through sacred canons and ecclesiastical regulations in accordance with Christian teaching against racial discrimination, with Orthodox ecclesiology and with canon law and pastoral requirements."[33] Ethnophyletism is the application of a particular nationality to an ecclesiastical domain. Or, stated simply, it is a conflation between Church and state. The

Orthodox Churches see this kind of national tribalism as inherently disordered because it risks oppressing an extant culture when the Orthodox Faith is introduced into a new area. When Sts. Cyril and Methodious proselytized Eastern Europe, they translated the Bible, liturgical books, and Philokalia (writings of the Church Fathers) into what is known today as Old Church Slavonic, a language they built for the Slavic peoples with whom they shared their Faith.[34] In doing so, they were able to avoid disturbing the local customs, traditions, and dialects while preserving the message of the Gospel. The spirit behind this practice acknowledges that the person receiving the Gospel is not inherently inferior just because he or she comes from a different culture. After all, St. Paul writes in Galatians 3:28 that "there is neither Jew nor Greek, slave nor free, male nor female, for you are all one in Christ." St. Paul, Sts. Cyril and Methodious, and Orthodox Christians today are expected to continue practicing this approach, which can be difficult to do in the West, especially in the United States, where one is able to observe a rise in ethnocentric nationalism.

In 2017, in response to the racist violence in Charlottesville, Virginia, the Assembly of Canonical Orthodox Bishops of the United States of America stated that they stood with all people of good will who condemned the hateful violence resulting in the loss of life, which was promoted by racial bigotry and an ideology of white supremacy. The Orthodox bishops were emphatic in their declaration against protecting, sanctioning, or promoting hatred, racism, or any discriminating behavior that is not rooted in respect of the law or love of God. The traditions of the Orthodox Church, which are founded upon the gospel of Jesus Christ are incompatible with any system of ideas that proclaims the superiority of one race over another. The Orthodox understanding of God is a Person who shows no partiality or favoritism (Deuteronomy 10:17, Romans 2:11). Jesus destroyed the wall that separated humanity from God and humanity from each other (Ephesians 2:14) and Christians are commanded not to associate with the unfruitful works of darkness, but to bring then to light (Ephesians 5:11). The Orthodox bishops rightly understand darkness to mean hatred, which bears every kind of injustice.

The person who hates his brother walks in darkness (1 John 2:11), which often looks like treating someone without regard for their justice. American Christians, Orthodox or otherwise, would do well to recall how Orthodox hierarchs from around the world assembled in Constantinople in 1872 to denounce every form of xenophobia and phyletism. A person or country cannot be just if she promotes racial or national superiority or ethnic bias. Proclamations made by Neo-Nazis, white nationalists, and fascists "betray the core human values of love and solidarity." If xenophobia continues to express itself within the contemporary American ethos, no matter how subtly, the distance between God will broaden, leaving room for injustice to prevail.

Conclusion

Any person or organization who seeks to follow the mandate of Christ to care for the least of his or her brethren, paying close attention to the various social problems that have plagued and continue to plague its most vulnerable members, does the work of the Spirit of God, Who cannot be separated from the other two members of the Trinity in the life of the Church, especially with concern for its building toward a just society.

It is the mission of the Spirit, and thus, the mission of the Church, to protect and give life to the people who need help. This mission is without condition, expecting no reward other than the ultimate reward: life with God. This work is not always explicit, but it is no less visible. Often, the implicit work of the Spirit of producing a just society can be seen whenever and wherever social ministry is taking place. The Church acts to liberate society from injustice. Social Justice is an act of worship, connecting a person with Christ as well as his or her neighbor.

It does not take place in a vacuum. Any person, Orthodox Christian or otherwise, who strives for a just society must realize that his or her actions affect people beyond his or her immediate encounter. Keeping this notion in mind is critical when reflecting on whether one's personal behavior might be received as justice to a stranger.

However, that is precisely why one's definition of "stranger" must diminish and an understanding of "neighbor" must necessarily broaden. Reaching back into Christian history, the reader is confronted with Church Fathers who received from Holy Tradition, the belief that it is necessary to take care of the most marginalized members of society in order to be a just steward of God's creation. In his homilies, St. Basil speaks Truth to power to the wealthy, encouraging them to consider how they might be able to use the gifts which they have been given by God for the sake of the poor.

Likewise, Christians today do well when every effort is made to spread prosperity and blessings of every kind (spiritual as well as material) instead of fetishizing poverty by the way it is attached to a caricaturization of morality. The practical steps one can take to alleviate the plight of the poor in society are simple: do not look to fix someone who is not broken. When a person is viewed as incomplete or un-whole, their inherent image bearing quality of the Spirit of God is diminished. Rather, serve those who have less, unconditionally.

Bibliography

11 Facts about Hunger in the US. 2014.
https://www.dosomething.org/facts/11-facts-about-
hunger-us. Chrysostom, John. *Second Sermon on Lazarus
and the Rich Man*; in *St. John Chrysostom: On Wealth and
Poverty*, trans. by Catherine P. Roth. Crestwood, NY: St.
Vladimir's Seminary Press, 1984.

Coleman-Jensen, A., Gregory, C., & Singh, A. "Household Food
Security in the United States in 2013." USDA Economic
Research Service, 2014.

Feeding America. "Map the Meal Gap: Child Food Insecurity 2011."
Feeding America, 2011.

Greek Orthodox Archdiocesan Statement on Racial Equality 1963.
http://civilrights.goarch.org/-/greek-orthodox-archdiocesan-
statement-on-racial-equality-1963?inheritRedirect=true.

Saint Gregory Nazianzen, Oration XLIII: Panegyric on Saint Basil
(ed. Philip Schaff and Henry Wace; trans. Charles Gordon
Browne, M.A. and James Edward Swallow, M.A.; NPNF 7,
Second Series; Grand Rapids, MI: Wm. Eerdmans Publishing
Co., 1983) 418-419

Gunder, Dana. "Wasted Food: How America Is Losing Up to 40
Percent of Its Food from Farm to Fork to Landfill." National
Resources Defense Council, 2012.

International Food Policy Research Institute. "2012 Global Hunger
Index." IFPRI, 2012.

Kopecek, Thomas A. "The Social Class of the Cappadocian Fathers,"
Church History, 42 (1973), 461-466.

St. Basil the Great, Trans. By C. Paul Schroeder. On Social Justice. Crestwood, NY: St. Vladimir's Seminary Press. 2009.

St. Cyril and Methodius. Lives of the Saints. Pravmir. http://www.pravmir.com/article_39.html.

The Assembly of Canonical Orthodox Bishops of the United States of America. Response to Racist Violence in Charlottesville, VA. http://civilrights.goarch.org/-/response to-racist-violence-in-charlottesville-va?

The Phenomenon of Ethnophyletism in Recent Years. http://civilrights.goarch.org/-/the-phenomenon-of-ethnophyletism-in-recent-years?inheritRedirect=true.

Chapter 15

Global Pentecostalism: A Spirit-Led Movement of, for, and by the Poor

Richard E. Waldrop

> Pentecostal churches are not "sects," "steered by U.S. capital and the CIA". They have sprung up out of the ground everywhere, like mushrooms. They are an independent popular movement of the poor. They have something to say to the whole of Christendom on earth, and have liberating experiences to pass on to all men and women.[1]

> Pentecostalism has arisen principally among the poorest and most excluded sectors of society, which, because of this condition, find themselves exposed to falling into all kinds of other social ills.[2]

Pentecostalism from the Perspective of the Poor

To write a complete work on the topic of "Pentecostals and the Poor" would be a gargantuan task given the amount of historical, theological, sociological and contextual information that would need to be covered. The subject could certainly be the topic of an entire volume or book series. Interestingly, the recent 47th Annual Meeting of the Society of Pentecostal Studies, held in March 2018, in

Cleveland, Tennessee, was dedicated to the topic of "The Good News of the Kingdom and the Poor in the Land." An excellent example from that conference was my colleague, Wilmer Estrada Carrasquillo's paper, *"A [not so] Poor Conversation: The Poor and their Contribution to Wesleyan and Pentecostal Thought,"*[3] in which he cites several scholars of Pentecostalism, and others, in regards to the pivotal role the poor have played, not only as privileged recipients of evangelistic and missionary efforts but, more importantly, as protagonists and central *subjects* in the rise and development of the movement worldwide. When Gustavo Gutiérrez wrote of *La fuerza historica de los pobres* [4] (The Power of the Poor u History) from Lima in 1979 he probably had little comprehension as to the implications of what was actually taking place on the ground in relation to Pentecostals and the poor. But to these issues, distinctions and developments we will turn our attention after some brief caveats.

For the purposes of this chapter, I will necessarily be selective in terms of how much time to spend in the different areas of emphasis that may help us understand better the chosen topic. Due to the broad range of practices and emphases in the constellation of Pentecostal values, here will also be some limitations as to which of those will be touched upon.

A note of clarification is also in order to establish the differentiation between the use of the terms "Pentecostals" and "Pentecostalism." My understanding is that there are many contextual iterations or manifestations of Pentecostal theology, thus many different Pentecostalisms. Time will not allow us to go into detail here but, for example, Euro-American Pentecostalism in North

America will generally have a different disposition toward the poor than African or Latin American Pentecostalisms, and even then, there are many nuances or hues in the matrix of the Pentecostal churches in those continents. For example, in Africa, the complexity is great if the African Instituted (or Initiated) Churches[5] are included in the mix of the "historic" missionary-related Pentecostal churches and the more indigenous or autochthonous national or regional Pentecostal bodies with little or no direct ties to Western Pentecostal churches. Similar observations can be made of the Pentecostal churches in Latin America and, to some extent, Asia.

Therefore, to reflect upon "Pentecostals and the Poor" seems to be a more accurate way of approaching the subject since I see my objective as being able to communicate something of the disposition of the Pentecostal churches, leaders, and people in general toward the poor. Still, the complicating question must be posed: "Which Pentecostals and from where?"

Recently, the global Lutheran-Pentecostal Dialog was held in Santiago, Chile (October 7-11, 2018) and the mutually agreed upon topic of the conversation was "Good News to the Poor". From the Pentecostal perspective, the location was ideal for the discussion of this subject. Chile is truly a laboratory for all things Pentecostal. The Chilean Pentecostal movement, one of the earliest on record, dates back to 1909, with no direct connection with the famed Los Angeles Azusa Street revival.[6] It was in Chile from which one of the first of a long list of sociological studies of Pentecostalism was executed and published in 1968 in Spanish by Christian Lalive D'Epinay, and later translated under the auspicious title *Haven of the Masses: A Study of the Pentecostal Movement in Chile*.[7] Interestingly, in that volume there is a printed Scripture text from Isaiah 61:1-2 included on the page of acknowledgments just before foreword:

> The spirit of the Lord is upon me,
> Because the Lord has anointed me;
> He has sent me to bring good new to the poor,
> To bind up the brokenhearted,
> To proclaim liberty to the captives,
> And release to the prisoners;
> To proclaim the year of the Lord's favor,
> And the day of vengeance of our God.

It was also in Chile where much later a study was developed on "Prophetic Pentecostalism"[8] which chronicles, among other things, the case of the Pentecostal support of the Allende socialist government and prophetic witness, together with Lutherans and others, against the atrocities of the Pinochet regime. In that volume is also the interesting case of social activism of a Pentecostal congregation in the working-class neighborhood of La Victoria in Santiago and the rise of the Pentecostal NGO, SEPADE (in English, Evangelical Service for Development)[9].

The subjects of "Pentecostals" and "poverty" or "the poor" have been heavily researched during the past 40 years from a variety of perspectives and with a broad variety of conclusions.[10] It is apparent that this very strong and intimate relationship does exist between the poor and Pentecostals.

Speaking of poverty, a second note of clarification, briefly, is needed in relation to the term "the poor". Although poverty may be understood as relative to specific cultures and contexts, here we will take, as a point of departure, the idea of the materially poor, or as Peruvian Pentecostal pastor and theologian Darío López Rodriquez writes in his seminal work, of 'God's Special Love for the Poor and Marginalized':

> Jesus's pronouncement in the synagogue of Nazareth had a very explicit social and political content. The Messiah had come to proclaim good news to the poor: euangelizō ptōchos (Luke 4:18). It is worth noting that this declaration began in the underdeveloped province of Galilee, a region populated by a mixed race that the pious of Jerusalem despised, an area inhabited by hundreds of widows, orphans, poor, and unemployed. From Galilee began the announcement of the good news of liberation to the poor and oppressed[11].

Unfortunately, however, it cannot be said that all Pentecostals share the same concern for the poor that may be evident in places like Chile, Peru, Ghana or Nigeria. So, the complex question remains to be further explicated, what is the nature of the relationship between Pentecostals and the poor?

Some Historical and Contextual Perspectives

From the multifaceted, multinational and multicultural genesis of the distinct but oftentimes related Pentecostal revivals around the turn of the 20th century, historical data, without a doubt, will prove a clear intimate relationship between the poor and the emerging

344

Pentecostal movements. There are so many examples that we will have to be very selective. I would want to be cautious, however, in making a claim that the relationship between Pentecostals and the poor is strictly exclusive of other socio-economic classes of people who may not fit neatly into those we describe as impoverished.

For example, history is quite clear that there have always been those of other classes who have joined or come to be a part of the movement from other Christian traditions, or who were converted to Christian faith from other social classes. These records show that at times these ministers from other established churches or denominations would come into the Pentecostal movement as a result of their own experience of Spirit baptism. And with the ongoing development of the movement, especially the Global North, Pentecostal churches have grown and become quite comfortable— too comfortable some would say—among the middle and upper classes of Europe and North America, and to a lesser degree on other continents.

In any case, the argument can be made, with clear statistical support, that the majority of Pentecostals are still poor in the Majority World where the vast majority of Pentecostals reside today. That would mean that, globally, Pentecostals are strongest among the impoverished masses. In other words, the majority of Pentecostals today are poor. One North American researcher, Philip Jenkins states it as follows: "African and Latin American Christians are people for whom the New Testament Beatitudes have a direct relevance inconceivable for most Christians in Northern societies. When Jesus told the 'poor' they were blessed, the word used does not imply relative deprivation, it means total poverty, or destitution. The great majority of Southern Christians (and increasingly of all Christians) really are the poor, the hungry, the persecuted, even the dehumanized. India has a perfect translation for Jesus' word in the term *Dalit*, literally "crushed" or "oppressed"[12].

In Latin America, according to Mexican Pentecostal historian, Daniel Chiquete[13], the first adherents of the Pentecostal movement lived, with their contemporary counterparts, the shared situations of sickness, unemployment, illiteracy, and lack of housing. This condition of material poverty seemed to be the common denominator among most or all Pentecostals in the early and subsequent stages of its development.

Although I am not as familiar with Pentecostalism on other continents, I believe that Latin America, more than any other place, has been where larger numbers of Pentecostals have come to terms consciously with their privileged place among the poor. One continental collective of national Pentecostal leaders, CEPLA (Comisión Evangélica Pentecostal Latinoamericana), was very active during the late 1900s in organizing a series of "Encounters" (*Encuentros*) dealing with a variety of issues directly relating to a Pentecostal commitment to and with the poor. The result of one such encounter was an edited English language volume, *Pentecostalism and Liberation: A Latin American Experience*[14]. Other Pentecostal denominations such as the Church of God and the Assemblies of God, in their various national or regional groupings, have also intentionally tried to come to terms with the meaning of their relationship and praxis among the poor. For example, in December 1985, the Latin American educational leadership of the Church of God (Cleveland, TN) organized a consultation in Puerto

346

Rico to discuss the import of "Liberation Theology" for the work of the churches. The findings of this consultation were published by the *Centro Evangélico Latinoamericano de Estudios Pastorales* (CELEP) in their journal *PASTORALIA*[15]. More recently, other mature Pentecostal voices, mostly from Latin America[16] have joined the chorus of pastors, educator, and denominational leaders, all showing the way forward toward a renewed understanding and commitment of the Pentecostal churches as seeing themselves as communities among, with, of, for and by the poor.

In reference to the Azusa Street revival in Los Angeles (1906-1913), Pentecostal historian, Cecil M. Robeck, Jr., writes that an "important aspect of the Azusa Street Mission and revival is that it continues to serve as an example for its outreach to the marginalized—the poor, women, and people of color"... and that "[o]ne of Pastor Seymour's favorite biblical texts was Luke 4:18-19."[17] William Seymour (1870-1922) was the African-American leader of the Azusa Street revival. According to one chronicler[18], Seymour was born in Louisiana, the oldest son of ex-slaves, and lived in abject poverty. Left with one eye and a scared face as a result of a childhood illness, he nevertheless rose to prominence as the founder and catalyst of the U.S. based Pentecostal movement with unparalleled global missionary influence.

Similar stories of poverty can be told of other branches of U.S. Pentecostalism, especially in the Appalachian South, where the Church of God (Cleveland, Tennessee) was birthed among poor white farmers and marginalized mountain folk[19].

According to scholars, Ogbu Kalu and Allan Anderson,[20] African Pentecostalism is so heterogeneous so that it is impossible

347

to contain it within rigid conventional definitions. However, poverty is the constant reality of life more so than on any other continent. It is in this context of extreme poverty that Pentecostal or Pentecostal-like churches have flourished. Anderson attributes the growth of these churches, in part, to their ability to "fulfill African aspirations, with roots in a marginalized and underprivileged society struggling to find dignity and identity in the face of brutal colonialism and oppression."[21] Today, Africa represents the continent where Christian churches are both the largest numerically and the poorest. According to Anderson and others, in most countries of Africa, Pentecostal churches represent the majority of Protestant Christians.

Asian Pentecostals are extremely culturally and contextually diverse as well. From Chinese house churches, Indian churches of the urban slums or of *Dalit* origins in Kerala, to Korean and Indonesian megachurches, the complexity of Pentecostalism is truly mind-boggling. From India comes a new volume by Ivan Satyavrata[22] in which he chronicles what he calls "the Pentecostal tradition of social engagement", taking his cue from Miller and Yamamori's edited volume.[23] Satyavrata's argument is that Indian Pentecostalism has a long history of engagement with the poor beginning with its indigenous roots in the Mukti Mission led by social reformer, Pandita Ramabai, and Minnie Abrams followed later by a Pentecostal revival movement in Kolkata led by missionaries, Alfred and Lilian Garr, from the Azusa Street mission. Here, Allan Anderson sheds additional light: "Pentecostals in various parts of the world have always had various programs of social action, ever since the involvement of Ramabai's Mukti Mission in India in the early 1900s or the work of Lilian Thrasher among orphans in Egypt from 1911. Early Pentecostals were involved in socio-political criticism, including opposition to war, capitalism and racial discrimination. African American Pentecostals have been in the forefront of the civil rights movement. Throughout the world today Pentecostals are involved in practical ways caring for the poor and the destitute, those often "unwanted" by the larger society." [24]

With the above rather "optimistic" overview of the organic, symbiotic, and dynamic relationship between Pentecostals and the poor, it is also necessary to point out some glaring exceptions and inadequacies. First, as a Pentecostal missionary from North America, I must clearly state that, as a general rule, the gospel taken from the North to the rest of the world has too often been limited in scope to the spiritual dimension of human existence. This truncated version of the gospel was given to and accepted by U.S. Pentecostals around the mid-1900s from our Fundamentalist counterparts who had fought to keep the gospel pure from "liberal" and "modernist" influences, as they understood it, earlier in the century. For one reason or another—perhaps due to the need for ecclesiastical and theological acceptability at the time— most Pentecostals in the U.S. bought into the Fundamentalist narrative and, together with the strange bedfellow of Dispensational eschatology, Pentecostal mission from North America was reduced primarily to "preaching the gospel and saving souls to go to heaven."[25] In this way, all but the most basic kinds of social service were frowned upon if not dismissed or prohibited. This was true in the case of most North American Pentecostal mission boards with few notable exceptions.

It must also be said that, in the worst of cases, North American missionaries and mission boards (Pentecostals and others) have been imperialistic in terms of their culture and politics as they have historically and uncritically sided with the policies of the U.S. government. In the case of Latin America, as in other places, by the 1960s through the 1980s the specter of Communism and Liberation Theology was being taunted by U.S.-based missionaries as an excuse for further prohibiting more advanced kinds of social service, especially those of the more activist or politically-engaged varieties. This set the stage for conflict between national Pentecostal churches, missionaries, North American denominations and sending agencies. Many national Pentecostal churches came out solidly in favor of a more wholistic understanding of mission even when it necessitated a rupture with the North American organizations representing paternalistic mission models and practices. Thankfully, many of us survived the conflicts with a few wounds and scars to prove it[26] and now we are attempting to move into an era of increased understanding and acceptance of the integrity of mission with the clear conviction of God's special love for the poor—even as many North American Pentecostal churches struggle to maintain their identity over against the prevailing influences of nationalism and neoliberal capitalism under the political pressures exerted by the so-called Religious Right and exacerbated further by the policies of the administration of President Donald Trump.

From these historical and contextual points of reference we will now move to some key theological emphasis that undergird the relationship between Pentecostals and the poor.

Biblical and Theological Perspectives

Here we will mention some salient features or contours of Pentecostal theology especially as they relate to the poor. First, Pentecostals have generally been touted as being "people of the book". This affirmation may be more complex than it appears. Globally speaking, and especially among the poor and illiterate, it can be questioned whether or not Pentecostals have the same view of Scripture as their Evangelical and Fundamentalist counterparts. The doctrine of biblical inerrancy does not necessarily play well into a Pentecostal understanding of the dynamic relationship that exists between Scripture, Spirit, and community of faith, as explained in the groundbreaking work of Pentecostal theologian, Kenneth J. Archer.[27] In any case, there can be no doubt of the very high regard that Pentecostals have of Scripture and their attempts to adhere to its teaching as they variously understand them to be. One of the early defining Pentecostal statements regarding Scripture comes from the Church of God (Cleveland, Tennessee) although it may not be original to that body. It states, "The Church of God stands for the whole Bible, rightly divided, and for the New Testament as the only rule of government and discipline"[28].

In terms of specific sections of Scripture, according to many Pentecostal scholars and pastoral practitioners,[29] the Gospel of Luke and the Acts of the Apostles, considered together to be Lucan literature, have the most prominent place in the Pentecostal "canon." In Luke, for example, much emphasis is given to various themes that have attracted Pentecostal interest such as the Holy Spirit at work in the lives of Zacharias, Mary, Elizabeth, Simeon, and John the Baptist, as well as the descent of the Spirit upon Jesus at his public baptism

351

by John, and Jesus' own reference to the Spirit's anointing at the beginning of his Messianic Proclamation in Nazareth (Luke 4: 18). Another theme in Luke with strong Pentecostal appeal is prayer. Jesus is shown to be in prayer on nine occasions while two exclusively Lucan parables are dedicated to the centrality of prayer in the life of the disciples (Lk. 18: 1-8; 18:9-14). Deliverance from demons is another topic dealt with on at least seven occasions in Luke. This appeal to the supernatural, miraculous power of God for divine healing and deliverance has been a staple of Pentecostal praxis from the beginning of the movement. The privileged place of women and children in Luke's gospel also points to the strong presence and participation of both of these groups in Pentecostal churches.

Moving on to Acts of the Apostles, there are obvious connections between Pentecostal experience and the outpouring of the Holy Spirit, not only in Acts 2, but in other references to receiving the Spirit in Acts 8, 9, 10, 11 and 19. The accompanying experience of speaking in tongues (Acts 2, 10 and 19) has been a hallmark of the Pentecostal movement from its inception. The earlier referenced prophethood of believers, in word and deed, is another mark of Luke-Acts that Pentecostals have taken very seriously. By prophethood, we refer to anointed speech as in preaching or prophetic utterances as gifts of the Spirit in order to communicate God's words in any given situation. In the Pentecostal churches, this ability is given even to the poorest, illiterate, most unlikely persons who yield themselves to become subjects and participants in the divine mission. Glossolalia becomes, in a real sense, a kind of speech by which socio-economic, linguistic, and cultural walls are broken down. It may even be understood to be a kind of social or political protest against those mighty oppressors who wield the powers of manipulation by wealth and worldly communication. Finally, Luke-Acts is very "Pentecostal" in the sense of the urgency of mission and evangelization. Pentecostals take quite literally Jesus' injunction to be filled with the Spirit and to be witness to the ends of the earth (Acts 1:8; Luke 24:47).

From Luke-Acts, by extension, the writings or letters of the Apostle Paul, especially as they impinge upon his missionary exploits and subsequent pastoral exhortations, also have historically struck a chord among Pentecostals since they speak to the everyday lived experience of being on a pilgrimage of mission in the world but having to deal with the mundane issues of shared live in community and in society at large.

Finally, for Pentecostals, many of the narratives of the Old Testament have a special meaning. The stories of slavery, exodus, deliverance, pilgrimage, conquest, and jubilation are signposts to help remind them of, or to rehearse as in the case of Israel, the great deeds of God in favor of his people through the ages.

Pentecostal Praxis and the Poor

Most Pentecostals would see worship as the center of their experience of "life in the Spirit" but this should be understood much more broadly than regular Sunday or weekly church services. Steven J. Land, in his seminal work [30], argues quite convincingly that the *gestalt* of Pentecostal identity is the *shared experience of Pentecostal spirituality*, which includes not only the liturgy of a worship service but, more importantly, the personal and shared *experience with God* at many different levels. For the poor, this shared experience is of vital importance since it is infused with communal concerns for a

353

broad range of issues and practices, most with very positive effects. These include healing practices, fasting, sacraments (sometimes expanded to include foot-washing or the use of natural elements such as water, for cleansing rituals in the case of some African Instituted Churches) smudging, or drumming circles in the case of some contextualized North American indigenous Pentecostals[31], dynamic narrative preaching, singing and drama, altar services (tarrying), street evangelism, mutual aid, spiritual retreats, testimony services, and corporate concert, and personal prayer, all-night prayer meetings (*vigilias*), to name a few.

Pentecostal spirituality is so fluid and adaptable as to be easily assimilated into diverse cultural contexts, from the "cold Northlands" of Canada and Scandinavia and the more "quietist" Pentecostals there to the many "underground" small groups of believers in Vietnam, China and in some Muslim contexts across North Africa and the Middle East, and on to the "hot" tropical lowlands of the Caribbean and Latin American coastlands where Pentecostals worship to the beats of *salsa, merengue, bachata, norteño*, reggae, or whatever their preferred musical genre may be. Even under austere Communist rule in Romania, Pentecostals were able to adapt and even flourish although forced to practically have an unseen and unheard presence. So much so, that after Communist rule was lifted, a prohibition against applause or the clapping or raising of hands continued in some churches, such was the extreme degree of its' inculturation.

If we consider the scope of the foundation of support that these kinds of practices provide for the poor, we may be able to begin to appreciate the meaning and value it has. Opportunities for self-

354

expression abound. Those who are considered to be "nobodies" in this world suddenly recuperate a sense of dignity and worth as they stand together to sing, to preach, to serve as ushers, deacons, or to work with the children or young people, and to literally find themselves, their Spirit-given gifts, and their individual place of service in the wider community of church and the Kingdom of God.

In terms of pedagogy, Pentecostal educator Cheryl Bridges Johns [32] and others, have critically examined Paulo Freire's *Pedagogy of the Oppressed*[33], and have been able to tease out some of the nuances of the more informal or non-formal way of knowing that many poor Pentecostals have most naturally used to strengthen their understanding of Scripture and the meaning of discipleship in the Christian life. In this way, Darío López also writes of the connection between Pentecostal discipleship, spirituality, and celebration in terms of the *fiesta* of the Spirit[34]. At best, it is jubilant and life-living experience, but also it is an alternative way of doing theology and means of shaping Pentecostals' life in the Spirit, especially in contexts where many Pentecostal believers still have limited access to formal education. Herein lies the great value of the oral nature of primal Pentecostalism. Hollenweger wrote about the black oral root of Pentecostalism but then expanded on that title and that root to include a number of global Pentecostal expressions[35]. All of this points to the favored status of the poor among Pentecostal churches that sing, shout, dance, dramatize, and preach their theology.

Since space is limited, we will mention only two or three additional issues that seem to be of universal import in the constellation of Pentecostal practices. Healing would certainly be toward the top of the list of Pentecostal praxes, and here I use the

355

term praxis advisedly. We not only pray for the sick publicly and privately, sometimes sacramentally anointing them with oil, but we also learn to reflect critically on those experiences. What happens when someone is not healed or when someone dies of the disease from which we had prayed for their healing? Miracles do happen but certainly not always and not as frequently as we would like. The poor have looked to the Divine Healer for deliverance when they seem to have absolutely no other options and certainly no money for or access to medical help, and on many occasions, they have been healed! Other forms of healing have also been incorporated into Pentecostal practice, such as Healing Homes and more recently, medical clinics, hospitals, and other services for the poor and needy. Historical theologian, Kimberly Ervin Alexander, has contributed a well-researched volume dealing with subject of Pentecostal healing but limited primarily to the North American context.[36]

Some apparent Pentecostal distinctives that may be more difficult to comprehend are the phenomena of glossolalia (speaking in tongues) and other related ecstatic experiences such as certain states of unconsciousness or, perhaps, subconsciousness, dreams, visions, physical and emotional outbursts, etc. While many North American classical Pentecostal denominations have maintained that Spirit baptism is always accompanied by glossolalia (as in the case of those Acts passages mentioned earlier), the reality in the Pentecostal rank and file is quite different. In fact, some non-North American Pentecostal groups (i.e. Chilean) have never held to this "initial evidence" doctrine while many other Pentecostal bodies around the world no longer hold, formally or informally, to this teaching. Although I am not aware of any global research or study on this issue,

Pentecostal believers are made up of those who speak in tongues, some often, occasionally, or rarely, or those who never do.

Many years ago, I remember a rather informal survey being conducted in Guatemala by one leader of the *Iglesia de Dios Evangelio Completo* (Cleveland, Tennessee affiliate) with the dire result (for that leader) that a low percentage of those surveyed had ever spoken in tongues. The leader then went on a campaign to promote more experiences of Spirit-baptism, but I never was able to ascertain any of the exact results. However, it should be clearly stated that many Pentecostal believers do speak in tongues and many others, especially the poor, are more open to experience what they consider to be supernatural phenomena such as visions, dreams and other physical or emotional manifestations of their relationship with God through the Spirit. My experience has shown that Africans and African-American Pentecostals, and Christians in general, seem to have a cultural "predisposition" toward speaking in tongues and other "Spirit-induced" types of religious behaviors. Many of these can be understood as a means of direct communication with God in ways that sometimes bypass the "normal" processes of human reasoning through altered, or alternative, states of consciousness. Of course, these experiences are not strictly unique to Pentecostal Christians or even to Christians in general, as they have been reported or recorded on many occasions in cultures, especially non-Western ones, which are more in tune to spiritual and supernatural influences and worldviews.

If worship is understood to be the center of life in the Spirit for Pentecostals, then mission and evangelization would be considered to be the dynamic cutting edge of Pentecostal experience.

Pentecostal churches have multiplied very rapidly throughout the 20th century, especially among the poor. Interestingly, it seems that Pentecostal churches are not now growing and expanding as rapidly in the Global North where Pentecostalism has become a more prominent feature in European and Euro-American middle- class societies. The inverse is true in the Global South where, on one hand, Pentecostal churches have retained their vibrant and passionate evangelistic zeal and, on the other, where the poor continue to flock to those churches in large numbers. This early missionary impulse of spreading the fires of Pentecost, about which Allan Anderson wrote[37], has continued to be a hallmark of the movement globally.

Some, perhaps in a triumphalistic way, would say that Pentecostalism has become the greatest missionary force in the history of Christianity. Many contemporary observers of Christianity[38] believe that Pentecostal/Charismatic Christianity now represents the largest family of believers in the world after Roman Catholicism. To the extent that this may be true, it is certainly due to the huge numbers of poor that have embraced Christian faith in these churches and have become the protagonists the movement. I suppose I will never forget that in Guatemala in the late 1970s, the *Iglesia de Dios Evangelio Completo* was growing so rapidly and spontaneously that even the leaders (overseers, bishops) could not keep track of its expansion. Wherever peasants or indigenous believers would migrate to work in the markets or the coffee plantations, or if they were displaced or migrate to the larger cities, they would naturally share their Pentecostal faith and many times raise up village and *barrio* groups of believers later to be formally organized into "local churches."

How can all of this be explained? It has perhaps become something of a simplistic quip or cliché, but the observation has been made by several authors[39] that in Latin America during the 1960s and 1970s, while liberation theology there developed its "preferential option for the poor," the poor opted for the Pentecostal churches.

Samuel Escobar explains this in the following terms:

"From the sixteenth to the eighteenth centuries the Roman Catholic Church provided ideological justification for a system that enslaved minorities and kept dominating elites in power. After independence in the nineteenth century, the church opposed modernizing groups who, in turn, welcomed Protestant churches with the promise of more democratic influences. The Cold War brought tensions and divisions, but also dreams of utopias. Globalization has brought painful realities to this rapidly urbanizing continent. Attempting to address the new reality, Catholic bishops at Medellin voiced "a preferential option for the poor."

Pentecostalism became the new, growing face of Protestantism in Latin America. In spite of the fact that the Catholic Church made an intentional option for the poor, the poor opted for the Pentecostal churches. A major reason for this lies in its presentation of the Christian message within the culture of poverty. The result is a movement that empowers the poor to improve

359

their own lives. A serious weakness in this new Christianity, however, is the tendency of those adherents who gain political power to repeat earlier patterns of corruption and self-enrichment.

As a consequence, it fails to transform corrupt social and political structures. Catholic and Protestant Christians must come to terms with their disunity and rivalry for the sake of Christian witness[40].

This brings us to a final area of Pentecostal praxis that may not be taken into consideration by many observers or critics of the movement, that of social responsibility, social service or social action. For most Pentecostals, social responsibility has been primarily limited—with some notable exceptions—to the spheres of mutual help and some forms of social and material assistance to neighbors in need. But in other situations, Pentecostal efforts at social transformation has led to the defense of human rights and other forms of social and political activism. Here, the results have been mixed. Some researchers[41] would argue for the more recent development of a "new face" of Pentecostal social engagement among and for the poor while others would prefer to trace Pentecostal social action back to the earlier days of the movement. Certainly, material can be found in both directions. However, if we are looking for formally organized, officially sanctioned, social or political action campaigns we may be sorely disappointed. There are certainly some cases of social activism that were undertaken among Pentecostals from some of the earliest days until now. One clear case in point—although not recognized by many Pentecostals today—are the many pronouncements made by early Pentecostal preachers, leaders and even denominations, against war, militarism, and even capitalism, many of them collected in the volume, *Early Pentecostals on Nonviolence and Social Justice: A Reader*[42]. Only one example from Charles Parham will have to suffice here:

> The past order of civilization was upheld by the power of nationalism, which in turn was upheld by the spirit of patriotism, which divided the peoples of the world by geographical boundaries, over which each fought the other until they turned the world into a shamble. The ruling power of this old order has always been the rich, who exploited the masses for profit or drove them en masse to war, to perpetuate their misrule. The principle teachers of patriotism maintaining nationalism were the churches, who have lost their spiritual power and been forsaken of God.
> Thus, on the side of the old order in the coming struggle, will be arrayed the governments, the rich, and the churches, and whatever forces they can drive or patriotically inspire to fight for them. On the other hand, the new order that rises out of the sea of humanity knows no national boundaries, believing in the universal brotherhood of mankind and the establishment of the teachings of Jesus Christ as a foundation for all laws, whether political or social.[43]

Another case in point briefly mentioned above is that of the social reformer and Indian Pentecostal pioneer, Pandita Ramabai, whose crusading work focused on the plight of impoverished women and children, establishing homes for widows, prostitutes, and orphaned children in many different locations around the turn of the 20th century in India. More recently, it has also been documented that many African and African-American Pentecostals have been engaged in the struggles for civil and human rights in the U.S.A. and in South Africa[44]. Another intriguing study was written by Brazilian sociologist Francisco Cartaxo Rolim which revealed the participation of Pentecostals in the *Ligas Campesinas* (Peasant Leagues or Movements) in their struggle against the injustices of the large landowners of the sugarcane plantations in the Brazilian States of Paraiba and Pernambuco from mid-1950 to the early 1960s.[45]

We have already made mention earlier of the Chilean Pentecostals' struggle against the dictatorship of Pinochet in the early 1980s. Some of the above three cases have been connected to Marxist theories of class struggles and it is quite possible that some Pentecostals would align themselves politically in that direction, as would be the case of the Unión Evangélica Pentecostal Venezolana (Venezuelan Evangelical Pentecostal Union) [46] that has given open support to the government of late president Hugo Chávez. There have also been cases of individual Pentecostals' support for armed resistance against military dictatorships in Central America where some church members gave aid to or actually fought or otherwise collaborated with guerrilla forces such as the Sandinistas in Nicaragua or the U.R.N.G in Guatemala[47].

Other recent clear examples of Pentecostal defense of human rights and solidarity with the poor have been, for example, the leadership given to the *pastoral de la guardarraya en Vieques, Puerto*

Rico, a protest movement against the military practice bombing of the island of Vieques, given by pastor Wilfredo Estrada Adorno[48]. Additionally, the thousands of Hispanic churches in the U.S., for many years have also served as true sanctuaries for undocumented Latin American immigrants, providing them with a spiritual covering, family networks, employment opportunities, and many times even going to the border to provide transportation after they have "illegally" crossed into U.S. territory.

Finally, in this section, we need to deal with the particularly problematic issue of the more recent Pentecostal participation in politics. Here, we understand that the category of "politics" is much broader than the recent incursion of Pentecostal individuals into "party politics" or the attempted creation of Evangelical or Pentecostal political parties in some countries. Amos Yong helps to address these issues as he writes of Pentecostalism and political theology in his volume on the subject[49]. Unfortunately, however, this seems to be one of the real weakness in the Pentecostal understanding and practice of political participation, although some, such as López Rodríguez[50], are attempting to address this deficiency. In short, in most cases where Pentecostals are emerging out of situations of poverty, their experiences in party politics have been disastrous. The worst situations come to mind from Guatemala and the cases of the "born-again dictator" General Efraín Ríos Montt and his protégé, Jorge Serrano Elías. Coming to power as a result of a military coup, Ríos Montt headed up the government's counter-insurrectionist efforts in the early 1980s and was responsible for the massacre of thousands of peasants and people of Mayan descent and the destruction of their villages through the widespread use of scorched-earth military tactics. Thousands of poor and indigenous Pentecostal pastors and believers lost their lives throughout the civil conflict which lasted four decades after the democratically elected president Jacobo Arbenz was deposed in 1954 as a result of a C.I.A. assisted military coup.[51] Tragically, some wealthy Pentecostals in the U.S. gave their full support to the likes of Ríos Montt and Serrano Elías, who after being elected president, after his mentor was ousted, proceeded to suspend the constitution and, as a result, was expelled in disgrace from office by yet another military coup. Serrano Elías was a member of the Elim Pentecostal church while Ríos Montt was a member of the Neo-Pentecostal El Verbo church with connections to a church group by the same name in California.[52]

It would be unfair, however, to paint all Pentecostal participation in party politics with a somber brush. For example, and in spite of the less than spectacular recent showing of Pentecostals in the Brazilian parliament, there are clear cases of genuine, ethical political contributions made by Benedita da Silva and Marina Silva Vaz. Benedita da Silva, now Presbyterian, rose to prominent political office in the Brazilian Worker's Party as a Pentecostal and a self-proclaimed egalitarian (which may be why she is now Presbyterian!!). Marina Silva Vaz is also a Pentecostal politician and was a front runner in a recent presidential election, representing the green Sustainability Party. She came up through the ranks in Brazil's poor Northwest region and was an understudy and coworker of the famed environmentalist Chico Méndez, until his assassination. Both women grew up in abject poverty, and were subject to physical abuse, but found their spiritual homes in Pentecostal churches.[53]

Recent Development and Challenges

Here, I will divide my observations into two categories. First, those challenges that I see as primarily internal to the Pentecostal movement and then I will move finally to the issue of the so-called "prosperity gospel."

Briefly, as the Pentecostal movement worldwide ages and has moved more into the middle classes and away from the poor, the tendency has been for its growth and expansion to lose impetus. Even in places such as Guatemala and Chile, where Pentecostalism seems to be relatively strong among the poor, the evidence suggests that its growth is beginning to decline or at least plateau[54]. This seems to have been the case for several years now in the Global North with the exception of Pentecostals' continuing vitality among immigrant and other minority populations such as Latin Americans (North America) and Africans (Europe). Although more research certainly needs to be done on these developments, we might ask the question of whether or not there is a direct correlation between the waning of Pentecostal growth and influence, and its retreat as an organic expression of ministry among the poor. Perhaps the experience of Pentecostals in Europe and North America can assist us in understanding better this situation.

Speaking of influence, or the loss thereof, the other current challenge facing Pentecostals, especially in the Global South, is the problematic role of its recent interest and incursion in the field of political engagement, as is mentioned earlier. According to Juan Sepúlveda, this issue is related to the breadth of scope of the contribution of the Pentecostal churches to society. As we have touched upon in the previous section of this paper, the challenge is that of abandoning this corrupting dream of becoming a political force since, according to Sepúlveda and others, Pentecostals have no experience or preparation for this task, and that the formation of Pentecostal or Evangelical political parties is at odds with the tendencies of internal competition and the fractious nature of interpersonal relationships among many Pentecostal leaders. Thus, the challenge is to re-appreciate and prioritize the great social and spiritual contributions that Pentecostal churches can continue to make to the quality of life in the *barrios*, for example, in the prevention of delinquency and other forms of threats. In other words, suggests Sepúlveda, we should "let our Pentecostal churches continue to be what they have traditionally been: therapeutic and healing communities that have the potential to give much more to society in terms of the overcoming of poverty than by creating an Evangelical block in parliament or forming a great Evangelical political party."[55]

Finally, what do Pentecostalism, the poor, and the "prosperity gospel" have in common? For some, quite a bit and for others, nothing! I will begin with "continuity" and finalize my observations with "discontinuity."

There is no doubt, in my understanding, that there has always been a strand of "prosperity teaching" that has run through most brands of Pentecostalism. This is true by the shear connection of Pentecostalism with the poor and the liberating ethos within the movement itself. We want the poor to prosper, to be healed and to have an abundant life. Therefore, it is not strange that this impulse would be prominent and that, unfortunately at times, it would be overstated and abused by some. The great Pentecostal healing evangelists and crusades of the mid- to late 20th century is a case in point. There certainly was much emphasis on "faith healing," "receiving your miracle," "claiming the victory over disease," "praying through to deliverance," "prayer lines," etc. But were these evangelists and crusades "made in America" and exported to the rest of the world? Pentecostal history is full of examples such as T.L. Osborn, Katherine Kuhlman, Tommy Hicks, Oral Roberts, A.A. Allen, Yiye Ávila, Reinhard Bonnke, to name a few. Can it be documented that there have been more or less simultaneous efforts and emphases on "divine healing" in other contexts and on other continents? Or were these, mostly U.S.-based "faith healers", the precursors to the "prosperity gospel" movement, or as it is also referred to, the "Word of Faith," "Positive Confession," or the "Prosperity Theology" movement?

Some would see extreme Prosperity Theology as an aberration of Pentecostal healing teaching and practice. Still, others would say that it is a child of the "Neo-Pentecostal Movement" and has little to do with classical or historic Pentecostalism. This latter argument is made on the basis of the distinct historical, sociological and theological origins of each movement.

Perhaps a definition taken from the Akropong Consultation[56] would be helpful: Prosperity Gospel is "the teaching that believers have a right to the blessings of health and wealth and that they can obtain these blessings through positive confessions of faith and the 'sowing of seeds' through the faithful payment of tithes and offerings."

So, for some, such as Pentecostal theologian, Eldin Villafañe, "prosperity theology is strange fire and, for that reason, is heresy."[57]

From Latin America, perhaps the best critique comes from Martín Ocaña Flores wherein he posits that Prosperity Theology is a *reelaboración teológica* [theological re-elaboration] directed toward the middle-upper classes in which classical Pentecostalism is intentionally being "civilized" and taken from the poor, making it acceptable to business men, military officers, and large enterprise owners.[58]

Back to the Akropong Consultation (2008-9), I will mention four comments regarding the "excesses of prosperity teaching as incompatible with evangelical biblical Christianity" included in the final Akropong Statement, 2008-9.

1. "We affirm the miraculous grace and power of God and welcome the growth of churches and ministries that demonstrate them and that lead people to exercise expectant faith in the living God and his supernatural power."

    "However, we reject as unbiblical the notion that God's miraculous power can be treated as automatic, or at the disposal of human techniques, or manipulated by human words, actions or rituals."

2. "We affirm that there is a biblical vision of human prospering, and that the Bible includes material welfare (both wealth and health) within its teaching about the blessing of God. This needs further study and explanation across the whole Bible in both Testaments.

"However, we reject the unbiblical notion that spiritual welfare can be measured in terms of material welfare; or that wealth is always a sign of God's blessing (since it can be obtained by oppression, deceit or corruption); or that poverty, illness or early death is always a sign of God's curse, or lack of faith, or human curses."

3. "We affirm the biblical teaching on the importance of hard work, and the positive use of all the resources that God has given us—abilities, gifts, the earth, education, wisdom, skills, wealth, etc. And to the extent that some prosperity teaching encourages these things, it can have a positive effect on people's lives."

    "However, we reject as dangerously contradictory to the sovereign grace of God the notion that success in life is entirely due to our own striving, wrestling, negotiation or cleverness. We reject those elements of prosperity teaching that are virtually identical to 'positive thinking' and other kinds of 'self-help' techniques."

4. "We recognize that prosperity teaching flourishes in contexts of terrible poverty, and that for many people, it presents their only hope, in the face of constant frustration, the failure of politicians and NGOs, etc., for a better future, or even for a more bearable present. We are angry that such poverty persists, and we affirm the Bible's view that it also angers God and that it is not his will that people should live in abject poverty."

"However, we do not believe that prosperity teaching provides a helpful or biblical response to the poverty of the people among whom it flourishes. And we observe that much of this teaching has come from North American sources where people are not materially poor in the same way."[59]

Conclusion

As we come to an end to our examination of the relationship between Pentecostals and the poor, I must recognize that there are several other areas of Pentecostal theology and praxis that could have been examined here, but time does not allow on this occasion.

1. We have barely touched upon the issue of "spiritual warfare" or conflict, which is also very real in the existence of many poor people.

2. The prominence of the place and role of women in Pentecostalism is powerful and can be liberating, especially among the poor.

3. The intersection of Christology and Pneumatology is also critical especially as many poor Pentecostals have understood Jesus to be the *divino compañero*[60] or Divine Companion in what some have called a Spirit Christology.

4. Eschatology and the Pentecostal poor is another much misunderstood subject that could be further explicated

and extracted from its North American dispensationalist prison.

5. Finally, the various Pentecostal understandings and practices related to sanctification and the life of holiness have had real life impacts on the ways in which the poor have conducted their lives in terms of personal piety, lifestyles, and ethics. There is a direct connection between culture, poverty and the way these understandings of holiness have been taught and applied.

Harvey Cox[61] and others have observed that Pentecostalism's gift to the world was the gift of the poor. Perhaps something of the inverse can also be said: A gift from the poor to the world has been the Pentecostal movement. My hope and my prayer are that the global Pentecostal movement will continue to provide a home for the poor for many, many years to come and that we will all learn more and more how to embrace the poor and receive the gifts of the poor with dignity, love and respect so that the Spirit of Life will continue to breathe in and through us.

Bibliography

Álvarez, Carmelo, ed. *Pentecostalismo y Liberación: Una Experiencia Latinoamericana*. D.E.I., 1992.

Anderson, Allan. *An Introduction to Pentecostalism*. Cambridge, UK: Cambridge University Press, 2004.

Anderson, Allan and Edmond Tang, eds. *Asian and Pentecostal: The Charismatic Face of Christianity in Asia*. Oxford, UK: Regnum Books, 2005.

Anderson, Robert Mapes. *Vision of the Disinherited: The Making of American Pentecostalism*. New York: Oxford University Press, 1979.

Archer, Kenneth J. *A Pentecostal Hermeneutic: Spirit, Scripture, and Community*. Cleveland, TN: CPT Press, 2009.

Ayegboyin, Deji and Ademola Ishola. *African Indigenous Churches: An Historical Perspective*. Greater Heights Publications, 1997.

Beaman, Jay. *Pentecostal Pacifism: The Origin, Development, and Rejection of Pacific Belief among the Pentecostals*. Eugene, OR: Wipf and Stock, 1989.

Bomann, Rebecca Pierce. *Faith in the Barrios: The Pentecostal Poor in Bogotá*. Boulder, CO: Lynne Rienner Publishers, 1999.

Bridges Johns, Cheryl. *Pentecostal Formation: A Pedagogy among the Oppressed*. Eugene, OR: Wipf and Stock, 2010.

Bueno, Ronald N. "Listening to the Margins: Re-historicizing Pentecostal Experiences and Identities," in Dempster, Murray, Byron Klaus, and Douglas Petersen, eds., *The Globalization of Pentecostalism: A Religion Made to Travel*. Oxford, UK: Regnum Books, 1999.

Cartaxo Rolim, Franciso. "El Pentecostalismo a Partir del Pobre", *Cristianismo y Sociedad.* 26:1 (1988).

Chestnut, R. Andrew. Born Again in Brazil: The Pentecostal Boom and the Pathogens of Poverty. New Brunswick, NJ: Rutgers University Press, 1997.

Chikane, Frank. *No Life of My Own: An Autobiography.* Eugene, OR: Wipf and Stock, 2010.

Chiquete, Daniel. *Escritos a Tiempo y Fuera de Tiempo: Sobre Espiritualidad, Biblia y Cultura en Vísperas del Primer Centenario del Pentecostalismo.* CEEP Ediciones, 2008.

Cox, Harvey. *Fire from Heaven: The Rise of Pentecostal Spirituality and the Reshaping of Religion in the Twenty-First Century.* Boston: Addison-Wesley, 1995.

Ervin Alexander, Kimberly. *Pentecostal Healing: Models in Theology and Practice.* Blandford, UK: Deo Publishing, 2006

Escobar, Samuel. "Latin American Christians in the New Christianity", *International Bulletin of Mission Research,* 2006.

Estrada-Adorno, Wilfredo. *100 Años Después: La Ruta del Ppentecostalismo Ppuertorriqueño.* Centro de Estudios Latinos Publicaciones, 2015.

_____*¿Pastores o Politicos con Sotanas? Pastoral de la Guardarraya en Vieques.* Editorial Guardarrayas, 2003.

Freire, Paulo. *Pedagogía del Oprimido.* Siglo Veintiuno Editores, 1970.

Freire de Alencar, Gedeon. *Matriz Pentecostal Brasileira: Assembleias de Deus 1911-2011.* Editora Novos Diálogos, 2013.

Garrard-Burnett, Virginia. *Living in the New Jerusalem: Protestantism in Guatemala*. Austin: The University of Texas Press, 1998.

Gutiérrez, Gustavo. *La Fuerza Histórica de los Ppobres*. Centro de Estudios y Publicaciones, 1979.

_____*The Power of the Poor in History*. Norwich, UK: SCM Press, 1983.

Hollenweger, Walter J. *Pentecostalism: Origins and Developments Worldwide*. Peabody, MA: Hendrickson Publishers, 1997.

_____*The Pentecostals: The Charismatic Movement in the Churches*. Norwich, UK: SCM Press, 1972.

Hoover, W.C., *Historia del Avivamiento Pentecostal en Chile*. Imprenta Excelsior, 1948.

Jenkins, Philip. *The Next Christendom: The Coming of Global Christianity*. New York: Oxford University Press, 2002.

Johnson, Todd M. "Counting Pentecostals Worldwide." *Pneuma* 36:2 (2014).

Kalu, Ogbu. *African Pentecostalism: An Introduction*. Oxford University Press, 2008.

Kamsteeg, Frans H. *Prophetic Pentecostalism in Chile: A Case Study on Religion and Development Policy*. The Scarecrow Press, 1998.

Lalive D'Epinay, Christian. *El Rrefugio de las Masas: Estudio Sociológico del Protestantismo Chileno*. Editorial Del Pacifico, 1968.

Land, Steven L. *Pentecostal Spirituality: A Passion for the Kingdom*. Cleveland, TN: CPT Press, 2010.

López Rodríguez, Darío. *Cuando Dios Incomoda: Reflexiones Bíblicas Sobre el Testimonio Cristiano en la Sociedad.* Ediciones Puma, 2005.

_____*El Nuevo Rostro del Pentecostalismo Latinoamericano.* Ediciones Puma, 2002.

_____*La Fiesta del Espíritu: Espiritualidad y Celebración Pentecostal.* Ediciones Puma, 2006.

_____*La Misión Liberadora de Jesús: El Mensaje del Evangelio de Lucas.* Ediciones Puma, 2017.

_____*La Propuesta Política del Reino de Dios: Estudios Bbíblicos Sobre Iglesia, Sociedad y Estado.* Ediciones Puma, 2009.

_____*The Liberating Message of Jesus: The Message of the Gospel of Luke.* Eugene, OR: Pickwick Publications, 2012.

"From Alternative Religion to Established Religion: The Deconstruction of the 'Subversive Memory' of the Church of God, *Pax Pneuma.*

Loreto Mariz, Cecília. *Coping with Poverty: Pentecostals and Christian Base Communities in Brazil.* Philadelphia: Temple University Press, 1994.

Mesquiati de Oliveira, David, org. *Pentecostalismo e Transformação Social.* Red Latinoamericano de Estudios Pentecostales, 2013.

Míguez Bonino, José. *Faces of Latin American Protestantism.* (Grand Rapids, MI: Wm. B. Eerdmans Publishing, 1995).

Miller, Donald E. and Tetsunao Yamamori. *Global Pentecostalism: The New Face of Christian Social Engagement.* (Berkeley, CA: University of California Press, 2007).

Ocaña Flores, Martín. *Los banquero de Dios: Una aproximación Evangélica a la Teología de la Prosperidad.* Ediciones Puma, 2002.

Orellana Urtubia, Luis. *El Fuego y la Nieve: Historia del Movimiento Pentecostal en Chile 1909-1932.* CEEP Ediciones, 2006.

Pastoralia: Pentecostalismo y Teología de la

Pollak-Eltz, Angelina y Yolanda Salas, coord. *El Pentecostalismo en América Latina: Entre Tradición y Glogalización.* Ediciones Abya-Yala, 1998.

Pope, Liston. *Millhands and Preachers: A Study of Gastonia.* New Haven, CT: Yale University Press, 1942.

Robeck, Jr., Cecil M. *The Azusa Street Mission and Revival: The Birth of the Global Pentecostal Movement. Nashville, TN:* Thomas Nelson, 2006.

Salinas, J. Daniel, ed. *Prosperity Theology and the Gospel: Good News or Bad News for the Poor?* Peabody, MA: Hendrickson Publishers, 2017.

Sanders, Rufus G.W. *William Joseph Seymour: Black Father of the 20th Century Pentecostal/Charismatic Movement. S. l.:* Xulon Press, 2003.

Satyavrata, Ivan. *Pentecostals and the Poor: Reflections from the Indian Context.* Baguio City, Philippines: Asia Pacific Theological Seminary Press, 2017.

Sepúlveda, Juan. "Another Way of Being Pentecostal", in Calvin L. Smith, ed., *Pentecostal Power: Expressions, Impact and Faith of Latin American Pentecostalism.* Brill, 2011.

Sepúlveda Fernandois, Victor. *La Pentecostalidad en Chile.* CEEP Ediciones, 2009.

Stronstad, Roger. *The Prophethood of All Believers: A Study in Luke's Charismatic Theology*. Sheffield, UK: Sheffield Academic Press, 1999.

Villafañe, Eldin. *Manda Fuego, Señor: Introducción al Pentecostalismo*. Nashville, TN: Abingdon Press, 2012.

Chapter 16

Write the Vision and Make it Plain!: A Homiletic Essay

Herbert R. Marbury

The shouts "Make it plain, Reverend! Make it plain," burst from the congregations at many traditional black churches on any given Sunday. The words serve notice whenever good preachers stray from the main ideas of their sermons or get bogged down by unnecessary details. That cry "Make it plain!" echoes Habakkuk 2:2 and speaks to black people's hope for a vision written on high that might be handed down and lead to freedom, liberation, empowerment, and fulfillment.[1]

Such a vision emerges in Genesis 1. Read it in its historical context, Genesis 1 becomes a powerful vision of hope from an ancient people living under Persian and Greek oppression. Its enduring legacy speaks a message to modern people living under the repressive force of white supremacy.

For Genesis 1, historical context becomes important. I am reminded of an occasion some years ago. I was helping a friend clean out her attic when we ran across a note that said, "Sandra, these past five years have been a blessing. Looking forward, as always, to our celebration this evening." It was signed, "Love, JJ." My friend's mother was named Sandra and her father was named James Junior. Naturally, we assumed that her father was sending a little romantic note before they celebrated their anniversary dinner that night.

Later, however, when my friend discussed the note with her mother, she told her a fuller story. Her father was stationed overseas when he wrote the note. He was one among so many black men who were disproportionally sent to the front lines and used for those tasks that white soldiers would not preform. The note was a tradition that the couple started when they were first married and continued through the war.

After hearing her mother's story, Sandra and I confirmed that we were right that the letter was a romantic note. But it was so much more. During his time overseas, the note was a symbol of their faith that he would come home safely from the war and that they would celebrate together once again. As history would have it, two years later, he returned to many anniversary celebrations thereafter. However, the conversation with my friend's mother gave the letter historical context and deeper meaning. In the same way, Genesis 1 finds deeper meaning in its own context.

First, Genesis 1 is one of the last stories to be written in the Old Testament.[2] Whenever I make that statement in class, I pause to let its implications sink in. Genesis 1 was written after the stories of Abraham and Noah, after the stories of David and Solomon, after the stories of Moses and Joshua, and after the stories of the Judges and Kings. For Christians, for over two millennia Genesis 1 has been our story of creation. The story is a narrative that communicates knowledge about who created humankind and why. However, just as the romantic note in the example above, Genesis one is also so much more. It is also a vision about a people's hope and their resilient faith that emerges from a community's destruction and subsequent political oppression. In response, Genesis 1 "writes the vision" about faith in God's power to overcome one's oppressors and evil in the world.

Context: Jerusalem's Destruction and a People's Devastation

The reference point for Genesis is the tragic destruction of Jerusalem. In 587 B.C.E. the Babylonians ransacked Jerusalem and exiled its inhabitants to the city of Babylon.[3] For almost fifty years they languish in captivity until Cyrus, the king of Persia, conquers the Babylonian Empire, set the descendants of the exiles free, and directs them to "return" to Jerusalem. However, when the "returnees" arrive, they find that Jerusalem is not the homeland described to them by their parents who had been taken into exile fifty years earlier.[4] Instead of the nostalgic visions of a homeland such as the one invoked in Psalm 139, they find devastation and destruction. Lamentations 5:1-6 describes their lives this way:

> Remember, O LORD, what has befallen us;
> look, and see our disgrace!
> Our inheritance has been turned over to strangers,
> our homes to aliens.
> We have become orphans, fatherless;
> our mothers are like widows.
> We must pay for the water we drink;
> the wood we get must be bought.
> With a yoke on our necks we are hard driven;
> we are weary, we are given no rest.

We have made a pact with Egypt and Assyria, to get enough bread.

When Nebuchadnezzar and the Babylonian army devastated Jerusalem, they devastated the city entirely. If one could imagine the Ninth Ward in New Orleans after the levees broke during Hurricane Katrina, such a scene might be an apt analogy. The descendants of the exiles returned and were surrounded by the devastation left by Babylon. While the physical destruction was everywhere evident, it was the damage to long held cultural beliefs that caused pain.

Extending the Hurricane Katrina analogy is helpful here: After the flood waters of Katrina devastated the Ninth Ward, federal and local government agencies could have easily rebuilt the buildings and repaired the destruction, but that would not have healed the pain. The U.S. government's inability, and in many cases its unwillingness, to protect its black, Brown and poor citizens in the ways that it protected a mostly well-to-do, white French Quarter only exacerbated the pain. The government's response after Katrina reopened old wounds inflicted by a nation that had long disregarded its citizens of color. The painful scenes shocked the world. Black families were holed-up in the Superdome without basic necessities such as food and running water.[5] The elderly died in the sweltering heat; their families had no choice but to leave their loved ones' remains behind.[6] Outside the Superdome, the scenes were just as horrific. Throngs of black survivors waded and swam to safety while others had no choice but to await rescue as they clung to life from their rooftops. Even more horrific, police executed black people as they tried to escape the city.[7] These painful scenes told the story of deeply entrenched poverty and long-established structures of discrimination.

Journalists called the survivors "refugees."[8] The term referred to those scenes that bore every mark of a disaster in a less developed nation. "Refugee" also signified that there was something about black people that was still not quite American. As if in response, black people across New Orleans held, waved, and draped themselves in American flags to remind the world what America refused to fully acknowledge: they were not refugees from a foreign nation, but American citizens. Their citizenship, their contributions by way taxes, hard work, and loyalty had been generationally invested in these United States. The policy disaster of Hurricane Katrina, similar to so many debacles in US history, such as the lynching of the Nadir, the Tuskegee syphilis experiment,[9] the federal policies that redlined black neighborhoods after World War II,[10] and the over-policing that has been a constant backdrop to black life, to name a few, all had a similar effect. Each eroded any legitimacy to the nation's creed articulated in the opening lines of Thomas Jefferson's Declaration of Independence, "We hold these truths to be self-evident that all men are created equal." It undermined the identity of African Americans as American citizens.

Ancient Israel experienced a pain similar to that of African Americans. It was also born out of a crisis of legitimation. The legitimacy of two promises that framed identity was at stake. First, what happened to God's promise to David? We read that account in 2 Samuel 7:12-17 where there was a promise that God would always keep a son of David on the throne:

When your days are fulfilled and you lie down with your ancestors, I will raise up your offspring after you, who shall come forth from your body, and I will establish his Kingdom. He shall build a house for my name, and I will establish the throne of his Kingdom forever. I will be a father to him, and he shall be a son to me... I will not take my steadfast love from him, as I took it from Saul, whom I put away from before you. Your house and your Kingdom shall be made sure forever before me; your throne shall be established forever. In accordance with all these words and with all this vision, Nathan spoke to David.

Such was the promise, but it lost legitimacy when the Babylonians led the last king away and killed his sons.[11] (2 Kgs 25:6-7). This meant that there were no more heirs of David to ascend the throne. Pain and confusion emerged in the aftermath of such a tragedy. How were they even a people anymore without a king? Every people had a king. Even worse, they had been embarrassed before the nations. They had been defeated and their people had been dragged off into exile.

A second question was more basic to peoples across the ancient world: How could another nation destroy the Temple in Jerusalem. For ancient Israel, the Temple was the Lord's house. And yet Babylon burned it to the ground. We read the account in 2 Kings 25:8-9:

In the fifth month, on the seventh day of the month—which was the nineteenth year of King Nebuchadnezzar, king of Babylon—Nebuzaradan, the captain of the bodyguard, a servant of the king of Babylon, came to Jerusalem. 9 He burned the house of the LORD, the king's house, and all the houses of Jerusalem; every great house he burned down.

If we were to put ourselves in ancient Israel's "shoes" for a moment, we can understand their angst. What they believed no longer made sense. Did they have a God without a temple? Their temple, their king, and their God had become a laughing stock in front of the world. Who would want to return to Jerusalem now? Everywhere they looked, the people were hurting; suffering children and families living among the ruins of Jerusalem.

In the ancient world, beliefs about losing or winning a war had less to do with the strength of one's army or the prowess of one's commanders than with the efficacy of one's God. In other words, losing a war gave rise to the belief that the victor's God was more powerful than the God of the conquered.

However, when the Jerusalem priesthood faced the question, "Did Babylon's God defeat our God?" Their answer was a resounding "No!" They turned to their faith and wrote a new vision. They never accepted the idea that their enemy's God prevailed.

Faith: A Response to Devastation

In response to the world around them, God gave them Genesis 1. It was their testimony of faith and their story of resistance. Although any cursory look at the evidence confirmed their defeat, they claimed the contrary. They wrote a testimony of victory. They began with the idea that what God had created in the beginning was fundamentally good, that is unchangeably good. The priests who wrote the three words bᵉrēʾšît̲ bārāʾ ʾᵉlōhîm, which translates as, "In the beginning, God created" or "When God began to create" take their community to a vision of what God intended from the beginning. By extension, they point to what was fundamentally good about their world. Their story testifies that because God's creation "in the beginning" was fundamentally good, Babylon's evil could not destroy it.

Although they did not see evidence of this "goodness" in the ruins, they did not need to see it to believe in God. And so they wrote not from what they saw but they wrote about what they knew. When I was growing up, we used to say it this way, "When you know what you know... " The phrase refers to a "knowing" about God's power that is so sure that it defies evidence to the contrary. In the midst of trial and struggle, those ancestors suffering under the slave regime could sing, "Over my head, I hear music in the air. There must be a God somewhere." Similarly, the priesthood, whose people had been devastated by Babylon, and were now living under Persian imperial oppression, wrote from a place of their faith.

The Vision

So here the priests in Jerusalem begin to write what would become the Bible's creation story. Despite the chaos and devastation around them, they testified that their God was a God of order. They testified to a God who created in seven days because seven for them was the symbol of completeness and perfection.

That orderliness and perfection become evident in the story's vivid descriptions. Days 1-3 correspond to days 4-6. On day one there is light. On day four, which corresponds to day one, there are moving lights, which mark time. As the lights move, they signify the movement of time, that is, hours and days and months. On day two, God creates the dome that separates the waters above from the waters below. On day five, which corresponds to day two, God creates life in the waters above and in the waters below, birds and fish respectively. On day three, the dry land appears. Finally, on day six, which corresponds to day three, God creates moving things in the land namely land animals and humans. On day seven, creation was complete and perfect, and God rested. The message is clear to those who thought that the Babylonians had defeated their God, they write not only about a God of order, but about a God of power—a God who creates by simply speaking. A God who can simply say, "Let there be," and it is done.

They even show God's power over Babylon, the nation that had devastated Jerusalem. We find it in the Hebrew in verse two: the earth was a formless void and darkness covered the face of the deep, while a wind, breath, or spirit from God hovered over the face of the waters. In the second verse, the word translated as "deep" is the Hebrew word *tehom*. The word is a Hebrew reference to the Babylonian concept of chaos and devastation. Their vision positions the spirit of God *over* the waters of the "deep." By doing so, they comunicate that God subdues the work of their oppressor. It is out of the waters of the "deep" that God begins to create. In that image, the priesthood in Jerusalem declares to the world that their testimony is that God controlled Babylon's evil and out of what Babylon meant for evil, God has the power to create something good.

Out of their painful questions about the loss of their king and the destruction of their temple, they come to see God as one who will overthrow the work of the oppressor. So Genesis 1 calls people back to Jerusalem to rebuild, and tells them that God had given them everything necessary to return. They turn to the beginning as a way of stating the fundamental character of the world around them. In effect, they assert that if the world was good then, that is in the beginning, then that is the fundamental character of what God created. And, so the world is good now. Nothing, not even the evil and devastation that they experience can destroy what God intended. Despite the devastation, they can rebuild, because it is good. Their testimony offers a powerful affirmation for African Americans who also have been devastated—not by the ancient empires of Babylon, Persia, and Greece, as was ancient Israel, but by generations of white supremacy and its violent and destructive manifestations.

The priesthood's vision continues by turning to the refrain "*tov*," which translates as "good" in Hebrew. They take "*tov*" to rehabilitate their world left in ruins. In Hebrew, "*tov*" or "good" has two meanings similar to English. The first is functionality, as in "does it work?" For exemple, "Is this lawn mower any good?" In other words, does the lawnmower work, or is it broken? Their testimony is that functionality is the fundamental character in or of the world. Simply stated: what God creates works. Despite what they see, their vision claims unequivocally that the world is not broken and, more importantly, they are not a broken people. Babylon has not crushed them.

They use this refrain, "good" as a testimony of functionality to rehabilitate and then to evaluate every aspect of creation. The light here is Good—for seasons and time. The land here is good; it is fertile. The water here is good—for drinking and for livestock. The vegetation here is good; it will sustain us.

Similar to English, "*tov*" in Hebrew has another meaning: It means morally good, as in a good person. In this regard, *tov* means nothing that God has created has been permanently tainted by Babylon's evil. As was its functionality, its moral nature is also fundamentally "good." This becomes important as a way of responding to claims that they deserved the calamity of 587. Their testimony is that irrespective of how the world may see them or may see Jerusalem, they will not be embarrassed because God has called them and Jerusalem fundamentally "good" from the beginning. So "good" becomes an affirmation of morality, exonerating them from the past. They are a "good" people even though they were defeated. It is also an affirmation of functionality. They are no longer a "broken people."

The priesthood takes the word up as a refrain. They are not defined by their embarrassment but defined by God who has brought them back. Their story will remind them that they are not inadequate, but good. They are not defeated, but good. They are not rejected, but good—they will be fruitful and multiply and renew their numbers once again. Ultimately, they, the people of Jerusalem, a people who had been utterly cast out and exiled testify that they have been reclaimed by God as "indeed, very good." (vs. 26) What is more amazing than the vision itself is the fact that they could see it and write about it with no evidence of "goodness" that they claimed. They had the faith to write about what they could not see.

What would it mean for African American pastors each Sunday to claim such a bold vision for black people? Such a reading of Genesis 1 calls African Americans, or people of African descent to declare boldly that irrespective of what has befallen the black community from the slave regime, to the degradation of generational deprivation and poverty, to mass incarceration that in black people God has created a fundamentally "good" people—both functionally and morally.

The ancient priesthood in Jerusalem understood that it was the Spirit of God that empowered them to overcome the horror and the violence of their experience with the Babylonian empire. The Hebrew word *rûaḥ*, can be translated as "a wind from God," "the breath of God," or "the Spirit of God." The *rûaḥ* hovered over the deep and subdued the power of Babylon's destruction. This same Spirit of God that was there—in the beginning—empowers people of faith to claim victory over the evils in our own world. The ancient priesthood in Jerusalem called upon that Spirit to give them a new vision. Those who face oppression now and claim God's power for their own liberation are their spiritual descendants, they call upon the *rûaḥ* as the breath of God to inspire new life into those who have become too weary to continue the struggle. They call upon the *rûaḥ* as the wind from God to subdue the devastation to black Life. And they must call upon the *rûaḥ* as the Spirit of God to lead people of faith to victory over the enemies of liberation just as God did for the people of Jerusalem.

The Spirit of God calls, challenges, and directs. So, might modern day black preachers, like the priesthood who wrote Genesis 1, envision a world that humanity has not seen—a world that God intended? Can black preachers and black communities follow the work of the example given in the Holy Scripture? Or has the evil of Babylon's destruction in this contemporary world, along with the chaos that attends to it so jaded even the marginalized, so that they can no longer envision what God intended... in the beginning?

As the Spirit of God called the ancient priesthood to do for their people in Genesis 1, the Spirit of God calls black preachers to write a vision each week; one that tells the people that they are not the images conjured by the white supremacist imagination. Such a vision should show that God is not the God of the oppressors, the God who enslaves, and who continues, especially during the Trump era, to wage war on the lives of African Americans and people of Latino descent. God has done something marvelous in black people even if it is not yet fully realized. It becomes incumbent upon black pastors and other religious leaders to show the faithful what they cannot yet see by painting a vision of a world that God intended "in the beginning." Instead of preaching respectability politics that acquiesces to white supremacy, the Spirit of God in Genesis 1 calls the faithful to paint a vision of a world in which the faithful dismantle white supremacy. Instead of preaching a prosperity gospel that holds the poor morally culpable for their own poverty, the Spirit of God calls upon those who proclaim God's Word to paint a vision of a world that points to God's call to eradicate poverty. Instead of accepting patriarchy as God's intended order, the Spirit of God calls preachers to paint a vision of a world that dismantles gender discrimination and that values people irrespective of their gender identity. The Spirit of God in Genesis 1 calls faithful communities to reject the destructive world of the oppressors and paint a vision of a world where marginalized people can live, can breathe, and can thrive.

This is what the ancient priesthood did in Genesis 1. They wrote a vision and made it plain for their people, the new inhabitants of Jerusalem. To follow their example is to do the same. If we rise to the task, then we too can begin to call a broken world out of the ruins of our own Babylonian devastation and point it toward the freedom and fulfillment that God intended—in the beginning.

Bibliography

Daunt, Tina, and Robin Abcarian. "Survivors, Others Take Offense at Word 'Refugees.'" *Los Angeles Times.*, September 8, 2005.

Davies, Philip R. *In Search of 'Ancient Israel'*, vol. 148. Journal for the Study of the Old Testament Supplement Series. Sheffield: Sheffield Academic Press, 1992.

Davies, Philip R., and John Rogerson. *The Old Testament World*, Second ed. Louisville, KY: Westminster John Knox, 2005.

Gold, Scott. "Trapped in the Superdome: Refuge Becomes a Hellhole." *The Seattle [Washington] Times.* Sep 1, 2005

Jones, James H. *Bad Blood: The Tuskegee Syphillis Experiment.* New York: The Free Press, 1993.

Liverani, Mario. *Israel's History and the History of Israel*, Bible World. London: Equinox, 2005.

Pesca, Mike. "Are Katrina's Victims 'Refugees' or 'Evacuees?'," *N.P.R. Special Series: Reporter's Notebok*(2005), https://www.npr.org/templates/story/story.php?storyId=4833613.

Robertson, Campbell. "5 Ex-Officers Sentenced in Post-Katrina Shootings." *The New York Times* Apr 4, 2012.

——————————. "New Orleans Police Officers Plead Guilty in Shooting of Civilians." The *New York Times*. New York, NY, Apr 20, 2016.

Rothstein, Richard. *The Color of Law: A Forgotten History of How Our Government Segregated America.* New York: Liverlight Publishing Corporation, 2017.

Thevenot, Brian, and Gordon Russell, "Rape. Murder. Gunfight." In *The Time-Picayune*. New Orleans, LA: The Times-Picayune, Sep 26, 2005.

Wellhausen, Julius. *Prolegomena to the History of Israel*, trans. J.S. Black and Allan Menzies, 2nd ed. Atlanta: Scholars Press, 1994.

Notes

Introduction

1. Willliam Frankena, "The Concept of Social Justice," in Brandt, ed. *Social Justice* Englewood Cliffs: NJ: Prentice Hall, 1964, 1-29.

2. David Miller, *Principles of Social Justice* Cambridge, MA: Harvard University Press, 1999), 1.

3. Cecil M. Robeck, Jr., "Pentecostals and Social Ethics." *Pneuma: The Journal of the Society for Pentecostal Studies,* 9 (Fall 1987), 103-107.

4. Vinson Synan, *The Holiness-Pentecostal Tradition*, Grand Rapids, MI: Wm. B. Eerdmans Publishing Co., 1971, 186.

5. Michael D. Palmer, "Ethical Formation: The Theological Virtues," in *The Holy Spirit and Christian Formation: Multidisciplinary Perspectives*, ed. Diane Chandler New York: Palgrave MacMillan, 2016), 107–26.

6. "Barth in Retirement," *Time Magazine,* LXXXI. 22 (May 31, 1963).

Chapter 1

1. José Comblin, "Espíritu Santo," in *Mysterium Liberationis: Conceptos Fundamentales de la Teología de la Liberación*, ed. Ignacio Ellacuría (Madrid: Editorial Trotta, 1990), 625.

2. Justo L. González, *Mañana: Christian Theology from a Hispanic Perspective* Nashville: Abingdon Press, 1990, 25–26.

3. Jon Sobrino, "Poverty Means Death to the Poor," *Cross Currents* 36 (1986), 267–76.

4. See Matt García, *A World of Its Own: Race, Labor, and Citrus in the Making of Greater Los Angeles, 1900–1970* Chapel Hill, NC: University of North Carolina Press, 2002; Abigail Licad, "A Brief History of Political Collaborations Between Latinos and Asians in America," *Hypen* (2014), Https://hyphenmagazine.com/blog/2014/11/4/brief-history-political-collaborations-between-latinos-and-asians-america; Elías Ortega-Aponte, "The Young Lords and the People's Church: Social Movement Theory, Telling of Brown Power Movements Impact on Latino/a Religious History," *Perspectivas* (2016), Http://perspectivasonline.com/downloads/the-young-lords-and-the-peoples-church-social-movement-theory-telling-of-brown-power-movements-impact-on-latinoa-religious-history/.

5. Roberto Chao Romero, "The Spiritual Praxis of César Chávez," *Perspetivas* (2016), Http://perspectivasonline.com/downloads/the-spiritual-praxis-of-cesar-chavez/.

6. For a fuller discussion of Tillich's work in relation to the cultural

see Néstor Medina, *Christianity, Empire, and the Spirit: (Re)Configuring Faith and the Cultural* (Leiden: Brill, 2018), 177–82.

7. Paul Tillich, *The Protestant Era*, translated with a concluding essay by James Luther Adams Chicago, IL: University of Chicago Press, 1948), 57.

8. Tillich, *The Protestant Era*, 55.

9. Paul Tillich, *On the Boundary: An Autobiographical Sketch* New York, NY: Charles Scribner's Sons, 1966), 62.

10. Jürgen Moltmann, *The Spirit of Life: A Universal Affirmation*, trans. Margaret Kohl (Minneapolis: Fortress Press, 2001). See also Néstor Medina, "Jürgen Moltmann and Pentecostalism(s): Toward a Cultural Theology of the Spirit," *Toronto Journal of Theology: Love and Freedom: Essay in Honour of Harold G. Wells* 24,: (2008), 99–111, ed. Rob Fennell and David John C. Zub.

11. Moltmann, *The Spirit of Life*, 117.

12. Moltmann, *The Spirit of Life*, 229–48.

13. Moltmann, *The Spirit of Life*, 229.

14. Moltmann, *The Spirit of Life*, 220.

15. Moltmann, *The Spirit of Life*, 217.

16. John Driver, "The Anabaptist Vision and Social Justice," in *Freedom and Discipleship: Liberation Theology in Anabaptist Perspective*, ed. Daniel Schipani Maryknoll, NY: Orbis Books, 1989, 109.

17. Driver, "The Anabaptist Vision and Social Justice," 110.

18. Driver, "The Anabaptist Vision and Social Justice," 109.

19. Driver, "The Anabaptist Vision and Social Justice," 110.

20. Elsa Tamez, *The Amnesty of Grace: Justification by Faith From a Latin American Perspective* Nashville: Abingdon Press, 1993.

21. Elsa Tamez, "La justificación por la fe desde los excluidos," in *Conceptos fundamentales del Cristianismo*, ed. Juan José Tamayo and Casiano Floristán. Madrid: Trotta, 1993.

22. Moltmann, *The Spirit of Life*, 130.

23. João Justino De Medeiros Silva, "Pneumatologia e Mariologia No Horizonte Teológico Latino-Americano" Ph.D. diss., Rome: Pontificiae Universitatis Gregorianae, 2004.

24. Jorge Boran, "Young People, Politics and Postmodernity," trans. Néstor Medina, in *The Latin American Agenda 2008*, ed. José María Vigil and Pedro Casaldáliga (Panama, 2008), 220–21, Http://agenda.latinoamericana.org/English/.

25. Leonardo Boff, *Church: Charism and Power: Liberation Theology and the Institutional Church*, trans. John W. Diercksmeier. New York: Crossroads, 1985.

26. Leonardo Boff, "Liberation Theology and Ecology: Alternative, Confrontation or Complementarity," trans. Paul Burns, in *Ecology and Poverty: Cry of the Earth, Cry of the Poor*, vol. 5, ed. Virgilio Elizondo and Leonardo Boff, Concilium Maryknoll: Orbis Books, 1995), 74.

27. José Comblin, *The Holy Spirit and Liberation*, trans. Paul Burns Maryknoll, NY: Orbis Books, 1989), 47.

28. Comblin, *The Holy Spirit and Liberation*, 48.

29. Comblin, "Espíritu Santo," 621.

30. Comblin, "Espíritu Santo," 632.

31. Comblin, "Espíritu Santo," 636–37.

32. Comblin, "Espíritu Santo," 622.

33. Eldin Villafañe, "The Socio-Cultural Matrix of Intergenerational Dynamics: An Agenda for the 90's," *Apuntes: Reflexiones Teológicas Desde el Márgen Hispano* 12:1 (Spring 1992), 13–30.

34. Elsewhere I have discussed the fact that Latina/o theologians often subsume the Holy Spirit to the person of Christ. This type of subordination prevents them from dealing with the Spirit on its own merits. See Néstor Medina, "Theological Musings Toward a Latina/o Pneumatology," in *Blackwell Companion to Latina/o Theology*, ed. Orlando Espín New York: Blackwell, 2015), 173–89.

35. Eldin Villafañe, *The Liberating Spirit: Toward an Hispanic American Pentecostal Social Ethic* Grand Rapids, MI: William B. Eerdmans Publishing Company, 1993).

36. Villafañe, *The Liberating Spirit*.

37. Samuel Solivan, "The Holy Spirit, A Pentecostal Perspective," in *Teología en Conjunto: A Collaborative Hispanic Protestant Perspective*, José David Rodríguez and Loida I. Martell-Otero Louisville, KY: Westminster John Knox, 1997, 62.

38. Solivan, "The Holy Spirit," 62.

39. Solivan, "The Holy Spirit," 63.

40. Solivan, "The Holy Spirit."

41. Néstor Medina, "A Decolonial Primer," *Toronto Journal of Theology* 33:2 (2017), 279–87.

42. Medina, *Christianity, Empire, and the Spirit*, Chapters 3–4.

43. For an introductory discussion of Decolonial thinking and its theological connections and implications see Medina, "A Decolonial Primer".

44. Nancy E. Bedford, "Little Moves Against Destructiveness: Theology and Practice of Discernment," in *Practicing Theology: Believes and Practices in Christian Life*, ed. Miroslav Volf and Dorothy C. Bass Grand Rapids, MI: William B. Eerdmanns Publishing Company, 2002), 164.

45. J. Kameron Carter, *Race: A Theological Account* (Oxford: Oxford University Press, 2008), 192. For a Fuller discussion of Carter's work and proposal see Néstor Medina, "Transgressing Theological Shibboleths: Culture as Locus of Divine (Pneumatological) Activity," *PNEUMA* 36:3 (2014), 1–15.

46. Grace Ji-Sun Kim, *Colonialism, Han, and the Transformative Spirit* New York, NY: Palgrave Pivot, 2013).

47. Grace Ji-Sun Kim, *Embracing the Other: The Transformative Spirit of Love*. Grand Rapids, MI: Eerdmans, 2015).

48. Emmanuel Levinas, *Existence and Existents*, trans. Alphonso Lingis The Hague, NL: Martinus Huhoff, 1978).

49. Moltmann, *The Spirit of Life*, 217. See also Medina, "Jürgen Moltmann and Pentecostalism(s)" *Toronto Journal of Theoogy* 24 Supplement 1, (January 2008), 101–114

50. For a fuller discussion on how the Trinity can be understood as a model for building a society see Leonardo Boff, *Trinity and Society*, trans. Paul Burns, Theology and Liberation Series Maryknoll: Orbis Books, 1988).

51. Comblin, *The Holy Spirit and Liberation*, 47.

52. Harvey Cox, *Fire from Heaven: The Rise of Pentecostal Spirituality and the Reshaping of Religion in the Twenty-First Century* Reading, MA: Perseus Books, 1995, 318.

53. Cox, *Fire from Heaven*, 318.

54. José María Vigil, "The Option for the Poor is an Option for Justice, and not Preferential. A New Theological-Systematic Framework for the Option for the Poor," *Koinonia* (2005), Http://servicioskoinonia.org/relat/371e.htm

Chapter 2

1. A line from *Adriana Lecouvreur*, the Italian opera (premiered in 1902) by Francesco Cilèa (composer) with Arturo Colautti (librettist); translation mine.

2. In Aramaic and Hebrew, as well in Greek, the word for "gift" can also mean "bribe."

3. Elijah resumes the instruction, and this portion of teaching becomes *Seder Eliyahu Zuta* ("The Minor Order of Elijah), while the previous set is now called *Seder Eliyahu Rabbah* ("The Major Order of

Elijah). See also Kristen H. Lindbeck, *Elijah and the Rabbis: Story and Theology*. New York: Columbia University Press, 2010, 100-3.

4. Søren Kierkegaard, *The Sickness unto Death*, tr. Walter Lowrie (Princeton: Princeton University Press, 1941), 39.

5. Klaus Koch, *The Prophets*, 2 vols., tr. Margaret Kohn (Philadelphia: Fortress, Press, 1983-1984). The first volume deals with the prophets of the Assyrian period, and the second, of the Babylonian and Persian periods.

6. Frederick E. Greenspahn, "Why Prophecy Ceased," *JBL* 108:1 (Spring, 1989), 37.

7. In the Bible, the mountain of God of Exodus is known by the various names of Mount Sinai, Mount Horeb, and Mount Paran, while "it is clear from the Bible that they are located in southern Sinai" (Yohanan Aharoni, *The Land of the Bible: A Historical Geography*, rev. and enlarged ed. Philadelphia: Westminster Press, 1979, 199.

8. The latter concern is linked with a caricature of Baalism as a fertility religion charged with sexual immoralities. This criticism is prominent in later prophets like Hosea, but Elijah's critique of Baalism does not focus on this matter. The ancient Near Eastern documents do not substantiate this, and it is possible that the moral critique is the product of later Israel prophets' polemic.

9. The LORD (in all capital letters) signifies the ineffable name of God, Yahweh.

10. This dramatic scene is captured in the majestic music of Mendelssohn's oratorio *Elijah*.

11. Michael Welker, *God the Spirit*, tr. John F. Hoffmeyer (Minneapolis: Fortress Press, 1994), 100.

12. Marvin Sweeney, "The Prophets and Priests in the Deuteronomistic History: Elijah and Elisha" in *Israelite Prophecy and the Deuteronomistic History: Portrait, Reality, and the Formation of a History*, eds. Mignon R. Jacobs and Raymond F. Person Jr., Ancient Israel and Its Literature 14 (Atlanta: Society of Biblical Literature, 2013), 46.

13. The theological point is underscored in the parts of prophetic literature commonly known as "oracles against the nations" (e.g., Amos 1-2; Isa 13-23; Jer 46-51; Ezk 25-31).

14. The English word "companion" has an interesting etymology. Its Latin root includes *panis*, which means "bread," indicating that companions share bread.

15. In historical critical studies, this difference between 1 Kings 17-19 and chap. 21 is commonly attributed to their different tradition history. See Steven McKenzie, *The Trouble with Kings: The Composition of the Book of Kings in the Deuteronomistic History* (Leiden: E. J. Brill, 1991), 84.

16. Walter Brueggemann, *The Prophetic Imagination*, 2nd ed. (Minneapolis: Fortress Press, 2001), 3; italics in the original.

17. René Girard, "The Bible's Distinctiveness and the Gospel" in *The Girard Reader*, ed. James G. Williams New York: Crossroad Publishing Co., 2000), 145.

18. Girard states, "Nietzsche was the first thinker to see clearly that the singularity of Judeo-Christianity was that it rehabilitates victims that myths would regard as justly immolated... for Nietzsche this was a dreadful mistake that first Judaism, then Christianity had inflicted on the world" (*The Girard Reader*, 272).

19. This accounts for the common practice of studying the prophets based on the books that bear their name. For example, see Carol J. Dempsey's uplifting study of the prophetic deconstruction of power and domination in *The Prophets: A Liberation-Critical Reading* (A Liberation-Critical Reading of the Old Testament; Minneapolis: Fortress Press, 2000), based on the canonical Major and Minor prophetic books. Her coverage includes Daniel, which the Jewish canon places not in the Latter Prophets (*Nevi'im 'aharonim*) but in the Writings (Kethuvim).

20. The Twelve (Minor Prophets) begins with the book of Hosea. While the size of the book must have been a contributing factor—not a deciding factor since the second book Joel has only three chapters. The rabbinic tradition recalls that Hosea is placed as the first because of the wording in Hosea 1:1.

21. Virginia Scott, *Women on the Stage in Early Modern France: 1540-1750* New York: Cambridge University Press, 2010), 222-23.

Chapter 3

1. This chapter was presented at the 47th Annual Meeting of the Society for Pentecostal Studies (March 8-10, 2018, Cleveland, TN).

2 Lee Roy Martin, ""Oh give thanks to the Lord for he is Good": Affective Hermeneutics, Psalm 107, and Pentecostal Spirituality," *Pneuma* 36 (2014), 355–378. See also L. R. Martin, 'Longing for God: Psalm 63 and Pentecostal Spirituality,' *Journal of Pentecostal Theology*, 22 (2013), 54-76.

3 Rickie D. Moore, "Altar Hermeneutics: Reflections on Pentecostal Biblical Interpretation," *Pneuma* 38:1-2 (2016), 148-59.

4. See, among others, Peter Althouse, "Toward a Theological Understanding of the Pentecostal Appeal to Experience," *JES* 38:4 (Fall 2001), 399-411; Terry L. Cross, "Divine-Human Encounter Towards a Pentecostal Theology of Experience," *Pneuma* 31 (2009), 3-34; Paul W. Lewis, "Towards a Pentecostal Epistemology: The Role of Experience in Pentecostal Hermeneutics," *The Church and Spirit* 2:1 (2000), 95-125; John McKay, "When the Veil is Taken Away: The impact of Prophetic Experience on Biblical Interpretation," *JPT* 5 (1994), 17-40; Peter D. Neumann, *Pentecostal Experience: An Ecumenical Encounter*, Princeton Theological Monographs Series 187 (Eugene, OR: Wipf and Stock Publishers, 2012).

5. Steven J. Land, *Pentecostal Spirituality: A Passion for the Kingdom*, JPT Supp 1 (Sheffield: Sheffield Academic Press, 1993) 74-5.

6. See Jacqueline Grey, *Three's A Crowd: Pentecostalism, Hermeneutics and the Old Testament* (Eugene, Oregon: Pickwick Publications, 2011).

7. Luke Timothy Johnson, *Religious Experience in Earliest Christianity: A Missing Dimension in New Testament Studies* (Minneapolis, MI: Fortress Press, 1998) 60.

8. David Perry, "Spirit Baptism and Social Action: The Pentecostal Experience of Spirit Baptism as a Rationale for Social Action and Mission," *Australasian Pentecostal Studies* Issue 16. Online: (http://aps-journal.com/aps/index.php/APS/article/view/138/135)

9. Kimberly Ervin Alexander, "Boundless Love Divine: A Re-evaluation of Early Understandings of the Experience of Spirit Baptism," in Land, S.J., Moore, R.D., & Thomas. J.C., *Passover, Pentecost & Parousia: Studies in Celebration of the Life and Ministry of T. Hollis Gause*, JPT Supplement Series 35. Dorset, UK: Deo Publishing, 2010, 145-170.

10. Alexander, "Boundless Love Divine," 161.

11. Perry, "Spirit Baptism and Social Action"

12. Yongnan Jeon Ahn, *Interpretation of Tongues and Prophecy in 1 Corinthians 12-14: With a Pentecostal Hermeneutics*, JPT Supp Series 41, Dorset, UK: Deo Publishing, 2013, 79.

13. These were the Syro-Ephraimite Crisis (735-32), Sargon's Philistia Campaign (713-711), and Sennacherib's campaign (705-701) – See J.J.M. Roberts, *First Isaiah: A Commentary*. Minneapolis, MN: Fortress Press, 2015), 107.

14. Mark Gray, *Rhetoric and Social Justice in Isaiah*. New York: T & T Clark, 2006) 19-20.

15. Gray, *Rhetoric and Social Justice in Isaiah*, 19-20.

16. Roberts, *First Isaiah*, 4.

17. For example, Mark Gray defines social justice as a function of a system of governance that puts people before profits. See Gray, *Rhetoric and Social Justice in Isaiah*, 23.

18. John Goldingay, *The Theology of the Book of Isaiah* (Downers Grove, IL: Intervarsity Press, 2014) 21.

19. Rudolf Otto, *The Idea of the Holy* (Oxford: OUP, 1982) 10.

20. Andrew T. Abernethy, *The Book of Isaiah and God's Kingdom: A Thematic-Theological Approach*, NSBT Series, (Downers Grove, IL: Intervarsity Press, 2016) 18.

21. Eryl W. Davies, *Prophecy and Ethics: Isaiah and the Ethical Tradition of Israel*, JSOT Supp Series 16, Sheffield: JSOT Press, 1981, 13.

22. Davies, *Prophecy and Ethics*, 14

23. John N. Oswalt, *The Holy One of Israel: Studies in the Book of Isaiah*. Eugene, OR: Wipf & Stock, 2014.58.

24. Davies, *Prophecy and Ethics*, 25.

25. Davies, *Prophecy and Ethics*, 25. Davies notes however that while some stipulations of the law were being neglected, some of the accusations made by Isaiah concerned behaviour and attitudes over which there was no law. For example, there was no legislation against drunkenness or extravagance. He also notes that it is probable that many were not actually violating the law, but instead exploiting loopholes for self-gain. While some scholars note the inadequacy of the law, others emphasise that the condemnation was based not on legal stipulations but on the failure of the people in relation to Yahweh. (Davies, 25)

26. Walter Brueggemann, *Isaiah 1-39*, *(Louisville*, KY: Westminster John Knox Press, 1998), 19.

27. Joseph Blenkinsopp, *Isaiah 1-39*, *Anchor Bible*. New York, NY: Doubleday, 2000, 213.

28. Goldingay, *The Theology of the Book of Isaiah*, 22.

29. As Brueggemann notes, 'The combination of "houses-fields" likely alludes to the warning against coveting in the tenth commandment (Deut. 5:21). In prophetic usage this warning does not pertain to particular acts of greed but to a general economic policy and frame of reference whereby big landowners buy up and crowd out small farmers in what we might now term agribusiness." (Brueggemann, *Isaiah 1-39*, 51).

30. Roberts, *First Isaiah*, 81.

31. It is noted that in terms of the canonical structure of the book, chapters 1 and 5 come before the call of the prophet in chapter 6. However, it is assumed that the first five chapters were placed before the call by the redactor as an introduction to the book and that most likely the call narrative precedes the message of chapters 1-5.

32. In fact, Roberts goes so far as to suggest that it should be read as part of the indictment of chapter 5 and so therefore places it between verse 24 and 25 of chapter 5 (Roberts, *First Isaiah*, 85).

33. Gray, *Rhetoric and Social Justice in Isaiah*, 23.

34. Brueggemann, *Isaiah 1-39*, 25.

35. Blenkinsopp, *Isaiah 1-39*, 250.

36. Andrew Davies, *Double Standards in Isaiah: Re-Evaluating Prophetic Ethics and Divine Justice*, Biblical Interpretation Series, (Leiden: Brill, 2000) 43.

37. Roberts, *First Isaiah*, 322.

38. Brueggemann, *Isaiah 1-39*, 203.

Chapter 4

1. The following texts from the Psalter suggest a direct link between worship and ethics, addressing, for the most part, either the ethical condition of the worshiper, the ethical requirements of the covenant, or the ethical character of Yahweh: Pss. 1:2; 5:4-6; 7:4-6, 15-17; 9:19; 10:2-11, 14, 17-18; 12:2-9; 14:4-6; 15:1-5; 18:26-28; 24:3-4; 25:8-10; 26:2-3; 31:17-18; 32:6; 33:5; 34:14-15; 37:1-3, 8, 21, 28-29; 39:12; 40:9; 41:2; 49:1-20; 50:5, 16-20; 52:3-7; 53:5; 62:11; 68:6-7; 72:1-14; 73:1-19; 74:21; 82:2-4; 84:11; 92:9, 13; 94:2, 6, 12; 96:9, 13; 97:10; 99:4, 5; 101:5, 7; 107:40-41; 112:5-10; 118:18; 119:9, 19, 29; 125:3; 130:3-8; 141:3-4; 143:2, 10; 146:9; 147:6:

2. For example, there is no entry for either "liturgy" or "worship" in John Macquarrie, *Dictionary of Christian Ethics* (Philadelphia: Westminster Press, 1967). Cf. Vigen Guroian, "Seeing Worship as Ethics: An Orthodox Perspective," *Journal of Religious Ethics* 13:2 (1985), 332-59, who observes the troubling "separation, if not an outright divorce, of worship, belief, and ethics in much of American religious discourse" (332).

3. Don Saliers, "Liturgy and Ethics: Some New Beginnings," *Journal of Religious Ethics* 7:2 (1979), 173-89 (174, emphasis original). Saliers asks, "... to what extent ought the church as liturgical community make moral and ethical transformation of persons and society the purpose of worship?" (183). Cf. Geoffrey Wainwright, "Eucharist and/as Ethics," *Worship* 62:2 (1988), 123-38.

4. Daniel Castelo, "Tarrying on the Lord: Affections, Virtues and Theological Ethics in Pentecostal Perspective," *Journal of Pentecostal Theology* 13:1 (2004), 31-56 (50).

5. Cf. Theresa F. Koernke, "Toward an Ethics of Liturgical Behavior," *Worship* 66:1 (1992), 25-38 (27).

6. Guroian, "Seeing Worship as Ethics," 335.

7. Eugene A. LaVerdiere, "Covenant Morality," *Worship* 38:5 (1964), 240-46 (240).

8. LaVerdiere, "Covenant Morality," 242.

9. Saliers, "Liturgy and Ethics," 175 (emphasis original). Cf. Castelo, "Tarrying on the Lord," who writes, "the inculcation and formation of the affections arise from a context of worship" (37). Cf. Philip J. Rossi, "Narrative, Worship, and Ethics: Empowering Images for the Shape of Christian Moral Life," *Journal of Religious Ethics* 7:2 (1979), 239-48 (244).

10. Gordon J. Wenham, "Reflections on Singing the Ethos of God," *European Journal of Theology* 18:2 (2009), 115-24 (121).

11. Saliers, "Liturgy and Ethics," 183.

12. Johannes Bremer, "'Doch den אֶבְיוֹן hob er aus dem עוֹנִי empor.' (Psa 107:41a)," *Biblische Notizen* 158 (2013), 57. Bremer argues that these transformations of society are not fleeting and ineffectual; rather, they are permanent (77).

13. Ludwig Köhler, *The Hebrew and Aramaic Lexicon of the Old Testament* (Leiden: E. J. Brill, 1994–2000), 856, hereafter *HALOT*; David J.A. Clines, ed., *The Dictionary of Classical Hebrew* (Sheffield, UK: Sheffield Academic Press; Sheffield Phoenix Press, 1993–2011), VI, 504, hereafter *DCH*; עני is found 41 times in the Psalms.

14. *HALOT*, 5; *DCH*, I, 104; אביון is found 23 times in the Psalms.

15. *HALOT*, 222-23; *DCH*, II, 437; דל is found 6 times in the Psalms.

16. *DCH*, VII, 455; Francis Brown, Samuel R. Driver, and Charles A. Briggs, *Enhanced Brown-Driver-Briggs Hebrew and English Lexicon* (Oxford: Clarendon Press, 1977), 930, hereafter, *BDB*; רוּשׁ is found twice in the Psalms.

17. *BDB*, 2.

18. Cf. Bremer, "'Doch den אֶבְיוֹן hob er aus dem עוֹנִי empor.'," 57.

19. The words "righteous" and "righteousness" come from the צדק root, and the words "justice," "just," and "judgment" come from the שפט root.

20. Jeffrey Bullock, "Forum: The Ethical Implications in Liturgy," *Worship* 59:3 (1985), 266-70 (269).

21. Donald Gray, "Liturgy and Morality," *Worship* 39:1 (1965), 28-35 (30).

22. Saliers, "Liturgy and Ethics," 187.

23. LaVerdiere, "Covenant Morality," 244.

24. Elias Brasil de Souza, "Worship and Ethics: A Reflection on Psalm 15," https://www.academia.edu/3089608/ Worship_and_Ethics_A_Reflection_on_Psalm_15_A_short_study_on_ the_inextricable_relation_between_worship_and_conduct_in_Psalm_15, 4.

25. Saliers, "Liturgy and Ethics," 182. Paul Ramsey, "Focus on Liturgy and Ethics," *Journal of Religious Ethics* 7:2 (1979), 139-248, agrees. He writes, "The notion of steadfast 'covenant' love, or agape, in Christian ethics must obviously be constantly nourished by liturgy" (150). It should be noted that Saliers and Ramsey are not without their critics; cf. William W. Everett, "Liturgy and Ethics: A Response to Saliers and Ramsey," *Journal of Religious Ethics* 7:2 (1979), 203-14; and Margaret A. Farley, "Beyond the Formal Principle: A Reply to Ramsey and Saliers," *Journal of Religious Ethics* 7:2 (1979), 191-202.

26. Cf. Pss. 5:3-7; 24:2-4; 50:15-20; 101:3-7.

27. Souza, "Worship and Ethics: A Reflection on Psalm 15," 1.

28. Souza, "Worship and Ethics," 4. Cf. Ellen T. Charry, *Psalms 1-50* (Brazos Theological Commentary on the Bible; Grand Rapids, MI: Brazos Press, 2015), who writes that Psalm 50 rebukes those who have failed to practice the covenant's ethical demands for justice.

29. Walter Brueggemann, *From Whom No Secrets Are Hid: Introducing the Psalms* (Louisville, KY: Westminster John Knox Press, 2014), 27.

30. Walter Brueggemann, *The Prophetic Imagination.* Philadelphia: Fortress Press, 1978.

31. Elizabeth Achtemeier, "Preaching the Praises and Laments," *Calvin Theological Journal* 36:1 (2001), 103-14 (104).

32. Patrick D. Miller, "Prayer and Worship," *Calvin Theological Journal* 36:1 (2001), 62.

33. Hans-Joachim Kraus, *Theology of the Psalms* (trans. K.R. Crim; Continental Commentaries; Minneapolis, MN: Augsburg Pub. House, 1986), 13. Kraus borrows the term "kerygmatic intention" from Gerhard von Rad, *Old Testament Theology* (2 vols.; New York: Harper, 1962), I, 106.

34. In his comments on Psalm 109, John Calvin calls upon the poor to suffer "meekly," while calling upon God for assistance and while praying for the oppressor, because the oppressor may or may not be among the "elect." John Calvin, *Commentary on the Book of Psalms* (Bellingham, WA: Logos Bible Software, 2010), IV, 283.

35. The terminology of "orientation" and "disorientation" is applied to the Psalter by Walter Brueggemann, *The Message of the Psalms: A Theological Commentary* (Augsburg Old Testament Studies; Minneapolis: Augsburg Pub. House, 1984), 9-23. In the New Testament, of course, the question of theodicy is related to eschatological redemption.

36. Although Calvin urged believers to assist the poor, he taught that one's economic state, whether wealth or poverty, is due to God's sovereignty, "for God gives his gifts as he wills" (W.S. Reid, "Jean Calvin: The Father of Capitalism?," *Themelios* 8:2 (1983), 23). Reid argues against the popular Weberian view that Calvin is the father of capitalism, but insists, instead, that broad economic forces came together to create capitalism. Reid, however, cannot deny Calvin's view that one's economic state (whether wealth or poverty) is a result of God's sovereign decrees. Nevertheless, Calvin rebuked oppressors in the strongest terms and urged the rich to be generous toward the poor. Calvin, *Commentary on the Book of Psalms*, I, 213. I find Calvin's ethics to be commendable, even if his theology is questionable.

37. Bremer, "'Doch den אֶבְיוֹן hob er aus dem עוֹנִי empor.",' 75, n. 59.

Chapter 5

1. This is adapted from my previous chapter entitled "The Gospel and Racial Reconciliation," pages 117-30, 181-90 in *The Gospel in Black & White: Theological Resources for Racial Reconciliation* (ed. Dennis L. Ockholm; Downers Grove, IL: InterVarsity, 1997), with permission from InterVarsity and Dennis Ockholm. It was originally presented at the Wheaton Theology Conference.

2. David Walker, a black Christian protesting injustice, applied the expression in 1829 to unrepentant white racists, long before Nation of Islam began (see Gayraud S. Wilmore, *Black Religion and Black Radicalism: An Interpretation of the Religious History of Afro-American People*, 2d rev. ed. Maryknoll, NY: Orbis, 1983), 40). Henry Highland Garnet applied similar language in 1843; see "Address to the Slaves of the United States of America,"165-69 in *Witness for Freedom: African American Voices on Race, Slavery, and Emancipation*, ed. C. Peter Ripley (Chapel Hill, NC: The University of North Carolina Press, 1993), 169.

3. See Frank M. Snowden, Jr., *Blacks in Antiquity: Ethiopians in the Greco-Roman Experience* (Cambridge, MA: The Belknap Press of Harvard University Press, 1970); idem, *Before Color Prejudice: The Ancient View of Blacks* (Cambridge: Harvard University Press, 1983).

4. When Paul uses "Greeks and Barbarians" to summarize all humanity (Rom 1:14), he adopts a schema standard among Greeks and many who followed their usage (e.g., Isoc. *Nicocles/Cyprians* 50, *Or.* 3.37; *Panegyricus* 108, *Or.* 4; *Helen* 67-68, *Or.* 10; Plato *Alcib.* 2, 141C; *Theaetetus* 175A; *Laws* 9.870AB; Strabo *Geog.* 6.1.2; 13.1.1; 15.3.23; Plut. *Agesilaus* 10.3; *Timoleon* 28.2; *Eumenes* 16.3; *Bride* 21, Mor. 141A; Dio Chrys. *1st Disc. on Kingship* 14; *9th or Isthmian Disc* 12; *12th or Olympic Disc.* 11, 27-28; *31st Disc.* 20; *32d Disc.* 35; *36th Disc.* 43; Sext. Emp. *Against the Ethicists* 1.15; Diog. Laert. 6.1.2; Athenaeus *Deipnosophists* 11.461b; Tatian 1, 21, 29). Some Roman texts add Romans as a third category (Juv. *Sat.* 10.138; Quint. *Inst. Or.* 5.10.24), though others are content to use the Greek categories (Cic. *De Invent.* 1.24.35; Sen. *Dial.* 5.2.1; cf. Cic. *De Offic.* 3.26.99). Although Jews sometimes classified themselves differently (cf. Philo *Spec.* 2.165), Greeks included Jews among "barbarians" (Strabo *Geog.* 16.2.38), and some Jews followed suit (Josephus, *War* 1. preamble 3). Jewish writers in Greek often summarized humanity as "Greeks and barbarians" (Josephus, *War* 5.17; *Ant.* 1.107; 15.136; 18.20; *Apion* 1.201; 2.39; Philo *Cher.* 91; *Ebr.* 193; *Abr.* 267; *Mos.* 2.20; *Decal.* 153; *Spec.* 2.18, 20, 44, 165; 4.120; *Prob.* 94, 98; *Cont.* 21; *Leg.* 145, 292). The basis for the contrast was sometimes primary linguistic (e.g., Plato *Cratylus* 409DE; 421D; 425E-426A; Plut. *Educ.* 6, *Mor.* 4A; Sext. Emp. *Outlines of Pyrrhonism* 3.267; Philo *Conf.* 6, 190).

5. The authorship of Ephesians is frequently disputed; against Pauline authorship, see e.g., Andrew T. Lincoln, *Ephesians*, WBC 42 (Dallas: Word, 1990), lix-lxxiii; D. E. Nineham, "The Case Against the Pauline Authorship," 21-35 in *Studies in Ephesians*, ed. F. L. Cross (London: A. R. Mowbray & Co., 1956); C. L. Mitton, *Ephesians*, NCBC (Greenwood, SC: Attic Press, 1976), 4-11; Wilfred L. Knox, *St. Paul and the Church of the Gentiles* (Cambridge: Cambridge University Press, 1939), 182; John C. Kirby, *Ephesians: Baptism and Pentecost. An Enquiry into the Structure and Purpose of the Epistle to the Ephesians* (Montreal: McGill University Press, 1968), 3-56. In favor of Pauline authorship, see J. N. Sanders, "The Case for the Pauline Authorship," 9-20 in *Studies*, ed. Cross; John A. T. Robinson, *Redating the New Testament* (Philadelphia: The Westminster Press; London: SCM Press, 1976), 63; Markus Barth, *Ephesians*, 2 vols., AB 34, 34A (Garden City, NY: Doubleday & Co., 1974) 1:3-60; cf. H. J. Cadbury, "The Dilemma of Ephesians," *NTS* 5 (2, Jan. 1959), 91-102. We believe that all the elements of this letter's style appear in undisputedly Pauline letters, although by this period in his ministry (cf. Acts 19:9-10) his language in such letters has moved in a more Stoicizing direction (attested also in Philippians). Ancient rhetorical training included the adoption of various styles.

6. Paul's *berakah* or blessing to God in 1:3-14 introduces many of the letter's themes, as was frequent in his letters; see e.g., Peter T. O'Brien, "Ephesians I: An Unusual Introduction to a New Testament Letter," *NTS* 25 (4, July 1979), 504-16, 512.

7. God's people also appear as a Temple (2:19-22) in some contemporary Jewish documents (e.g., 1QS 8.5-9; Bertril Gärtner, *The Temple and the Community in Qumran and the New Testament* (Cambridge: Cambridge University, 1965), 16-46).

8. Josephus, *War* 2.266-70, 457-58. For other massacres in reprisal, see *War* 2.458-68; *Life* 25.

9. I intentionally use "hearers" rather than the less precise "readers": one person in the congregation would read, while others would simply hear, his letter (cf. e.g., Rev 1:3).

10. Purity rules were common in ancient sanctuaries (e.g., inscriptions in Frederick C. Grant, *Hellenistic Religions: The Age of Syncretism* (Indianapolis: Bobbs-Merrill, Liberal Arts Press, 1953), 6-7). Cf. an eschatological ideal excluding Gentiles portrayed in Joel 3:17 (MT 4:17); Zech 14:21; but cf. the coming of Gentiles to Jerusalem for homage, tribute or worship in Is 18:7; 60:3-16; Zech 14:17; Tobit 13:11-12; Sib. Or. 3.716-19, 772-74; 1QM 12.14. Jesus cites Is 56:3-8, the text most decisively supporting his position.

11. Josephus, *Ant.* 15.417; *War* 5.193-200; 6.124-26. For the extant inscription, see Efrat Carmon, ed., *Inscriptions Reveal: Documents from the Time of the Bible, the Mishna and the Talmud*, tr. R. Grafman (Jerusalem: Israel Museum, 1973), 76, 167-68, §169; Josephus, *The Jewish War*, ed. Gaalya Cornfeld Grand Rapids: Zondervan, 1982), 354-56. The penalty probably applied even to Roman citizens like Paul (pace Alfredo Mordechai Rabello, "The Legal Condition of the Jews in the Roman Empire," *ANRW* 10.13.662-762 (Berlin: Walter de Gruyter, 1980), 737-38). Although Romans otherwise withheld the right of capital jurisdiction from subject peoples, they sometimes permitted it for temple violations; one may compare their permission for violation of the Eleusis sanctuary (John J. O'Rourke, "Roman Law and the Early Church," 165-86 in *The Catacombs and the Colosseum: The Roman Empire as the Setting of Primitive Christianity*, ed. Stephen Benko and John J. O'Rourke (Valley Forge, PA: Judson, 1971), 174.

12. Several paragraphs in this section overlap with my rough draft for material in chapter six of Glenn Usry and Craig Keener, *Black Man's Religion: Can Christianity be Afrocentric?* (Downers Grove: InterVarsity, 1996), although we have added more detailed information here.

13. Paul's activity, if understood, would have appeared virtuous within Judaism; cf. Acts 18:18; 21:24 with Josephus, *Ant.* 19.293-94; *War* 2.313-14.

14. The governor provided extra troops for the Roman garrison in the Fortress Antonia during the crowded festivals. Riots could easily occur in the crowded Temple area, leading to the trampling of many people (Josephus, *War* 2.224-27); the garrison thus took special precautions during the festivals (*War* 5.244).

15. On the fortress, see e.g., Josephus, *War* 1.118, 121, 401; 5.238-45; 6.68, 74; *Life* 20; Tac. *Hist.* 5.11.

16. On this Egyptian Jew, who had recently escaped Felix's grasp, see more fully Josephus, *War* 2.261-63. The proposed identification with Ben Stada in rabbinic texts (Joseph Klausner, *Jesus: His Life, Times, and Teaching* New York: Menorah) 1979; s.l.: Macmillan, 1925, 21-22) is fanciful.

17. By extension, the term *sicarii* could apply to any murderers (Quint. 10.1.12), but in this period in Judea it applied specifically to nationalistic Jewish terrorists who frequently carried daggers resembling Roman *sicae*; see Josephus, *Ant.* 20.185-89, 208-10; *War* 4.516; 7.253, 262, 437; see further R. A. Horsley, "The Sicarii: Ancient Jewish 'Terrorists,'" *Journal of Religion* 59 (1979), 435-58. It is not surprising that Paul's interlocutor might have viewed various revolutionary movements (*sicarii* and the Egyptian) as related (cf. Josephus, *War* 2.259-60).

18. On bilingualism, see e.g., John Meier, *A Marginal Jew: Rethinking the Historical Jesus*, vol. 1: *The Roots of the Problem and the Person* New York: Doubleday, 1991), 255-68. On the usual lack of proficiency, see G. H. R. Horsley, *New Documents Illustrating Early Christianity*, vol. 5 (North Ryde, N.S.W.: The Ancient History Documentary Research Centre, Macquarie University, 1989), 23-24; Josephus, *Ant.* 20.263-64. If Luke refers to the *level* of Paul's Greek, we must regard as ill-founded Haenchen's suspicion of Lukan inaccuracy because "the Egyptian Jews spoke Greek by preference" (Ernst Haenchen, *The Acts of the Apostles: A Commentary* (Philadelphia: Westminster, 1971), 621. Paul would not have needed Latin here; the Roman administration of Syropalestine conducted its public affairs in Greek (see A. N. Sherwin-White, *Roman Society and Roman Law in the New Testament* Grand Rapids: Baker, 1978; Oxford: Oxford University, 1963), 150-51).

Romans in the western Mediterranean resented the encroachments of Greek there (e.g., Juv. *Sat.* 6.184-99; on the fluency of Roman Jews' Greek, see Harry J. Leon, *The Jews of Ancient Rome* (Philadelphia: Jewish Publication Society of America), 75-92), but in the East it remained the lingua franca (e.g., Apul. *Metam.* 9.39), and was spoken, albeit not as the only language, in Palestine (cf. e.g., A. W. Argyle, "Greek Among the Jews of Palestine in New Testament Times," *NTS* 20 (1, Oct. 1973): 87-89; G. Mussies, "Greek as the Vehicle of Early Christianity," *NTS* 29 (1983): 356-69; J. N. Sevenster, *Do You Know Greek?*, NovTSup 19 (Leiden: E. J. Brill, 1968), 176-91). In *CIJ*, more Palestinian Jewish inscriptions appear in Greek than in Aramaic or Hebrew, and even rabbinic texts attest the early use of Greek (e.g., p. Sot. 7:1, §4).

19. Citizens of cities ranked higher socially than the numerous resident aliens present (Ramsay MacMullen, *Roman Social Relations: 50 B.C. to A.D. 284* (New Haven: Yale, 1974), 59); one could be born in or voted in by the citizen assembly (Char. *Chaer.* 8.8.13-14). On civic pride or honor, see e.g., Aelius Aristides on Rome; Isocrates *Panegyricus*; *Panathenaicus*; Diog. Laert. *Lives* 7.1.12; Heraclitus *Ep.* 9, to Hermodorus; Quint. *Inst. Or.* 3.7.26; *Rhet. ad Herenn.* 3.3.4; Gen. Rab. 34:15; cf. Dieter Georgi, "Socioeconomic Reasons for the 'Divine Man' as a Propagandistic Pattern," 27-42 in *Aspects of Religious Propaganda in Judaism and Early Christianity*, ed. Elisabeth Schüssler Fiorenza, UNDCSJCA 2 (Notre Dame: University of Notre Dame, 1976), 2:27-28; Henry J. Cadbury, *The Book of Acts in History* (London: Adam & Charles Black, 1955), 32-33. Local municipal citizenship and Roman citizenship were viewed as compatible by this period (John E. Stambaugh and David L. Balch, *The New Testament in Its Social Environment*, LEC 2 (Philadelphia: Westminster, 1986), 31). For Paul's wording, compare Rendel Harris, "Did St. Paul Quote Euripides?" *ExpT* 31 (1, Oct. 1919), 36-37; Josephus, *Life* 1. Haenchen's skepticism (*Acts*, 621) is thus unwarranted.

20. Some evidence exists for some learning of Hebrew for Scripture study and prayer (e.g., Ep. Arist. 11, 30, 38; Jub. 12:25-27; tos. Hag. 1:2; Sifre Num. 39.2.1; Sifre Deut. 46.1.2; cf. J. M. Grintz, "Hebrew as the Spoken and Written Language in the Last Days of the Second Temple," *JBL* 79 (1960): 32-47), but Aramaic was far more pervasive as a spoken language (see e.g., Matthew Black, "The Recovery of the Language of Jesus," *NTS* 3 (4, July 1957): 305-13; Martin Goodman, *State and Society in Roman Galilee, A. D. 132-212*, Oxford Centre for Postgraduate Hebrew Studies (Totowa, NJ: Rowman & Allanheld, Publishers, 1983), 66; cf. Josephus' rhetorical understatement in *War* 1.3; *Ant.* 1.7; 20.263-64). The crowd likely would not have understood a long address in biblical Hebrew.

21. On the sense of "raised in Jerusalem," see especially W. C. Van Unnik, *Tarsus or Jerusalem: The City of Paul's Youth* (London: Epworth, 1962). Emphasizing particular aspects of one's account for a particular audience was standard rhetorical practice (e.g., Callirhoe in Char. *Chaer.* 2.5.10-11 omits Chaereas' kick).

22. Stephen's speech also decentralizes God's presence in Israel's history, challenging traditions about the Temple (Acts 6:13). The similarity of the charge against Paul in Acts 21:28 creates suspense, although Paul, unlike Stephen, survives through Roman intervention (cf. similarly 19:30-31).

23. Josephus, *War* 6.301-5.

24. Josephus, *War* 5.194; 6.124-26; *Ant.* 15.417.

25. It is unlikely that the issue is economic exploitation per se; given varying local currencies, moneychangers were necessary (Goodman 1983: 57; Sanders 1992: 63-65), and the Temple moneychangers reportedly made little profit (m. Shek. 1.6-7; though compare m. Ker. 1:7). Some charged the Sadducean aristocracy with corruption (1QpHab 9.4-5; 11.6-7; CD 5.6-7; cf. Psa Sol. 8:11-13; Test. Levi 14:1, if not an interpolation) or false teaching (various rabbinic texts), but Jesus may oppose especially their refusal to recognize his mission (Mk 11:27-12:12).

26. Various factors support the authenticity of Jesus' prediction: First, some of Jesus' contemporaries shared the expectation (Test. Mos. 6:8-9; 1 En. 90:28-29; 11QTemple 29:8-10; Josephus, *War* 6.301, 304, 306, 309); an accurate warning of Roman conquest hardly need be a "prophecy after the event" (e.g., 1QpHab 9.6-7). Second, if Jewish people recognized the first destruction as judgment (Psa Sol. 2:1-10; 17:5; cf. Song Rab. 8:12, §1) and many later so recognized the second destruction (e.g., Josephus, *War* 6.288-315; Pes. Rab. 26:6; cf. Apoc. Abr. 27:3-7), one has no reason to suppose that a prophet of judgment might not expect the event. Third, one creating a prophecy to fit a past event would likely have conformed it better to historical reality: the fire, some stones remaining attached, etc. Fourth, the prophecy fits the criterion of embarrassment in the early period: Jewish Christians continued to respect and worship in the Temple (Acts 2:46; 21:26-27). Finally, the point is multiply attested in various forms: a symbolic act of judgment (Mt 21:12), testimony of witnesses later Christians believed to be false (26:61; cf. Mk 15:29; Jn 2:19; Acts 6:14), and Q material (the house being left desolate--Mt 23:38//Lk 13:35).

27. Suet. *Claudius* 25.4. Scholars currently debate the extent of Claudius' expulsion (cf. Dio Cassius 60.6); one may wish to compare the analogous expulsion under Tiberius in Suet. *Tiberius* 36, but also the relatively uninterrupted Jewish life in Rome (*CIJ* 1:lxxiii).

28. Although various schools (Plut. *R.Q.* 95, *Mor.* 286D; *Eating of Flesh* 1.1, *Mor.* 993A; Philost. *V.A.* 1.8; Diog. Laert. 8.1.12-13, 24; 8.19), cults (e.g., Plut. *Isis* 2, 5, *Mor.* 351F, 352F; Apul. *Metam.* 11.21), rituals (e.g., *PGM* 4.52-55, 3079-81) and ethnic groups (Herod. *Hist.* 3.100; Epict. *Disc.* 1.11.12-13; 1.22.4; Artem. *Oneir.* 1.8; Plut. *R.Q.* 21, *Mor.* 268E; *Isis* 7, *Mor.* 353C; Lucian *Syrian Goddess* 54; Sextus Emp. *Outlines of Pyrrh.* 3.220-25) practiced diverse food customs, but Greeks and Romans particularly mocked Jews for these (Plut. *Table-Talk* 4.4.4, *Mor.* 669C; Molly Whittaker, *Jews and Christians: Graeco-Roman Views* (Cambridge: Cambridge University, 1984), 73-80; John G. Gager, *The Origins of Anti-Semitism: Attitudes Toward Judaism in Pagan and Christian Antiquity* New York: Oxford, 1983), 57; J. N. Sevenster, *The Roots of Pagan Anti-Semitism in the Ancient World*, NovTSup 41 (Leiden: E. J. Brill, 1975), 136-39). Gentiles likewise ridiculed Jewish practice of the Sabbath (Plut. *Superst.* 8, *Mor.* 169C; cf. Ex 5:8, 17).

29. For denunciations of idolatry, which was largely (though not exclusively) a Gentile sin, see e.g., Bel and Dragon; Ep. Jer.; Ep. Arist. 134-38; Sib. Or. 3.8-35; 4.4-23; Test. Sol. 26; tos. Bek. 3:12; Peah 1:2; Sanh. 13:8; Sifra VDDeho. par. 1.34.1.3; Sifre Num. 112.2.2; Sifre Deut. 43.4.1; 54.3.2; ARN 40A. Jews regarded homosexual behavior much more exclusively as a Gentile vice, virtually inconceivable among themselves in this period (e.g., Ep. Arist. 152; Sib. Or. 3.185-86, 596-600, 764; 4.34; 5.166, 387, 430; tos. Hor. 2:5-6).

30. Sins such as envy (e.g., Wisd. 6:23; Ep. Arist. 224; Josephus, *Ant.* 2.13; *War* 1.77; Philo *Prob.* 13; Sib. Or. 3.660-64; Test. Gad 7:2; Test. Sim. 3; Test. Sol. 6:4), pride (e.g., 1QS 4.9; Sir. 3:28; 10:7, 12-13; 13:1, 20; 22:22; 25:1; Philo *Post.* 52; Test. Reub. 3:5; Test. Jud. 13:2; Test. Job 15:8-10; m. Ab. 1:13), and slander (e.g., 1QS 7.15-16; Philo *Spec. Laws* 4.59-60; Sifre Deut. 1.8.2-3; 275.1.1; ARN 9; 40A; 16, §36; 41, §116B) also appear in condemnations of Jewish vices or warnings to Jewish hearers. Vice-lists were a standard rhetorical form (e.g., Plato *Law* 1.649D; Arist. *E.E.* 2.3.4, 1220b-21a; *V.V.* 1249a-51b; Epict. *Disc.* 2.8.23; Diogenes *Ep.* 36, to Timomachus; Maximus of Tyre *Disc.* 36.4; 1QS 4.9-11; Wisd. 14:25-26; Philo *Sac.* 32; *Post.* 52; Sib. Or. 2.255-82; Test. Levi 17:11; Did. 5).

31. See e.g., C. G. Montefiore, "The Spirit of Judaism," 1:35-81 in *The Beginnings of Christianity*, ed. F. J. Foakes Jackson and Kirsopp Lake Grand Rapids: Baker, 1979), 43. For Abraham as a model proselyte, see e.g., *Mekilta Nezikin* 18:36ff; b. Suk. 49b; Gen. Rab. 39:8; Num. Rab. 8:9.

32. Cf. e.g., Sirach 25:24; 1 En. 98:4; Life of Adam and Eve 44.3-4; Sifre Deut. 323.5.1; 339.1.2; and especially 4 Ezra 3:7, 20-22, 30; 7:118-26; 2 Bar. 17:2-3; 23:4; 48:42-45; 54:15, 19; 56:5-6.

33. E.g., Arist. *Pol.* 1.2.13, 1254b; Seneca *Dial.* 2.16.1; *Ep. Lucil.* 8.5; Epict. *Disc.* 1.3.3; Plut. *Isis* 78, *Mor.* 382F; Marc. Aur. *Med.* 2.2; Ep. Arist. 245, 277; 4 Macc. 1:29; 2:18, 21-22; 3:2-5; Philo *Gig.* 29; Sent. Sext. 139, 204-9.

34. E.g., 1QS 3.25-4.1; CD 2.15-16; Jub. 35:9; 4 Ezra 7:92; Test. Jud. 20:1-2; m. Ab. 2:11; Sifra Shemini Mekhilta deMiluim 99.2.3; Sifra A.M. pq. 13.194.2.11; Sifre Num. 40.1.3; Sifre Deut. 32.3.1; 45.1.3.

35. Rom 10:6-10 borrows the language of Deut 30, comparing Jesus with Torah. Cf. discussions in M. Jack Suggs, "'The Word is Near You': Romans 10:6-8 within the Purpose of the Letter," 289-312 in *Christian History and Interpretation: Studies Presented to John Knox*, ed. W. R. Farmer, C. F. D Moule, R. R. Niebuhr (Cambridge: University, 1967), 299-308; Daniel P. Fuller, *Gospel and Law: Contrast or Continuum?* Grand Rapids: Eerdmans, 1980), 66-86; Archibald M. Hunter, *The Gospel According to St. Paul* (Philadelphia: Westminster, 1966), 68; W. D. Davies, *Torah in the Messianic Age and/or the Age to Come*, JBLM 7 (Philadelphia: Society of Biblical Literature, 1952), 87; compare also relevant texts in Pes. Rab. 47:4; Ruth Rab. 2:3; Ephraim E. Urbach, *The Sages: Their Concepts and Beliefs*, 2d ed., 2 vols., tr. Israel Abrahams (Jerusalem: Magnes Press, 1979), 1:329. For possible polemical imagery, cf. Sifre Deut. 49.2.1, but the language may simply reflect a common hyperbolic image of the day (cf. Char. *Chaer.* 3.2.5, 7).

36. This is one of the most controversial passages in Romans, but it seems unlikely to me that Paul means something by "Israel" here different from what he meant in the preceding context. Cf. Johannes Munck, *Christ & Israel: An Interpretation of Romans 9-11* (Philadelphia: Fortress, 1967), 136; George E. Ladd, "Israel and the Church," *EQ* 36 (1964), 206-13.

37. On the Gentile mission in Luke-Acts, see e.g., Jacques Dupont, *The Salvation of the Gentiles: Essays on the Acts of the Apostles*, tr. John R. Keating New York: Paulist Press, 1979). On Luke's geographical schema, see especially James M. Scott, "Luke's Geographical Horizon," 483-544 in *The Book of Acts in Its Graeco-Roman Setting*, ed. David W. J. Gill and Conrad Gempf, vol. 2 in *The Book of Acts in its First-Century Setting* Grand Rapids: Eerdmans; Carlisle: Paternoster Press).

38. See more fully my forthcoming commentary on Matthew.

39. M. Aboth 1:5; b. Ber. 43b; Erub. 53b; p. Sot. 1:1, §7; A.Z. 2:3, §1; in some later traditions even, God avoids talking with women (Gen. Rab. 48:20; 63:7).

40. Asking for water would not be considered promiscuous (cf. b. Kid. 9a), but could have conjugal connotations (e.g., the girl who acts like Rebekah and wishes R. Joshua to act like Eliezer, in Lam. Rab. 1.1.19). Also recall that Jacob, whose well this reportedly was, had met Rachel at a well (Gen 29:9-10); for echoes of conjugal tradition in Gen 24, compare Norman R. Bonneau, "The Woman at the Well--John 4 and Genesis 24," *BiT* 67 (Oct. 1973), 1252-59; for Jacob traditions in the passage, see Jerome H. Neyrey, "Jacob Traditions and the Interpretation of John 4:10-26," *CBQ* 41 (3, July 1979), 419-37. The woman's assertion of singleness (4:17a) could have been construed as a sexual invitation (cf. b. Sotah 10a).

41. For Samaritan religious strictness, see S. Dar, "Three *Menorot* from Western Samaria," *IEJ* 34 (2-3, 1984),177-79 and plate 20BC.

42. See m. Toh. 5:8; Nid. 4:1; tos. Nid. 5:1; b. Shab. 17a; cf. Yeb. 86a.

43. Jewish people also often used "our father Jacob" (e.g., the later Pes. Rab Kah. 23:2), and sometimes complained that Samaritans identified themselves with the Jewish people only when it was convenient (Josephus, *Ant.* 11.340-41).

44. See Josephus, *War* 1.63-66; R. J. Bull, "Field Report XII," *BASOR* 180 (Dec. 1965), 37-41, 41; idem, "An Archaeological Context for Understanding John 4:20," *BA* 38 (1, March 1975), 54-59; Finegan, *Archaeology*, 35.

45. I have borrowed these examples from my research for *Black Man's Religion*, although they appear at various locations in that manuscript.

46. Compare Ida Rousseau Mukenge, *The Black Church in Urban America: A Case Study in Political Economy* (Lanham: University Press of America, 1983), 27.

47. Mark Noll, *A History of Christianity in the United States and Canada* Grand Rapids: Eerdmans, 1992), 138. On Liele and David George, see also James Melvin Washington, *Frustrated Fellowship: The Black Baptist Quest for Social Power* (Macon, GA: Mercer University, 1986), 8-9; Owen D. Pelt and Ralph Lee Smith, *The Story of the National Baptists* New York: Vantage Press, 1960), 29-41; on Bryan, see Pelt and Smith, *National Baptists*, 41-45; Milton C. Sernett, ed., *Afro-American History: A Documentary Witness* (Durham, NC: Duke University Press, 1985), 48-50.

48. Noll, *History*, 138-39.

49. Washington, *Fellowship*, 11.

50. See Lamin Sanneh, *West African Christianity: The Religious Impact* Maryknoll, NY: Orbis, 1983), 76; Noll, *History*, 136. On George, see more fully Grant Gordon, *From Slavery to Freedom: The Life of David George, Pioneer Black Baptist Minister* (Hantsport, Novia Scotia: Lancelot Press, 1993).

51. Albert J. Raboteau, *Slave Religion: The "Invisible Institution" in the Antebellum South* New York: Oxford University, 1978), 132; cf. 148; John Brown Childs, *The Political Black Minister: A Study in Afro-American Politics and Religion* (Boston: G. K. Hall, 1980), 29-30.

52. Raboteau, *Slave Religion*, 133-141.

53. Noll, *History*, 109, emphasizing that the Great Awakening bridged "the chasm between white and black cultures."

54. Lerone Bennett, Jr., *Before the Mayflower: A History of the Negro in America, 1619-1964*, Rev. ed. (Baltimore, MD: Penguin, 1966), 63.

55. Monroe Fordham, *Major Themes in Northern Black Religious Thought, 1800-1860* (Hicksville, NY: Exposition Press, 1975), 111.

56. See Herbert S. Klein, "Anglicanism, Catholicism, and the Negro Slave," 137-90 in *The Debate Over Slavery*, ed. Ann Lane (Urbana, IL: University of Illinois, 1971), 172-73.

57. John Woolman, *Some Considerations on the Keeping of Negroes 1754; Considerations on Keeping Negroes 1762* (Philadelphia: James Chattin, 1754; reprinted by New York: Viking, 1976).

58. Raboteau, *Slave Religion*, 143; Childs, *Political Black Minister*, 27-28.

59. Wilmore, *Black Radicalism*, 34.

60. Alice Dana Adams, *The Neglected Period of Anti-Slavery in America (1808-1831)* (Gloucester, MA: Peter Smith, 1964), 97.

61. Friends (Quakers) were strongly antislavery (Adams, *Anti-Slavery*, 101-3; Daniel P. Mannix with Malcolm Cowley, *Black Cargoes: A History of the Atlantic Slave Trade 1518-1865* New York: The Viking Press, 1962), 171-90).

62. Although Baptists by their polity had no central organization from which to make pronouncements, some ministers even in the South and as early as 1808 were working against slavery (Adams, *Anti-Slavery*, 100-1; Leonard L. Haynes, Jr. *The Negro Community Within American Protestantism, 1619-1844* (Boston: Christopher Publishing House, 1953), 111-12). For Baptist antislavery work, see further Washington, *Fellowship*, 27-38.

63. Adams, *Anti-Slavery*, 98-100.

64. Episcopalians and Catholics apparently remained largely neutral (Adams, *Anti-Slavery*, 101). On the Unitarians (lamenting their slow response to abolitionism), see Samuel J. May, *Some Recollections of our Antislaery Conflict* (Boston: Fields, Osgood, & Co., 1869); for Congregationalist antislavery, cf. Calvin Montague Clark, *American Slavery and Maine Congregationalists* (Bangor, Maine: C. M. Clark, 1940).

65. Pelt and Smith, *National Baptists*, 27.

66. Wilmore, *Black Radicalism*

67. See documents in *Witness for Freedom*, 201-10.

68. See Wilmore, *Black Radicalism*, 31.

69. See Wilmore, *Black Radicalism*, 32.

70. Bennett, *Mayflower*, 196.

71. Sara Bullard, *Free At Last: A History of the Civil Rights Movement and Those Who Died in the Struggle*, introduction by Julian Bond New York: Oxford; Southern Poverty Law Center, 1993), 66-67. For some other whites who served the black community, see Cornel West, *Race Matters* (Boston: Beacon Press, 1993), 85.

72. See Lester B. Scherer, *Slavery and the Churches in Early America 1619-1819* Grand Rapids: Wm. B. Eerdmans, 1975).

73. Dorothy Sterling, *We Are Your Sisters: Black Women in the Nineteenth Century* New York: W. W. Norton & Company, 1984), 115.

74. On the dichotomy, see e.g., Ronald J. Sider, *One-Sided Christianity? Uniting the Church to Heal a Lost and Broken World* Grand Rapids: Zondervan; San Francisco: Harper San Francisco, 1993).

75. We survey this more fully in Usry and Keener, *Religion*, 98-109.

76. For the social activism of nineteenth century evangelicals, see e.g., Timothy L. Smith, *Revivalism and Social Reform: American Protestantism on the Eve of the Civil War* (Baltimore: Johns Hopkins, 1980; Norris Magnuson, *Salvation in the Slums: Evangelical Social Work, 1865-1920*, ATLAM 190 (Metuchen: Scarecrow, 1977; Grand Rapids: Baker, 1990).

77. Even in the social gospel movement of the early twentieth century, when the polarization that would lead to the modernist-fundamentalist controversy of the 1920s was beginning, "More often in the black church one encounters a figure like Francis J. Grimké, who was a theological conservative making liberal social pronouncements," than the reverse (Ronald C. White, Jr., *Liberty and Justice for All: Racial Reform & the Social Gospel (1877-1925)*, The Rauschenbusch Lectures, New Series, II (San Francisco: Harper & Row, Publishers, 1990), 120).

78. The quotes from Jeremiah, Isaiah and James are from the NASB.

Chapter 6

1. Passel, Jeffrey, and D'Vera Cohn. "As Mexican Share Declined, U.S. Unauthorized Immigrant Population Fell in 2015 below Recession Level." Pew Research Center. April 25, 2017. http://www.pewresearch.org/fact-tank/2017/04/25/as-mexican-share-declined-u-s-unauthorized-immigrant-population-fell-in-2015-below-recession-level/.

2. Miroslav Volf, "The Trinity Is Our Social Program: The Doctrine of the Trinity and the Shape of Social Engagement," *Modern Theology* 14:3, (July 1998).

3. NIV Gen. 1:26-27

4. Volf, "The Trinity Is Our Social Program," 404.

5. Volf, "The Trinity Is Our Social Program," 406.

6. Volf, "The Trinity Is Our Social Program,". Rather than approaching the matter of a social vision from the vantage point of restructuring the social arrangements that shape human agents, Volf's approach focuses on the human agents that in fact shape those social arrangements that are in large part the result of human social relations. The target then is the difference that can be made at the micro-level of social relations so that a reshaping of the agents who constitute those relations can in turn reform social arrangements at the macro-level. Volf is not denying that social arrangements at the macro-level forcefully shape social agents and their relations, but he is strongly advocating that just social agents are better equipped, more likely, and have a greater possibility of bringing about a more just society not because their plans will be better plans, but also the way in which that social vision is accomplished and because the actual social vision will has a greater chance of being just and establishing justice because it will be brought about by agents who not only desire justice, but are themselves just and possess the will do justice. (Give pages for reference.)

7. NIV. The actual passage under discussion reads as such, "44But I tell you: Love your enemies and pray for those who persecute you, 45 that you may be sons of your Father in heaven. He causes his sun to rise on the evil and the good, and sends rain on the righteous and the unrighteous. 46 If you love those who love you, what reward will you get? Are not even the tax collectors doing that? 47 And if you greet only your brothers, what are you doing more than others? Do not even pagans do that? 48 Be perfect, therefore, as your heavenly Father is perfect (Matt 5:44-48)."

8. In Matthew 5:48, the main verb is to be or *esesqe* which is a verb conjugated as indicative future middle deponent 2nd person plural OR verb imperative present active 2nd person plural. The preferential conjugation here is the sense of Jesus charging the disciples to be perfect rather than simply suggesting that the disciples will somehow be perfect in the future. Therefore, a preference toward the conjugation as a verb imperative present active 2nd plural is chosen over the future middle deponent conjugation. It is not the case that the disciples will be perfect in the future but that they are to strive towards that perfection for perfection truly only comes in the eschaton.

9. The main verb in the first part of I Peter 1:15 is to be or *genhqhte* which is a verb conjugated as an imperative aorist passive 2nd person plural. The significance of the verb in its textual form is a command.

416

10. This is a roundabout way of getting at the same idea found in the Great Commandment, "Love the Lord your God will all your heart and with all your soul and with all your mind. This is the first and greatest commandment. And the second is like it: 'Love your neighbor as yourself'" (Matt 22:37-41). The connection between the vertical direction of one's love towards God and the horizontal emphasis of one's love towards one's neighbor are inseparably linked to one another. The horizontal demand to love one's neighbor flows out of the vertical command to love God so as to suggest that a love for one's neighbor finds it footing or foundation in one's love for God.

11. Volf, "The Trinity Is Our Social Program," 107.

12. Volf, *Exclusion and Embrace : A Theological Exploration of Identity, Otherness and Reconciliation*, Nashville, TN: Abingdon Press, 1996), 179.

14. Miroslav Volf, "The Trinity Is Our Social Program: The Doctrine of the Trinity and the Shape of Social Engagement," *Modern Theology* 14:3, (July 1998).

14. Miroslav Volf, "Being as God Is: Trinity and the Character of Human Living," (New Haven: Yale University Divinity School, 2001), 12.

15. See Charles Taylor, "The Politics of Recognition," in *Multiculturalism: Examining the Politics of Recognition*, ed. Amy Gutman (Princeton: Princeton University Press, 1994).

16. Volf, "The Trinity Is Our Social Program:" The Doctrine of the Trinity and the Shape of Social Engagement," 409.

17. Volf, "The Trinity Is Our Social Program:"

18. Volf, "The Trinity Is Our Social Program:"

19. See *After Our Likeness: The Church as the Image of the Trinity*, Grand Rapids: Wm. B, Eerdmans, 1997), 184-85.

20. Volf, "Being as God Is: Trinity and the Character of Human Living," 13.

21. "The Trinity Is Our Social Program": The Doctrine of the Trinity and the Shape of Social Engagement," 413.

22. Volf, "Being as God Is: Trinity and the Character of Human Living," 14.

23. Volf, "Being as God Is, 15.

24. Romans 5:5 (NIV).

25. Acts 2:17 (NIV).

26. Volf, *Exclusion and Embrace: A Theological Exploration of Identity, Otherness and Reconciliation*, 126-29.

27. Volf, *Exclusion and Embrace*, 126.

28. Volf, *Exclusion and Embrace*.

29. Volf, *Exclusion and Embrace*, 126-27.

30. NIV, Matthew 5:45 reads, "He (God) causes his sun to rise on the evil and the good and sends rain on the righteous and the unrighteous."

31. Miroslav Volf, *Exclusion and Embrace: A Theological Exploration of Identity, Otherness and Reconciliation* Nashville: Abingdon, 1996), 23. In the section that follows I will extend this view to those who are suffering and not just enemies – although those who are suffering may in fact yet be our enemies.

Chapter 7

1. The "Hexameron narrative" refers to the six-day Creation story in Genesis 1.

2. Traditional Jewish and Christian interpretations of Genesis assume male dominance over women. Throughout the chapter, I will make this case. Moreover, other forms of oppression have used Genesis as justification of oppression. For example, American slavery convoluted the equality of humanity with the assertion that people of African descent are not fully part of the human race with white people. Slavery is tailored for the African people who are cursed to be less than human beings. See Shaniqua Janeè Wells, "A Basis of the Civil War: The Theological Views of Nineteenth Century Christians on the Justification of Slavery." Honors Thesis: The University of Southern Mississippi, 2015. https://aquila.usm.edu/cgi/viewcontent.cgi?article=1319&context=honors_ theses. For more information on how the originators of apartheid grounded their argument in God as "One who separates," according to interpretations of Genesis 1–2, see Christo Lombaard, 2009. "Does contextual exegesis require an affirming Bible? Lessons from 'apartheid' and 'Africa' as narcissistic hermeneutical keys." *Scriptura* 101, p 276. Also, see CB Brink, "The Fundamental Principles of the Mission Policy of the "Nederduitse Gereformeerde" Churches in South Africa," in F.J. Van Wyk, ed.., *Christian principles in multi-racial South Africa*. Johannesburg: Voortrekkerpers, 1954, 33.

3. Some Ancient Near Eastern Sumerian, Akkadian and Egyptian texts suggest the notion of visual and character representation, especially in regard to the king and divine images, which contained the deity's essence and carried out the work of the deity. Ancient Near Eastern texts that address what "image" represents include the Mesopotamian *Epic of Tukulti-Ninurta I, Letter to Esarhaddon from Adad-šumu-uṣur, Letter to Esarhaddon from Ašredu*, and the *Bit Meseri Incantation*. Egyptian letters that address the image of god in human beings focus on either a function the person performs or an attribute they possess and includes *Instruction of Merikare* and *Instruction of Ani*.

Sumerian writings include *Song of the Hoe, Hymn to E-engura, and KAR 4*. Akkadian writings include *Atrahasis* and *Enuma Elish*. Also see Victor Matthews and Don C. Benjamin, *Old Testament Parallels* (4th ed.; New York, Paulist Press, 2016); Victor Harold Matthews, Mark W. Chavalas, and John H. Walton, *The IVP Bible Background Commentary: Old Testament* (Downers Grove, IL: InterVarsity Press, 2000), Genesis 1:26-27, and John H. Walton, *Genesis 1 as Ancient Cosmology* (Winona Lake, IN, Eisenbrauns, 2011), 74-86.

4. Humanity created in the likeness and image of God is also addressed in Genesis 5:1-3 and 9:6. See Peter C. Bouteneff, *Beginnings: Ancient Christian Readings of the Biblical Creation Narratives* Grand Rapids, MI: Baker Academic, 2008), 5.

5. Douglas John Hall, "Two Historical Conceptions of Imago Dei," in *Imaging God: Dominion as Stewardship* Grand Rapids: 2004), 88-112.

6. Richard S. Briggs, "Humans in the Image of God and Other Things Genesis Does Not Make Clear." *Journal of Theological Interpretation* 4:1 (2010), 120, 123.

7. Andreas Schüle, "Made in the Image of God: The Concepts of Divine Images in Gen 1-3," *ZAW* 117 (2005), 5.

8. W. Sibley Towner, "Clones of God: Genesis 1:26-28 and the Image of God in the Hebrew Bible." *Interpretation: A Journal of Bible & Theology* 59:4 (October 2005), 349-50.

9. Stephen L. Herring, "A 'Transubstantiated" Humanity: The Relationship between the Divine Image and the Presence of God in Genesis I 26f." *Vetus Testamentum* 58 (2008), 480.

10. Towner, "Clones of God," 348

11. Ellen F. Davis, *Scripture, Culture, and Agriculture: An Agrarian Reading of the Bible (*Cambridge, UK: Cambridge University Press, 2009), 55-56; cf. 42-65 for her reading of Gen 1.

12. Ellen van Wolde, "The Creation of Coherence," ed. Daniel Patte, *Semeia* 81 (1998), 166.

13. Mary Phil Korsak, "A Fresh Look at the Garden of Eden," ed. Daniel Patte, *Semeia* 81 (1998), 134.

14. John H. Sailhamer, "Genesis," in *The Expositor's Bible Commentary: Genesis, Exodus, Leviticus, Numbers*, ed. Frank E. Gaebelein, vol. 2 Grand Rapids, MI: Zondervan Publishing House, 1990), 40.

15. Sailhamer, "Genesis," 45.

16. Sailhamer, "Genesis," 47.

17. Sailhamer, "Genesis," 46.

18. Phyllis Trible. *God and the Rhetoric of Sexuality*. Minneapolis: Fortress Press, 1986.

19. Mark S. Smith, "Before Human Sin and Evil: Desire and Fear in the Garden of God." *Catholic Bible Quarterly* 80:2 (April 2018), 221.

20. Smith, "Before Human Sin and Evil," 225.

21. Joseph Abraham, *Eve: Accused or Acquitted?: An Analysis of Feminist Readings of the Creation Narrative Texts in Genesis 1–3* (Eugene, OR: Wipf & Stock Publishers, 2006), 90.

22. Smith, "Before Human Sin and Evil," 226.

23. Walter Vogels, "Like One of Us, Knowing *ṬÔB* and *RA* (Gen 3:22)," ed. Daniel Patte, *Semeia* 81 (1998), 154.

24. Briggs, "Humans in the Image," 124.

25. Briggs, "Humans in the Image," 125.

26. The first temple is known as Solomon's temple, which was destroyed by the Babylonians in 586 BCE. For deeper study on the History of the Second Temple period, please see Paolo Sacchi, *The History of the Second Temple Period* (London: T&T Clark, 2000); Lester L. Grabbe, *A History of the Jewish and Judaism in the Second Temple Period, Vols. 1 and 2* (London: T&T Clark, 2004 and 2008, respectively), Frederick J. Murphy, *Early Judaism: The Exile to the Time of Jesus* Grand Rapids: Baker, 2010); John J. Collins and Daniel C. Harlow, eds., *Early Judaism: A Comprehensive Overview* Grand Rapids: Eerdmans, 2012); and Brad Embry, Archie Wright, and Ronald Herms, ed. *Early Jewish Literature: An Anthology* Grand Rapids: Eerdmans, 2018).

27. Lyn M. Bechtel, "Adam and Eve: A Myth about Human Maturation." *Continuum* 3 (1994),153.

28. Bechtel, "Adam and Eve," 153.

29. Jubilees 3:15-31.

30. 2 Enoch 30:8.

31. 2 Enoch 30:9.

32. 2 Enoch 30:11-14.

33. 2 Enoch 30:16.

34. 2 Enoch 30:17-18.

35. 2 Enoch 31:1.

36. 2 Enoch 31:2-8.

37. Sir 25:24.

38. Sir 42:14.

39. Wis 2:23-24.

40. Wis 1:13-14.

41. 1QS iv.23, 1QHa xvii.15, CD iii.20 are a few examples.

42. *Leg. all.* 1.31.

43. *Opif.* 69–71.

44. *Opif.* 136-42.

45. *Opif.* 152.

46. *Opif.* 165.

47. *Ant.* 1.1.4.

48. Bouteneff, *Beginnings*, 45.

49. Bouteneff, *Beginnings*, 45.

49. James Barr, *The Garden of Eden and the Hope of Immortality* (Minneapolis: Fortress Press, 1993), 4.

50. Robert Saler, "The Transformation of Reason in Genesis 2-3: Two Options for Theological Interpretation," *Currents in Theology and Mission* 36:4 (August 2009), 276.

51. Saler, "The Transformation," 277.

52. Craig S. Keener, *The Mind of the Spirit* Grand Rapids: Baker, 2016), 49.

53. Keener, *The Mind of the Spirit*, 50.

54. Keener, *The Mind of the Spirit*, 50.

55. The author of Matthew's Gospel also makes a point of including Ruth, Rahab, Bathsheba and Tamar in Jesus' genealogy (Matt 1:16). Mary, who is a betrothed but unwed teenager, is the mother of Jesus (Matthew 1:18-25 and Luke 2:4-6). The wise men from the East are included the birth narrative of Jesus in Matthew 2:1-12. Mary, Joseph, and Jesus flee to Egypt because Jesus' life was in danger, and they live as immigrants there for a time (Matt 2: 13-18). In Luke's rendition of Jesus' birth narrative, shepherds working in fields just outside of Bethlehem were his first visitors (Luke 2:8-20). Anna, the widowed prophetess recognizes Jesus and proclaims him as the Redeemer of Jerusalem in Luke 2:36-38. From before the time he was born and throughout his birth narratives in Matthew and Luke's gospels, Jesus is presented as the one whose life brings about the reality of what it means to treat people as being made in the image of God.

56. Some authors who address the equality of all people from a feminist or womanist perspective include Renita Weems, *Just a Sister Away* (San Diego: Lura Media, 1988); Luise Schottroff, *Lydia's Impatient Sisters: A Feminist Social History of Early Christianity* (Louisville: Westminster/John Knox , 1995), Deborak Rause, "Keeping It Real: The Image of God in the New Testament," *Interpretation* (October 2005), 358-68; Carolyn Osiek and Margaret Y. MacDonald with Janet M. Tulloch, *A Woman's Place: House Churches in Earliest Christianity* (Minneapolis: Augsburg Fortress Press, 2005); Elsa Tamez and Matthew J. O'Connell (trans.) *Bible of the Oppressed* (Eugene, OR: Wipf & Stock, 2006).

57. Derek Kidner, *Genesis: An Introduction and Commentary* vol. 1. Tyndale Old Testament Commentaries (Downers Grove, IL: InterVarsity Press, 2008), 51.

58. See Howard W. Stone & James O. Duke, *How to Think Theologically* 3d ed.; (Minneapolis: Augsburg Fortress Press, 2013), 43-58.

Chapter 8

1 Alice L. Laffey, and Mahri Leonard-Fleckman, *Ruth*, ed. Amy-Jill Levine, vol. 8, *Wisdom Commentary*, ed. Barbara Reid (Collegeville, MN: Liturgical Press, 2017), xliii–xliv.

2. See Herbert Haag, and Dorothee Soelle, eds., et al., *Great Couples of the Bible*, trans. Brian McNeil, (Minneapolis: Fortress Press, 2006); Miki Raver, *Listen to Her Voice: Women of the Hebrew Bible* (San Francisco: Chronicle Books, 1998); and Dorothée Sölle, et al., *Great Women of the Bible in Art and Literature* Grand Rapids, Eerdmans, 1994).

3. Ironically, "Bethlehem" means "house of bread."

4. The names in this story may have symbolic import and speak to the antiquity of the narrative: Naomi ("my pleasant one"); Elimelech ("my god is king"); Mahlon ("sickness"); Chilion ("pining"); Ruth ("friend," "companion," or "refreshment"); Orpah ("back of the neck," perhaps meaning "disloyal"); and (Boaz ("strength"). "Melek" (of "Elimelech") appears in the Amarna Letters as early as 1400 BCE (from Egypt) and only occurs in pre-exilic texts of the Bible (pre-586 BCE). "Naomi" also appears in the 14th century Ras Shamra texts (northwestern Syria). Both names are ancient. Even the meanings of Ruth and Orpah are not certain; they are Moabite in form and not Hebrew (see J. B. Baldwin, "Ruth," in *The New Bible Commentary: Revised,* ed. D. Guthrie, et al. Grand Rapids: Eerdmans, 1970), 279). Thus, the meanings of Mahlon, Chilion, Orpah, and Ruth remain conjecture.

5. In Deut 24:19 widows are identified with orphans and resident aliens—outside of society but not necessarily poor. They could and did inherit land, as Naomi did in this story (4:3).

6. Childless widows typically returned to their fathers' homes in the ancient Near East and the Bible (Gen 38:11; Lev 22:13). Moreover, a childless widow usually married her deceased husband's brother to ensure the continuation of the family line via "levirate marriage" (from Latin *levir* "brother-in-law"); Num 35:19–27; Deut 25:5–10. The initial son of this new union was considered to be the legal son of the deceased husband for inheritance purposes. See also, Dvora E. Weisberg, "The Widow of Our Discontent: Levirate Marriage in the Bible and the Ancient Near East," *JSOT* 28 (2004), 403–29.

7. For a positive reassessment of Orpah's decision, see Laura E. Donaldson, "The Sign of Orpah: Reading Ruth Through Native Eyes," in *FCB* 3, 2nd Ser., ed. Athalya Brenner (Sheffield: SAP, 1999), 130–44.

8. See a similar commitment by Elisha (Elijah directed his protégé, Elisha, to "Stay here," but Elisha responded, "I will not leave you," 2 Kgs 2:2, 4).

9. Adele Reinhartz, Introduction to "Ruth," *The Jewish Study Bible*, 2nd ed., ed. Adele Berlin and Marc Zvi Brettler (Oxford: Oxford University Press, 2014), 1573. She also holds that the story does not hint at formal conversion to Judaism because "that institution did not exist until rabbinic times" (1574).

10 Biblical laws direct that landowners should not harvest their fields "to the corners," but leave some of the produce for the poor who would then "glean the remains" (Lev 19:9, 23:22; Deut 24:19).

11 Gillian M. Rowell, "Ruth," in *The IVP Women's Bible Commentary: An Indispensable Resource for All Who to View Scripture Through Different Eyes*, ed. Catherine Clark Kroeger and Mary J. Evans (Downers Grove: IVP, 2002), 152.

12 The Hebrew word here is significant; *goel* is a "redeeming kinsman"—in modern terms, a "hero" with family connections and someone who would fight for the family's rights and assets (see Lev 25:25).

13 See Kathleen R. Farmer, "Ruth," *NISB*, ed. Walter J. Harrelson Nashville, Abingdon Press, 2003), 387–88.

14 Ruth returned to Naomi prematurely following the nocturnal meeting with Boaz, and just as he was shocked at Ruth's appearance at his bedside, so too Naomi was surprised at Ruth's early arrival. This is another pivotal moment in the narrative. The NRSV translation unfortunately misses this point in the story when it translates, "How did things go with you my daughter" (3:16). In contrast, the Hebrew reads, "Who are you my daughter" which highlights Naomi's surprise that Ruth returned so soon from her nighttime "meeting" with Boaz. Naomi did not expect her to return so quickly. Had her plan failed? See also, Marnie Legaspi, "Ruth: The So-Called Scandal," in *Vindicating the Vixens: Revisiting Sexualized, Vilified, and Marginalized Women of the Bible*, ed. Sandra Glahn Grand Rapids: Kregel Academic, 2017), 59–80.

15. *Hesed* is an important word in the HB, and scholars have invested significant effort in studying it. Peter H. W. Lau and Gregory Goswell's recent book, *Unceasing Kindness: A Biblical Theology of Ruth*, takes its title from this word. For more on *hesed* see, Danna Nolan Fewell, "Space for Moral Agency in the Book of Ruth" *JSOT* 40:1 (2015), 90, n.33. Reinhartz's translation of *hesed* is convincing: "loyalty and commitment that go (well) beyond the bounds of law and duty" (*JSB*, 1573). Ruth is an example of loyalty at its best. She deftly moves from loyalty to her mother-in-law, to loyalty to Boaz, to loyalty to the people of her mother-in-law and Boaz, ultimately becoming great grandmother of King David.

16. Torah Redemption Laws (Lev 25:23–28, 47–55) apply to both land and people. Land sold during hard times or people forced into servitude may later be redeemed from these situations. If not redeemed outright, they were to be released once every 50 years during the Jubilee year. Thus, there would be no generational indentured servitude or bondage in ancient Israel.

17 "All the people who were at the gate, along with the elders" (4:11).

18 Farmer, 390.

19 The Ketubim. From ancient times, the Hebrew Bible (HB) or Old Testament (OT) has been passed down to subsequent generations with three primary divisions: the Law, the Prophets, and the Writings. (See Matt 5:17; 7:12; Luke 24:17, 44; Acts 13:15; Rom 3:21 for New Testament references for these ancient subdivisions.) The Writings, like the Prophets, contain further divisions, and Ruth is part of a smaller subdivision of the Writings called the Five Megillot (scrolls). They include Song of Songs (sometimes called the Song of Solomon), Ruth, Lamentations, Qohelet (Ecclesiastes), and Esther. Ruth usually follows the Song of Songs, which is read during Passover; Ruth is read during the Feast of Weeks *(Shavuot)*— the length of the story in Ruth roughly spans the seven-week period between the barley harvest and the wheat harvest. Two later rabbinic interpretations warrant placing Ruth here: a. King David is understood to have died on *Shavuot (b. Hag (Chagiga))*. *b.* The Feast of Weeks "had been identified since the early postbiblical period as the time of the giving of the Torah to Moses on Mount Sinai (cf. Exod 19–20)." In this context, Ruth is seen as the "ideal convert to Judaism who takes the Torah upon herself just as the Israelites did at Mount Sinai." (Reinhartz, 1574).

20 Among scholars who place Ruth in the Persian period are André LaCocque, *The Feminine Unconventional: Four Subversive Figures in Israel's Tradition* (Minneapolis: Fortress Press, 1990), and Peter H. W. Lau, "Another Postcolonial Reading of the Book of Ruth," *Reading Ruth in Asia*, ed. Jione Havea and Peter H. W. Lau (Atlanta: SBL Press, 2015), 15–34.

21 Like the HB divisions, Christian Bibles also preserve textual divisions, including the Pentateuch, Historical Books, Poetic Books, and Prophecy, each with corresponding subdivisions (e.g., Major and Minor Prophets). This ancient biblical book order comes from the Septuagint written in Greek and arranged by Jews living in Alexandria, Egypt, ca. 250 BCE. Josephus, in his *Antiquities of the Jews* (5.11), attests to the placement of Ruth immediately after Judges. It was this division that influenced Jerome's Latin Vulgate compiled 383–95 CE, and all subsequent Christian Bibles followed his lead. Moreover, the Babylonian Talmud also connects Ruth with Judges and holds that both books were written by Samuel (*Baba Batra* 14b).

22 Toward the end of Judges, this phrase is repeated four times (17:6; 18:1; 19:1; and 21:25) and summarizes the declining mood of the book, the rapid unravelling of society, and the desperate need of new leadership. In "The Book of Ruth: A Contrast to the End of the Book of Judges," Jennifer Raskas examines multiple linguistic connections that establish a close connection with the Book with Judges. *JBQ* 43:4 (2015), 223–232.

23 For differing perspectives on the historical context of Ruth, see Laffey and Leonard-Fleckman, lvi–lxii.

24 Phyllis Trible, *God and the Rhetoric of Sexuality* (Philadelphia: Fortress Press, 1978), 166.

25 L. Julianna M. Claassens, "Resisting Dehumanization: Ruth, Tamar, and the Quest for Human Dignity" *CBQ* 74:4 (2012), 659.

26. Phyllis Trible reads Ruth as liberating, and she warns against contentious interpretive methods. "Two approaches, however, are best avoided: to interpret the book as protest literature (or) to relate its purpose to one specific historic setting. Neither in tone nor content is it polemical, and the date is uncertain." (Phyllis Trible, "Book of Ruth," vol. 5 of *The Anchor Bible Dictionary*, ed. David Noel Freedman New York: Doubleday, 1992): 846).

27. Bronner states, "Ruth may be regarded as the paragon of (what) all the sages believe a woman ought to embody. Ruth's role is to be a faithful, modest daughter-in-law and, by remarrying and bearing a male child, to continue the male line of her deceased husband... As attractive as her character is, Ruth is not independent, autonomous and free of male control; on the contrary she is docile and submissive, and this is why the sages laud and honor her" (L. L. Bronner, "A Thematic Approach to Ruth in Rabbinic Literature," in *A Feminist Companion to Ruth*, ed. Athalya Brenner (Sheffield: SAP, 1993), 168–169). For Fuchs evaluation, see Esther Fuchs, "The History of Women in Ancient Israel: Theory, Method, and the Book of Ruth," *Her Master's Tools: Feminist and Postcolonial Engagements of Historical-Critical Discourse,* ed. Caroline Vander Stichele and Todd Penner (Atlanta: SBL Press, 2005), 211–32.

28. "Role dedifferentiation is defined as the process by which persons respond to a crisis through adding roles, including roles that would be socially inappropriate in normal times" (Sarojini Nadar, "A South African Indian Womanist Reading of the Character of Ruth," *Other Ways of Reading: African Women and the Bible*, ed. Musa W. Dube (Atlanta: SBL, 2001), 164).

29. Nadar, 164.

30. Nadar, 164.

31. The word for "cling" *(dabaq)* is never used of a woman. See Jon L. Berquist, "Role Dedifferentiation in the Book of Ruth" *JSOT* 18 (1993), 27.

32. Trible, "Ruth," 146.

33. For additional information on women on the margins in the Bible, see: Carey Walsh, "Women on the Edge," *Imagining the Other and Constructing Israelite Identity in the Early Second Temple Period*, ed. Ehud ben Zvi and Diana V. Edleman, (London: Bloomsbury, 2016), 122–43.

34. Katherine Dobb Sakenfeld, *Just Wives? Stories of Power and Survival in the Old Testament and Today,* (Louisville: WJKP, 2003), 32.

35. See Num 22–25:5; Judg 3:12–30; 11:26; 1 Sam 14:47; 2 Sam 8:2.

36. Doubly shocking are the words of Deut 23:2, "Those born of an illicit union shall not be admitted to the assembly of the LORD. Even to the tenth generation, none of their descendants shall be admitted to the assembly of the LORD." The Hebrew idiom, "to the tenth generation" in this verse strengthens the prohibition. It means "forever"; Moabites could *never* become members Israel.

37. "Ruth" 1:4, 14, 16; 2:8, 21 (Ruth, "(Naomi's) daughter-in-law"); 3:9 ("(Ruth's) servant"); 4:13, "Ruth the Moabitess" 1:21; 2:2, 21; 4:5, 10.

38. Sakenfeld, 44.

39. Johana W. H. Bos, "Out of the Shadows: Genesis 38; Judges 4:17–22; Ruth 3," *Semeia* 42, ed. J. Cheryl Exum and Johana W. H. Bos (Atlanta: SBL, 1988), 37–67. See also Susan Niditch, *War in the Hebrew Bible: A Study of the Ethics of Violence* New York: Oxford University Press, 1993), 106–22.

40. Bos, 62. Ruth appeals to Boaz's sense of duty by reminding him "for you are a redeemer." This aggressive and presumptuous act is in opposition to the more passive directive from Naomi to wait and see what Boaz would tell her (Ruth).

41. Bos, 64.

42. Bos, 58.

Chapter 9

1. William K. Kay, *Pentecostalism* (London: SCM Press, 2009), 305.

2. Kay, 300.

3. See e.g., Lisa P. Stephenson, "Made in the Image of God: A Theological Reflection for Women Preachers," in *Toward a Pentecostal Theology of Preaching*, ed. Lee Roy Martin (Cleveland, TN: CPT Press, 2015), 141–53; John Christopher Thomas, "Biblical Reflections on Women in Ministry," in *Toward a Pentecostal Theology of Preaching*, ed. Lee Roy Martin (Cleveland, TN: CPT Press, 2015), 135–39.

4. Peter Althouse and Robby Waddell, "The Transformation of Pentecostalism: Migration, Globalization, and Ethic Identity," *Pneuma* 39:1–2 (2017), 1.

5. Peter Althouse, "Waxing and Waning of Social Deprivation as a Model for Understanding the Class Composition of Early American Pentecostalism: A Theological Assessment," in *A Liberating Spirit: Pentecostals and Social Action in North America*, ed. Michael Wilkinson and Steven M. Studebaker (Eugene, OR: Wipf & Stock, 2010), 124–25.

6. Althouse, 125.

7. Peter Garnsey and Richard Saller, *The Roman Empire: Economy, Society and Culture* (London & New York: Bloomsbury, 2014), 107.

8. Garnsey and Saller, 71–72.

9. Garnsey and Saller, 78.

10. David J. Downs, "Economics, Taxes, and Tithes," in *The World of the New Testament: Cultural, Social, and Historical Contexts*, ed. Joel B Green and Lee Martin McDonald Grand Rapids, MI: Baker Academic, 2017), 160; Garnsey and Saller, *The Roman Empire*, 78–79.

11. Steven J. Friesen, "Prospects for the Demography of the Pauline Mission: Corinth among the Churches," in *Urban Religion in Roman Corinth: Interdisciplinary Approaches*, ed. Daniel N. Schowalter and Steven J. Friesen, HTS 53 (Cambridge, MA: Harvard University Press, 2005), 364.

12. Friesen, 365. The percentiles given here are from a subsequent table where he measures the actual percentage of people in each category based on a city of 10,000 people or more

13. Friesen, 370.

14. Dale B. Martin, *The Corinthian Body* (New Haven: Yale University Press, 1999), xvi–xvii.

15. See, e.g., David W. J. Gill, "In Search of the Social Elite in the Corinthian Church," *TynBul* 44:2 (1993), 323–37; Dale B. Martin, "Review Essay: Justin J. Meggitt, Paul, Poverty and Survival," *JSNT* 84 (2001), 51–64; Gerd Theissen, "The Social Structure of Pauline Communities: Some Critical Remarks on J.J. Meggitt, Paul, Poverty and Survival," *JSNT* 84 (2001), 65–84; Gerd Theissen, "Social Conflicts in the Corinthian Community: Further Remarks on J.J. Meggitt, Paul, Poverty and Survival," *JSNT* 25:3 (2003), 371–91; Wayne A. Meeks, *The First Urban Christians: The Social World of the Apostle Paul* (New Haven: Yale University Press, 2003), 51–73; E. A. Judge, "The Social Pattern of the Christian Groups in the First Century," in *Social Distinctives of the Christians in the First Century: Pivotal Essays*, ed. David M. Scholer (Peabody, MA: Hendrickson, 2008), 1–56.

16. Martin, *The Corinthian Body*, xvii.

17. G.D.R. Sanders, "Landlords and Tenants: Sharecroppers and Subsistence Farming in Corinthian Historical Context," in *Corinth in Contrast: Studies in Inequality*, ed. Steven J Friesen, et al. (Leiden: Brill, 2014), 120.

18. Sanders, 120.

19. Anthony Spawforth, "Roman Corinth: The Formation of a Colonial Elite," in *Roman Onomastics in the Greek East: Social and Political Aspects*, ed. A. D. Rizakis, Meletemata 21 (Athens: Research Centre for Greek and Roman Antiquity, 1996), 171–72. See also Dirk Jongkind, "Corinth in the First Century AD: The Search for Another Class," *TynBul* 52:1 (2001), 148.

20. David K. Pettegrew, "The Diolkos and the Emporion: How a Land Bridge Framed the Commercial Economy of Roman Corinth," in *Corinth in Contrast: Studies in Inequality*, ed. Steven J Friesen, et al. (Leiden: Brill, 2014), 139.

21. Pettegrew, 139–40.

22. Pettegrew, 141.

23. Benjamin W. Millis, "The Social and Ethnic Origins of the Colonists on Early Roman Corinth," in *Corinth in Context*, ed. James C. Walters, et al. (Leiden: Brill, 2010), 13–35.

24. Sanders, "Landlords and Tenants", 122.

25. Sanders, 123.

26. A number of the Corinthians appear to be people of significant means. Chloe (1 Cor 1:11) was able to supply the provisions for members of her household to travel to Ephesus in order to report to Paul on the state of the church. Stephanas had a household (1 Cor 16:15–17) as did Gaius (1 Cor 1:11; Rom 16:23); the latter could apparently accommodate the whole congregation. Crispus (Acts 18:8; 1 Cor 1:14), as the former *archēsynagōgos*, must have been a man of significant means to fulfil that role. It is very likely, too, that Erastus (Rom 16:23) would have filled the official role of *aedile*, a position that required significant means. For discussion of these names, see, e.g., Floyd V. Filson, "The Significance of the Early House ChurcheEs," *JBL* 58:2 (1939), 105–12; Tessa Rajak and David Noy, "Archisynagogoi: Office, Title and Social Status in the Greco-Jewish Synagogue," *JRS* 83 (1993), 75–93; Bruce W. Winter, *Seek the Welfare of the City: Christians as Benefactors and Citizens* Grand Rapids: Eerdmans, 1994), 195; Meeks, *The First Urban Christians*, 57; Theissen, "Social Conflicts"; Gerd Theissen, *The Social Setting of Pauline Christianity: Essays on Corinth*, ed. and trans. John H. Schütz (Eugene, Ore.: Wipf & Stock, 2004), 83; L. L. Welborn, *An End to Enmity: Paul and the "Wrongdoer" of Second Corinthians* (Berlin: De Gruyter, 2011), 234–38.

27. Martin, *The Corinthian Body*, xvii.

28. Adam White, *Where Is the Wise Man? Graeco-Roman Education as a Background to the Division in 1 Corinthians 1-4*, LNTS 536 (London: Bloomsbury T & T Clark, 2015), 71–79.

29. See Bruce W. Winter, *After Paul Left Corinth: The Influence of Secular Ethics and Social Change* Grand Rapids: Eerdmans, 2001), 44–57.

30. See Winter, 76–109.

31. See John K. Chow, *Patronage and Power: A Study of Social Networks in Corinth*, JSNTSS 75 (Sheffield: JSOT, 1992), 110–12.

32. Christopher Forbes, *Prophecy and Inspired Speech: In Early Christianity and Its Hellenistic Environment* (Peabody, MA: Hendrickson, 1997), 173–74.

33. See Winter, *After Paul Left Corinth*, 26–28.

34. See E. A. Judge, "The Reaction Against Classical Education in the New Testament," *JCE* 77 (1983), 11; L. L. Welborn, *Paul, the Fool of Christ: A Study of 1 Corinthians 1-4 in the Comic-Philosophic Tradition*, JSNTSS 293 (Edinburgh: T&T Clark, 2005), 177–78; Friedrich Lang, *Die Briefe an die Korinther*, NTD (Göttingen: Vandenhoeck & Ruprecht, 1986), 29. For discussion of the terms, see Bruce W. Winter, *Philo and Paul among the Sophists: Alexandrian and Corinthian Responses to a Julio-Claudian Movement* Grand Rapids: Eerdmans, 2001), 188–89; Roy E. Ciampa and Brian S. Rosner, *The First Letter to the Corinthians*, PNTC Grand Rapids: Eerdmans, 2010), 94–95. Contra Richard A. Horsley, *1 Corinthians*, ANTC Nashville: Abingdon Press, 1998), 48–49; Hans Conzelmann, *First Corinthians*, Hermeneia (Philadelphia: Fortress Press, 1975), 43. They see these as simply the wise of this age without specific reference.

35. See Ronald F. Hock, "Paul and Greco Roman Education," in *Paul in the Greco-Roman World: A Handbook*, ed. J. Paul Sampley (Harrisburg, PA: Trinity Press, 2003), 204–8.

36. Welborn, *Paul, the Fool of Christ*, 125. Similarly, see Eckhard J. Schnabel, *Der erste Brief des Paulus an die Korinther*, HTA (Brunnen: Brockhaus, 2006), 140; Simon J. Kistemaker, *1 Corinthians*, NTC Grand Rapids: Baker, 1993), 62; Horsley, *1 Corinthians*, 51.

37. Conzelmann, *First Corinthians*, 51; Dieter Sänger, "Die 'Dynatoí' in 1 Kor 1:26," *ZNW* 76 (1985), 290.

38. See also *Adul. amic.* 58E; Dio, *Or.* 15.29; George A. Kennedy, ed., *Progymnasmata*, trans. George A. Kennedy, SBLWGRW 10 (Atlanta: SBL, 2003), 50.

39. See Raymond F. Collins, *First Corinthians*, SP (Collegeville, Minn.: Liturgical Press, 2006), 109; Ciampa and Rosner, *The First Letter to the Corinthians*, 104.

40. See Collins, *First Corinthians*, 109; Ciampa and Rosner, *The First Letter to the Corinthians*, 104.

41. For discussion, see Archibald Robertson and Alfred Plummer, *A Critical and Exegetical Commentary on the First Epistle of St Paul to the Corinthians*, ICC (Edinburgh: T&T Clark, 1914), 25; Judge, "The Social Pattern," 43; Andrew D. Clarke, *Secular and Christian Leadership in Corinth: A Socio-Historical and Exegetical Study of 1 Corinthians 1-6*, PBMS (Eugene, Ore.: Wipf & Stock, 2006), 41–45; L. L. Welborn, "On the Discord in Corinth: 1 Corinthians 1-4 and Ancient Politics," *JBL* 106:1 (1987), 96–97; Collins, *First Corinthians*, 98–99; Ben Witherington, *Conflict and Community in Corinth: A Socio-Rhetorical Commentary on 1 and 2 Corinthians* Grand Rapids: Eerdmans, 1995), 113–14.

42. Cf. Anthony C. Thiselton, *The First Epistle to the Corinthians*, NIGTC Grand Rapids: Eerdmans, 2000), 183.

43. Weiss notes the same structure, Johannes Weiss, *Der erste Korintherbrief*, KEK 9 (Göttingen: Vandenhoeck & Ruprecht, 1910), 36.

44. Georg Bertram, "Μωρός, Μωραίνω, Μωρία, Μωρολογία," in TDNT, 832.

45. Similarly, *Inst.* 12.10.52; Welborn, *Paul, the Fool of Christ*, 32–33.

46. David Alan Black, *Paul, Apostle of Weakness: Astheneia and Its Cognates in the Pauline Literature* New York: Peter Lang, 1984), 13. See also for Paul's use of the term in 1 Cor 1–4.

47. Epictetus, *Diatr.* 1.8.8.

48. BDAG.

49. David E. Garland, *1 Corinthians*, BECNT Grand Rapids: Baker, 2003), 77.

50. Schnabel, *Der erste Brief*, 142.

51. Peter Althouse and Robby Waddell, "The Promises and Perils of the Asuza Street Myth," *Pneuma* 38:4 (2016), 369.

52 Jacqueline Grey, "Embodiment and the Prophetic Message in Isaiah's Memoir," *Pneuma* 39:4 (2017), 452.

53. Sanders, "Landlords and Tenants," 103.

54. Andrew Wallace-Hadrill, *Houses and Society in Pompeii and Herculaneum* (Princeton: Princeton University Press, 1994), 118–19; Glenn R. Storey, "Housing and Domestic Architecture," in *The Cambridge Companion to Ancient Rome*, ed. Paul Erdkamp New York: Cambridge University Press, 2013), 153–54.

55. This is particularly evident in opening greetings of his letters, which are addressed to the *ekklēsiai* as wholes. When individuals are given special mention, it is on account of their service to the rest of the community, not their social standing (see e.g., 1 Cor 16 and Rom 16).

Chapter 10

1. S. J. Hafemann, "Letters to the Corinthians," in *Dictionary of Paul and His Letters*, eds. Gerald Hawthorne and Ralph P. Martin. (Downers Grove, IL: InterVarsity Press, 1993) 173.

2. All scriptural quotations are from the NRSV unless otherwise noted.

3. Alexandra Brown, "The Gospel Takes Place: Paul's Theology of Power-in-Weakness in 2 Corinthians," *Int* 52 (1998), 279. Scriptural citation added.

4. Richard Hays, *First Corinthians*. Interpretation: A Bible Commentary for Teaching and Preaching (Louisville, John Knox Press, 1997), 194.

5. Raymond Collins, *First Corinthians*. Sacra Pagina 7 (Collegeville, Minnesota: Liturgical Press, 1999), 422; Hans Conzelman, *1 Corinthians: A Commentary on the First Epistle to the Corinthians*. Hermenia (Philadelphia: Fortress Press, 1975), 194; Gordon Fee, *The First Epistle to the Corinthians*, NICNT Grand Rapids, MI: Eerdmans, 1987), 540.

6. See the discussions of the various possibilities in Barton, "Historical Criticism and Social-Scientific Perspectives," 56-58; Collins, *First Corinthians*, 416-435; Fee, *The First Epistle to the Corinthians*, 534-558; Fowl, "The New Testament, Theology, and Ethics," 406-412.

7. John Barclay, "I Corinthians," *Oxford Bible Commentary*, 1126; Campbell, "Does Paul Acquiesce?" 61; Gerd Thiessen's analysis regarding the Lord' Supper in *The Social Setting of Pauline Christianity* (Edinburgh, 1983) was groundbreaking. See especially 145-168.

8. Fee, *The First Epistle to the Corinthians*, 542.

9. Lampe, "The Eucharist," *Int* 48 (January 2001), 40.

10. Lampe, "The Eucharist," 40

11. Lampe, "The Eucharist," 40-41.

12. Barton, "Historical Criticism and Social-Scientific," 57.

13. Collins, *First Corinthians*, 423; Fee, *The First Epistle to the Corinthians*, 543.

14. Collins, *First Corinthians*, 423; Fee, *The First Epistle to the Corinthians*, 544.

15. Fee, *The First Epistle to the Corinthians*, 544.

16. Collins, *First Corinthians*, 419.

17. Hays, *First Corinthians*, 4.

18. Chilton, "Traditio-Historical Criticism," 48.

19. For example, the NRSV reads in the following manner: "For I received from the Lord what I also <u>handed on</u> to you, that the Lord Jesus

on the night when he was betrayed took a loaf of bread" so there is no indication that Paul repeats the same verb.

20. Hays, *First Corinthians*, 198. See also Beverly Gaventa, *Our Mother Saint Paul*. (Louisville: Westminster John Knox Press, 2007), 122-123.

21. Hays, *First Corinthians*, 198. See also Gaventa, *Our Mother Saint Paul*, 122-123.

22. Hays, *First Corinthians*, 198; Robertson and Plummer, *A Critical and Exegetical Commentary*, 243.

23. Sampley, *First Letter to the Corinthians*, 935.

24. Hays, *First Corinthians*, 199-200.

25. Lampe, "The Eucharist," 45.

26. Julia Foote, "A Brand Plucked from the Fire: An Autobiographical Sketch by Mrs. Julia A. J. Foote" Cleveland, Ohio: W. F. Schneider, 1879 in *Sisters of the Spirit: Three Black Women's Autobiographies of the Nineteenth Century*, ed. William L. Andrews (Bloomington: Indiana University Press, 1986), 167.

Chapter 11

1. James' language resembles Greek rhetorical handbooks, specifically *progymnasmata* in the flow of the argument (see headings). "The argument that the thought in James jumps illogically from one topic to another holds little weight in the light of the elementary exercises in composition (*the progymnasmata*) and the rhetorical handbooks." Wesley Hiram Wachob, *The Voice of Jesus in the Social Rhetoric of James* (Cambridge: University Press, 2000), 170.

2. G. A. Kennedy, *Aristotle "On Rhetoric": A Theory of Civic Discourse* (Oxford: Oxford University Press, 1991), 182; "an opinion given as a judgment or advice."

3. The subjective genitive is chosen, "trust *of* our Lord Jesus Christ," for in the Book of James, trust "is directed to God, the Father, rather than to Jesus." Patrick J. Hartin, *James* (Collegeville, MN: Liturgical Press, 2003), 117; Wachob, 64-66. *Contra* Ralph P. Martin, *James* (Dallas: Nelson Reference & Electronic, 1988), 59; Sophie Laws, *A Commentary on the Epistle of James* (San Francisco: Harper & Row Publishers, 1980), 93; James Hardy Ropes, *A Critical and Exegetical Commentary on the Epistle of St. James* (Edinburgh: T & T Clark, 1978), 187. The term "trust" is chosen rather than "faith," in that in the English language, faith is often equated with mental assent, which James pairs with demonic knowledge (James 2:19). In the biblical sense, the πιστ-word family can be both a verb, noun, and adjective—it indicates a personal entrustment of oneself to another.

4. Many scholars interpret the genitive "of glory" (τῆς δόξης) in apposition to "our Lord Jesus Christ, the glory." E.g. Laws, 94-97; Joseph B. Mayor, *The Epistle of St. James* Grand Rapids: Baker Book House, 1978), 76-78.

5. H. E. Daney, Julius R. Mantey, *A Manual Grammar of the Greek New Testament* (Toronto: The Macmillan Company, 1927), 301-302. Some scholars, e.g. Adamson, 102, and Martin, 56, suggest the conative sense, "do not try to combine."

6. Dana & Mantey, 174.

7. For a discussion of socialization in the context of paraenesis, and its bearing upon James, see Leo G. Perdue, "Paraenesis and the Epistle of James" *ZNW* 72 (1981), 241-256.

8. Luke Timothy Johnson, *Brother of Jesus, Friend of God* (William B. Eerdmans Publishing Company, 2004), 32.

9. Wachob, 70.

10. I am indebted to the many contributions from Wachob.

11. Many scholars, e.g. Laws, 105, suggest a baptismal allusion with this formula; Dibelius, 141.

12. Wachob, 160.

13. Dibelius, 39 presents a full discussion, 39-45. Bammel notes, "As far as the situation in James is concerned, one can merely say that the rich were beginning to seek entry into the church and the poor had already come to be esteemed less highly, ἠτιμάσατε τὸν πτῶχον 2:6." E. Bammel, "πτῶχος", *TDNT*, VI, 911.

14. Bruce J. Malina, "Wealth and Poverty in the New Testament and Its World," *Interpretation* 41/4 (1987), 354-367. For another discussion of the cultural scripts of honor and shame, see Hartin, 140-148.

15. Malina, 356.

16. Wachob, 180.

17. The expression, "you have become divided against yourselves" (διεκρίθητε ἐν ἑαυτοῖς 4:4), would suggest that both the poor man and the gold fingered man are part of the community.

18. For a full discussion of the term, "rich," in light of an overvalue of money, see Paul H. Furfey, "ΠΛΟΥΣΙΟΣ and Cognates in the New Testament," *CBQ* 5/3 (1943), 243-263.

19. B. L. Mack, *Rhetoric in the New Testament* (Minneapolis: Fortress Press, 1990), 30.

20. For a full discussion of the term, συναγωγή, see Dibelius, 132-135; W. Schrage, "συναγωγή", *TDNT*, VII, 837-838, for the only New Testament use of the term for Christians.

433

21. The verb, "pay attention" (ἐπιβλέπω) can denote, "to look upon with favor."

22. Cheung interprets the verb, "to be divided" (διακρίνω) in the light of its use in James 1:6, "doubting/being double-minded." Luke L. Cheung, *The Genre, Composition and Hermeneutics of James* (Carlisle CA: Paternoster Press, 2003), 196-239.

23. Martin's translation of κριταὶ διαλογισμῶν πονηρῶν.

24. See Burchard for a full discussion of the plurals. Christoph Burchard, *Der Jakobusbrief* (Heidelbert: Mohr Siebeck, 2000), 99.

25. Signs of opulence and extravagance.

26. I well remember the visible anger of a retired senator when a visitor sat in his seat in his pew in a church that I pastored.

27. Martin Dibelius, *James*, (ed. Helmut Koester; trans. Michael A. Williams; Philadelphia: Fortress Press, 1976), 125.

28. Douglas J. Moo, *The Letter of James* Grand Rapids: William B. Eerdmans Publishing Company, 2000), 102.

29. Hartin, 116.

30. Laws, 98.

31. BDF §371.4

32. Martin, 60-61.

33. Ropes, 191; Moo, 103-104; Dibelius, 131-132; James B. Adamson, *The Epistle of James* Grand Rapids: William B. Eerdmans Publishing Company, 1976), 105.

34. Roy Bowen Ward, "Partiality in the Assembly," *HTR*, 62 (1969), 87-97.

35. Ward, 91.

36. Martin, 57; Wachob, 75; Peter H. Davids, *The Epistle of James* Grand Rapids: William B. Eerdmans Publishing Company, 1982), 109.

37. K. Jason Coker, "Identifying the Imperial Presence," in *Identifying the Imperial Presence* (Augsburg, Fortress Publishers, 2015), 121; Laws, 98.

38. Leander E. Keck, "The Poor Among the Saints in the New Testament, *ZNW* 56 (1966), 117.

39. The suggested translation of τῷ κόσμῳ|, as an ethical dative, "poor in the estimation of the world" BDAG, 728; Moule renders the expression, "the literally, i.e. materially poor." C. F. D. Moule, *An Idiom Book of New Testament* (Cambridge: At the University Press, 1963), 46.

40. "They become rich only by election. The two accusatives are bound up with election." W. Schrenk, "ἐκλέγομαι", *TDNT*, IV, 175.

41. Vernon K. Robinson, "Writing as a Rhetorical Act in Plutarch and the Gospels," in *Persuasive Artistry: Studies in New Testament Rhetoric in Honor of George A Kennedy* (ed. D. F. Watson; Sheffield, JSOT Press, 1991), 120.

42. See Wachob, 137-150, for a full discussion of the particular comparisons and differences in this macarism.

43. "James seems to leave the impression that he is familiar with the oral gospel of Jesus but not with the books of the NT." Simon J. Kistemaker, "The Theological Message of James," *JETS* 29/1 (1986), 55.

44. Wachob, 150. See Michael D. Fiorello, "The Ethical Implication of Holiness in James 2," *JETS* 55/3 (2012), 562, for an extensive list of parallels in James with Jesus' teaching, particularly the Sermon on the Mount. Also, George M. Stulac, *James* (Downers Grove: InterVarsity Press, 1993), 91-93. Lockett also approaches James 2 with the perspective of purity stressed in 1:27. Darian Lockett, *Purity and Worldview in the Epistle of James* New York: T & T Clark, 2008), 96.

45. See J. Eichler, "Inheritance", *NIDNTT*, 2, 300-301 for arguments concerning the present and future aspects of the inheritance.

46. This story, along with others (with name changes) is taken from an interview with Dr. Wayne Lewis, who has worked extensively with the poor in Washington DC.

47. The mention of sin (ἁμαρτία) recalls 1:14-15 in terms of a negative progression: one's own desire > conceives > gives birth to sin > when sin is fully grown > brings forth death.

48. See Coker, 133-135 for a full discussion. *Contra* Martin, 67.

49. Wachob, 182.

50. BDAG, 136.

51. Martin, 67.

52. Moo, 112.

53. For a thoroughgoing critique against Freud's give arguments against the love commandment, see Ernest Wallwork, "Thou Shalt Love Thy Neighbor as Thyself: The Freudian Critique," *The Journal of Religious Ethics* 10:2 (1982), 264-319.

54. Luke Timothy Johnson, "The Use of Leviticus 19 in the Letter of James," *HTR* 101 (1982), 392.

55. Johnson draws attention to the same motifs of judgment and law elsewhere in James and Pseudo-Phocylides. 391-401.

56. Fiorello, 559.

57. BDAG, 450.

58. The nouns and verbal forms are plural and point to the community as a whole.

59. Perhaps a deliberate counter to the rabbinic "light" and "heavy" principle as a way of distinguishing commandments.

60. Martin, 70.

61. Darian R. Lockett has argued from the numerous contrasts (positive and negative commands) in the Book of James that James' strategy builds upon the Jewish doctrine of the "two ways." "Structure or Communicative Strategy? The 'Two Ways' Motif in James' Theological Instruction," *Neotestamentica* 42/2 (2008), 269-287.

62. Laws, 116, suggests that the repeated adverb, "thus," should be understood as "in every respect."

63. See Richard Bauckham, *James*, (London: Routledge, 1999), 170-172.

64. John H. Elliot, "The Epistle of James in Rhetorical and Social-Scientific Perspective," *BTB* 23:2 (1993), 75.

65. Moo, 117, interprets the "freedom" as "an obligation we discharged in the joyful knowledge that God has both 'liberated' us, in his Spirit, the power to obey his will."

66. Wachob, 105.

67. Dibelius' argument, 147-148, that 2:13 is an isolated and independent saying that is unrelated to the paragraph is unconvincing.

68. William Dyrness, "Mercy Triumphs over Justice: James 2:13 and the Theology of Faith and Works," *Themelios* 6:3 (1981), 13. Mayor, 92 suggests, "the very essence of the Christian law of liberty ... supplying the rule for the believer's daily life." On the verb, "boast" (κατακαυχάομαι), Bultmann notes that "it brings out strongly the element of comparative superiority expressed in boasting, 'to boast in triumphant comparison with others.'" "κατακαυχάομαι", *TDNT*, III, 653.

69. David P. Nystrom, *James: The NIV Application Commentary* Grand Rapids: Zondervan Publishing House, 1997), 134.

70. The writer has discussed at length some of the socio-economic issues in the global community with his colleague, Dr. Douglas Walker, Professor of Economics, in the Robertson School of Government of Regent University (Virginia Beach, VA).

71. Nystrom, 137, from Lord Acton in a letter to Creighton, April 4, 1887.

72. This last affirmation of Isa 40:5 is not found in the parallel accounts of Mark 1:3 or Matt 3:3.

73. Wachob, 198.

Chapter 12

1. This chapter is adapted and revised from the conference paper, "Healing the 'Us vs. Them' Divide: Inter-Group Cooperation, Spirit Baptism, and Naturalistic Ethics," presented at the Ethics Interest Group in the 46th Annual Meeting of the *Society for Pentecostal Studies* (SPS) on March 10, 2017, in St. Louis, Missouri. I thank Michael Palmer, Antipas Harris, Amos Yong, Mark Cartledge, Michael Di Fuccia, Daniela Augustine, and Martin Mittelstadt along with Andrew Thrasher and Andrew Youd for the encouragement, inputs, and support offered in various ways in the writing, presenting, and revising process. I remain fully responsible for any error in this piece.

2. Joshua Greene, *Moral Tribes: Emotion, Reason, and the Gap Between Us and Them* New York: Penguin Books, 2013).

3. At a basic metaphysical level, naturalism (as a worldview) asserts two ideas: (1) the natural (implying, physical) world is all that exists; and (2) there are no spiritual or supernatural entities that transcend this world. For a more detailed unpacking of naturalism, please see Kelly James Clark, "Naturalism and Its Discontents," in *The Blackwell Companion to Naturalism*, ed. Kelly James Clark (Chichester, West Sussex, UK: Wiley Blackwell, 2016), 1–15. Naturalistic ethics, therefore, seeks to understand the nature and experience of human morality without appealing to any spiritual truth (that comes in the form of divine revelation) or transcendental moral framework rooted in the idea of God as a universal moral lawgiver. For many naturalistic ethicists including Joshua Greene, human evolutionary history (as understood by evolutionary biology and its related scientific disciplines) becomes the primary vantage point for all moral theorizing.

4. John Hare, *God's Command* (Oxford: Oxford University Press, 2015); Craig A. Boyd, "Neuroscience, the Trolley Problem, and Moral Virtue," in *Theology and the Science of Moral Action: Virtue Ethics, Exemplarity, and Cognitive Neuroscience*, eds. James A. Van Slyke et al New York: Routledge, 2013), 130–47.

5. Michael D. Palmer, "Ethical Formation: The Theological Virtues," in *The Holy Spirit and Christian Formation: Multidisciplinary Perspectives*, ed. Diane Chandler New York: Palgrave MacMillan, 2016), 107–26.

6. Alasdair MacIntyre, *After Virtue*, 3rd ed. (Notre Dame, IN: University of Notre Dame Press, 2007). MacIntyre argues for the superiority of the Aristotelian virtue tradition in comparison to the modern moral philosophical tradition. For him, "from the standpoint of an ongoing way of life informed by and expressed through Aristotelian concepts it is possible to understand what the predicament of moral

437

modernity is and why the culture of moral modernity lacks the resources to proceed further with its own moral enquiries" (ix).

7. Renewal, in general, represents the Classical Pentecostal, neo-Pentecostal or charismatic, and the 'Third Wave' streams of the global church. A Renewal perspective in theology or ethics pays significant emphasis to the person and work of the third person of the Trinity, the Holy Spirit, while ensuring theological and moral reflection is done in light of the Pentecostal-charismatic experience and spirituality, and fully embracing the affective and embodied aspects of human nature. In this chapter, the general usage of the word "Renewal" would mean "Pentecostal-Charismatic" and in a theological sense, "Renewal" can be synonymous with "pneumatological."

8. Palmer, "Ethical Formation," 107–26. Also, for more Pentecostal theological explorations into virtue ethics, see Paul W. Lewis, "A Pneumatological Approach to Virtue Ethics," *Asian Journal of Pentecostal Studies* 1:1 (1998), 42–61, idem, "Value Formation and the Role of the Holy Spirit in the Writings of J. Rodman Williams." *Asian Journal of Pentecostal Studies* 14:2 (2011), 272–309, Daniel Castelo, "Tarrying on the Lord: Affections, Virtues, and Theological Ethics in a Pentecostal Perspective." Journal of Pentecostal Theology 13:1 (2004), 31–56, and idem, *Revisioning Pentecostal Ethics: The Epicletic Community*. Cleveland, TN: CPT Press, 2012.

9. Greene, *Moral Tribes*, 23.

10. Greene, *Moral Tribes*, 23.

11. Greene, *Moral Tribes*, 26.

12. Jonathan Haidt, *The Righteous Mind* New York: Vintage Books, 2012), 284.

13. Frans de Waal, "Morally Evolved: Primate Social Instincts, Human Morality, and the Rise and Fall of 'Veneer Theory,'" in *Primates and Philosophers: How Morality Evolved*, eds. Stephen Macedo and Josiah Ober (Princeton, NJ: Princeton University Press, 2006), 53.

14. Frans de Waal, "Morally Evolved," 53–54.

15. For example, see Haidt, *Righteous Mind*; de Waal, "Morally Evolved." Haidt and de Waal, for example, empathize with the limitations of human ability to cooperate with one another due to the evolutionary hardwiring of human morality as explained earlier. Hence, they do not push strongly for universal human cooperation because it fundamentally runs against the grain of human nature, which is groupish and tribal.

16. Greene, *Moral Tribes*, 26.

17. Greene, *Moral Tribes*, 26.

18. Greene, *Moral Tribes*, 153–54.

19. Greene uses the Trolley problem, which is a classic moral dilemma in which a trolley is moving down the track where there are five people stuck, unable to move. If nothing is done, the trolley will proceed to kill the five. But there are at least two different situations given as a thought experiment to stop this trolley from killing these people. In the first case, there is a switch that one can flip which in turn causes the trolley to change its course to another track, thereby saving the five, although unfortunately killing the one person who is stuck in the new track. In the second case, there is a footbridge above the trolley's course and a fat person is standing on it. One could push the fat man over the bridge onto the track, thus killing him and saving the five.

20. Greene, *Moral Tribes*, 105–43.

21. Greene, *Moral Tribes*, 251.

22. Greene, *Moral Tribes*, 147–89.

23. Greene, *Moral Tribes*, 183.

24. See Hare, *God's Command*, ch. 8. Also see Hare, "Evolutionary Theory and Theological Ethics," *Studies in Christian Ethics* 25:2 (2012), 244–54, where he critically engages the moral theories of the primatologist Frans de Waal, moral psychologist Mark Hauser, and game theorist, Ken Binmore.

25. Hare, *God's Command*, 308; emphasis mine.

26. Hare, *God's Command*, 286–92.

27. Greene, *Moral Tribes*, 268.

28. Greene, *Moral Tribes*, 266

29. It should be noted that not all utilitarian philosophers make such a claim.

30. Hare, *God's Command*, 5–11. This idea is basically a moral argument from Immanuel Kant that Hare adapts and develops further.

31. Greene, *Moral Tribes*, 268.

32. Hare, *God's Command*, 290. This idea of the human need for assistance to fix an inherent "moral gap" has been a persistent theme in the moral philosophy of John Hare. See his *The Moral Gap* New York: Oxford University Press, 1996) and "the argument from grace" developed in his *God's Command*, 11–16.

33. Boyd, "Neuroscience," 136–38. Also, see William D. Casebeer, "Moral Cognition and Its Neural Constituents," *Nature Reviews Neuroscience* 4 (2003), 841–47.

34. Boyd, "Neuroscience," 141.

35. Boyd, "Neuroscience," 140.

36. Boyd, "Neuroscience," 141–42.

37. Thomas Jay Oord, *Defining Love: A Philosophical, Scientific, and Theological Engagement* Grand Rapids, MI: Brazos Press, 2010), 128.

38. Stephen J. Pope, *Human Evolution and Christian Ethics* New York: Cambridge University Press, 2007), 225.

39. William FitzPatrick, "Why Darwinism Does Not Debunk Objective Morality?" in *Cambridge Companion to Evolutionary Ethics*, eds. Michael Ruse and Robert J. Richards (Cambridge, UK: Cambridge University Press, 2017), 198.

40. See Boyd, "Neuroscience," 137–39.

41. See Daniel C. Dennett and Alvin Plantinga, *Science and Religion: Are They Compatible?* New York: Oxford University Press, 2011). For a detailed exposition of the EAAN, see Alvin Plantinga, *Where the Conflict Really Lies: Science, Religion, and Naturalism* (Oxford, UK: Oxford University Press, 2011), ch. 10. Also see, idem, "The Evolutionary Argument against Naturalism," in *Blackwell Companion to Science and Christianity*, eds. J. B. Stump and Alan G. Padgett (Hoboken, GB: Wiley-Blackwell, 2012), 103–15.

42 Pope, *Human Evolution and Christian Ethics*, 228.

43 Palmer, "Ethical Formation," 107–26. One can also use the word "love" instead of "charity."

44 Palmer, "Ethical Formation," 113.

45 Palmer, "Ethical Formation," 116.

46 Palmer, "Ethical Formation," 117–19.

47 Palmer, "Ethical Formation," 118; Also, see Thomas Aquinas, *Summa Theologiae* II-II 23.5.

48 Palmer, "Ethical Formation," 118.

49 Joseph A. Fitzmeyer, *The Acts of the Apostles: A New Translation with Introduction and Commentary*, The Anchor Bible New York: Doubleday, 1997), 454.

50 F. F. Bruce, *The Book of Acts*, rev. ed. Grand Rapids, MI: Eerdmans, 1988), 205. Bruce sees a correlation between Peter's hunger and the vision on food.

51. For a helpful unpacking of the idea of the Spirit walking alongside, please see Mark J. Cartledge, "Spirit-Empowered 'Walking Alongside': Towards a Renewal Theology of Public Life," *Journal of Pentecostal Theology* 27:1 (2018), 14–36. Cartledge's article is based on a careful exegesis and theological analysis of the Paraclete texts in John 14–16.

52. Palmer, "Ethical Formation," 118.

53. Frank Macchia, *Baptized in the Spirit: A Global Pentecostal Theology* Grand Rapids, MI: Zondervan, 2006), 281.

54. Amos Yong, *Spirit of Love: A Trinitarian Theology of Grace* (Waco, TX: Baylor University Press, 2012), 37.

55. Yong, *Spirit of Love*, 55.

56 Aaron J. Kuecker, *The Spirit and the 'Other': Social Identity, Ethnicity, and Intergroup Reconciliation in Luke-Acts* (London: T & T Clark, 2011), 187.

57 Kuecker, *Spirit and the 'Other,'* 213.

58 Kuecker, *Spirit and the 'Other'*, 214; emphasis mine.

59 Kuecker, *Spirit and the 'Other'*, 188.

60 Murray Dempster, "The Church's Moral Witness: A Study of Glossolalia in Luke's Theology of Acts" *Paraclete* 23 (Winter 1989), 4–5.

61 Dempster, "Church's Moral Witness," 5.

62. Dempster, "Church's Moral Witness," 5.

63. See Enoch S. Charles, "Toward a Pneumatological-Participatory Theology of Divine Moral Assistance: An Apologetic Dialogue with Naturalistic Ethics and Kantian Ethics of John Hare" (PhD diss., Regent University, 2018), ProQuest Dissertations & Theses Global.

64. The virtue of inter-group hospitality explored in this chapter could be further enriched using the works on Pentecost and hospitality by Amos Yong and Daniela Augustine. See Amos Yong, *Hospitality and the Other: Pentecost, Christian Practices, and the Neighbor* Maryknoll, NY: Orbis Books, 2008) and Daniela Augustine, *Pentecost, Hospitality, and Transfiguration*. Also, see idem, "Pentecost and the Hospitality of God as Justice for the Others," in *Brethren Life and Thought* 57:1 (Spring 2012), 17–26. Moreover, the politics of friendship by Nimi Wariboko developed in his *The Charismatic City and the Public Resurgence of Religion: A Pentecostal Social Ethics of Cosmopolitan Urban Life* New York: Palgrave Macmillan, 2014) could be useful. Miroslav Volf's *Exclusion and Embrace: A Theological Exploration of Identity, Otherness, and Reconciliation* Nashville, TN: Abingdon Press, 1996) could also be helpful. Finally, this research could be enriched by the works of Brendan Byrne, *The Hospitality of God: A Reading of Luke's Gospel*, rev. ed. (Collegeville, MN: Liturgical Press, 2015) and Martin Mittelstadt, *Reading Luke-Acts in the Pentecostal Tradition* (Cleveland, TN: CPT Press, 2010).

Chapter 13

1. I am using "Pentecostal" in a looser way dependent on scholars identifying themselves and/or their work as Pentecostal. Rather than tying this term to a specific confessional group or an overly particular theological commitment, I understand Pentecostal more inclusively as including explicitly Classical Pentecostal groups/theologies,

Oneness/Apostolic groups/theologies, and groups/theologies that emphasis the continuity of Christ's ministry through the Spirit who empowers the church community.

2. Steven Jack Land, *Pentecostal Spirituality: A Passion for the Kingdom* (Cleveland, Tennessee: CPT Press, 2010), 12.

3. Amos Yong, *The Spirt Poured Out On All Flesh: Pentecostalism and the Possibility of Global Theology* Grand Rapids, MI: Baker Academic, 2005), 27-30.

4. Acts 2:42-47.

5. C. Paul Schroeder, "Introduction" in *On Social Justice: St. Basil the Great*, trans. C. Paul Schroeder (Crestwood, New York: St. Vladimir's Press, 2009), 15-21. It is necessary to see Basil's social commitments against the background of his own privileged upbringing. Through his monastic lifestyle and use of the resources he had because of his privilege, Basil reorients himself to the wealth that was at his disposal.

6. Demetrios Constantelos, "Basil the Great's Social Thought and Involvement," *The Greek Theological Review* 26 (1981), 81.

7. Basil the Great, "To the Rich," in *On Social Justice: St. Basil the Great*, trans. C. Paul Schroeder (Crestwood, New York: St. Vladimir's Press, 2009), 43.

8. Basil the Great, "To the Rich," 43

9. Basil the Great, "To the Rich,"44.

10. Basil the Great, "To the Rich," 60.

11. Basil the Great, "In Time of Famine and Drought," in *On Social Justice: St. Basil the Great*, trans. C. Paul Schroeder (Crestwood, New York: St. Vladimir's Press, 2009), 76.

12. Basil the Great, "In Time of Famine and Drought," 86.

13 Basil the Great, *On the Spirit*. Beloved Publishing, 2015.

14 William J. Abraham, "Divine Action and Pneumatology in the Cappadocians," in Divine Agency and Divine Action, Volume II: Soundings in the Christian Tradition (Oxford, UK: Oxford University Press, 2017), 74.

15 Lewis Ayres, ""Basil of Caesarea and the Development of Pro-Nicene Theology," in Nicaea and its Legacy: An Approach to Fourth-Century Trinitarian Theology (Oxford, UK: Oxford University Press, 2004), 28.

16. Dwight N. Hopkins, *Being Human: Race, Culture, and Religion* (Minneapolis, Minnesota: Fortress Press, 2005), 183.

17. Hopkins, *Being Human*, 184.

18. Hopkins, *Being Human*, 184.

19. Hopkins, *Being Human*, 186.

20. Hopkins, *Being Human*, 186.

Chapter 14

1. Thomas A. Kopecek. "The Social Class of the Cappadocian Fathers," *Church History*, 42 (1973), 461-466.

2. Basil the Great, *On Social Justice,* Trans. By C. Paul Schroeder (Crestwood, NY: St. Vladimir's Seminary Press. 2009), 43.

3. Basil the Great, *On Social Justice,* 43.

4. Basil the Great, *On Social Justice,* 93.

5. Basil the Great, *On Social Justice,* 63.

6. Basil the Great, *On Social Justice. I Will Tear Down My Barns,* Trans. By C. Paul Schroeder (Crestwood, NY: St. Vladimir's Seminary Press, 2009), 18.

7. Basil the Great, *On Social Justice. I Will Tear Down My Barns,* Trans. By C. Paul Schroeder (Crestwood, NY: St. Vladimir's Seminary Press. 2009), 21.

8. Basil the Great, *On Social Justice,* 22.

9. Basil the Great, *On Social Justice. I will Tear Down My Barns,* Trans. By C. Paul Schroeder (Crestwood, NY: St. Vladimir's Seminary Press. 2009), 23.

10. Basil the Great, *On Social Justice,* 24.

11. Basil the Great, *On Social Justice. I will Tear Down My Barns,* Trans. By C. Paul Schroeder (Crestwood, NY: St. Vladimir's Seminary Press. 2009), 25.

12. Basil the Great, *On Social Justice,* 27.

13. Basil the Great, On Social Justice. 5.

14. Basil the Great, *On Social Justice,* 7.

15. John Chrysostom, *Second Sermon on Lazarus and the Rich Man*; in *St. John Chrysostom: On Wealth and Poverty*, trans. by Catherine P. Roth, (Crestwood, NY: St. Vladimir's Seminary Press, 1984), 49.

16. Basil the Great, *On Social Justice,* 6.

17. Basil the Great, *On Social Justice,* 7.

18. Basil the Great, *On Social Justice,* 30.

19. Basil the Great, Trans. By C. Paul Schroeder. On Social Justice. *I will Tear Down My Barns* (Crestwood, NY: St. Vladimir's Seminary Press. 2009), 32.

20. Gregory of Nazianzus, *Panegyric on St. Basil*, 63 (NPNF 7:416), 33 of Schroeder's book.

21. FOCUS is a dual acronym: Fellowship of Orthodox Christians United in Service; Food Occupation Clothing Understanding and Shelter. This basic-needs organization, which seeks to live out the vision of Basil's *Basiliad*, has centers primarily in the rust belt of the United States and

further west, as well as ministry sites in dozens of US cities.

22. Basil the Great, *On Social Justice,* 36.

23. Basil the Great, *On Social Justice,* 8.

24. Coleman-Jensen, A., C. Gregory, and A. "Household Food Security in the United States in 2013." Washington, DC: USDA Economic Research Service, 2014.

25. Feeding America. "Map the Meal Gap: Child Food Insecurity 2011." Feeding America, 2011.

26. Coleman-Jensen, Gregory, and Singh. "Household Food Security in the United States in 2013." Washington, DC: USDA Economic Research Service, 2014.

27. Dana. Gunder, "Wasted Food: How America Is Losing Up to 40 Percent of Its Food from Farm to Fork to Landfill." National Resources Defense Council, 2012.

28. International Food Policy Research Institute. "2012 Global Hunger Index." Washington, DC: IFPRI, 2012.

29. 11 Facts about Hunger in the US. 2014. https://www.dosomething.org/facts/11-facts-about-hunger-us.

30. Coleman-Jensen, Alisha, M. Nord, M. Andrews, and S. Carlson. "Household Food Security in the United States in 2011." Washington, DC: U.S. Department of Agriculture, Economic Research Service, 2012.

31. Greek Orthodox Archdiocesan Statement on Racial Equality 1963. http://civilrights.goarch.org/-/greek-orthodox-archdiocesan-statement-on-racial-equality-1963?inheritRedirect=true.

32. Greek Orthodox Archdiocesan Statement on Racial Equality 1963.

33. The Phenomenon of Ethnophyletism in Recent Years. http://civilrights.goarch.org/-/the-phenomenon-of-ethnophyletism-in-recent-years?inheritRedirect=true.

34. Sts. Cyril and Methodius. Lives of the Saints. Pravmir. http://www.pravmir.com/article_39.html.

Chapter 15

1. Jürgen Moltmann, "Preface" in Veli-Matti Kärkkäinen, ed., *The Spirit in the World: Emerging Pentecostal Theologies in Global Contexts,* Grand Rapids, MI: Wm. B. Eerdmans, 2009, ix.

2. Juan Sepúlveda, "Reflections on the Pentecostal Contribution to the Mission of the Church in Latin America", in *Journal of Pentecostal Theology* 1 (1992), 98.

3. Estrada-Carrasquillo, Wilmer, paper presented to the Annual Meeting of the Society of Pentecostal Studies, Cleveland, Tennessee, March 8-10, 2018.

4. Gutiérrez, Centro de Estudios y Publicaciones, 1979, later published in English as *The Power of the Poor in History*, New York: Orbis Publications, 1983.

5. See Allan Anderson, *African Reformation: African Initiated Christianity in the 20th Century*. Trenton, NJ: African World Press, 2001.

6 See historians of Chilean Pentecostalism, including W.C. Hoover, *Historia del avivamiento Pentecostal en Chile*. Excelsior, 1948; Luis Orellana Urtubia, *El fuego y la nieve: Historia del movimiento pentecostal en Chile 1909-1932*. CEEP Ediciones, 2006; and Victor Sepúlveda Fernandois, *La pentecostalidad en Chile*. CEEP Publicaciones, 2009.

7 See, Christian Lalive d'Epinay, *El refugio de las masas: Estudio sociológico del protestantismo chileno*. Editorial Del Pacifico, 1968; in English, Cambridge, UK: Lutterworth Press, 1969.

8 See Frans H. Kamsteeg, *Prophetic Pentecostalism in Chile: A Case Study on Religion and Development Policy*. Lanham, MD: The Scarecrow Press, 1998.

9 See www.sepade.cl

10 To mention just a few, see Rebecca Pierce Bomann, *Faith in the Barrios: The Pentecostal Poor in Bogotá*, Boulder, CO: Lynne Reinner Publishers, 1999; Robert Mapes Anderson, *Vision of the Disinherited: The Making of American Pentecostalism*. New York: Oxford University Press, 1979; Cecilia Loreto Mariz. *Coping with Poverty: Pentecostals and Christian Base Communities in Brazil*. Philadelphia: Temple University Press, 1994; and R. Andrew Chestnut, Born *Again in Brazil: The Pentecostal Boom and the Pathogens of Poverty*, New Brunswick, NJ: Rutgers University Press, 1997.

11 Darío López Rodríguez, *The Liberating Mission of Jesus: The Message of the Gospel of Luke*. Translated from the Spanish by Stefanie E. Israel and Richard E. Waldrop. Eugene, OR: Pickwick Publications, 2012, 16.

12 Philip Jenkins. *The Next Christendom: The Coming of Global Christianity*, Oxford University Press, 2002, 216.

13 See Daniel Chiquete, *Escritos a tiempo y fuera de tiempo: Sobre espiritualidad, Biblia y cultura en vísperas del primer centenario del pentecostalismo*. CEEP Ediciones, 2008, 33.

14 See Carmelo Álvarez, ed., *Pentecostalismo y Liberación: Una Experiencia Latinoamericana*. Departamento Ecuménico de Investigaciones, 1992.

15 Centro Evangélico de Estudios Pastorales, *Pastoralia: Pentecostalismo y Teología de la Liberación* 7 (1985).

445

16 For example, see Darío López Rodríguez' signature titles (mostly in Spanish), such as *Pentecostalismo y misión integral: Teología del Espíritu, teología de la vida* (Pentecostalism and Integral Mission: Theology of the Spirit, Theology of Life) Ediciones Puma, 2008 and *La propuesta política del reino de Dios: Estudios bíblicos sobre iglesia, sociedad y estado* (The Political Proposal of the Reign of God: Biblical Studies on Church, Society and State), Ediciones Puma, 2009; Néstor Medina and Sammy Alfaro, eds., *Pentecostals and Charismatics in Latin America and Latino Communities.* Palgrave Macmillan, 2015; David Mesquiati de Oliveira, org. *Pentecostalismos e transformação social* (Pentecostalisms and Social Transformation). Red Latinoamericana de Estudios Pentecostales, 2013; Douglas Petersen, *Not by Might, nor by Power: A Pentecostal Theology of Social Concern in Latin America.* (Oxford, UK: Regnum, 1996).

17 See Cecil M. Robeck, Jr., *The Azusa Street Mission and Revival: The Birth of the Global Pentecostal Movement.* Nashville, TN: Thomas Nelson, 2006, 13.

18 See Rufous G.W. Sanders, *William Joseph Seymour: Black Father of the 20th Century Pentecostal/Charismatic Movement. s.l.:* Xulon Press, 2003).

19 For example, see R.C. Robins, *A.J. Tomlinson: Plainsfolk Modernist.* New York: Oxford University Press, 2006, 33-34.

20. See Ogbu Kalu, *African Pentecostalism: An Introduction.* Oxford University Press, 2008 and Allan Anderson, *An Introduction to Pentecostalism,* (Cambridge, UK: University Press, 2004).

21. Anderson, *An Introduction to Pentecostalism,* 122.

22. See Ivan Satvayrata, *Pentecostals and the Poor: Reflections from the Indian Context.* Asia Pacific Theological Seminary Press, 2017. 2-18.

23. Donald E. Miller and Tetsunao Yamamori, *Global Pentecostalism: The New Face of Christian Social Engagement.* Berkeley, CA: University of California Press, 2007.

24. Anderson, *An Introduction to Pentecostalism,* 276-277.

25. For an excellent critical analysis this topic, see Cheryl Bridges Johns' 1993 presidential address to the Society of Pentecostal Studies, published as "The Adolescence of Pentecostalism: In Search of a Legitimate Sectarian Identity", in *Pnuema* 17 (1995), 3-17.

26. See Rodney A. Coeller's Ph.D. dissertation American University, 2012), *Beyond the Borders: Radicalized Evangelical Missionaries in Central America from the 1950s through the 1980s,* in which he chronicles the conflictive nature of the relationships between North American evangelical missionary sending agencies and seven related missionary couples, including parts of my history with Church of God World Missions.

27. Kenneth J. Archer, *A Pentecostal Hermeneutic: Spirit, Scripture and Community.* Cleveland, TN: CPT Press, 2009.

28. *Minutes of the 68th General Assembly of the Church of God.* Cleveland, TN: Church of God Publishing House, 2000, 96.

29. For example, see Roger Stronstad's major work, *The Prophethood of All Believers.* Sheffield, UK: Sheffield Academic Press, 1999, and Darío López Rodríguez', *La Misión Liberadora de Jesús: El Mensaje del Evangelio de Lucas* (Third Expanded Edition). *Ediciones Puma,* 2017.

30. See Steven J. Land's groundbreaking work, *Pentecostal Spirituality: A Passion for the Kingdom.* Cleveland, TN: CPT Press, 2010.

31. For theory and praxis related to the Christian/Pentecostal contextual indigenous movement in North America, see Casey Church, *Holy Smoke: The Contextual Use of Native American Ritual and Ceremony.* Cherohala Press, 2017; Randy S. Woodley, *Shalom and the Community of Creation: An Indigenous Vision.* Wm. B. Eerdmans, 2012; and Corky Alexander, *Native American Pentecost: Praxis, Contextualization, Transformation.* Cleveland, TN: Cherohala Press, 2012.

32. See Cheryl Bridges Johns, early work, *Pentecostal Formation: A Pedagogy among the Oppressed.* Cleveland, TN: CPT Press, 1970.

33. This was the mid-20th century critique of the traditional "banking" or schooling model of education as seen in the acclaimed classic, Paolo Freire, *Pedagogy of the Oppressed.* New York: Continuum, 2000.

34. Further explicated in Darío López Rodríguez' *La Fiesta del Espíritu: Espiritualidad y Celebración Pentecostal. Ediciones Puma,* 2006.

35. See Walter Hollenweger's expanded section on "The Oral Root of Pentecostalism", in *Pentecostalism: Origins and Developments Worldwide.* Peabody, MA: Hendrikson Publishers, 1997, 18-141.

36. See Kimberly Ervin Alexander, *Pentecostal Healing: Models in Theology and Practice.* Blandford, UK: Deo Publishing, 2006.

37. See Allan Anderson's *Spreading Fires: The Missionary Nature of Early Pentecostalism.* New York: Orbis, 2007.

447

38. See, for example, Philip Jenkin's more recent work, *The New Faces of Christianity: Believing the Bible in the Global South*. New York: Oxford University Press, 2006, and Todd M Johnson's "Counting Pentecostals Worldwide", in Pneuma 36:2 (2014).

39. Perhaps one unlikely source would be Gideon Van der Watt, "...'but the poor opted for the Evangelicals—Evangelicals, Poverty and Prosperity", in *Acta Theologica*, suppl. 16 (2012).

40. Samuel Escobar, "Latin American Christians in the New Christianity", *International Bulletin of Mission Research*, 2006, 579-602.

41. For example, see Darío López Rodríguez, *El Nuevo Rostro del Pentecostalismo Latinoamericano*. Edicones Puma, 2002, Miller and Yamamori, *Global Pentecostalism*, and Kalu's section on "Pentecostalism in the African Public Space", in African *Pentecostalism*, 169-246.

42. Brian K. Pipkin and Jay Beaman, eds., *Early Pentecostals on Nonviolence and Social Justice: A Reader. Eugene, OR:* Pickwick Publications, 2016. Also see Jay Beaman, *Pentecostal Pacifism: The Origin, Development, and Rejection of Pacific Belief among the Pentecostals. Eugene, OR:* Wipf and Stock, 2009, and Paul Alexander, ed., *Pentecostals and Nonviolence: Reclaiming a Heritage.* Eugene, OR: Pickwick Publications, 2012. These three volumes are published in Pickwick Publication's Pentecostals, Peacemaking, and Social Justice series.

43. Charles Fox Parham, "Imminent Events in the United States", in Pipkin and Beaman, *Early Pentecostals on Nonviolence*, 2-3.

44. See Frank Chikane's own account of his struggle against apartheid in *No Life of My Own: An Autobiography.* Eugene, OR: Wipf and Stock, 2010, and Hollenweger, "A Kite Flies Against the Wind: Black Power and Black Pentecostalism in the USA", *Pentecostalism: Origins and Developments Worldwide*, 25-40.

45. Francisco Cartaxo Rolim, "El pentecostalismo a partir el pobre", in *Cristianismo y Sociedad* 26:1 (1988), 51-69.

46. See Carmelo Álvarez' narrative regarding the ministry shared between Disciples of Christ and the Unión Evangélica Pentecostal Venezolana, *Compartiendo la misión de Dios: Discípulos y pentecostales en Venezuela.* CLAI Ediciones, 2007.

47. This is according to my personal communication with members of the Church of God in Guatemala and Nicaragua during the civil wars in those countries (1979-1994).

48. See, pastor Wilfredo Estrada-Adorno's account in *¿Pastores o políticos con sotanas? Pastoral de la guardarraya en Vieques.* Editorial Guardarrayas, 2003.

49. See, Amos Yong, *In the Days of Caesar: Pentecostalism and Political Theology.* Grand Rapids, MI: Wm. B. Eerdmans Publishers, 2010).

50. López Rodríguez, *La Propuesta Política.*

51. See Stephen Schlesinger and Stephen Kinzer, *Bitter Fruit: The Story of the American Coup in Guatemala.* Harvard University Press, 2005, Eduardo Galeano, *Open Veins of Latin America: Five Centuries of the Pillage of a Continent.* Monthly Review Press, 1973, 113-115, and Tom Barry, *Roots of Rebellion: Land and Hunger in Central America.* Boston, MA: South End Press, 1987.

52. Virginia Garrard-Burnett, *Living in the New Jerusalem: Protestantism in Guatemala.* (Austin, TX: University of Texas Press, 1998).

53. In regard to Silva Vaz, see Ziporah Hildebrandt, *Marina Silva: Defending Rainforest Communities in Brazil. New York*: Feminist Press, 2001).

54. According to my personal conversations with Juan Sepúlveda (Chile) and Roberto Aldana (Guatemala). Also, see Sepulveda, panelmission2111052017-JS.docx.

55. Correspondence with Juan Sepúlveda, September 25, 2018.

56. See the Akropong Consultation, in J. Daniel Salinas, ed., *Prosperity Theology and the Gospel: Good News or Bad News for the Poor?* Peabody, MA: Hendrickson Publishers, 2017), 172-175.

57. Eldin Villafañe, *Manda fuego, Señor: Introducción al pentecostalismo. Nashville*, TN: Abingdon Press, 2012), 148-150.

58. Martin Ocaña Flores, *Los Banqueros de Dios: Una aproximación evangélica a la Teología de la Prosperidad.* Ediciones Puma, 2002, 32.

59 Salinas, ed., *Prosperity Theology,* 182-186.

60See Sammy Alfaro, *Divino Compañero: Toward a Hispanic Pentecostal Christology.* Eugene, OR: Pickwick Publications, 2010).

61. Harvey Cox, *Fire from Heaven: The Rise of Pentecostal Spirituality and the Reshaping of Religion in the Twenty-First Century.* Boston, MA: Addison-Wesley, 1995.

Chapter 16

1. Habakkuk's setting is, in many ways, analogous to the contemporary moment. The book is set in the late 7th or early 6th century B.C.E., a time when Jerusalem faced Babylonian oppression. In 605 B.C.E. the Babylonians defeated a coalition of Egyptian and Assyrian forces and established itself as the new dominant power in 597 B.C.E. the Babylonians initiated the first deportations from Jerusalem. It was clear that they were facing a new enemy and they feared for their survival.

Those fears were realized in 587 B.C.E. when the Babylonians ransacked Jerusalem. {Hassler, 2015 #344}

2. Genesis 1:1-2:4 is identified as the Priestly story of creation. It has been contrasted with the Yahwist story in Genesis 2:4b-3, which was written earlier. Since Julius Wellhausen's *Prolegomena*, the documentary sequence JEDP, that is Yahwist, Elohist, Deuteronomist, and Priestly compositions of the Pentateuch have been understood to be composed in that order. For the full exposition of the Documentary Hypothesis, see Julius Wellhausen, *Prolegomena to the History of Israel*, trans. J.S. Black and Allan Menzies, 2nd ed. Atlanta: Scholars Press, 1994; repr., (Edinburgh: A.C.& Black, 1885)). The accepted dating of the Priestly literature is no earlier than the Persian period, although many scholars will date it to the Hellenistic Period. See Philip R. Davies, *In Search of 'Ancient Israel'*, vol. 148, Journal for the Study of the Old Testament Supplement Series Sheffield: Sheffield Academic Press, 1992). 90-92.

3. For an excellent discussion on the history of ancient Israel and particularly the impact of the Babylonian devastation, see Mario Liverani, *Israel's History and the History of Israel*, Bible World London: Equinox, 2005). especially 183-98. See also Philip R. Davies and John Rogerson, *The Old Testament World*, Second ed. Louisville, KY: Westminster John Knox, 2005). 86-95.

4. See Davies and Rogerson, *The Old Testament World*: 145-46.

5. Scott Gold, "Trapped in the Superdome: Refuge Becomes a Hellhole," in *The Seattle Times* Seattle, WA: The Seattle Times Company, 2005).

6. Brian Thevenot and Gordon Russell, "Rape. Murder. Gunfight.," in *The Time-Picayune* New Orleans, LA: The Times-Picayune, 2005).

7. For the account see, Campbell Robertson, "5 Ex-Officers Sentenced in Post-Katrina Shootings," in *The New York Times*, 2012). See also Campbell Robertson, "New Orleans Police Officers Plead Guilty in Shooting of Civilians," in The New York Times), 2016).

8. See Mike Pesca, "Are Katrina's Victims 'Refugees' or 'Evacuees?'," *N.P.R. Special Series: Reporter's Notebook*(2005), https://www.npr.org/templates/story/ story.php?storyId=4833613.   See also Tina Daunt and Robin Abcarian, "Survivors, Others Take Offense at Word 'Refugees'," in *Los Angeles Times* Los Angeles, CA), 2005.

9. For the classic discussion, see James H. Jones, *Bad Blood: The Tuskegee Syphillis Experiment* New York: The Free Press, 1993).

10. A new erudite treatment can be found in Richard Rothstein, *The Color of Law: A Forgotten History of How Our Government Segregated America* New York: Liverlight Publishing Corporation), 2017.

11. 2 Kings 25:6-7 When they captured the king and brought him up to the king of Babylon at Riblah, and they passed sentence on him. They slaughtered the sons of Zedekiah before his eyes and put out the eyes of Zedekiah and bound him in chains and took him to Babylon.

Made in the USA
Coppell, TX
14 August 2023

20366200R00266